*Collector's Library*

# LEAVES OF GRASS

# LEAVES OF GRASS

Walt Whitman

*with an Afterword by*

PETER HARNESS

BARNES & NOBLE
NEW YORK

M 10 9 8 7 6 5 4

ISBN 0 7607 5782 8



Typeset in Great Britain by Antony Gray
Printed and bound in China by Imago

*Contents*

CHILDREN OF ADAM



CALAMUS

SEA-DRIFT



BY THE ROADSIDE

MEMORIES OF PRESIDENT LINCOLN



AUTUMN RIVULETS

SONGS OF PARTING

SANDS AT SEVENTY (*First Annex*)

GOOD-BYE MY FANCY (*Second Annex*)

# INSCRIPTIONS

## *One's-Self I Sing*

One's-self I sing, a simple separate person,
Yet utter the word Democratic, the word En-Masse.
Of physiology from top to toe I sing,
Not physiognomy alone nor brain alone is worthy
for the Muse, I say the Form complete is
worthier far,
The Female equally with the Male I sing.
Of Life immense in passion, pulse, and power,
Cheerful, for freest action form'd under the laws divine,
The Modern Man I sing.

## *As I Ponder'd in Silence*

As I Ponder'd in Silence,
Returning upon my poems, considering, lingering
long,
A Phantom arose before me with distrustful aspect,
Terrible in beauty, age, and power,
The genius of poets of old lands,
As to me directing like flame its eyes,
With finger pointing to many immortal songs,
And menacing voice, *What singest thou?* it said,
*Know'st thou not there is but one theme for
ever-enduring bards?*
*And that is the theme of War, the fortune of battles,*
*The making of perfect soldiers.*

*Be it so*, then I answer'd,
*I too haughty Shade also sing war, and a longer and
greater one than any,*
*Waged in my book with varying fortune, with flight,
advance and retreat, victory deferr'd and wavering,*

*(Yet methinks certain, or as good as certain, at the last,)*
*the field the world,*
*For life and death, for the Body and for the eternal Soul,*
*Lo, I too am come, chanting the chant of battles,*
*I above all promote brave soldiers.*

## *In Cabin'd Ships at Sea*

In cabin'd ships at sea,
The boundless blue on every side expanding,
With whistling winds and music of the waves, the
large imperious waves,
Or some lone bark buoy'd on the dense marine,
Where joyous full of faith, spreading white sails,
She cleaves the ether mid the sparkle and the foam
of day, or under many a star at night,
By sailors young and old haply will I, a reminiscence
of the land, be read,
In full rapport at last.

*Here are our thoughts, voyagers' thoughts,*
*Here not the land, firm land, alone appears*, may then
by them be said,
*The sky o'erarches here, we feel the undulating deck*
*beneath our feet,*
*We feel the long pulsation, ebb and flow of endless motion.*
*The tones of unseen mystery, the vague and vast*
*suggestions of the briny world, the liquid-flowing*
*syllables,*
*The perfume, the faint creaking of the cordage, the*
*melancholy rhythm,*
*The boundless vista and the horizon far and dim are all*
*here,*
*And this is ocean's poem.*

Then falter not O book, fulfil your destiny,
You not a reminiscence of the land alone,
You too as a lone bark cleaving the ether, purpos'd I
know not whither, yet ever full of faith,
Consort to every ship that sails, sail you!
Bear forth to them folded my love, (dear mariners,
for you I fold it here in every leaf;)
Speed on my book! spread your white sails my little
bark athwart the imperious waves,
Chant on, sail on, bear o'er the boundless blue from
me to every sea,
This song for mariners and all their ships.

## *To Foreign Lands*

I heard that you ask'd for something to prove this
puzzle the New World,
And to define America, her athletic Democracy,
Therefore I send you my poems that you behold in
them what you wanted.

## *To a Historian*

You who celebrate bygones,
Who have explored the outward, the surfaces of the
races, the life that has exhibited itself,
Who have treated of man as the creature of politics,
aggregates rulers and priests,
I, habitan of the Alleghanies, treating of him as he is
in himself in his own rights,
Pressing the pulse of the life that has seldom exhibited
itself, (the great pride of man in himself),
Chanter of Personality, outlining what is yet to be,
I project the history of the future.

## *To Thee Old Cause*

To thee old cause!
Thou peerless, passionate, good cause,
Thou stern, remorseless, sweet idea,
Deathless throughout the ages, races, lands,
After a strange sad war, great war for thee,
(I think all war through time was really fought, and
ever will be really fought, for thee,)
These chants for thee, the eternal march of thee.
(A war O soldiers not for itself alone,
Far, far more stood silently waiting behind, now to
advance in this book.)

Thou orb of many orbs!
Thou seething principle! thou well-kept, latent germ!
thou centre!
Around the idea of thee the war revolving,
With all its angry and vehement play of causes,
(With vast results to come for thrice a thousand
years,)
These recitatives for thee, – my book and the war are
one,
Merged in its spirit I and mine, as the contest hinged
on thee,
As a wheel on its axis turns, this book unwitting to
itself,
Around the idea of thee.

## *Eidólons*

I met a seer,
Passing the hues and objects of the world,
The fields of art and learning, pleasure, sense,
To glean eidólons.

Put in thy chants said he,
No more the puzzling hour nor day, nor segments,
parts, put in,
Put first before the rest as light for all and entrance-
song of all,
That of eidólons.

Ever the dim beginning,
Ever the growth, the rounding of the circle,
Ever the summit and the merge at last, (to surely
start again,)
Eidólons! eidólons!

Ever the mutable,
Ever materials, changing, crumbling, re-cohering,
Ever the ateliers, the factories divine,
Issuing eidólons.

Lo, I or you,
Or woman, man, or state, known or unknown,
We seeming solid wealth, strength, beauty build,
But really build eidólons.

The ostent evanescent,
The substance of an artist's mood or savan's studies
long,
Or warrior's, martyr's, hero's toils,
To fashion his eidólon.

Of every human life,
(The units gather'd, posted, not a thought, emotion, deed, left out,)
The whole or large or small summ'd, added up,
In its eidólon.

The old, old urge,
Based on the ancient pinnacles, lo, newer, higher pinnacles,
From science and the modern still impell'd,
The old, old urge, eidólons.

The present now and here,
America's busy, teeming, intricate whirl,
Of aggregate and segregate for only thence releasing,
To-day's eidólons.

These with the past,
Of vanish'd lands, of all the reigns of kings across the sea,
Old conquerors, old campaigns, old sailor's voyages,
Joining eidólons.

Densities, growth, façades,
Strata of mountains, soils, rocks, giant trees,
Far-born, far-dying, living long, to leave,
Eidólons everlasting.

Exaltè, rapt, ecstatic,
The visible but their womb of birth,
Of orbic tendencies to shape and shape and shape,
The mighty earth-eidólon.

All space, all time,
(The stars, the terrible perturbations of the suns,
Swelling, collapsing, ending, serving their longer, shorter use,)
Fill'd with eidólons only.

The noiseless myriads,
The infinite oceans where the rivers empty,
The separate countless free identities, like eyesight,
The true realities, eidólons.

Not this the world,
Nor these the universes, they the universes,
Purport and end, ever the permanent life of life,
Eidólons, eidólons.

Beyond thy lectures learn'd professor,
Beyond thy telescope or spectroscope observer keen,
beyond all mathematics,
Beyond the doctor's surgery, anatomy, beyond the
chemist with his chemistry,
The entities of entities, eidólons.

Unfixed yet fix'd,
Ever shall be, ever have been and are,
Sweeping the present to the infinite future,
Eidólons, eidólons, eidólons.

The prophet and the bard,
Shall yet maintain themselves, in higher stages yet,
Shall mediate to the Modern, to Democracy,
interpret yet to them,
God and eidólons.

And thee my soul,
Joys, ceaseless exercises, exaltations,
Thy yearning amply fed at last, prepared to meet,
Thy mates, eidólons.

Thy body permanent,
The body lurking there within thy body,
The only purport of the form thou art, the real I myself,
An image, an eidólon.

Thy very songs not in thy songs,
No special strains to sing, none for itself,
But from the whole resulting, rising at last and
floating,
A round full-orb'd eidólon.

## *For him I Sing*

For him I sing,
I raise the present on the past,
(As some perennial tree out of its roots, the present
on the past,)
With time and space I him dilate and fuse the
immortal laws,
To make himself by them the law unto himself.

## *When I Read the Book*

When I read the book, the biography famous,
And is this then (said I) what the author calls a
man's life?
And so will some one when I am dead and gone
write my life?
(As if any man really knew aught of my life,
Why even I myself I often think know little or
nothing of my real life,
Only a few hints, a few diffused faint clews and
indirections
I seek for my own use to trace out here.)

## *Beginning My Studies*

Beginning my studies the first step pleas'd me so much,
The mere fact consciousness, these forms, the power
 of motion,
The least insect or animal, the senses, eyesight, love,
The first step I say awed me and pleas'd me so much,
I have hardly gone and hardly wish'd to go any farther,
But stop and loiter all the time to sing it in ecstatic
 songs.

## *Beginners*

How they are provided for upon the earth,
 (appearing at intervals,)
How dear and dreadful they are to the earth,
How they inure to themselves as much as to any –
 what a paradox appears their age,
How people respond to them, yet know them not,
How there is something relentless in their fate all
 times,
How all times mischoose the objects of their
 adulation and reward,
And how the same inexorable price must still be
 paid for the same great purchase.

## *To The States*

To the States or any one of them, or any city of the
States, *Resist much, obey little,*
Once unquestioning obedience, once fully enslaved,
Once fully enslaved, no nation, state, city, of this
earth, ever afterward resumes its liberty.

## *On Journeys through The States*

On journeys through the States we start,
(Ay through the world, urged by these songs,
Sailing henceforth to every land, to every sea,)
We willing learners of all, teachers of all, and lovers
of all.

We have watch'd the seasons dispensing themselves
and passing on,
And have said, Why should not a man or woman do
as much as the seasons, and effuse as much?

We dwell a while in every city and town,
We pass through Kanada, the North-east, the vast
valley of the Mississippi, and the Southern States,
We confer on equal terms with each of the States,
We make trial of ourselves and invite men and
women to hear,
We say to ourselves, Remember, fear not, be candid,
promulge the body and the soul,
Dwell a while and pass on, be copious, temperate,
chaste, magnetic,
And what you effuse may then return as the seasons
return,
And may be just as much as the seasons.

## *To a Certain Cantatrice*

Here, take this gift,
I was reserving it for some hero, speaker, or general,
One who should serve the good old cause, the great
 idea, the progress and freedom of the race,
Some brave confronter of despots, some daring rebel;
But I see that what I was reserving belongs to you
 just as much as to any.

## *Me Imperturbe*

Me imperturbe, standing at ease in Nature,
Master of all or mistress of all, aplomb in the midst
 of irrational things,
Imbued as they, passive, receptive, silent as they,
Finding my occupation, poverty, notoriety, foibles,
 crimes, less important than I thought,
Me toward the Mexican sea, or in the Mannahatta
 or the Tennessee, or far north or inland,
A river man, or a man of the woods or of any farm-life of
 these States or of the coast, or the lakes or Kanada,
Me wherever my life is lived, O to be self-balanced
 for contingencies,
To confront night, storms, hunger, ridicule,
 accidents, rebuffs, as the trees and animals do.

## *Savantism*

Thither as I look I see each result and glory retracing
 itself and nestling close, always obligated,
Thither hours, months, years – thither trades,
 compacts, establishments, even the most minute,
Thither every-day life, speech, utensils, politics,
 persons, estates;
Thither we also, I with my leaves and songs, trustful,
 admirant,
As a father to his father going takes his children
 along with him.

## *The Ship Starting*

Lo, the unbounded sea,
On its breast a ship starting, spreading all sails,
 carrying even her moonsails,
The pennant is flying aloft as she speeds she speeds
 so stately – below emulous waves press forward,
They surround the ship with shining curving
 motions and foam.

## *I Hear America Singing*

I hear America singing, the varied carols I hear,
Those of mechanics, each one singing his as it should be blithe and strong,
The carpenter singing his as he measures his plank or beam,
The mason singing his as he makes ready for work, or leaves off work,
The boatman singing what belongs to him in his boat, the deck-hand singing on the steamboat deck,
The shoemaker singing as he sits on his bench, the hatter singing as he stands,
The wood-cutter's song, the ploughboy's on his way in the morning, or at noon intermission or at sundown,
The delicious singing of the mother, or of the young wife at work, or of the girl sewing or washing,
Each singing what belongs to him or her and to none else,
The day what belongs to the day – at night the party of young fellows, robust, friendly,
Singing with open mouths their strong melodious songs.

## *What Place is Besieged?*

What place is besieged, and vainly tries to raise the siege?
Lo, I send to that place a commander, swift, brave, immortal,
And with him horse and foot, and parks of artillery,
And artillery-men, the deadliest that ever fired gun.

## *Still though the One I Sing*

Still though the one I sing,
(One, yet of contradictions made,) I dedicate to Nationality,
I leave in him revolt, (O latent right of insurrection! O quenchless, indispensable fire!)

## *Shut not Your Doors*

Shut not your doors to me proud libraries,
For that which was lacking on all your well-fill'd shelves, yet needed most, I bring,
Forth from the war emerging, a book I have made,
The words of my book nothing, the drift of it every thing,
A book separate, not link'd with the rest nor felt by the intellect,
But you ye untold latencies will thrill to every page.

## *Poets to Come*

Poets to come! orators, singers, musicians to come!
Not to-day is to justify me and answer what I am for,
But you, a new brood, native, athletic, continental, greater than before known,
Arouse! for you must justify me.

I myself but write one or two indicative words for the future,
I but advance a moment only to wheel and hurry back in the darkness.

I am a man who, sauntering along without fully
 stopping, turns a casual look upon you and then
 averts his face,
Leaving it to you to prove and define it,
Expecting the main things from you.

## *To You*

Stranger, if you passing meet me and desire to speak
 to me, why should you not speak to me?
And why should I not speak to you?

## *Thou Reader*

Thou reader throbbest life and pride and love the
 same as I,
Therefore for thee the following chants.

## *Starting from Paumanok*

1

Starting from fish-shape Paumanok where I was born,
Well-begotten, and rais'd by a perfect mother,
After roaming many lands, lover of populous pavements,
Dweller in Mannahatta my city, or on southern savannas,
Or a soldier camp'd or carrying my knapsack and gun, or a miner in California,
Or rude in my home in Dakota's woods, my diet meat, my drink from the spring,
Or withdrawn to muse and meditate in some deep recess,
Far from the clank of crowds intervals passing rapt and happy,
Aware of the fresh free giver the flowing Missouri, aware of mighty Niagara,
Aware of the buffalo herds grazing the plains, the hirsute and strong-breasted bull,
Of earth, rocks, Fifth-month flowers experienced, stars, rain, snow, my amaze,
Having studied the mocking-bird's tones and the flight of the mountain-hawk,
And heard at dawn the unrivall'd one, the hermit thrush from the swamp-cedars,
Solitary, singing in the West, I strike up for a New World.

2

Victory, union, faith, identity, time,
The indissoluble compacts, riches, mystery,
Eternal progress, the kosmos, and the modern reports.

This then is life,
Here is what has come to the surface after so many throes and convulsions.
How curious! how real!
Underfoot the divine soil, overhead the sun.
See revolving the globe,
The ancestor-continents away group'd together,
The present and future continents north and south, with the isthmus between.

See, vast trackless spaces,
As in a dream they change, they swiftly fill,
Countless masses debouch upon them,
They are now cover'd with the foremost people, arts, institutions, known.

See, projected through time,
For me an audience interminable.

With firm and regular step they wend, they never stop,
Successions of men, Americanos, a hundred millions,
One generation playing its part and passing on,
Another generation playing its part and passing on in its turn,
With faces turn'd sideways or backward towards me to listen,
With eyes retrospective towards me.

3

Americanos! conquerors! marches humanitarian!
Foremost! century marches! Libertad! masses!
For you a programme of chants.

Chants of the prairies,
Chants of the long-running Mississippi, and down to the Mexican sea,
Chants of Ohio, Indiana, Illinois, Iowa, Wisconsin and Minnesota,
Chants going forth from the centre from Kansas, and thence equidistant,
Shooting in pulses of fire ceaseless to vivify all.

4

Take my leaves America, take them South and take them North,
Make welcome for them everywhere, for they are your own offspring,
Surround them East and West, for they would surround you,
And you precedents, connect lovingly with them, for they connect lovingly with you.
I conn'd old times,
I sat studying at the feet of the great masters,
Now if eligible O that the great masters might return and study me.

In the name of these States shall I scorn the antique?
Why these are the children of the antique to justify it.

5

Dead poets, philosophs, priests,
Martyrs, artists, inventors, governments long since,
Language-shapers on other shores,
Nations once powerful, now reduced, withdrawn, or desolate,
I dare not proceed till I respectfully credit what you have left wafted hither,

I have perused it, own it is admirable, (moving
awhile among it,)
Think nothing can ever be greater, nothing can ever
deserve more than it deserves,
Regarding it all intently a long while, then dismissing it,
I stand in my place with my own day here.

Here lands female and male,
Here the heir-ship and heiress-ship of the world,
here the flame of materials,
Here spirituality the translatress, the openly-avow'd,
The ever-tending, the finalè of visible forms,
The satisfier, after due long-waiting now advancing,
Yes here comes my mistress the soul.

6

The soul,
Forever and forever – longer than soil is brown and
solid – longer than water ebbs and flows.

I will make the poems of materials, for I think they
are to be the most spiritual poems,
And I will make the poems of my body and of mortality,
For I think I shall then supply myself with the poems
of my soul and of immortality.

I will make a song for these States that no one State
may under any circumstances be subjected to
another State.
And I will make a song that there shall be comity by
day and by night between all the States, and
between any two of them,
And I will make a song for the ears of the President,
full of weapons with menacing points,
And behind the weapons countless dissatisfied faces;

And a song make I of the One form'd out of all,
The fang'd and glittering One whose head is over all,
Resolute warlike One including and over all,
(However high the head of any else that head is over all.)

I will acknowledge contemporary lands,
I will trail the whole geography of the globe and
salute courteously every city large and small,
And employments! I will put in my poems that with
you is heroism upon land and sea,
And I will report all heroism from an American
point of view.

I will sing the song of companionship,
I will show what alone must finally compact these,
I believe these are to found their own ideal of manly
love, indicating it in me,
I will therefore let flame from me the burning fires
that were threatening to consume me,
I will lift what has too long kept down those
smouldering fires,
I will give them complete abandonment,
I will write the evangel-poem of comrades and of love,
For who but I should understand love with all its
sorrow and joy?
And who but I should be the poet of comrades?

7

I am the credulous man of qualities, ages, races,
I advance from the people in their own spirit,
Here is what sings unrestricted faith.

Omnes! omnes! let others ignore what they may,
I make the poem of evil also, I commemorate that
part also,

I am myself just as much evil as good, and my
nation is – and I say there is in fact no evil,
(Or if there is I say it is just as important to you, to
the land or to me, as any thing else.)

I too, following many and follow'd by many,
inaugurate a religion, I descend into the arena,
(It may be I am destin'd to utter the loudest cries
there, the winner's pealing shouts,
Who knows? they may rise from me yet, and soar
above every thing.)

Each is not for its own sake,
I say the whole earth and all the stars in the sky are
for religion's sake.
I say no man has ever yet been half devout enough,
None has ever yet adored or worship'd half enough,
None has begun to think how divine he himself is,
and how certain the future is.
I say that the real and permanent grandeur of these
States must be their religion,
Otherwise there is no real and permanent grandeur;
(Nor character nor life worthy the name without
religion,
Nor land nor man or woman without religion.)

8

What are you doing young man?
Are you so earnest, so given up to literature, science,
art, amours?
These ostensible realities, politics, points?

Your ambition or business whatever it may be?
It is well – against such I say not a word, I am their
poet also,

But behold! such swiftly subside, burnt up for
religion's sake,
For not all matter is fuel to heat, impalpable flame,
the essential life of the earth,
Any more than such are to religion.

9

What do you seek so pensive and silent?
What do you need camerado?
Dear son do you think it is love?

Listen dear son – listen America, daughter or son,
It is a painful thing to love a man or woman to
excess, and yet it satisfies, it is great,
But there is something else very great, it makes the
whole coincide,
It, magnificent, beyond materials, with continuous
hands sweeps and provides for all.

10

Know you, solely to drop in the earth the germs of a
greater religion,
The following chants each for its kind I sing.

My comrade!
For you to share with me two greatnesses, and a
third one rising inclusive and more resplendent,
The greatness of Love and Democracy, and the
greatness of Religion.

Melange mine own, the unseen and the seen,
Mysterious ocean where the streams empty,
Prophetic spirit of material shifting and flickering
around me,
Living beings, identities now doubtless near us in the
air that we know not of,

Contact daily and hourly that will not release me,
These selecting, these in hints demanded of me.

Not he with a daily kiss onward from childhood
kissing me,
Has winded and twisted around me that which holds
me to him,
Any more than I am held to the heavens and all the
spiritual world,
After what they have done to me, suggesting themes.
O such themes – equalities! O divine average!
Warblings under the sun, usher'd as now, or at
noon, or setting,
Strains musical flowing through ages, now reaching
hither,
I take to your reckless and composite chords, add to
them, and cheerfully pass them forward.

II

As I have walk'd in Alabama my morning walk,
I have seen where the she-bird the mocking-bird sat
on her nest in the briers hatching her brood.

I have seen the he-bird also,
I have paus'd to hear him near at hand inflating his
throat and joyfully singing.

And while I paus'd it came to me that what he really
sang for was not there only,
Nor for his mate nor himself only, nor all sent back
by the echoes,
But subtle, clandestine, away beyond,
A charge transmitted and gift occult for those being
born.

12

Democracy! near at hand to you a throat is now
inflating itself and joyfully singing.

Ma femme! for the brood beyond us and of us,
For those who belong here and those to come,
I exultant to be ready for them will now shake out
carols stronger and haughtier than have ever yet
been heard upon earth.
I will make the songs of passion to give them their way,
And your songs outlaw'd offenders, for I scan you
with kindred eyes, and carry you with me the
same as any.

I will make the true poem of riches,
To earn for the body and the mind whatever adheres
and goes forward and is not dropt by death;
I will effuse egotism and show it underlying all, and I
will be the bard of personality,
And I will show of male and female that either is but
the equal of the other,
And sexual organs and acts! do you concentrate in
me, for I am determin'd to tell you with
courageous clear voice to prove you illustrious,
And I will show that there is no imperfection in the
present, and can be none in the future,
And I will show that whatever happens to anybody it
may be turn'd to beautiful results,
And I will show that nothing can happen more
beautiful than death,
And I will thread a thread through my poems that
time and events are compact,
And that all the things of the universe are perfect
miracles, each as profound as any.

I will not make poems with reference to parts,
But I will make poems, songs, thoughts, with
reference to ensemble,
And I will not sing with reference to a day, but with
reference to all days,
And I will not make a poem nor the least part of a
poem but has reference to the soul,
Because having look'd at the objects of the universe,
I find there is no one nor any particle of one but
has reference to the soul.

## 13

Was somebody asking to see the soul?
See, your own shape and countenance, persons,
substances, beasts, the trees, the running rivers,
the rocks and sands.

All hold spiritual joys and afterwards loosen them;
How can the real body ever die and be buried?

Of your real body and any man's or woman's real body,
Item for item it will elude the hands of the corpse-
cleaners and pass to fitting spheres,
Carrying what has accrued to it from the moment of
birth to the moment of death.

Not the types set up by the printer return their
impression, the meaning, the main concern,
Any more than a man's substance and life or a woman's
substance and life return in the body and the soul,
Indifferently before death and after death.

Behold, the body includes and is the meaning, the
main concern, and includes and is the soul;
Whoever you are, how superb and how divine is
your body, or any part of it!

14

Whoever you are, to you endless announcements!

Daughter of the lands did you wait for your poet?
Did you wait for one with a flowing mouth and indicative hand?
Toward the male of the States, and toward the female of the States,
Exulting words, words to Democracy's lands.

Interlink'd, food-yielding lands!
Land of coal and iron! land of gold! land of cotton, sugar, rice!
Land of wheat, beef, pork! land of wool and hemp! land of the apple and the grape!
Land of the pastoral plains, the grass-fields of the world! land of those sweet-air'd interminable plateaus!
Land of the herd, the garden, the healthy house of adobie!
Lands where the north-west Columbia winds, and where the south-west Colorado winds!
Land of the eastern Chesapeake! land of the Delaware!
Land of Ontario, Erie, Huron, Michigan!
Land of the Old Thirteen! Massachusetts land! land of Vermont and Connecticut!
Land of the ocean shores! land of sierras and peaks!
Land of boatmen and sailors! fishermen's land!
Inextricable lands! the clutch'd together! the passionate ones!
The side by side! the elder and younger brothers! the bony-limb'd!
The great women's land! the feminine! the experienced sisters and the inexperienced sisters!

Far breath'd land! Arctic braced! Mexican breez'd! the
diverse! the compact!
The Pennsylvanian! the Virginian! the double
Carolinian!
O all and each well-loved by me! my intrepid nations! O
I at any rate include you all with perfect love!
I cannot be discharged from you! not from one any
sooner than another!
O death! O for all that, I am yet of you unseen this
hour with irrepressible love,
Walking New England, a friend, a traveler,
Splashing my bare feet in the edge of the summer
ripples of Paumanok's sands,
Crossing the prairies, dwelling again in Chicago,
dwelling in every town,
Observing shows, births, improvements, structures,
arts,
Listening to orators and oratresses in public halls,
Of and through the States as during life, each man
and woman my neighbor,
The Louisianian, the Georgian, as near to me, and I
as near to him and her,
The Mississippian and Arkansian yet with me, and I
yet with any of them,
Yet upon the plains west of the spinal river, yet in
my house of adobie,
Yet returning eastward, yet in the Seaside State or in
Maryland,
Yet Kanadian cheerily braving the winter, the snow
and ice welcome to me,
Yet a true son either of Maine or of the Granite State, or
the Narragansett Bay State, or the Empire State,
Yet sailing to other shores to annex the same, yet
welcoming every new brother,

Hereby applying these leaves to the new ones from the hour they unite with the old ones,
Coming among the new ones myself to be their companion and equal, coming personally to you now,
Enjoining you to acts, characters, spectacles, with me.

15

With me with firm holding, yet haste, haste on.
For your life adhere to me,
(I may have to be persuaded many times before I consent to give myself really to you, but what of that?
Must not Nature be persuaded many times?)
No dainty dolce affettuoso I,
Bearded, sun-burnt, gray-neck'd, forbidding, I have arrived,
To be wrestled with as I pass for the solid prizes of the universe,
For such I afford whoever can persevere to win them.

16

On my way a moment I pause,
Here for you! and here for America!
Still the present I raise aloft, still the future of the States I harbinge glad and sublime,
And for the past I pronounce what the air holds of the red aborigines.
The red aborigines,
Leaving natural breaths, sounds of rain and winds, calls as of birds and animals in the woods, syllabled, to us for names,
Okonee, Koosa, Ottawa, Monongahela, Sauk, Natchez, Chattahoochee, Kaqueta, Oronoco,

Wabash, Miami, Saginaw, Chippewa, Oshkosh,
Walla-Walla,
Leaving such to the States they melt, they depart,
charging the water and the land with names.

17

Expanding and swift, henceforth,
Elements, breeds, adjustments, turbulent, quick and
audacious,
A world primal again, vistas of glory incessant and
branching,
A new race dominating previous ones and grander
far, with new contests,
New politics, new literatures and religions, new
inventions and arts.
These, my voice announcing – I will sleep no more
but arise,
You oceans that have been calm within me! how I
feel you, fathomless, stirring, preparing
unprecedented waves and storms.

18

See, steamers steaming through my poems,
See, in my poems immigrants continually coming
and landing,
See, in arriere, the wigwam, the trail, the hunter's
hut, the flatboat, the maize-leaf, the claim, the
rude fence, and the backwoods village,
See, on the one side the Western Sea and on the other
the Eastern Sea, how they advance and retreat upon
my poems as upon their own shores,
See, pastures and forests in my poems – see, animals
wild and tame – see, beyond the Kaw, countless
herds of buffalo feeding on short curly grass,

See, in my poems, cities, solid, vast, inland, with
paved streets, with iron and stone edifices,
ceaseless vehicles, and commerce,
See, the many-cylinder'd steam printing-press – see,
the electric telegraph stretching across the
continent,
See, through Atlantica's depths pulses American
Europe reaching, pulses of Europe duly return'd,
See, the strong and quick locomotive as it departs,
panting, blowing the steam-whistle,
See, ploughmen ploughing farms – see, miners
digging mines – see, the numberless factories,
See, mechanics busy at their benches with tools – see
from among them superior judges, philosophs,
Presidents, emerge, drest in working dresses,
See, lounging through the shops and fields of the States,
me well-belov'd, close-held by day and night,
Hear the loud echoes of my songs there – read the
hints come at last.

19

O camerado close! O you and me at last, and us two
only.
O a word to clear one's path ahead endlessly!
O something ecstatic and undemonstrable! O music
wild!
O now I triumph – and you shall also;
O hand in hand – O wholesome pleasure – O one
more desirer and lover!
O to haste firm holding – to haste, haste on with me.

## *Song of Myself*

### 1

I celebrate myself, and sing myself,
And what I assume you shall assume,
For every atom belonging to me as good belongs to you.

I loafe and invite my soul,
I lean and loafe at my ease observing a spear of summer grass.

My tongue, every atom of my blood, form'd from this soil, this air,
Born here of parents born here from parents the same, and their parents the same,
I, now thirty-seven years old in perfect health begin,
Hoping to cease not till death.
Creeds and schools in abeyance,
Retiring back a while sufficed at what they are, but never forgotten,
I harbor for good or bad, I permit to speak at every hazard,
Nature without check with original energy.

### 2

Houses and rooms are full of perfumes, the shelves are crowded with perfumes,
I breathe the fragrance myself and know it and like it,
The distillation would intoxicate me also, but I shall not let it.

The atmosphere is not a perfume, it has no taste of the distillation, it is odorless,
It is for my mouth forever, I am in love with it,

I will go to the bank by the wood and become
undisguised and naked,
I am mad for it to be in contact with me.

The smoke of my own breath,
Echoes, ripples, buzz'd whispers, love-root, silk-
thread, crotch and vine,
My respiration and inspiration, the beating of my heart,
the passing of blood and air through my lungs,
The sniff of green leaves and dry leaves, and of the shore
and dark-color'd sea-rocks, and of hay in the barn,
The sound of the belch'd words of my voice loos'd
to the eddies of the wind,
A few light kisses, a few embraces, a reaching
around of arms,
The play of shine and shade on the trees as the
supple boughs wag,
The delight alone or in the rush of the streets, or
along the fields and hill-sides,
The feeling of health, the full-noon trill, the song of
me rising from bed and meeting the sun.

Have you reckon'd a thous and acres much? have
you reckon'd the earth much?
Have you practis'd so long to learn to read?
Have you felt so proud to get at the meaning of
poems?

Stop this day and night with me and you shall
possess the origin of all poems,
You shall possess the good of the earth and sun,
(there are millions of suns left,)
You shall no longer take things at second or third
hand, nor look through the eyes of the dead, nor
feed on the spectres in books,

You shall not look through my eyes either, nor take things from me,
You shall listen to all sides and filter them from your self.

3

I have heard what the talkers were talking, the talk of the beginning and the end,
But I do not talk of the beginning or the end.

There was never any more inception than there is now,
Nor any more youth or age than there is now,
And will never be any more perfection than there is now,
Nor any more heaven or hell than there is now.

Urge and urge and urge,
Always the procreant urge of the world.
Out of the dimness opposite equals advance, always substance and increase, always sex,
Always a knit of identity, always distinction, always a breed of life.

To elaborate is no avail, learn'd and unlearn'd feel that it is so.

Sure as the most certain sure, plumb in the uprights, well entretied, braced in the beams,
Stout as a horse, affectionate, haughty, electrical,
I and this mystery here we stand.

Clear and sweet is my soul, and clear and sweet is all that is not my soul.

Lack one lacks both, and the unseen is proved by the seen,
Till that becomes unseen and receives proof in its turn.

Showing the best and dividing it from the worst age vexes age,
Knowing the perfect fitness and equanimity of things, while they discuss I am silent, and go bathe and admire myself.
Welcome is every organ and attribute of me, and of any man hearty and clean,
Not an inch nor a particle of an inch is vile, and none shall be less familiar than the rest.

I am satisfied – I see, dance, laugh, sing;
As the hugging and loving bed-fellow sleeps at my side through the night, and withdraws at the peep of the day with stealthy tread,
Leaving me baskets cover'd with white towels swelling the house with their plenty,
Shall I postpone my acceptation and realization and scream at my eyes,
That they turn from gazing after and down the road,
And forthwith cipher and show me to a cent,
Exactly the value of one and exactly the value of two, and which is ahead?

4

Trippers and askers surround me,
People I meet, the effect upon me of my early life or the ward and city I live in, or the nation,
The latest dates, discoveries, inventions, societies, authors old and new,
My dinner, dress, associates, looks, compliments, dues,
The real or fancied indifference of some man or woman I love,
The sickness of one of my folks or of myself, or ill-doing or loss or lack of money, or depressions or exaltations,

Battles, the horrors of fratricidal war, the fever of doubtful news, the fitful events;
These come to me days and nights and go from me again,
But they are not the Me myself.

Apart from the pulling and hauling stands what I am,
Stands amused, complacent, compassionating, idle, unitary,
Looks down, is erect, or bends an arm on an impalpable certain rest,
Looking with side-curved head curious what will come next,
Both in and out of the game and watching and wondering at it.

Backward I see in my own days where I sweated through fog with linguists and contenders,
I have no mockings or arguments, I witness and wait.

5

I believe in you my soul, the other I am must not abase itself to you,
And you must not be abased to the other.

Loafe with me on the grass, loose the stop from your throat,
Not words, not music or rhyme I want, not custom or lecture, not even the best,
Only the lull I like, the hum of your valvèd voice.

I mind how once we lay such a transparent summer morning,
How you settled your head athwart my hips and gently turn'd over upon me,

And parted the shirt from my bosom-bone, and
plunged your tongue to my bare-stript heart,
And reach'd till you felt my beard, and reach'd till
you held my feet.

Swiftly arose and spread around me the peace and
knowledge that pass all the argument of the earth,
And I know that the hand of God is the promise of
my own,
And I know that the spirit of God is the brother of
my own,
And that all the men ever born are also my brothers,
and the women my sisters and lovers,
And that a kelson of the creation is love,
And limitless are leaves stiff or drooping in the fields,
And brown ants in the little wells beneath them,
And mossy scabs of the worm fence, heap'd stones,
elder, mullein and poke-weed.

6

A child said *What is the grass?* fetching it to me with
full hands;
How could I answer the child? I do not know what it
is any more than he.

I guess it must be the flag of my disposition, out of
hopeful green stuff woven.
Or I guess it is the handkerchief of the Lord,
A scented gift and remembrancer designedly dropt,
Bearing the owner's name someway in the corners,
that we may see and remark, and say *Whose*?

Or I guess the grass is itself a child, the produced
babe of the vegetation.

Or I guess it is a uniform hieroglyphic,
And it means, Sprouting alike in broad zones and
 narrow zones,
Growing among black folks as among white,
Kanuck, Tuckahoe, Congressman, Cuff, I give them
 the same, I receive them the same.

And now it seems to me the beautiful uncut hair of
 graves.

Tenderly will I use you curling grass,
It may be you transpire from the breasts of young men,
It may be if I had known them I would have loved them,
It may be you are from old people, or from offspring
 taken soon out of their mothers' laps,
And here you are the mothers' laps.

This grass is very dark to be from the white heads of
 old mothers,
Darker than the colorless beards of old men,
Dark to come from under the faint red roofs of
 mouths.

O I perceive after all so many uttering tongues,
And I perceive they do not come from the roofs of
 mouths for nothing.

I wish I could translate the hints about the dead
 young men and women,
And the hints about old men and mothers, and the
 offspring taken soon out of their laps.

What do you think has become of the young and old
 men?
And what do you think has become of the women
 and children?

They are alive and well somewhere,
The smallest sprout shows there is really no death,
And if ever there was it led forward life, and does
not wait at the end to arrest it,
And ceas'd the moment life appear'd.

All goes onward and outward, nothing collapses,
And to die is different from what any one supposed,
and luckier.

7

Has any one supposed it lucky to be born?
I hasten to inform him or her it is just as lucky to
die, and I know it.

I pass death with the dying and birth with the new-
wash'd babe, and am not contain'd between my
hat and boots,
And peruse manifold objects, no two alike and every
one good,
The earth good and the stars good, and their
adjuncts all good.

I am not an earth nor an adjunct of an earth,
I am the mate and companion of people, all just as
immortal and fathomless as myself,
(They do not know how immortal, but I know.)

Every kind for itself and its own, for me mine male
and female,
For me those that have been boys and that love
women,
For me the man that is proud and feels how it stings
to be slighted,
For me the sweet-heart and the old maid, for me
mothers and the mothers of mothers,

For me lips that have smiled, eyes that have shed tears,
For me children and the begetters of children.

Undrape! you are not guilty to me, nor stale nor discarded,
I see through the broadcloth and gingham whether or no,
And am around, tenacious, acquisitive, tireless, and cannot be shaken away.

8

The little one sleeps in its cradle,
I lift the gauze and look a long time, and silently brush away flies with my hand.
The youngster and the red-faced girl turn aside up the bushy hill,
I peeringly view them from the top.
The suicide sprawls on the bloody floor of the bedroom,
I witness the corpse with its dabbled hair, I note where the pistol has fallen.

The blab of the pave, tires of carts, sluff of boot-soles, talk of the promenaders,
The heavy omnibus, the driver with his interrogating thumb, the clank of the shod horses on the granite floor,
The snow-sleighs, clinking, shouted jokes, pelts of snow-balls,
The hurrahs for popular favorites, the fury of rous'd mobs,
The flap of the curtain'd litter, a sick man inside borne to the hospital,
The meeting of enemies, the sudden oath, the blows and fall,

The excited crowd, the policeman with his star quickly
working his passage to the centre of the crowd,
The impassive stones that receive and return so
many echoes,
What groans of over-fed or half-starv'd who fall
sunstruck or in fits,
What exclamations of women taken suddenly who
hurry home and give birth to babes,
What living and buried speech is always vibrating
here, what howls restrain'd by decorum,
Arrests of criminals, slights, adulterous offers made,
acceptances, rejections with convex lips,
I mind them or the show or resonance of them – I
come and I depart.

9

The big doors of the country barn stand open and ready,
The dried grass of the harvest-time loads the
slow-drawn wagon,
The clear light plays on the brown gray and green
intertinged,
The armfuls are pack'd to the sagging mow.

I am there, I help, I came stretch'd atop of the load,
I felt its soft jolts, one leg reclined on the other,
I jump from the cross-beams and seize the clover
and timothy,
And roll head over heels and tangle my hair full of wisps.

10

Alone far in the wilds and mountains I hunt,
Wandering amazed at my own lightness and glee,
In the late afternoon choosing a safe spot to pass the
night,

Kindling a fire and broiling the fresh-kill'd game,
Falling asleep on the gather'd leaves with my dog
and gun by my side.

The Yankee clipper is under her sky-sails, she cuts
the sparkle and scud,
My eyes settle the land, I bend at her prow or shout
joyously from the deck.

The boatmen and clam-diggers arose early and stopt
for me,
I tuck'd my trowser-ends in my boots and went and
had a good time;
You should have been with us that day round the
chowder-kettle.

I saw the marriage of the trapper in the open air in
the far west, the bride was a red girl,
Her father and his friends sat near cross-legged and
dumbly smoking, they had moccasins to their
feet and large thick blankets hanging from their
shoulders,
On a bank lounged the trapper, he was drest mostly
in skins, his luxuriant beard and curls protected
his neck, he held his bride by the hand,
She had long eyelashes, her head was bare, her
coarse straight locks descended upon her
voluptuous limbs and reach'd to her feet.

The runaway slave came to my house and stopt
outside,
I heard his motions crackling the twigs of the woodpile,
Through the swung half-door of the kitchen I saw
him limpsy and weak,
And went where he sat on a log and led him in and
assured him,

And brought water and fill'd a tub for his sweated body
    and bruis'd feet,
And gave him a room that enter'd from my own,
    and gave him some coarse clean clothes,
And remember perfectly well his revolving eyes and
    his awkwardness,
And remember putting plasters on the galls of his
    neck and ankles;
He staid with me a week before he was recuperated
    and pass'd north,
I had him sit next me at table, my fire-lock lean'd in
    the corner.

11

Twenty-eight young men bathe by the shore,
Twenty-eight young men and all so friendly;
Twenty-eight years of womanly life and all so
    lonesome.

She owns the fine house by the rise of the bank,
She hides handsome and richly drest aft the blinds
    of the window.

Which of the young men does she like the best?
Ah the homeliest of them is beautiful to her.

Where are you off to, lady? for I see you,
You splash in the water there, yet stay stock still in
    your room.

Dancing and laughing along the beach came the
    twenty-ninth bather,
The rest did not see her, but she saw them and loved
    them.

The beards of the young men glisten'd with wet, it
ran from their long hair,
Little streams pass'd all over their bodies.

An unseen hand also pass'd over their bodies,
It descended tremblingly from their temples and ribs.

The young men float on their backs, their white
bellies bulge to the sun, they do not ask who
seizes fast to them,
They do not know who puffs and declines with
pendant and bending arch,
They do not think whom they souse with spray.

12

The butcher-boy puts off his killing-clothes, or
sharpens his knife at the stall in the market,
I loiter enjoying his repartee and his shuffle and
breakdown.

Blacksmiths with grimed and hairy chests environ
the anvil,
Each has his main-sledge, they are all out, there is a
great heat in the fire.

From the cinder-strew'd threshold I follow their
movements,
The lithe sheer of their waists plays even with their
massive arms,
Overhand the hammers swing, overhand so slow,
overhand so sure,
They do not hasten, each man hits in his place.

13

The negro holds firmly the reins of his four horses, the block swags underneath on its tied-over chain,
The negro that drives the long dray of the stone-yard, steady and tall he stands pois'd on one leg on the string-piece,
His blue shirt exposes his ample neck and breast and loosens over his hip-band,
His glance is calm and commanding, he tosses the slouch of his hat away from his forehead,
The sun falls on his crispy hair and mustache, falls on the black of his polish'd and perfect limbs.

I behold the picturesque giant and love him, and I do not stop there,
I go with the team also.

In me the caresser of life wherever moving, backward as well as forward sluing,
To niches aside and junior bending, not a person or object missing
Absorbing all to myself and for this song.

Oxen that rattle the yoke and chain or halt in the leafy shade, what is that you express in your eyes?
It seems to me more than all the print I have read in my life.
My tread scares the wood-drake and wood-duck on my distant and day-long ramble,
They rise together, they slowly circle around.

I believe in those wing'd purposes,
And acknowledge red, yellow, white, playing within me,
And consider green and violet and the tufted crown intentional,

And do not call the tortoise unworthy because she is
not something else,
And the jay in the woods never studied the gamut,
yet trills pretty well to me,
And the look of the bay mare shames silliness out of me.

14

The wild gander leads his flock through the cool
night,
*Ya-honk* he says, and sounds it down to me like an
invitation,
The pert may suppose it meaningless, but I listening
close,
Find its purpose and place up there toward the
wintry sky.

The sharp-hoof'd moose of the north, the cat on the
house-sill, the chickadee, the prairie-dog,
The litter of the grunting sow as they tug at her
teats,
The brood of the turkey-hen and she with her half-
spread wings,
I see in them and myself the same old law.

The press of my foot to the earth springs a hundred
affections,
They scorn the best I can do to relate them.

I am enamour'd of growing out-doors,
Of men that live among cattle or taste of the ocean
or woods,
Of the builders and steerers of ships and the wielders
of axes and mauls, and the drivers of horses,
I can eat and sleep with them week in and week out.

What is commonest, cheapest, nearest, easiest, is Me,
Me going in for my chances, spending for vast returns,
Adorning myself to bestow myself on the first that will take me,
Not asking the sky to come down to my good will,
Scattering it freely forever.

## 15

The pure contralto sings in the organ loft,
The carpenter dresses his plank, the tongue of his foreplane whistles its wild ascending lisp,
The married and unmarried children ride home to their Thanksgiving dinner,
The pilot seizes the king-pin, he heaves down with a strong arm,
The mate stands braced in the whale-boat, lance and harpoon are ready,
The duck-shooter walks by silent and cautious stretches,
The deacons are ordain'd with cross'd hands at the altar,
The spinning-girl retreats and advances to the hum of the big wheel,
The farmer stops by the bars as he walks on a First-day loafe and looks at the oats and rye,
The lunatic is carried at last to the asylum a confirm'd case,
(He will never sleep any more as he did in the cot in his mother's bedroom;)
The jour printer with gray head and gaunt jaws works at his case,
He turns his quid of tobacco while his eyes blurr with the manuscript;

The malform'd limbs are tied to the surgeon's table,
What is removed drops horribly in a pail;
The quadroon girl is sold at the auction-stand, the
drunkard nods by the bar-room stove,
The machinist rolls up his sleeves, the policeman
travels his beat, the gate-keeper marks who pass,
The young fellow drives the express-wagon, (I love
him, though I do not know him;)
The half-breed straps on his light boots to compete
in the race,
The western turkey-shooting draws old and young,
some lean on their rifles, some sit on logs,
Out from the crowd steps the marksman, takes his
position, levels his piece;
The groups of newly-come immigrants cover the
wharf or levee,
As the woolly-pates hoe in the sugar-field, the
overseer views them from his saddle,
The bugle calls in the ball-room, the gentlemen run
for their partners, the dancers bow to each other,
The youth lies awake in the cedar-roof'd garret and
harks to the musical rain,
The Wolverine sets traps on the creek that helps fill
the Huron,
The squaw wrapt in her yellow-hemm'd cloth is
offering moccasins and bead-bags for sale,
The connoisseur peers along the exhibition-gallery
with half-shut eyes bent sideways,
As the deck-hands make fast the steamboat the
plank is thrown for the shore-going passengers,
The young sister holds out the skein while the elder
sister winds it off in a ball, and stops now and
then for the knots,

The one-year wife is recovering and happy having a
week ago borne her first child,
The clean-hair'd Yankee girl works with her sewing-
machine or in the factory or mill,
The paving-man leans on his two-handed rammer, the
reporter's lead flies swiftly over the note-book, the
sign-painter is lettering with blue and gold,
The canal boy trots on the tow-path, the book-keeper
counts at his desk, the shoemaker waxes his thread,
The conductor beats time for the band and all the
performers follow him,
The child is baptized, the convert is making his first
professions,
The regatta is spread on the bay, the race is begun,
(how the white sails sparkle!)
The drover watching his drove sings out to them
that would stray,
The pedler sweats with his pack on his back, (the
purchaser higgling about the odd cent;)
The bride unrumples her white dress, the minute-
hand of the clock moves slowly,
The opium-eater reclines with rigid head and just-
open'd lips,
The prostitute draggles her shawl, her bonnet bobs
on her tipsy and pimpled neck,
The crowd laugh at her blackguard oaths, the men
jeer and wink to each other,
(Miserable! I do not laugh at your oaths nor jeer you;)
The President holding a cabinet council is
surrounded by the great Secretaries,
On the piazza walk three matrons stately and
friendly with twined arms,
The crew of the fish-smack pack repeated layers of
halibut in the hold,

The Missourian crosses the plains toting his wares
and his cattle,
As the fare-collector goes through the train he gives
notice by the jingling of loose change,
The floor-men are laying the floor, the tinners are
tinning the roof, the masons are calling for mortar,
In single file each shouldering his hod pass onward
the laborers;
Seasons pursuing each other the indescribable crowd
is gather'd, it is the fourth of Seventh-month,
(what salutes of cannon and small arms!)
Seasons pursuing each other the plougher ploughs,
the mower mows, and the winter-grain falls in
the ground;
Off on the lakes the pike-fisher watches and waits by
the hole in the frozen surface,
The stumps stand thick round the clearing, the
squatter strikes deep with his axe,
Flatboatmen make fast towards dusk near the
cotton-wood or pecan-trees,
Coon-seekers go through the regions of the Red
river or through those drain'd by the Tennessee,
or through those of the Arkansas,
Torches shine in the dark that hangs on the
Chattahooche or Altamahaw,
Patriarchs sit at supper with sons and grandsons and
great-grandsons around them,
In walls of adobie, in canvas tents, rest hunters and
trappers after their day's sport,
The city sleeps and the country sleeps,
The living sleep for their time, the dead sleep for
their time,
The old husband sleeps by his wife and the young
husband sleeps by his wife;

And these tend inward to me, and I tend outward to them,
And such as it is to be of these more or less I am,
And of these one and all I weave the song of myself.

16

I am of old and young, of the foolish as much as the wise,
Regardless of others, ever regardful of others,
Maternal as well as paternal, a child as well as a man,
Stuff'd with the stuff that is coarse and stuff'd with the stuff that is fine,
One of the Nation of many nations, the smallest the same and the largest the same,
A Southerner soon as a Northerner, a planter nonchalant and hospitable down by the Oconee I live,
A Yankee bound my own way ready for trade, my joints the limberest joints on earth and the sternest joints on earth,
A Kentuckian walking the vale of the Elkhorn in my deer-skin leggings, a Louisianian or Georgian,
A boatman over lakes or bays or along coasts, a Hoosier, Badger, Buck-eye;
At home on Kanadian snow-shoes or up in the bush, or with fishermen off Newfoundland,
At home in the fleet of ice-boats, sailing with the rest and tacking,
At home on the hills of Vermont or in the woods of Maine, or the Texan ranch,
Comrade of Californians, comrade of free North-Westerners, (loving their big proportions,)
Comrade of raftsmen and coalmen, comrade of all who shake hands and welcome to drink and meat,

A learner with the simplest, a teacher of the thoughtfullest
A novice beginning yet experient of myriads of seasons,
Of every hue and caste am I, of every rank and religion,
A farmer, mechanic, artist, gentleman, sailor, quaker,
Prisoner, fancy-man, rowdy, lawyer, physician, priest.

I resist any thing better than my own diversity,
Breathe the air but leave plenty after me,
And am not stuck up, and am in my place.

(The moth and the fish-eggs are in their place,
The bright suns I see and the dark suns I cannot see are in their place,
The palpable is in its place and the impalpable is in its place.)

17

These are really the thoughts of all men in all ages and lands, they are not original with me,
If they are not yours as much as mine they are nothing, or next to nothing,
If they are not the riddle and the untying of the riddle they are nothing,
If they are not just as close as they are distant they are nothing.

This is the grass that grows wherever the land is and the water is,
This the common air that bathes the globe.

18

With music strong I come, with my cornets and my drums,
I play not marches for accepted victors only, I play marches for conquer'd and slain persons.

Have you heard that it was good to gain the day?
I also say it is good to fall, battles are lost in the same
spirit in which they are won.

I beat and pound for the dead,
I blow through my embouchures my loudest and
gayest for them.

Vivas to those who have fail'd!
And to those whose war-vessels sank in the sea!
And to those themselves who sank in the sea!
And to all generals that lost engagements, and all
overcome heroes!
And the numberless unknown heroes equal to the
greatest heroes known!

## 19

This is the meal equally set, this the meat for natural
hunger,
It is for the wicked just the same as the righteous, I
make appointments with all,
I will not have a single person slighted or left away,
The kept-woman, sponger, thief, are hereby invited,
The heavy-lipp'd slave is invited, the venerealee is
invited;
There shall be no difference between them and the
rest.

This is the press of a bashful hand, this the float and
odor of hair,
This the touch of my lips to yours, this the murmur
of yearning,
This the far-off depth and height reflecting my own
face,
This the thoughtful merge of myself, and the outlet
again.

Do you guess I have some intricate purpose?
Well I have, for the Fourth-month showers have,
and the mica on the side of a rock has.

Do you take it I would astonish?
Does the daylight astonish? does the early redstart
twittering through the woods?
Do I astonish more than they?

This hour I tell things in confidence,
I might not tell everybody, but I will tell you.

20

Who goes there? hankering, gross, mystical, nude;
How is it I extract strength from the beef I eat?

What is a man anyhow? what am I? what are you?

All I mark as my own you shall offset it with your own,
Else it were time lost listening to me.

I do not snivel that snivel the world over,
That months are vacuums and the ground but
wallow and filth.

Whimpering and truckling fold with powders for
invalids, conformity goes to the fourth-remov'd,
I wear my hat as I please indoors or out.

Why should I pray? why should I venerate and be
ceremonious?

Having pried through the strata, analyzed to a hair,
counsel'd with doctors and calculated close,
I find no sweeter fat than sticks to my own bones.
In all people I see myself, none more and not one a
barley-corn less,
And the good or bad I say of myself I say of them.

I know I am solid and sound,
To me the converging objects of the universe perpetually flow,
All are written to me, and I must get what the writing means.

I know I am deathless,
I know this orbit of mine cannot be swept by a carpenter's compass,
I know I shall not pass like a child's carlacue cut with a burnt stick at night.

I know I am august,
I do not trouble my spirit to vindicate itself or be understood,
I see that the elementary laws never apologize,
(I reckon I behave no prouder than the level I plant my house by, after all.)

I exist as I am, that is enough,
If no other in the world be aware I sit content,
And if each and all be aware I sit content.

One world is aware and by far the largest to me, and that is myself,
And whether I come to my own to-day or in ten thousand or ten million years,
I can cheerfully take it now, or with equal cheerfulness I can wait.

My foothold is tenon'd and mortis'd in granite,
I laugh at what you call dissolution,
And I know the amplitude of time.

## 21

I am the poet of the Body and I am the poet of the Soul,
The pleasures of heaven are with me and the pains of hell are with me,
The first I graft and increase upon myself, the latter I translate into a new tongue.
I am the poet of the woman the same as the man,
And I say it is as great to be a woman as to be a man,
And I say there is nothing greater than the mother of men.

I chant the chant of dilation or pride,
We have had ducking and deprecating about enough,
I show that size is only development.

Have you outstript the rest? are you the President?
It is a trifle, they will more than arrive there every one, and still pass on.

I am he that walks with the tender and growing night,
I call to the earth and sea half-held by the night.

Press close bare-bosom'd night – press close magnetic nourishing night!
Night of south winds – night of the large few stars!
Still nodding night – mad naked summer night.

Smile O voluptuous cool-breath'd earth!
Earth of the slumbering and liquid trees!
Earth of departed sunset – earth of the mountains misty-topt!
Earth of the vitreous pour of the full moon just tinged with blue!
Earth of shine and dark mottling the tide of the river!

Earth of the limpid gray of clouds brighter and
clearer for my sake!
Far-swooping elbow'd earth – rich apple-blossom'd
earth!
Smile, for your lover comes.

Prodigal, you have given me love – therefore I to you
give love!
O unspeakable passionate love.

## 22

You sea! I resign myself to you also – I guess what
you mean,
I behold from the beach your crooked inviting fingers,
I believe you refuse to go back without feeling of me,
We must have a turn together, I undress, hurry me
out of sight of the land,
Cushion me soft, rock me in billowy drowse,
Dash me with amorous wet, I can repay you.
Sea of stretch'd ground-swells,
Sea breathing broad and convulsive breaths,
Sea of the brine of life and of unshovell'd yet always-
ready graves,
Howler and scooper of storms, capricious and dainty
sea,
I am integral with you, I too am of one phase and of
all phases.

Partaker of influx and efflux, I, extoller of hate and
conciliation,
Extoller of amies and those that sleep in each others'
arms.

I am he attesting sympathy,
(Shall I make my list of things in the house and skip
the house that supports them?)

I am not the poet of goodness only, I do not decline
to be the poet of wickedness also.

What blurt is this about virtue and about vice?
Evil propels me and reform of evil propels me, I
stand indifferent,
My gait is no fault-finder's or rejecter's gait,
I moisten the roots of all that has grown.

Did you fear some scrofula out of the unflagging
pregnancy?
Did you guess the celestial laws are yet to be work'd
over and rectified?

I find one side a balance and the antipodal side a
balance,
Soft doctrine as steady help as stable doctrine,
Thoughts and deeds of the present our rouse and
early start.

This minute that comes to me over the past
decillions,
There is no better than it and now.

What behaved well in the past or behaves well
to-day is not such a wonder,
The wonder is always and always how there can be a
mean man or an infidel.

23

Endless unfolding of words of ages!
And mine a word of the modern, the word
En-Masse.
A word of the faith that never balks,
Here or henceforward it is all the same to me, I accept
Time absolutely.

It alone is without flaw, it alone rounds and
completes all,
That mystic baffling wonder alone completes all.

I accept Reality and dare not question it,
Materialism first and last imbuing.

Hurrah for positive science! long live exact
demonstration!
Fetch stonecrop mixt with cedar and branches of lilac,
This is the lexicographer, this the chemist, this made
a grammar of the old cartouches,
These mariners put the ship through dangerous
unknown seas,
This is the geologist, this works with the scalpel, and
this is a mathematician.

Gentlemen, to you the first honors always!
Your facts are useful, and yet they are not my dwelling,
I but enter by them to an area of my dwelling.

Less the reminders of properties told my words,
And more the reminders they of life untold, and of
freedom and extrication,
And make short account of neuters and geldings,
and favor men and women fully equipt,
And beat the gong of revolt, and stop with fugitives
and them that plot and conspire.

24

Walt Whitman, a kosmos, of Manhattan the son,
Turbulent, fleshy, sensual, eating, drinking and
breeding,
No sentimentalist, no stander above men and
women or apart from them,
No more modest than immodest.

Unscrew the locks from the doors!
Unscrew the doors themselves from their jambs!
Whoever degrades another degrades me,
And whatever is done or said returns at last to me.

Through me the afflatus surging and surging,
through me the current and index.

I speak the pass-word primeval, I give the sign of
democracy,
By God! I will accept nothing which all cannot have
their counterpart of on the same terms.

Through me many long dumb voices,
Voices of the interminable generation of prisoners
and slaves,
Voices of the diseas'd and despairing and of thieves
and dwarfs,
Voices of cycles of preparation and accretion,
And of the threads that connect the stars, and of
wombs and of the father-stuff,
And of the rights of them the others are down upon,
Of the deform'd, trivial, flat, foolish, despised,
Fog in the air, beetles rolling balls of dung.

Through me forbidden voices,
Voices of sexes and lusts, voices veil'd and I remove
the veil,
Voices indecent by me clarified and transfigur'd.

I do not press my fingers across my mouth,
I keep as delicate around the bowels as around the
head and heart,
Copulation is no more rank to me than death is.
I believe in the flesh and the appetites,

Seeing, hearing, feeling, are miracles, and each part
and tag of me is a miracle.
Divine am I inside and out, and I make holy
whatever I touch or am touch'd from,
The scent of these arm-pits aroma finer than prayer,
This head more than churches, bibles, and all the
creeds.

If I worship one thing more than another it shall be
the spread of my own body, or any part of it,
Translucent mould of me it shall be you!
Shaded ledges and rests it shall be you!
Firm masculine colter it shall be you!
Whatever goes to the tilth of me it shall be you!
You my rich blood! your milky stream pale
strippings of my life!
Breast that presses against other breasts it shall be you!
My brain it shall be your occult convolutions!
Root of wash'd sweet-flag! timorous pond-snipe!
nest of guarded duplicate eggs! it shall be you!
Mix'd tussled hay of head, beard, brawn, it shall be you!
Trickling sap of maple, fibre of manly wheat, it shall
be you!
Sun so generous it shall be you!
Vapors lighting and shading my face it shall be you!
You sweaty brooks and dews it shall be you!
Winds whose soft-tickling genitals rub against me it
shall be you!
Broad muscular fields, branches of live oak, loving
lounger in my winding paths, it shall be you!

Hands I have taken, face I have kiss'd, mortal I have
ever touch'd, it shall be you.

I dote on myself, there is that lot of me and all so
luscious,

Each moment and whatever happens thrills me with joy,
I cannot tell how my ankles bend, nor whence the cause of my faintest wish,
Nor the cause of the friendship I emit, nor the cause of the friendship I take again.

That I walk up my stoop, I pause to consider if it really be,
A morning-glory at my window satisfies me more than the metaphysics of books.

To behold the day-break!
The little light fades the immense and diaphanous shadows,
The air tastes good to my palate.

Hefts of the moving world at innocent gambols silently rising, freshly exuding,
Scooting obliquely high and low.

Something I cannot see puts upward libidinous prongs,
Seas of bright juice suffuse heaven.
The earth by the sky staid with, the daily close of their junction,
The heav'd challenge from the east that moment over my head,
The mocking taunt, See then whether you shall be master!

25

Dazzling and tremendous how quick the sun-rise would kill me,
If I could not now and always send sun-rise out of me.

We also ascend dazzling and tremendous as the sun,

We found our own O my soul in the calm and cool
of the day-break.

My voice goes after what my eyes cannot reach,
With the twirl of my tongue I encompass worlds and
volumes of worlds.

Speech is the twin of my vision, it is unequal to
measure itself,
It provokes me forever, it says sarcastically,
*Walt you contain enough, why don't you let it out then?*

Come now I will not be tantalized, you conceive too
much of articulation,
Do you not know O speech how the buds beneath
you are folded?
Waiting in gloom, protected by frost,
The dirt receding before my prophetical screams,
I underlying causes to balance them at last,
My knowledge my live parts, it keeping tally with the
meaning of all things,
Happiness, (which whoever hears me let him or her
set out in search of this day.)

My final merit I refuse you, I refuse putting from me
what I really am,
Encompass worlds, but never try to encompass me,
I crowd your sleekest and best by simply looking
toward you.

Writing and talk do not prove me,
I carry the plenum of proof and every thing else in
my face,
With the hush of my lips I wholly confound the skeptic.

26

Now I will do nothing but listen,
To accrue what I hear into this song, to let sounds
contribute toward it.

I hear bravuras of birds, bustle of growing wheat,
gossip of flames, clack of sticks cooking my meals.
I hear the sound I love, the sound of the human voice,
I hear all sounds running together, combined, fused
or following,
Sounds of the city and sounds out of the city,
sounds of the day and night,
Talkative young ones to those that like them, the
loud laugh of work-people at their meals,
The angry base of disjointed friendship, the faint
tones of the sick,
The judge with hands tight to the desk, his pallid lips
pronouncing a death-sentence,
The heave'e'yo of stevedores unlading ships by the
wharves, the refrain of the anchor-lifters,
The ring of alarm-bells, the cry of fire, the whirr of
swift-streaking engines and hose-carts with
premonitory tinkles and color'd lights,
The steam-whistle, the solid roll of the train of
approaching cars,
The slow march play'd at the head of the association
marching two and two,
(They go to guard some corpse, the flag-tops are
draped with black muslin.)

I hear the violoncello, ('tis the young man's heart's
complaint,)
I hear the key'd cornet, it glides quickly in through
my ears,
It shakes mad-sweet pangs through my belly and breast.

I hear the chorus, it is a grand opera,
Ah this indeed is music – this suits me.

A tenor large and fresh as the creation fills me,
The orbic flex of his mouth is pouring and filling me full.

I hear the train'd soprano (what work with hers is this?)
The orchestra whirls me wider than Uranus flies,
It wrenches such ardors from me I did not know I
possess'd them,
It sails me, I dab with bare feet, they are lick'd by the
indolent waves,
I am cut by bitter and angry hail, I lose my breath,
Steep'd amid honey'd morphine, my windpipe
throttled in fakes of death,
At length let up again to feel the puzzle of puzzles,
And that we call Being.

## 27

To be in any form, what is that?
(Round and round we go, all of us, and ever come
back thither,)
If nothing lay more develop'd the quahaug in its
callous shell were enough.

Mine is no callous shell,
I have instant conductors all over me whether I pass
or stop,
They seize every object and lead it harmlessly
through me.

I merely stir, press, feel with my fingers, and am hungry,
To touch my person to some one else's is about as
much as I can stand.

28

Is this then a touch? quivering me to a new identity,
Flames and ether making a rush for my veins,
Treacherous tip of me reaching and crowding to
help them,
My flesh and blood playing out lightning to strike
what is hardly different from myself,
On all sides prurient provokers stiffening my limbs,
Straining the udder of my heart for its withheld drip,
Behaving licentious toward me, taking no denial,
Depriving me of my best as for a purpose,
Unbuttoning my clothes, holding me by the bare waist,
Deluding my confusion with the calm of the sunlight
and pasture-fields,
Immodestly sliding the fellow-senses away,
They bribed to swap off with touch and go and graze
at the edges of me,
No consideration, no regard for my draining
strength or my anger,
Fetching the rest of the herd around to enjoy them a
while,
Then all uniting to stand on a headland and worry
me.
The sentries desert every other part of me,
They have left me helpless to a red marauder,
They all come to the headland to witness and assist
against me.

I am given up by traitors,
I talk wildly, I have lost my wits, I and nobody else
am the greatest traitor,
I went myself first to the headland, my own hands
carried me there.

You villain touch! what are you doing? my breath is tight in its throat,
Unclench your floodgates, you are too much for me.

## 29

Blind loving wrestling touch, sheath'd hooded sharp-tooth'd touch!
Did it make you ache so, leaving me?
Parting track'd by arriving, perpetual payment of perpetual loan,
Rich showering rain, and recompense richer afterward.

Sprouts take and accumulate, stand by the curb prolific and vital,
Landscapes projected masculine, full-sized and golden.

## 30

All truths wait in all things,
They neither hasten their own delivery nor resist it,
They do not need the obstetric forceps of the surgeon,
The insignificant is as big to me as any,
(What is less or more than a touch?)

Logic and sermons never convince,
The damp of the night drives deeper into my soul.

(Only what proves itself to every man and woman is so,
Only what nobody denies is so.)

A minute and a drop of me settle my brain,
I believe the soggy clods shall become lovers and lamps,
And a compend of compends is the meat of a man or woman,
And a summit and flower there is the feeling they have for each other,

And they are to branch boundlessly out of that
 lesson until it becomes omnific,
And until one and all shall delight us, and we them.

## 31

I believe a leaf of grass is no less than the journey-
 work of the stars,
And the pismire is equally perfect, and a grain of
 sand, and the egg of the wren,
And the tree-toad is a chef-d'œuvre for the highest,
And the running blackberry would adorn the parlors
 of heaven,
And the narrowest hinge in my hand puts to scorn
 all machinery,
And the cow crunching with depress'd head
 surpasses any statue,
And a mouse is miracle enough to stagger sextillions
 of infidels.

I find I incorporate gneiss, coal, long-threaded moss,
 fruits, grains, esculent roots,
And am stucco'd with quadrupeds and birds all over,
And have distanced what is behind me for good reasons,
But call any thing back again when I desire it.

In vain the speeding or shyness,
In vain the plutonic rocks send their old heat against
 my approach,
In vain the mastodon retreats beneath its own
 powder'd bones,
In vain objects stand leagues off and assume
 manifold shapes,
In vain the ocean setting in hollows and the great
 monsters lying low,
In vain the buzzard houses herself with the sky,

In vain the snake slides through the creepers and logs,
In vain the elk takes to the inner passes of the woods,
In vain the razor-bill'd auk sails far north to Labrador,
I follow quickly, I ascend to the nest in the fissure of the cliff.

## 32

I think I could turn and live with animals, they're so placid and self-contain'd,
I stand and look at them long and long.

They do not sweat and whine about their condition,
They do not lie awake in the dark and weep for their sins,
They do not make me sick discussing their duty to God,
Not one is dissatisfied, not one is demented with the mania of owning things,
Not one kneels to another, nor to his kind that lived thousands of years ago,
Not one is respectable or unhappy over the whole earth.
So they show their relations to me and I accept them,
They bring me tokens of myself, they evince them plainly in their possession.

I wonder where they get those tokens,
Did I pass that way huge times ago and negligently drop them?
Myself moving forward then and now and forever,
Gathering and showing more always and with velocity,
Infinite and omnigenous, and the like of these among them,
Not too exclusive toward the reachers of my remembrancers,
Picking out here one that I love, and now go with him on brotherly terms.

A gigantic beauty of a stallion, fresh and responsive
    to my caresses,
Head high in the forehead, wide between the ears,
Limbs glossy and supple, tail dusting the ground,
Eyes full of sparkling wickedness, ears finely cut,
    flexibly moving.

His nostrils dilate as my heels embrace him,
His well-built limbs tremble with pleasure as we race
    around and return.
I but use you a minute, then I resign you, stallion,
Why do I need your paces when I myself out-gallop
    them?
Even as I stand or sit passing faster than you.

## 33

Space and Time! now I see it is true, what I guess'd at,
What I guess'd when I loaf'd on the grass,
What I guess'd while I lay alone in my bed,
And again as I walk'd the beach under the paling
    stars of the morning.
My ties and ballasts leave me, my elbows rest in sea-
    gaps,
I skirt sierras, my palms cover continents,
I am afoot with my vision.
By the city's quadrangular houses – in log huts,
    camping with lumbermen,
Along the ruts of the turnpike, along the dry gulch
    and rivulet bed,
Weeding my onion-patch or hoeing rows of carrots
    and parsnips, crossing savannas, trailing in
    forests,
Prospecting, gold-digging, girdling the trees of a new
    purchase,

Scorch'd ankle-deep by the hot sand, hauling my
boat down the shallow river,
Where the panther walks to and fro on a limb
overhead, where the buck turns furiously at the
hunter,
Where the rattlesnake suns his flabby length on a
rock, where the otter is feeding on fish,
Where the alligator in his tough pimples sleeps by
the bayou,
Where the black bear is searching for roots or honey,
where the beaver pats the mud with his
paddle-shaped tail;
Over the growing sugar, over the yellow-flower'd
cotton plant, over the rice in its low moist field,
Over the sharp-peak'd farm house, with its scallop'd
scum and slender shoots from the gutters,
Over the western persimmon, over the long-leav'd
corn, over the delicate blue-flower flax,
Over the white and brown buckwheat, a hummer
and buzzer there with the rest,
Over the dusky green of the rye as it ripples and
shades in the breeze;
Scaling mountains, pulling myself cautiously up,
holding on by low scragged limbs,
Walking the path worn in the grass and beat through
the leaves of the brush,
Where the quail is whistling betwixt the woods and
the wheat-lot,
Where the bat flies in the Seventh-month eve, where
the great gold-bug drops through the dark,
Where the brook puts out of the roots of the old tree
and flows to the meadow,
Where cattle stand and shake away flies with the
tremulous shuddering of their hides,

Where the cheese-cloth hangs in the kitchen, where
andirons straddle the hearth-slab, where
cobwebs fall in festoons from the rafters;
Where trip-hammers crash, where the press is
whirling its cylinders,
Where the human heart beats with terrible throes
under its ribs,
Where the pear-shaped balloon is floating aloft,
(floating in it myself and looking composedly
down,)
Where the life-car is drawn on the slip-noose, where the
heat hatches pale-green eggs in the dented sand,
Where the she-whale swims with her calf and never
forsakes it,
Where the steam-ship trails hind-ways its long
pennant of smoke,
Where the fin of the shark cuts like a black chip out
of the water,
Where the half-burn'd brig is riding on unknown
currents,
Where shells grow to her slimy deck, where the dead
are corrupting below;
Where the dense-starr'd flag is borne at the head of
the regiments,
Approaching Manhattan up by the long-stretching
island,
Under Niagara, the cataract falling like a veil over
my countenance,
Upon a door-step, upon the horse-block of hard
wood outside,
Upon the race-course, or enjoying picnics or jigs or a
good game of base-ball,
At he-festivals, with blackguard gibes, ironical
license, bull-dances, drinking, laughter,

At the cider-mill tasting the sweets of the brown mash, sucking the juice through a straw,
At apple-peelings wanting kisses for all the red fruit I find,
At musters, beach-parties, friendly bees, huskings, house-raisings;
Where the mocking-bird sounds his delicious gurgles, cackles, screams, weeps,
Where the hay-rick stands in the barn-yard, where the dry-stalks are scatter'd, where the brood-cow waits in the hovel,
Where the bull advances to do his masculine work, where the stud to the mare, where the cock is treading the hen,
Where the heifers browse, where geese nip their food with short jerks,
Where sun-down shadows lengthen over the limitless and lonesome prairie,
Where herds of buffalo make a crawling spread of the square miles far and near,
Where the humming-bird shimmers, where the neck of the long-loved swan is curving and winding,
Where the laughing-gull scoots by the shore, where she laughs her near-human laugh,
Where bee-hives range on a gray bench in the garden half hid by the high weeds,
Where band-neck'd partridges roost in a ring on the ground with their heads out,
Where burial coaches enter the arch'd gates of a cemetery,
Where winter wolves bark amid wastes of snow and icicled trees,
Where the yellow-crown'd heron comes to the edge of the marsh at night and feeds upon small crabs,

Where the splash of swimmers and divers cools the
warm noon,
Where the katy-did works her chromatic reed on the
walnut-tree over the wall,
Through patches of citrons and cucumbers with
silver-wired leaves,
Through the salt-lick or orange glade, or under
conical firs,
Through the gymnasium, through the curtain'd
saloon, through the office or public hall;
Pleas'd with the native and pleas'd with the foreign,
pleas'd with the new and old,
Pleas'd with the homely woman as well as the
handsome,
Pleas'd with the quakeress as she puts off her bonnet
and talks melodiously,
Pleas'd with the tune of the choir of the whitewash'd
church,
Pleas'd with the earnest words of the sweating
Methodist preacher, impress'd seriously at the
camp-meeting;
Looking in at the shop-windows of Broadway the
whole forenooon, flatting the flesh of my nose on
the thick plate glass,
Wandering the same afternoon with my face turn'd up
to the clouds, or down a lane or along the beach,
My right and left arms round the sides of two
friends, and I in the middle;
Coming home with the silent and dark-cheek'd bush-
boy, (behind me he rides at the drape of the day,)
Far from the settlements studying the print of
animals' feet, or the moccasin print,
By the cot in the hospital reaching lemonade to a
feverish patient,

Nigh the coffin'd corpse when all is still, examining
with a candle;
Voyaging to every port to dicker and adventure,
Hurrying with the modern crowd as eager and fickle
as any,
Hot toward one I hate, ready in my madness to knife
him,
Solitary at midnight in my back yard, my thoughts
gone from me a long while,
Walking the old hills of Judaea with the beautiful
gentle God by my side,
Speeding through space, speeding through heaven
and the stars,
Speeding amid the seven satellites and the broad
ring, and the diameter of eighty thousand miles,
Speeding with tail'd meteors, throwing fire-balls like
the rest,
Carrying the crescent child that carries its own full
mother in its belly,
Storming, enjoying, planning, loving, cautioning,
Backing and filling, appearing and disappearing,
I tread day and night such roads.

I visit the orchards of spheres and look at the product,
And look at quintillions ripen'd and look at
quintillions green.

I fly those flights of a fluid and swallowing soul,
My course runs below the soundings of plummets.

I help myself to material and immaterial,
No guard can shut me off, no law prevent me.

I anchor my ship for a little while only,
My messengers continually cruise away or bring
their returns to me.

I go hunting polar furs and the seal, leaping chasms
with a pike-pointed staff, clinging to topples of
brittle and blue.

I ascend to the foretruck,
I take my place late at night in the crow's-nest,
We sail the arctic sea, it is plenty light enough,
Through the clear atmosphere I stretch around on
the wonderful beauty,
The enormous masses of ice pass me and I pass
them, the scenery is plain in all directions,
The white-topt mountains show in the distance, I
fling out my fancies toward them,
We are approaching some great battle-field in which
we are soon to be engaged,
We pass the colossal outposts of the encampment,
we pass with still feet and caution,
Or we are entering by the suburbs some vast and
ruin'd city,
The blocks and fallen architecture more than all the
living cities of the globe.

I am a free companion, I bivouac by invading
watchfires,
I turn the bridegroom out of bed and stay with the
bride myself,
I tighten her all night to my things and lips.
My voice is the wife's voice, the screech by the rail of the
stairs,
They fetch my man's body up dripping and
drown'd.

I understand the large hearts of heroes,
The courage of present times and all times,

How the skipper saw the crowded and rudderless wreck of the steamship, and Death chasing it up and down the storm,
How he knuckled tight and gave not back an inch, and was faithful of days and faithful of nights,
And chalk'd in large letters on a board, *Be of good cheer, we will not desert you;*
How he follow'd with them and tack'd with them three days and would not give it up,
How he saved the drifting company at last,
How the lank loose-gown'd women look'd when boated from the side of their prepared graves,
How the silent old-faced infants and the lifted sick, and the sharp-lipp'd unshaved men;
All this I swallow, it tastes good, I like it well, it becomes mine,
I am the man, I suffer'd, I was there.

The disdain and calmness of martyrs,
The mother of old, condemn'd for a witch, burnt with dry wood, her children gazing on,
The hounded slave that flags in the race, leans by the fence, blowing, cover'd with sweat,
The twinges that sting like needles his legs and neck, the murderous buckshot and the bullets,
All these I feel or am.

I am the hounded slave, I wince at the bite of the dogs,
Hell and despair are upon me, crack and again crack the marksmen,
I clutch the rails of the fence, my gore dribs, thinn'd with the ooze of my skin,
I fall on the weeds and stones,
The riders spur their unwilling horses, haul close,

Taunt my dizzy ears and beat me violently over the
    head with whip-stocks.

Agonies are one of my changes of garments,
I do not ask the wounded person how he feels, I
    myself become the wounded person,
My hurts turn livid upon me as I lean on a cane and
    observe.

I am the mash'd fireman with breast-bone broken,
Tumbling walls buried me in their debris,
Heat and smoke I inspired, I heard the yelling shouts
    of my comrades,
I heard the distant click of their picks and shovels,
They have clear'd the beams away, they tenderly lift
    me forth.
I lie in the night air in my red shirt, the pervading
    hush is for my sake,
Painless after all I lie exhausted but not so unhappy,
White and beautiful are the faces around me, the
    heads are bared of their fire-caps,
The kneeling crowd fades with the light of the
    torches.
Distant and dead resuscitate,
They show as the dial or move as the hands of me, I
    am the clock myself.

I am an old artillerist, I tell of my fort's bombardment,
I am there again.

Again the long roll of the drummers,
Again the attacking cannon, mortars,
Again to my listening ears the cannon responsive.

I take part, I see and hear the whole,
The cries, curses, roar, the plaudits for well-aim'd shots,

The ambulanza slowly passing trailing its red drip,
Workmen searching after damages, making
indispensable repairs,
The fall of grenades through the rent roof, the fan-shaped explosion,
The whizz of limbs, heads, stone, wood, iron, high
in the air.

Again gurgles the mouth of my dying general, he
furiously waves with his hand,
He gasps through the clot *Mind not me – mind – the
entrenchments.*

## 34

Now I tell what I knew in Texas in my early youth,
(I tell not the fall of Alamo,
Not one escaped to tell the fall of Alamo,
The hundred and fifty are dumb yet at Alamo,)
Tis the tale of the murder in cold blood of four
hundred and twelve young men.
Retreating they had form'd in a hollow square with
their baggage for breastworks,
Nine hundred lives out of the surrounding enemy's,
nine times their number, was the price they took
in advance,
Their colonel was wounded and their ammunition
gone,
They treated for an honorable capitulation, receiv'd
writing and seal, gave up their arms and march'd
back prisoners of war.

They were the glory of the race of rangers,
Matchless with horse, rifle, song, supper, courtship,
Large, turbulent, generous, handsome, proud, and
affectionate,

Bearded, sunburnt, drest in the free costume of
hunters,
Not a single one over thirty years of age.
The second First-day morning they were brought
out in squads and massacred, it was beautiful
early summer,
The work commenced about five o'clock and was
over by eight.

None obey'd the command to kneel,
Some made a mad and helpless rush, some stood
stark and straight,
A few fell at once, shot in the temple or heart, the
living and dead lay together,
The maim'd and mangled dug in the dirt, the
new-comers saw them there,
Some half-kill'd attempted to crawl away,
These were dispatch'd with bayonets or batter'd
with the blunts of muskets.
A youth not seventeen years old seiz'd his assassin
till two more came to release him,
The three were all torn and cover'd with the boy's
blood.

At eleven o'clock began the burning of the bodies;
That is the tale of the murder of the four hundred
and twelve young men.

35

Would you hear of an old-time sea-fight?
Would you learn who won by the light of the moon
and stars?
List to the yarn, as my grandmother's father the
sailor told it to me.
Our foe was no skulk in his ship I tell you, (said he,)

His was the surly English pluck, and there is no tougher or truer, and never was, and never will be;
Along the lower'd eve he came horribly raking us.

We closed with him, the yards entangled, the cannon touch'd,
My captain lash'd fast with his own hands.

We had receiv'd some eighteen pound shots under the water,
On our lower-gun-deck two large pieces had burst at the first fire, killing all around and blowing up overhead.

Fighting at sun-down, fighting at dark,
Ten o'clock at night, the full moon well up, our leaks on the gain, and five feet of water reported,
The master-at-arms loosing the prisoners confined in the after-hold to give them a chance for themselves.

The transit to and from the magazine is now stopt by the sentinels,
They see so many strange faces they do not know whom to trust.

Our frigate takes fire,
The other asks if we demand quarter?
If our colors are struck and the fighting done?

Now I laugh content, for I hear the voice of my little captain,
*We have not struck*, he composedly cries, *we have just begun our part of the fighting.*

Only three guns are in use,
One is directed by the captain himself against the enemy's main-mast,

Two well serv'd with grape and canister silence his
musketry and clear his decks.
The tops alone second the fire of this little battery,
especially the main-top,
They hold out bravely during the whole of the
action.

Not a moment's cease,
The leaks gain fast on the pumps, the fire eats
toward the powder-magazine.
One of the pumps has been shot away, it is generally
thought we are sinking.

Serene stands the little captain,
He is not hurried, his voice is neither high nor low,
His eyes give more light to us than our battle-
lanterns.

Toward twelve there in the beams of the moon they
surrender to us.

36

Stretch'd and still lies the midnight,
Two great hulls motionless on the breast of the
darkness,
Our vessel riddled and slowly sinking, preparations
to pass to the one we have conquer'd,
The captain on the quarter-deck coldly giving his
orders through a countenance white as a sheet,
Near by the corpse of the child that serv'd in the
cabin,
The dead face of an old salt with long white hair and
carefully curl'd whiskers,
The flames spite of all that can be done flickering
aloft and below,

The husky voices of the two or three officers yet fit
for duty,
Formless stacks of bodies and bodies by themselves,
dabs of flesh upon the masts and spars,
Cut of cordage, dangle of rigging, slight shock of the
soothe of waves,
Black and impassive guns, litter of powder-parcels,
strong scent,
A few large stars overhead, silent and mournful
shining,
Delicate sniffs of sea-breeze, smells of sedgy grass
and fields by the shore, death-messages given in
charge to survivors,
The hiss of the surgeon's knife, the gnawing teeth of
his saw,
Wheeze, cluck, swash of falling blood, short wild
scream, and long, dull, tapering groan,
These so, these irretrievable.

37

You laggards there on guard! look to your arms!
In at the conquer'd doors they crowd! I am
possess'd!
Embody all presences outlaw'd or suffering,
See myself in prison shaped like another man,
And feel the dull unintermitted pain,
For me the keepers of convicts shoulder their
carbines and keep watch,
It is I let out in the morning and barr'd at night.

Not a mutineer walks handcuff'd to jail but I am
handcuff'd to him and walk by his side,
(I am less the jolly one there, and more the silent
one with sweat on my twitching lips.)

Not a youngster is taken for larceny but I go up too,
and am tried and sentenced.

Not a cholera patient lies at the last gasp but I also
lie at the last gasp,
My face is ash-color'd, my sinews gnarl, away from
me people retreat.

Askers embody themselves in me and I am
embodied in them,
I project my hat, sit shame-faced, and beg.

38

Enough! enough! enough!
Somehow I have been stunn'd. Stand back!
Give me a little time beyond my cuff'd head,
slumbers, dreams, gaping,
I discover myself on the verge of a usual mistake.
That I could forget the mockers and insults!
That I could forget the trickling tears and the blows
of the bludgeons and hammers!
That I could look with a separate look on my own
crucifixion and bloody crowning!

I remember now,
I resume the overstaid fraction,
The grave of rock multiplies what has been confided
to it, or to any graves,
Corpses rise, gashes heal, fastenings roll from me.

I troop forth replenish'd with supreme power, one of
an average unending procession,
Inland and sea-coast we go, and pass all boundary lines,
Our swift ordinances on their way over the whole earth,
The blossoms we wear in our hats the growth of
thousands of years.

Eleves, I salute you! come forward!
Continue your annotations, continue your questionings.

39

The friendly and flowing savage, who is he?
Is he waiting for civilization, or past it and mastering it?

Is he some Southwesterner rais'd out-doors? is he Kanadian?
Is he from the Mississippi country? Iowa, Oregon, California?
The mountains? prairie-life, bush-life? or sailor from the sea?

Wherever he goes men and women accept and desire him,
They desire he should like them, touch them, speak to them, stay with them.

Behavior lawless as snow-flakes, words simple as grass, uncomb'd head, laughter, and naivetè,
Slow-stepping feet, common features, common modes and emanations,
They descend in new forms from the tips of his fingers,
They are wafted with the odor of his body or breath, they fly out of the glance of his eyes.

40

Flaunt of the sunshine I need not your bask – lie over!
You light surfaces only, I force surfaces and depths also.

Earth! you seem to look for something at my hands,
Say, old top-knot, what do you want?

Man or woman, I might tell you I like you, but cannot,
And might tell what it is in me and what it is in you,
    but cannot,
And might tell that pining I have, that pulse of my
    nights and days.

Behold, I do not give lectures or a little charity,
When I give I give myself.

You there, impotent, loose in the knees,
Open your scarf'd chops till I blow grit within you,
Spread your palms and lift the flaps of your pockets,
I am not to be denied, I compel, I have stores plenty
    and to spare,
And any thing I have I bestow.

I do not ask who you are, that is not important to me,
You can do nothing and be nothing but what I will
    infold you.

To cotton-field drudge or cleaner of privies I lean,
On his right cheek I put the family kiss,
And in my soul I swear I never will deny him.

On women fit for conception I start bigger and
    nimbler babes,
(This day I am jetting the stuff of far more arrogant
    republics.)

To any one dying, thither I speed and twist the knob
    of the door,
Turn the bed-clothes toward the foot of the bed,
Let the physician and the priest go home.

I seize the descending man and raise him with
    resistless will,
O despairer, here is my neck,

By God, you shall not go down! hang your whole
 weight upon me.

I dilate you with tremendous breath, I buoy you up,
Every room of the house do I fill with an arm'd force,
Lovers of me, bafflers of graves.

Sleep – I and they keep guard all night,
Not doubt, not disease shall dare to lay finger upon you,
I have embraced you, and henceforth possess you to
 myself,
And when you rise in the morning you will find what
 I tell you is so.

## 41

I am he bringing help for the sick as they pant on
 their backs,
And for strong upright men I bring yet more needed
 help.

I heard what was said of the universe,
Heard it and heard it of several thousand years;
It is middling well as far as it goes – but is that all?
Magnifying and applying come I,
Outbidding at the start the old cautious hucksters,
Taking myself the exact dimensions of Jehovah,
Lithographing Kronos, Zeus his son, and Hercules
 his grandson,
Buying drafts of Osiris, Isis, Belus, Brahma, Buddha,
In my portfolio placing Manito loose, Allah on a
 leaf, the crucifix engraved,
With Odin and the hideous-faced Mexitli and every
 idol and image,
Taking them all for what they are worth and not a
 cent more,

Admitting they were alive and did the work of their
days,
(They bore mites as for unfledg'd birds who have
now to rise and fly and sing for themselves,)
Accepting the rough deific sketches to fill out better
in myself, bestowing them freely on each man
and woman I see,
Discovering as much or more in a framer framing a
house,
Putting higher claims for him there with his roll'd-up
sleeves driving the mallet and chisel,
Not objecting to special revelations, considering a
curl of smoke or a hair on the back of my hand
just as curious as any revelation,
Lads ahold of fire-engines and hook-and-ladder ropes
no less to me than the gods of the antique wars,
Minding their voices peal through the crash of
destruction,
Their brawny limbs passing safe over charr'd laths,
their white foreheads whole and unhurt out of
the flames;
By the mechanic's wife with her babe at her nipple
interceding for every person born,
Three scythes at harvest whizzing in a row from three
lusty angels with shirts bagg'd out at their waists,
The snag-tooth'd hostler with red hair redeeming
sins past and to come,
Selling all he possesses, traveling on foot to fee
lawyers for his brother and sit by him while he is
tried for forgery;
What was strewn in the amplest strewing the square
rod about me, and not filling the square rod then,
The bull and the bug never worshipp'd half enough,
Dung and dirt more admirable than was dream'd,

The supernatural of no account, myself waiting my time
to be one of the supremes,
The day getting ready for me when I shall do as
much good as the best, and be as prodigious;
By my life-lumps! becoming already a creator,
Putting myself here and now to the ambush'd womb
of the shadows.

## 42

A call in the midst of the crowd,
My own voice, orotund sweeping and final.

Come my children,
Come my boys and girls, my women, household and
intimates,
Now the performer launches his nerve, he has pass'd
his prelude on the reeds within.

Easily written loose-finger'd chords – I feel the
thrum of your climax and close.

My head slues round on my neck,
Music rolls, but not from the organ,
Folks are around me, but they are no household of
mine.
Ever the hard unsunk ground,
Ever the eaters and drinkers, ever the upward and
downward sun, ever the air and the ceaseless
tides,
Ever myself and my neighbors, refreshing, wicked,
real,
Ever the old inexplicable query, ever that thorn'd
thumb, that breath of itches and thirsts,
Ever the vexer's *hoot! hoot!* till we find where the sly
one hides and bring him forth,

Ever love, ever the sobbing liquid of life,
Ever the bandage under the chin, ever the trestles of
death.

Here and there with dimes on the eyes walking,
To feed the greed of the belly the brains liberally
spooning,
Tickets buying, taking, selling, but in to the feast
never once going,
Many sweating, ploughing, thrashing, and then the
chaff for payment receiving,
A few idly owning, and they the wheat continually
claiming.

This is the city and I am one of the citizens,
Whatever interests the rest interests me, politics,
wars, markets, newspapers, schools,
The mayor and councils, banks, tariffs, steamships,
factories, stocks, stores, real estate and personal
estate.
The little plentiful manikins skipping around in
collars and tail'd coats,
I am aware who they are, (they are positively not
worms or fleas,)
I acknowledge the duplicates of myself, the weakest
and shallowest is deathless with me,
What I do and say the same waits for them,
Every thought that flounders in me the same
flounders in them.

I know perfectly well my own egotism,
Know my omnivorous lines and must not write any less,
And would fetch you whoever you are flush with
myself.

Not words of routine this song of mine,
But abruptly to question, to leap beyond yet nearer bring;
This printed and bound book – but the printer and the printing-office boy?
The well-taken photographs – but your wife or friend close and solid in your arms?
The black ship mail'd with iron, her mighty guns in her turrets – but the pluck of the captain and engineers?
In the houses the dishes and fare and furniture – but the host and hostess, and the look out of their eyes?
The sky up there – yet here or next door, or across the way?
The saints and sages in history – but you yourself?
Sermons, creeds, theology – but the fathomless human brain,
And what is reason? and what is love? and what is life?

43

I do not despise you priests, all time, the world over,
My faith is the greatest of faiths and the least of faiths,
Enclosing worship ancient and modern and all between ancient and modern,
Believing I shall come again upon the earth after five thousand years,
Waiting responses from oracles, honoring the gods, saluting the sun,
Making a fetich of the first rock or stump, powowing with sticks in the circle of obis,
Helping the llama or brahmin as he trims the lamps of the idols,
Dancing yet through the streets in a phallic procession, rapt and austere in the woods a gymnosophist,

Drinking mead from the skull-cap, to Shastas and
 Vedas admirant, minding the Koran,
Walking the teokallis, spotted with gore from the
 stone and knife, beating the serpent-skin drum,
Accepting the Gospels, accepting him that was
 crucified, knowing assuredly that he is divine,
To the mass kneeling or the puritan's prayer rising,
 or sitting patiently in a pew,
Ranting and frothing in my insane crisis, or waiting
 dead-like till my spirit arouses me,
Looking forth on pavement and land, or outside of
 pavement and land,
Belonging to the winders of the circuit of circuits.

One of that centripetal and centrifugal gang I turn and
 talk like a man leaving charges before a journey.

Down-hearted doubters dull and excluded,
Frivolous, sullen, moping, angry, affected,
 dishearten'd, atheistical,
I know every one of you, I know the sea of torment,
 doubt, despair and unbelief.

How the flukes splash!
How they contort rapid as lightning, with spasms
 and spouts of blood!

Be at peace bloody flukes of doubters and sullen
 mopers,
I take my place among you as much as among any.
The past is the push of you, me, all, precisely the
 same,
And what is yet untried and afterward is for you, me,
 all precisely the same.

I do not know what is untried and afterward,

But I know it will in its turn prove sufficient, and
cannot fail.

Each who passes is consider'd, each who stops is
consider'd, not a single one can it fail.

It cannot fail the young man who died and was
buried,
Nor the young woman who died and was put by his
side,
Nor the little child that peep'd in at the door, and
then drew back and was never seen again,
Nor the old man who has lived without purpose,
and feels it with bitterness worse than gall,
Nor him in the poor house tubercled by rum and the
bad disorder,
Nor the numberless slaughter'd and wreck'd, nor
the brutish koboo call'd the ordure of humanity,
Nor the sacs merely floating with open mouths for
food to slip in,
Nor any thing in the earth, or down in the oldest
graves of the earth,
Nor any thing in the myriads of spheres, nor the
myriads of myriads that inhabit them,
Nor the present, nor the least wisp that is known.

44

It is time to explain myself – let us stand up.

What is known I strip away,
I launch all men and women forward with me into
the Unknown.

The clock indicates the moment – but what does
eternity indicate?

We have thus far exhausted trillions of winters and summers,
There are trillions ahead, and trillions ahead of them.

Births have brought us richness and variety,
And other births will bring us richness and variety.

I do not call one greater and one smaller,
That which fills its period and place is equal to any.

Were mankind murderous or jealous upon you, my brother, my sister?
I am sorry for you, they are not murderous or jealous upon me,
All has been gentle with me, I keep no account with lamentation,
(What have I to do with lamentation?)
I am an acme of things accomplish'd, and I an encloser of things to be.

My feet strike an apex of the apices of the stairs,
On every step bunches of ages, and larger bunches between the steps,
All below duly travel'd, and still I mount and mount.

Rise after rise bow the phantoms behind me,
Afar down I see the huge first Nothing, I know I was even there,
I waited unseen and always, and slept through the lethargic mist,
And took my time, and took no hurt from the fetid carbon.

Long I was hugg'd close – long and long.

Immense have been the preparations for me,
Faithful and friendly the arms that have help'd me.

Cycles ferried my cradle, rowing and rowing like
cheerful boatmen,
For room to me stars kept aside in in their own rings,
They sent influences to look after what was to hold me.

Before I was born out of my mother generations
guided me,
My embryo has never been torpid, nothing could
overlay it.

For it the nebula cohered to an orb,
The long slow strata piled to rest it on,
Vast vegetables gave it sustenance,
Monstrous sauroids transported it in their mouths
and deposited it with care.

All forces have been steadily employ'd to complete
and delight me,
Now on this spot I stand with my robust soul.

45

O span of youth! ever-push'd elasticity!
O manhood, balanced, florid and full.
My lovers suffocate me,
Crowding my lips, thick in the pores of my skin
Jostling me through streets and public halls, coming
naked to me at night,
Crying by day *Ahoy!* from the rocks of the river,
swinging and chirping over my head,
Calling my name from flower-beds, vines, tangled
underbrush,
Lighting on every moment of my life,
Bussing my body with soft balsamic busses,
Noiselessly passing handfuls out of their hearts and
giving them to be mine.

Old age superbly rising! O welcome, ineffable grace
of dying days!

Every condition promulges not only itself, it
promulges what grows after and out of itself,
And the dark hush promulges as much as any.

I open my scuttle at night and see the far-sprinkled
systems,
And all I see multiplied as high as I can cipher edge
but the rim of the farther systems.

Wider and wider they spread, expanding, always
expanding,
Outward and outward and forever outward.

My sun has his sun and round him obediently wheels,
He joins with his partners a group of superior circuit,
And greater sets follow, making specks of the
greatest inside them.

There is no stoppage and never can be stoppage,
If I, you, and the worlds, and all beneath or upon
their surfaces, were this moment reduced back to
a pallid float, it would not avail in the long run,
We should surely bring up again where we now stand,
And surely go as much farther, and then farther and
farther.

A few quadrillions of ears, a few octillions of cubic
leagues, do not hazard the span or make it
impatient,
They are but parts, any thing is but a part.
See ever so far, there is limitless space outside of that,
Count ever so much, there is limitless time around
that.
My rendezvous is appointed, it is certain,

The Lord will be there and wait till I come on perfect terms,
The great Camerado, the lover true for whom I pine will be there.

## 46

I know I have the best of time and space, and was never measured and never will be measured.

I tramp a perpetual journey, (come listen all!)
My signs are a rain-proof coat, good shoes, and a staff cut from the woods,
No friend of mine takes his ease in my chair,
I have no chair, no church, no philosophy,
I lead no man to a dinner-table, library, exchange,
But each man and each woman of you I lead upon a knoll,
My left hand hooking you round the waist,
My right hand pointing to landscapes of continents and the public road.

Not I, not any one else can travel that road for you,
You must travel it for yourself.

It is not far, it is within reach,
Perhaps you have been on it since you were born and did not know,
Perhaps it is everywhere on water and on land.

Shoulder your duds dear son, and I will mine, and let us hasten forth,
Wonderful cities and free nations we shall fetch as we go.

If you tire, give me both burdens, and rest the chuff of your hand on my hip,

And in due time you shall repay the same service to me,
For after we start we never lie by again.

This day before dawn I ascended a hill and look'd at the crowded heaven,
And I said to my spirit *When we become the enfolders of those orbs, and the pleasure and knowledge of every thing in them, shall we be fill'd and satisfied then?*
And my spirit said *No, we but level that lift to pass and continue beyond.*

You are also asking me questions and I hear you,
I answer that I cannot answer, you must find out for yourself.
Sit a while dear son,
Here are biscuits to eat and here is milk to drink,
But as soon as you sleep and renew yourself in sweet clothes,
I kiss you with a good-by kiss and open the gate for your egress hence.

Long enough have you dream'd contemptible dreams,
Now I wash the gum from your eyes,
You must habit yourself to the dazzle of the light and of every moment of your life.

Long have you timidly waded holding a plank by the shore,
Now I will you to be a bold swimmer,
To jump off in the midst of the sea, rise again, nod to me, shout, and laughingly dash with your hair

## 47

I am the teacher of athletes,
He that by me spreads a wider breast than my own proves the width of my own,
He most honors my style who learns under it to destroy the teacher.

The boy I love, the same becomes a man not through derived power, but in his own right,
Wicked rather than virtuous out of conformity or fear,
Fond of his sweetheart, relishing well his steak,
Unrequited love or a slight cutting him worse than sharp steel cuts,
First-rate to ride, to fight, to hit the bull's eye, to sail a skiff, to sing a song or play on the banjo,
Preferring scars and the beard and faces pitted with smallpox over all latherers,
And those well-tann'd to those that keep out of the sun.

I teach straying from me, yet who can stray from me?
I follow you whoever you are from the present hour,
My words itch at your ears till you understand them.

I do not say these things for a dollar or to fill up the time while I wait for a boat,
(It is you talking just as much as myself, I act as the tongue of you,
Tied in your mouth, in mine it begins to be loosen'd.)
I swear I will never again mention love or death inside a house,
And I swear I will never translate myself at all, only to him or her who privately stays with me in the open air.

If you would understand me go to the heights or
watershore,
The nearest gnat is an explanation, and a drop or
motion of waves a key,
The maul, the oar, the hand-saw, second my words.

No shutter'd room or school can commune with me,
But roughs and little children better than they.

The young mechanic is closest to me, he knows me well,
The woodman that takes his axe and jug with him
shall take me with him all day,
The farm-boy ploughing in the field feels good at the
sound of my voice,
In vessels that sail my words sail, I go with fishermen
and seamen and love them.

The soldier camp'd or upon the march is mine,
On the night ere the pending battle many seek me,
and I do not fail them,
On that solemn night (it may be their last) those that
know me seek me.

My face rubs to the hunter's face when he lies down
alone in his blanket,
The driver thinking of me does not mind the jolt of
his wagon,
The young mother and old mother comprehend me,
The girl and the wife rest the needle a moment and
forget where they are,
They and all would resume what I have told them.

48

I have said that the soul is not more than the body,
And I have said that the body is not more than the
soul,

And nothing, not God, is greater to one than one's
 self is,
And whoever walks a furlong without sympathy
 walks to his own funeral drest in his shroud,
And I or you pocketless of a dime may purchase the
 pick of the earth,
And to glance with an eye or show a bean in its pod
 confounds the learning of all times,
And there is no trade or employment but the young
 man following it may become a hero,
And there is no object so soft but it makes a hub for
 the wheel'd universe,
And I say to any man or woman, Let your soul stand
 cool and composed before a million universes.

And I say to mankind, Be not curious about God,
For I who am curious about each am not curious
 about God,
(No array of terms can say how much I am at peace
 about God and about death.)

I hear and behold God in every object, yet
 understand God not in the least,
Nor do I understand who there can be more
 wonderful than myself.
Why should I wish to see God better than this day?
I see something of God each hour of the twenty-
 four, and each moment then,
In the faces of men and women I see God, and in
 my own face in the glass,
I find letters from God dropt in the street, and every
 one is sign'd by God's name,
And I leave them where they are, for I know that
 wheresoe'er I go,
Others will punctually come for ever and ever.

49

And as to you Death, and you bitter hug of
 mortality, it is idle to try to alarm me.

To his work without flinching the accoucheur comes,
I see the elder-hand pressing receiving supporting,
I recline by the sills of the exquisite flexible doors,
And mark the outlet, and mark the relief and escape.

And as to you Corpse I think you are good manure,
 but that does not offend me,
I smell the white roses sweet-scented and growing,
I reach to the leafy lips, I reach to the polish'd
 breasts of melons.

And as to you Life I reckon you are the leavings of
 many deaths,
(No doubt I have died myself ten thousand times
 before.)

I hear you whispering there O stars of heaven,
O suns – O grass of graves – O perpetual transfers
 and promotions,
If you do not say any thing how can I say any thing?

Of the turbid pool that lies in the autumn forest,
Of the moon that descends the steeps of the
 soughing twilight,
Toss, sparkles of day and dusk – toss on the black
 stems that decay in the muck,
Toss to the moaning gibberish of the dry limbs.

I ascend from the moon, I ascend from the night,
I perceive that the ghastly glimmer is noonday
 sunbeams reflected,
And debouch to the steady and central from the
 offspring great or small.

## 50

There is that in me – I do not know what it is – but I
know it is in me.

Wrench'd and sweaty – calm and cool then my body
becomes,
I sleep – I sleep long.

I do not know it – it is without name – it is a word unsaid,
It is not in any dictionary, utterance, symbol.

Something it swings on more than the earth I swing on,
To it the creation is the friend whose embracing
awakes me.

Perhaps I might tell more. Outlines! I plead for my
brothers and sisters.

Do you see O my brothers and sisters?
It is not chaos or death – it is form, union, plan – it
is eternal life – it is Happiness.

## 51

The past and present wilt – I have fill'd them,
emptied them,
And proceed to fill my next fold of the future.
Listener up there! what have you to confide to me?
Look in my face while I snuff the sidle of evening,
(Talk honestly, no one else hears you, and I stay
only a minute longer.)

Do I contradict myself?
Very well then I contradict myself,
(I am large, I contain multitudes.)

I concentrate toward them that are nigh, I wait on
the doorslab.

Who has done his day's work? who will soonest be
through with his supper?
Who wishes to walk with me?

Will you speak before I am gone? will you prove
already too late?

52

The spotted hawk swoops by and accuses me, he
complains of my gab and my loitering.

I too am not a bit tamed, I too am untranslatable,
I sound my barbaric yawp over the roofs of the world.

The last scud of day holds back for me,
It flings my likeness after the rest and true as any on
the shadow'd wilds,
It coaxes me to the vapor and the dusk.

I depart as air, I shake my white locks at the
runaway sun,
I effuse my flesh in eddies, and drift it in lacy jags.

I bequeath myself to the dirt to grow from the grass I
love,
If you want me again look for me under your boot-soles.

You will hardly know who I am or what I mean,
But I shall be good health to you nevertheless,
And filter and fibre your blood.

Failing to fetch me at first keep encouraged,
Missing me one place search another,
I stop somewhere waiting for you.

# CHILDREN OF ADAM

## *To the Garden the World*

To the garden the world anew ascending,
Potent mates, daughters, sons, preluding,
The love, the life of their bodies, meaning and being,
Curious here behold my resurrection after slumber,
The revolving cycles in their wide sweep having
brought me again,
Amorous, mature, all beautiful to me, all wondrous,
My limbs and the quivering fire that ever plays
through them, for reasons, most wondrous,
Existing I peer and penetrate still,
Content with the present, content with the past,
By my side or back of me Eve following,
Or in front, and I following her just the same.

## *From Pent-up Aching Rivers*

From pent-up aching rivers,
From that of myself without which I were nothing,
From what I am determin'd to make illustrious,
even if I stand sole among men,
From my own voice resonant, singing the phallus,
Singing the song of procreation,
Singing the need of superb children and therein
superb grown people,
Singing the muscular urge and the blending,
Singing the bedfellow's song, (O resistless yearning!
O for any and each the body correlative attracting!
O for you whoever you are your correlative body! O
it, more than all else, you delighting!)
From the hungry gnaw that eats me night and day,
From native moments, from bashful pains, singing
them,

Seeking something yet unfound though I have
diligently sought it many a long year,
Singing the true song of the soul fitful at random,
Renascent with grossest Nature or among animals,
Of that, of them and what goes with them my poems
informing,
Of the smell of apples and lemons, of the pairing of
birds,
Of the wet of woods, of the lapping of waves,
Of the mad pushes of waves upon the land, I them
chanting,
The overture lightly sounding, the strain
anticipating,
The welcome nearness, the sight of the perfect body,
The swimmer swimming naked in the bath, or
motionless on his back lying and floating,
The female form approaching, I pensive, love-flesh
tremulous aching,
The divine list for myself or you or for any one making,
The face, the limbs, the index from head to foot,
and what it arouses,
The mystic deliria, the madness amorous, the utter
abandonment,
(Hark close and still what I now whisper to you,
I love you, O you entirely possess me,
O that you and I escape from the rest and go utterly
off, free and lawless,
Two hawks in the air, two fishes swimming in the
sea not more lawless than we;)
The furious storm through me careering, I
passionately trembling,
The oath of the inseparableness of two together, of
the woman that loves me and whom I love more
than my life, that oath swearing,

(O I willingly stake all for you,
O let me be lost if it must be so!
O you and I! what is it to us what the rest do or think?
What is all else to us? only that we enjoy each other
  and exhaust each other if it must be so;)
From the master, the pilot I yield the vessel to,
The general commanding me, commanding all,
  from him permission taking,
From time the programme hastening, (I have
  loiter'd too long as it is,)
From sex, from the warp and from the woof,
From privacy, from frequent repinings alone,
From plenty of persons near and yet the right person
  not near,
From the soft sliding of hands over me and thrusting
  of fingers through my hair and beard,
From the long sustain'd kiss upon the mouth or bosom,
From the close pressure that makes me or any man
  drunk, fainting with excess,
From what the divine husband knows, from the
  work of fatherhood,
From exultation, victory and relief from the
  bedfellow's embrace in the night,
From the act-poems of eyes, hands, hips and bosoms,
From the cling of the trembling arm,
From the bending curve and the clinch,
From side by side the pliant coverlet off-throwing,
From the one so unwilling to have me leave, and me
  just as unwilling to leave,
(Yet a moment O tender waiter, and I return,)
From the hour of shining stars and dropping dews,
From the night a moment I emerging flitting out,
Celebrate you act divine and you children prepared for,
And you stalwart loins.

## *I Sing the Body Electric*

I

I sing the body electric,
The armies of those I love engirth me and I engirth them,
They will not let me off till I go with them, respond to them,
And discorrupt them, and charge them full with the charge of the soul.
Was it doubted that those who corrupt their own bodies conceal themselves?
And if those who defile the living are as bad as they who defile the dead?
And if the body does not do fully as much as the soul?
And if the body were not the soul, what is the soul?

2

The love of the body of man or woman balks account, the body itself balks account,
That of the male is perfect, and that of the female is perfect.

The expression of the face balks account,
But the expression of a well-made man appears not only in his face,
It is in his limbs and joints also, it is curiously in the joints of his hips and wrists,
It is in his walk, the carriage of his neck, the flex of his waist and knees, dress does not hide him,
The strong sweet quality he has strikes through the cotton and broadcloth,
To see him pass conveys as much as the best poem, perhaps more,

You linger to see his back, and the back of his neck
 and shoulder-side.

The sprawl and fulness of babes, the bosoms and
 heads of women, the folds of their dress, their
 style as we pass in the street, the contour of their
 shape downwards,
The swimmer naked in the swimming-bath, seen as
 he swims through the transparent green-shine, or
 lies with his face up and rolls silently to and fro
 in the heave of the water,
The bending forward and backward of rowers in
 row-boats, the horseman in his saddle,
Girls, mothers, house-keepers, in all their
 performances,
The group of laborers seated at noon-time with their
 open dinner-kettles, and their wives waiting,
The female soothing a child, the farmer's daughter
 in the garden or cow-yard,
The young fellow hoeing corn, the sleigh-driver
 driving his six horses through the crowd,
The wrestle of wrestlers, two apprentice-boys, quite
 grown, lusty, good-natured, native-born, out on
 the vacant lot at sundown after work,
The coats and caps thrown down, the embrace of
 love and resistance,
The upper-hold and under-hold, the hair rumpled
 over and blinding the eyes;
The march of firemen in their own costumes, the
 play of masculine muscle through clean-setting
 trowsers and waist-straps,
The slow return from the fire, the pause when the
 bell strikes suddenly again, and the listening on
 the alert,

The natural, perfect, varied attitudes, the bent head,
the curv'd neck and the counting;
Such-like I love – I loosen myself, pass freely, am at
the mother's breast with the little child,
Swim with the swimmers, wrestle with wrestlers, march
in line with the firemen, and pause, listen, count.

3

I knew a man, a common farmer, the father of five sons,
And in them the fathers of sons, and in them the
fathers of sons.

This man was of wonderful vigor, calmness, beauty
of person,
The shape of his head, the pale yellow and white of his
hair and beard, the immeasurable meaning of his
black eyes, the richness and breadth of his manners,
These I used to go and visit him to see, he was wise also,
He was six feet tall, he was over eighty years old, his
sons were massive, clean, bearded, tan-faced,
handsome,
They and his daughters loved him, all who saw him
loved him,
They did not love him by allowance, they loved him
with personal love,
He drank water only, the blood show'd like scarlet
through the clear-brown skin of his face,
He was a frequent gunner and fisher, he sail'd his
boat himself, he had a fine one presented to him
by a ship-joiner, he had fowling-pieces presented
to him by men that loved him,
When he went with his five sons and many grand-
sons to hunt or fish, you would pick him out as
the most beautiful and vigorous of the gang,

You would wish long and long to be with him, you
would wish to sit by him in the boat that you and
he might touch each other.

4

I have perceiv'd that to be with those I like is
enough,
To stop in company with the rest at evening is
enough,
To be surrounded by beautiful, curious, breathing,
laughing flesh is enough,
To pass among them or touch any one, or rest my
arm ever so lightly round his or her neck for a
moment, what is this then?
I do not ask any more delight, I swim in it as in a sea.

There is something in staying close to men and
women and looking on them, and in the contact
and odor of them, that pleases the soul well,
All things please the soul, but these please the soul well

5

This is the female form,
A divine nimbus exhales from it from head to foot,
It attracts with fierce undeniable attraction,
I am drawn by its breath as if I were no more than a
helpless vapor, all falls aside but myself and it,
Books, art, religion, time, the visible and solid earth,
and what was expected of heaven or fear'd of
hell, are now consumed,
Mad filaments, ungovernable shoots play out of it,
the response likewise ungovernable,
Hair, bosom, hips, bend of legs, negligent falling
hands all diffused, mine too diffused,

Ebb stung by the flow and flow stung by the ebb,
love-flesh swelling and deliciously aching,
Limitless limpid jets of love hot and enormous,
quivering jelly of love, white-blow and delirious
juice,
Bridegroom night of love working surely and softly
into the prostrate dawn,
Undulating into the willing and yielding day,
Lost in the cleave of the clasping and sweet-flesh'd
day.

This the nucleus – after the child is born of woman,
man is born of woman,
This the bath of birth, this the merge of small and
large, and the outlet again.

Be not ashamed women, your privilege encloses the
rest, and is the exit of the rest,
You are the gates of the body, and you are the gates
of the soul.

The female contains all qualities and tempers them,
She is in her place and moves with perfect balance,
She is all things duly veil'd, she is both passive and
active,
She is to conceive daughters as well as sons, and
sons as well as daughters.

As I see my soul reflected in Nature,
As I see through a mist, One with inexpressible
completeness, sanity, beauty,
See the bent head and arms folded over the breast,
the Female I see.

## 6

The male is not less the soul nor more, he too is in his place,
He too is all qualities, he is action and power,
The flush of the known universe is in him,
Scorn becomes him well, and appetite and defiance become him well,
The wildest largest passions, bliss that is utmost, sorrow that is utmost become him well, pride is for him,
The full-spread pride of man is calming and excellent to the soul,
Knowledge becomes him, he likes it always, he brings every thing to the test of himself,
Whatever the survey, whatever the sea and the sail he strikes soundings at last only here,
(Where else does he strike soundings except here?)
The man's body is sacred and the woman's body is sacred,
No matter who it is, it is sacred – is it the meanest one in the laborer's gang?
Is it one of the dull-faced immigrants just landed on the wharf?
Each belongs here or anywhere just as much as the well-off, just as much as you,
Each has his or her place in the procession.

(All is a procession,
The universe is a procession with measured and perfect motion.)

Do you know so much yourself that you call the meanest ignorant?
Do you suppose you have a right to a good sight, and he or she has no right to a sight?

Do you think matter has cohered together from its
  diffuse float, and the soil is on the surface, and
  water runs and vegetation sprouts,
For you only, and not for him and her?

7

A man's body at auction,
(For before the war I often go to the slave-mart and
  watch the sale,)
I help the auctioneer, the sloven does not half know
  his business.

Gentlemen look on this wonder,
Whatever the bids of the bidders they cannot be high
  enough for it,
For it the globe lay preparing quintillions of years
  without one animal or plant,
For it the revolving cycles truly and steadily roll'd.

In this head the all-baffling brain,
In it and below it the makings of heroes.

Examine these limbs, red, black, or white, they are
  cunning in tendon and nerve,
They shall be stript that you may see them.
Exquisite senses, life-lit eyes, pluck, volition,
Flakes of breast-muscle, pliant backbone and neck,
  flesh not flabby, good-sized arms and legs,
And wonders within there yet.

Within there runs blood,
The same old blood! the same red-running blood!
There swells and jets a heart, there all passions,
  desires, reachings, aspirations,
(Do you think they are not there because they are
  not express'd in parlors and lecture-rooms?)

This is not only one man, this the father of those
who shall be fathers in their turns,
In him the start of populous states and rich
republics,
Of him countless immortal lives with countless
embodiments and enjoyments.
How do you know who shall come from the
offspring of his offspring through the centuries?
(Who might you find you have come from yourself,
if you could trace back through the centuries?)

8

A woman's body at auction,
She too is not only herself, she is the teeming mother
of mothers,
She is the bearer of them that shall grow and be
mates to the mothers.

Have you ever loved the body of a woman?
Have you ever loved the body of a man?
Do you not see that these are exactly the same to all
in all nations and times all over the earth?
If any thing is sacred the human body is sacred,
And the glory and sweat of a man is the token of
manhood untainted,
And in man or woman a clean, strong, firm-fibred body,
is more beautiful than the most beautiful face.
Have you seen the fool that corrupted his own live
body? or the fool that corrupted her own live
body?
For they do not conceal themselves, and cannot
conceal themselves.

9

O my body! I dare not desert the likes of you in
other men and women, nor the likes of the parts
of you,
I believe the likes of you are to stand or fall with the
likes of the soul, (and that they are the soul,)
I believe the likes of you shall stand or fall with my
poems, and that they are my poems,
Man's, woman's, child's, youth's, wife's, husband's,
mother's, father's, young man's, young woman's
poems,
Head, neck, hair, ears, drop and tympan of the ears,
Eyes, eye-fringes, iris of the eye, eyebrows, and the
waking or sleeping of the lids,
Mouth, tongue, lips, teeth, roof of the mouth, jaws,
and the jaw-hinges,
Nose, nostrils of the nose, and the partition,
Cheeks, temples, forehead, chin, throat, back of the
neck, neck-slue,
Strong shoulders, manly beard, scapula, hind-
shoulders, and the ample side-round of the chest,
Upper-arm, armpit, elbow-socket, lower-arm, arm-
sinews, arm-bones,
Wrist and wrist-joints, hand, palm, knuckles, thumb,
fore-finger, finger-joints, finger-nails,
Broad breast-front, curling hair of the breast, breast-
bone, breast-side,
Ribs, belly, backbone, joints of the backbone,
Hips, hip-sockets, hip-strength, inward and outward
round, man-balls, man-root,
Strong set of thighs, well carrying the trunk above,
Leg-fibres, knee, knee-pan, upper-leg, under-leg,
Ankles, instep, foot-ball, toes, toe-joints, the heel;

All attitudes, all the shapeliness, all the belongings of my
  or your body or of any one's body, male or female,
The lung-sponges, the stomach-sac, the bowels
  sweet and clean,
The brain in its folds inside the skull-frame,
Sympathies, heart-valves, palate-valves, sexuality,
  maternity,
Womanhood and all that is a woman, and the man
  that comes from woman,
The womb, the teats, nipples, breast-milk, tears,
  laughter, weeping, love-looks, love-perturbations
  and risings,
The voice, articulation, language, whispering,
  shouting aloud,
Food, drink, pulse, digestion, sweat, sleep, walking,
  swimming,
Poise on the hips, leaping, reclining, embracing,
  arm-curving and tightening,
The continual changes of the flex of the mouth, and
  around the eyes,
The skin, the sunburnt shade, freckles, hair,
The curious sympathy one feels when feeling with
  the hand the naked meat of the body,
The circling rivers the breath, and breathing it in
  and out,
The beauty of the waist, and thence of the hips, and
  thence downward toward the knees,
The thin red jellies within you or within me, the
  bones and the marrow in the bones,
The exquisite realization of health;
O I say these are not the parts and poems of the
  body only, but of the soul,
O I say now these are the soul!

## *A Woman Waits for Me*

A woman waits for me, she contains all, nothing is lacking,
Yet all were lacking if sex were lacking, or if the moisture of the right man were lacking.

Sex contains all, bodies, souls,
Meanings, proofs, purities, delicacies, results, promulgations,
Songs, commands, health, pride, the maternal mystery, the seminal milk,
All hopes, benefactions, bestowals, all the passions, loves, beauties, delights of the earth,
All the governments, judges, gods, follow'd persons of the earth,
These are contain'd in sex as parts of itself and justifications of itself.
Without shame the man I like knows and avows the deliciousness of his sex,
Without shame the woman I like knows and avows hers.

Now I will dismiss myself from impassive women,
I will go stay with her who waits for me, and with those women that are warm-blooded and sufficient for me,
I see that they understand me and do not deny me,
I see that they are worthy of me, I will be the robust husband of those women.

They are not one jot less than I am,
They are tann'd in the face by shining suns and blowing winds,
Their flesh has the old divine suppleness and strength,

They know how to swim, row, ride, wrestle, shoot, run,
strike, retreat, advance, resist, defend themselves,
They are ultimate in their own right – they are calm,
clear, well-possess'd of themselves.

I draw you close to me, you women,
I cannot let you go, I would do you good,
I am for you, and you are for me, not only for our
own sake, but for others' sakes,
Envelop'd in you sleep greater heroes and bards,
They refuse to awake at the touch of any man but me.

It is I, you women, I make my way,
I am stern, acrid, large, undissuadable, but I love you,
I do not hurt you any more than is necessary for you,
I pour the stuff to start sons and daughters fit for
these States, I press with slow rude muscle,
I brace myself effectually, I listen to no entreaties,
I dare not withdraw till I deposit what has so long
accumulated within me.

Through you I drain the pent-up rivers of myself,
In you I wrap a thousand onward years,
On you I graft the grafts of the best-beloved of me
and America,
The drops I distil upon you shall grow fierce and
athletic girls, new artists, musicians, and singers,
The babes I beget upon you are to beget babes in
their turn,
I shall demand perfect men and women out of my
love-spendings,
I shall expect them to interpenetrate with others, as I
and you interpenetrate now,

I shall count on the fruits of the gushing showers of
them, as
I count on the fruits of the gushing showers I give now,
I shall look for loving crops from the birth, life,
death, immortality, I plant so lovingly now.

## *Spontaneous Me*

Spontaneous me, Nature,
The loving day, the mounting sun, the friend I am
happy with,
The arm of my friend hanging idly over my shoulder,
The hillside whiten'd with blossoms of the mountain
ash,
The same late in autumn, the hues of red, yellow,
drab, purple, and light and dark green,
The rich coverlet of the grass, animals and birds, the
private untrimm'd bank, the primitive apples,
the pebble-stones,
Beautiful dripping fragments, the negligent list of
one after another as I happen to call them to me
or think of them,
The real poems, (what we call poems being merely
pictures,)
The poems of the privacy of the night, and of men
like me,
This poem drooping shy and unseen that I always
carry, and that all men carry,
(Know once for all, avow'd on purpose, wherever
are men like me, are our lusty lurking masculine
poems,)
Love-thoughts, love-juice, love-odor, love-yielding,
love-climbers, and the climbing sap,

Arms and hands of love, lips of love, phallic thumb
of love, breasts of love, bellies press'd and glued
together with love,
Earth of chaste love, life that is only life after love,
The body of my love, the body of the woman I love,
the body of the man, the body of the earth,
Soft forenoon airs that blow from the south-west,
The hairy wild-bee that murmurs and hankers up
and down, that gripes the full-grown lady-flower,
curves upon her with amorous firm legs, takes
his will of her, and holds himself tremulous and
tight till he is satisfied;
The wet of woods through the early hours,
Two sleepers at night lying close together as they
sleep, one with an arm slanting down across and
below the waist of the other,
The smell of apples, aromas from crush'd sage-
plant, mint, birch-bark,
The boy's longings, the glow and pressure as he
confides to me what he was dreaming,
The dead leaf whirling its spiral whirl and falling still
and content to the ground,
The no-form'd stings that sights, people, objects,
sting me with,
The hubb'd sting of myself, stinging me as much as
it ever can any one,
The sensitive, orbic, underlapp'd brothers, that only
privileged feelers may be intimate where they are,
The curious roamer the hand roaming all over the
body, the bashful withdrawing of flesh where the
fingers soothingly pause and edge themselves,
The limpid liquid within the young man,
The vex'd corrosion so pensive and so painful,

The torment, the irritable tide that will not be at rest,
The like of the same I feel, the like of the same in others,
The young man that flushes and flushes, and the young woman that flushes and flushes,
The young man that wakes deep at night, the hot hand seeking to repress what would master him,
The mystic amorous night, the strange half-welcome pangs, visions, sweats,
The pulse pounding through palms and trembling encircling fingers, the young man all color'd, red, ashamed, angry;
The souse upon me of my lover the sea, as I lie willing and naked,
The merriment of the twin babies that crawl over the grass in the sun, the mother never turning her vigilant eyes from them,
The walnut-trunk, the walnut-husks, and the ripening or ripen'd long-round walnuts,
The continence of vegetables, birds, animals,
The consequent meanness of me should I skulk or find myself indecent, while birds and animals never once skulk or find themselves indecent,
The great chastity of paternity, to match the great chastity of maternity,
The oath of procreation I have sworn, my Adamic and fresh daughters,
The greed that eats me day and night with hungry gnaw, till I saturate what shall produce boys to fill my place when I am through,
The wholesome relief, repose, content,
And this bunch pluck'd at random from myself,
It has done its work – I toss it carelessly to fall where it may.

## *One Hour to Madness and Joy*

One hour to madness and joy! O furious! O confine me not!
(What is this that frees me so in storms?
What do my shouts amid lightnings and raging winds mean?)

O to drink the mystic deliria deeper than any other man!
O savage and tender achings! (I bequeath them to you, my children,
I tell them to you, for reasons, O bridegroom and bride.)

O to be yielded to you whoever you are, and you to be yielded to me in defiance of the world!
O to return to Paradise! O bashful and feminine!
O to draw you to me, to plant on you for the first time the lips of a determin'd man.

O the puzzle, the thrice-tied knot, the deep and dark pool, all untied and illumin'd!
O to speed where there is space enough and air enough at last!
To be absolv'd from previous ties and conventions, I from mine and you from yours!
To find a new unthought-of nonchalance with the best of Nature!
To have the gag remov'd from one's mouth!
To have the feeling to-day or any day I am sufficient as I am.

O something unprov'd! something in a trance!
To escape utterly from others' anchors and holds!
To drive free! to love free! to dash reckless and dangerous!
To court destruction with taunts, with invitations!

To ascend, to leap to the heavens of the love
  indicated to me!
To rise thither with my inebriate soul!
To be lost if it must be so!
To feed the remainder of life with one hour of
  fulness and freedom!
With one brief hour of madness and joy.

## *Out of the Rolling Ocean the Crowd*

Out of the rolling ocean the crowd came a drop
  gently to me,
Whispering *I love you, before long I die,*
*I have travel'd a long way merely to look on you to touch*
  *you,*
*For I could not die till I once look'd on you,*
*For I fear'd I might afterward lose you.*

Now we have met, we have look'd, we are safe,
Return in peace to the ocean my love,
I too am part of that ocean my love, we are not so
  much separated,
Behold the great rondure, the cohesion of all, how
  perfect!
But as for me, for you, the irresistible sea is to
  separate us,
As for an hour carrying us diverse, yet cannot carry
  us diverse forever;
Be not impatient – a little space – know you I salute
  the air, the ocean and the land,
Every day at sundown for your dear sake my love.

## *Ages and Ages Returning at Intervals*

Ages and ages returning at intervals,
Undestroy'd, wandering immortal,
Lusty, phallic, with the potent original loins, perfectly sweet,
I, chanter of Adamic songs,
Through the new garden the West, the great cities calling,
Deliriate, thus prelude what is generated, offering these, offering myself,
Bathing myself, bathing my songs in Sex,
Offspring of my loins.

## *We Two, How Long We were Fool'd*

We two, how long we were fool'd,
Now transmuted, we swiftly escape as Nature escapes,
We are Nature, long have we been absent, but now we return,
We become plants, trunks, foliage, roots, bark,
We are bedded in the ground, we are rocks,
We are oaks, we grow in the openings side by side,
We browse, we are two among the wild herds spontaneous as any,
We are two fishes swimming in the sea together,
We are what locust blossoms are, we drop scent around lanes mornings and evenings,
We are also the coarse smut of beasts, vegetables, minerals,
We are two predatory hawks, we soar above and look down,
We are two resplendent suns, we it is who balance ourselves orbic and stellar, we are as two comets,

We prowl fang'd and four-footed in the woods, we
spring on prey,
We are two clouds forenoons and afternoons driving
overhead,
We are seas mingling, we are two of those cheerful
waves rolling over each other and interwetting
each other,
We are what the atmosphere is, transparent,
receptive, pervious, impervious,
We are snow, rain, cold, darkness, we are each
product and influence of the globe,
We have circled and circled till we have arrived
home again, we two,
We have voided all but freedom and all but our own joy.

## *O Hymen! O Hymenee!*

O hymen! O hymenee! why do you tantalize me thus?
O why sting me for a swift moment only?
Why can you not continue? O why do you now cease?
Is it because if you continued beyond the swift
moment you would soon certainly kill me?

## *I am He that Aches with Love*

I am he that aches with amorous love;
Does the earth gravitate? does not all matter, aching,
attract all matter?
So the body of me to all I meet or know.

## *Native Moments*

Native moments – when you come upon me – ah you are here now,
Give me now libidinous joys only,
Give me the drench of my passions, give me life coarse and rank,
To-day I go consort with Nature's darlings, to-night too,
I am for those who believe in loose delights, I share the mid-night orgies of young men,
I dance with the dancers and drink with the drinkers,
The echoes ring with our indecent calls, I pick out some low person for my dearest friend,
He shall be lawless, rude, illiterate, he shall be one condemned by others for deeds done,
I will play a part no longer, why should I exile myself from my companions?
O you shunn'd persons, I at least do not shun you,
I come forthwith in your midst, I will be your poet,
I will be more to you than to any of the rest

## *Once I Pass'd Through a Populous City*

Once I pass'd through a populous city imprinting
my brain for future use with its shows,
architecture, customs, traditions,
Yet now of all that city I remember only a woman I
casually met there who detain'd me for love of me,
Day by day and night by night we were together – all
else has long been forgotten by me,
I remember I say only that woman who passionately
clung to me,
Again we wander, we love, we separate again,
Again she holds me by the hand, I must not go,
I see her close beside me with silent lips sad and
tremulous.

## *I Heard You Solemn-Sweet Pipes of the Organ*

I heard you solemn-sweet pipes of the organ as last
Sunday morn I pass'd the church,
Winds of autumn, as I walk'd the woods at dusk I heard
your long-stretch'd sighs up above so mournful,
I heard the perfect Italian tenor singing at the opera,
I heard the soprano in the midst of the quartet
singing;
Heart of my love! you too I heard murmuring low
through one of the wrists around my head,
Heard the pulse of you when all was still ringing
little bells last night under my ear.

## *Facing West from California's Shores*

Facing west from California's shores,
Inquiring, tireless, seeking what is yet unfound,
I, a child, very old, over waves, towards the house of maternity, the land of migrations, look afar,
Look off the shores of my Western sea, the circle almost circled;
For starting westward from Hindustan, from the vales of Kashmere,
From Asia, from the north, from the God, the sage, and the hero,
From the south, from the flowery peninsulas and the spice islands,
Long having wander'd since, round the earth having wander'd,
Now I face home again, very pleas'd and joyous,
(But where is what I started for so long ago?
And why is it yet unfound?)

## *As Adam Early in the Morning*

As Adam early in the morning,
Walking forth from the bower refresh'd with sleep,
Behold me where I pass, hear my voice, approach,
Touch me, touch the palm of your hand to my body as I pass,
Be not afraid of my body.

# CALAMUS

## *In Paths Untrodden*

In paths untrodden,
In the growths by margins of pond-waters,
Escaped from the life that exhibits itself,
From all the standards hitherto publish'd, from the
    pleasures, profits, conformities,
Which too long I was offering to feed my soul,
Clear to me now standards not yet publish'd, clear
    to me that my soul,
That the soul of the man I speak for rejoices in
    comrades,
Here by myself away from the clank of the world,
Tallying and talk'd to here by tongues aromatic,
No longer abash'd, (for in this secluded spot I can
    respond as I would not dare elsewhere,)
Strong upon me the life that does not exhibit itself,
    yet contains all the rest,
Resolv'd to sing no songs to-day but those of manly
    attachment,
Projecting them along that substantial life,
Bequeathing hence types of athletic love,
Afternoon this delicious Ninth-month in my
    forty-first year,
I proceed for all who are or have been young men,
To tell the secret of my nights and days,
To celebrate the need of comrades.

## *Scented Herbage of My Breast*

Scented herbage of my breast,
Leaves from you I glean, I write, to be perused best
afterwards,
Tomb-leaves, body-leaves growing up above me
above death,
Perennial roots, tall leaves, O the winter shall not
freeze you delicate leaves,
Every year shall you bloom again, out from where
you retired you shall emerge again;
O I do not know whether many passing by will
discover you or inhale your faint odor, but I
believe a few will;
O slender leaves! O blossoms of my blood! I permit you
to tell in your own way of the heart that is under you,
O I do not know what you mean there underneath
yourselves, you are not happiness,
You are often more bitter than I can bear, you burn
and sting me,
Yet you are beautiful to me you faint-tinged roots,
you make me think of death,
Death is beautiful from you, (what indeed is finally
beautiful except death and love?)
O I think it is not for life I am chanting here my
chant of lovers, I think it must be for death,
For how calm, how solemn it grows to ascend to the
atmosphere of lovers,
Death or life I am then indifferent, my soul declines
to prefer,
(I am not sure but the high soul of lovers welcomes
death most,)
Indeed O death, I think now these leaves mean
precisely the same as you mean,

Grow up taller sweet leaves that I may see! grow up
out of my breast!
Spring away from the conceal'd heart there!
Do not fold yourself so in your pink-tinged roots
timid leaves!
Do not remain down there so ashamed, herbage of
my breast!
Come I am determin'd to unbare this broad breast
of mine, I have long enough stifled and choked;
Emblematic and capricious blades I leave you, now
you serve me not,
I will say what I have to say by itself,
I will sound myself and comrades only, I will never
again utter a call only their call,
I will raise with it immortal reverberations through
the States,
I will give an example to lovers to take permanent
shape and will through the States,
Through me shall the words be said to make death
exhilarating.
Give me your tone therefore O death, that I may
accord with it,
Give me yourself, for I see that you belong to me
now above all, and are folded inseparably
together, you love and death are,
Nor will I allow you to balk me any more with what
I was calling life,
For now it is convey'd to me that you are the
purports essential,
That you hide in these shifting forms of life, for
reasons, and that they are mainly for you,
That you beyond them come forth to remain, the
real reality,

That behind the mask of materials you patiently
wait, no matter how long,
That you will one day perhaps take control of all,
That you will perhaps dissipate this entire show of
appearance,
That may-be you are what it is all for, but it does not
last so very long,
But you will last very long.

## *Whoever You are Holding Me Now in Hand*

Whoever you are holding me now in hand,
Without one thing all will be useless,
I give you fair warning before you attempt me further,
I am not what you supposed, but far different.

Who is he that would become my follower?
Who would sign himself a candidate for my
affections?
The way is suspicious, the result uncertain, perhaps
destructive,
You would have to give up all else, I alone would
expect to be your sole and exclusive standard,
Your novitiate would even then be long and
exhausting,
The whole past theory of your life and all conformity
to the lives around you would have to be
abandon'd,
Therefore release me now before troubling yourself
any further, let go your hand from my shoulders,
Put me down and depart on your way.

Or else by stealth in some wood for trial,
Or back of a rock in the open air,

(For in any roof'd room of a house I emerge not,
 nor in company,
And in libraries I lie as one dumb, a gawk, or
 unborn, or dead,)
But just possibly with you on a high hill, first
 watching lest any person for miles around
 approach unawares,
Or possibly with you sailing at sea, or on the beach
 of the sea or some quiet island,
Here to put your lips upon mine I permit you,
With the comrade's long-dwelling kiss or the new
 husband's kiss,
For I am the new husband and I am the comrade.

Or if you will, thrusting me beneath your clothing,
Where I may feel the throbs of your heart or rest
 upon your hip,
Carry me when you go forth over land or sea;
For thus merely touching you is enough, is best,
And thus touching you would I silently sleep and be
 carried eternally.

But these leaves conning you con at peril,
For these leaves and me you will not understand,
They will elude you at first and still more afterward,
 I will certainly elude you,
Even while you should think you had
 unquestionably caught me, behold!
Already you see I have escaped from you.

For it is not for what I have put into it that I have
 written this book,
Nor is it by reading it you will acquire it,
Nor do those know me best who admire me and
 vauntingly praise me,

Nor will the candidates for my love (unless at most a very few) prove victorious,
Nor will my poems do good only, they will do just as much evil, perhaps more,
For all is useless without that which you may guess at many times and not hit, that which I hinted at;
Therefore release me and depart on your way.

## *For You O Democracy*

Come, I will make the continent indissoluble,
I will make the most splendid race the sun ever shone upon,
I will make divine magnetic lands,
With the love of comrades,
With the life-long love of comrades.

I will plant companionship thick as trees along all the rivers of America, and along the shores of the great lakes, and all over the prairies,
I will make inseparable cities with their arms about each other's necks,
By the love of comrades,
By the manly love of comrades.

For you these from me, O Democracy, to serve you ma femme!
For you, for you I am trilling these songs.

## *These I Singing in Spring*

These I singing in spring collect for lovers,
(For who but I should understand lovers and all
their sorrow and joy?
And who but I should be the poet of comrades?)
Collecting I traverse the garden the world, but soon
I pass the gates,
Now along the pond-side, now wading in a little,
fearing not the wet,
Now by the post-and-rail fences where the old
stones thrown there, pick'd from the fields, have
accumulated,
(Wild-flowers and vines and weeds come up through
the stones and partly cover them, beyond these I
pass,)
Far, far in the forest, or sauntering later in summer,
before I think where I go,
Solitary, smelling the earthy smell, stopping now and
then in the silence,
Alone I had thought, yet soon a troop gathers
around me,
Some walk by my side and some behind, and some
embrace my arms or neck,
They the spirits of dear friends dead or alive, thicker
they come, a great crowd, and I in the middle,
Collecting, dispensing, singing, there I wander with
them,
Plucking something for tokens, tossing toward
whoever is near me,
Here, lilac, with a branch of pine,
Here, out of my pocket, some moss which I pull'd
off a live-oak in Florida as it hung trailing down,

Here, some pinks and laurel leaves, and a handful of sage,
And here what I now draw from the water, wading in the pond-side,
(O here I last saw him that tenderly loves me, and returns again never to separate from me,
And this, O this shall henceforth be the token of comrades, this calamus-root shall,
Interchange it youths with each other! let none render it back!)
And twigs of maple and a bunch of wild orange and chestnut,
And stems of currants and plum-blows, and the aromatic cedar,
These I compass'd around by a thick cloud of spirits,
Wandering, point to or touch as I pass, or throw them loosely from me,
Indicating to each one what he shall have, giving something to each;
But what I drew from the water by the pond-side, that I reserve,
I will give of it, but only to them that love as I myself am capable of loving.

## *Not Heaving from my Ribb'd Breast Only*

Not heaving from my ribb'd breast only,
Not in sighs at night in rage dissatisfied with myself,
Not in those long-drawn, ill-suppress sighs,
Not in many an oath and promise broken,
Not in my wilful and savage soul's volition,
Not in the subtle nourishment of the air,

Not in this beating and pounding at my temples and
wrists,
Not in the curious systole and diastole within which
will one day cease,
Not in many a hungry wish told to the skies only,
Not in cries, laughter, defiances, thrown from me
when alone far in the wilds,
Not in husky pantings through clinch'd teeth,
Not in sounded and resounded words, chattering
words, echoes, dead words,
Not in the murmurs of my dreams while I sleep,
Nor the other murmurs of these incredible dreams
of every day,
Nor in the limbs and senses of my body that take
you and dismiss you continually – not there,
Not in any or all of them O adhesiveness! O pulse of
my life!
Need I that you exist and show yourself any more
than in these songs.

## *Of the Terrible Doubt of Appearances*

Of the terrible doubt of appearances,
Of the uncertainty after all, that we may be deluded,
That may-be reliance and hope are but speculations
after all,
That may-be identity beyond the grave is a beautiful
fable only,
May-be the things I perceive, the animals, plants,
men, hills, shining and flowing waters,
The skies of day and night, colors, densities, forms,
may-be these are (as doubtless they are) only
apparitions, and the real something has yet to be
known,

(How often they dart out of themselves as if to
confound me and mock me!
How often I think neither I know, nor any man
knows, aught of them,)
May-be seeming to me what they are (as doubtless
they indeed but seem) as from my present point
of view, and might prove (as of course they
would) nought of what they appear, or nought
anyhow, from entirely changed points of view;
To me these and the like of these are curiously
answer'd by my lovers, my dear friends,
When he whom I love travels with me or sits a long
while holding me by the hand,
When the subtle air, the impalpable, the sense that
words and reason hold not, surround us and
pervade us,
Then I am charged with untold and untellable
wisdom, I am silent, I require nothing further,
I cannot answer the question of appearances or that
of identity beyond the grave,
But I walk or sit indifferent, I am satisfied,
He ahold of my hand has completely satisfied me.

## *The Base of All Metaphysics*

And now gentlemen,
A word I give to remain in your memories and minds,
As base and finalè too for all metaphysics.

(So to the students the old professor,
At the close of his crowded course.)

Having studied the new and antique, the Greek and
Germanic systems,

Kant having studied and stated, Fichte and
Schelling and Hegel,
Stated the lore of Plato, and Socrates greater than Plato,
And greater than Socrates sought and stated, Christ
divine having studied long,
I see reminiscent to-day those Greek and Germanic
systems,
See the philosophies all, Christian churches and
tenets see,
Yet underneath Socrates clearly see, and underneath
Christ the divine I see,
The dear love of man for his comrade, the attraction
of friend to friend,
Of the well-married husband and wife, of children
and parents,
Of city for city and land for land.

## *Recorders Ages Hence*

Recorders ages hence,
Come, I will take you down underneath this impassive
exterior, I will tell you what to say of me,
Publish my name and hang up my picture as that of
the tenderest lover,
The friend the lover's portrait, of whom his friend
his lover was fondest,
Who was not proud of his songs, but of the
measureless ocean of love within him, and freely
pour'd it forth,
Who often walk'd lonesome walks thinking of his
dear friends, his lovers,
Who pensive away from one he lov'd often lay
sleepless and dissatisfied at night,

Who knew too well the sick, sick dread lest the one
he lov'd might secretly be indifferent to him,
Whose happiest days were far away through fields, in
woods, on hills, he and another wandering hand
in hand, they twain apart from other men,
Who oft as he saunter'd the streets curv'd with his
arm the shoulder of his friend, while the arm of
his friend rested upon him also.

## *When I Heard at the Close of the Day*

When I heard at the close of the day how my name
had been receiv'd with plaudits in the capitol,
still it was not a happy night for me that follow'd,
And else when I carous'd, or when my plans were
accomplish'd, still I was not happy,
But the day when I rose at dawn from the bed of
perfect health, refresh'd, singing, inhaling the
ripe breath of autumn,
When I saw the full moon in the west grow pale and
disappear in the morning light,
When I wander'd alone over the beach, and
undressing bathed, laughing with the cool
waters, and saw the sun rise,
And when I thought how my dear friend my lover
was on his way coming, O then I was happy,
O then each breath tasted sweeter, and all that day
my food nourish'd me more, and the beautiful
day pass'd well,
And the next came with equal joy, and with the next
at evening came my friend,
And that night while all was still I heard the waters
roll slowly continually up the shores,

I heard the hissing rustle of the liquid and sands as
directed to me whispering to congratulate me,
For the one I love most lay sleeping by me under the
same cover in the cool night,
In the stillness in the autumn moonbeams his face
was inclined toward me,
And his arm lay lightly around my breast – and that
night I was happy.

## *Are You The New Person Drawn Toward Me?*

Are you the new person drawn toward me?
To begin with take warning, I am surely far different
from what you suppose;
Do you suppose you will find in me your ideal?
Do you think it is so easy to have me become your lover?
Do you think the friendship of me would be
unalloy'd satisfaction?
Do you think I am trusty and faithful?
Do you see no further than this façade, this smooth
and tolerant manner of me?
Do you suppose yourself advancing on real ground
toward a real heroic man?
Have you no thought O dreamer that it may be all
maya, illusion?

## *Roots and Leaves Themselves Alone*

Roots and leaves themselves alone are these,
Scents brought to men and women from the wild
  woods and pond-side,
Breast-sorrel and pinks of love, fingers that wind
  around tighter than vines,
Gushes from the throats of birds hid in the foliage of
  trees as the sun is risen,
Breezes of land and love set from living shores to
  you on the living sea, to you O sailors!
Frost-mellow'd berries and Third-month twigs
  offer'd fresh to young persons wandering out in
  the fields when the winter breaks up,
Love-buds put before you and within you whoever
  you are,
Buds to be unfolded on the old terms,
If you bring the warmth of the sun to them they will
  open and bring form, color, perfume, to you,
If you become the aliment and the wet they will
  become flowers, fruits, tall branches and trees.

## *Not Heat Flames Up and Consumes*

Not heat flames up and consumes,
Not sea-waves hurry in and out,
Not the air delicious and dry, the air of ripe summer,
  bears lightly along white down-balls of myriads
  of seeds,
Wafted, sailing gracefully, to drop where they may;
Not these, O none of these more than the flames of
  me, consuming, burning for his love whom I love,
O none more than I hurrying in and out;

Does the tide hurry, seeking something, and never
give up? O I the same,
O nor down-balls nor perfumes, nor the high
rain-emitting clouds, are borne through the open
air,
Any more than my soul is borne through the open air,
Wafted in all directions O love, for friendship, for you.

## *Trickle Drops*

Trickle drops! my blue veins leaving!
O drops of me! trickle, slow drops,
Candid from me falling, drip, bleeding drops,
From wounds made to free you whence you were
prison'd,
From my face, from my forehead and lips,
From my breast, from within where I was conceal'd,
press forth red drops, confession drops,
Stain every page, stain every song I sing, every word
I say, bloody drops,
Let them know your scarlet heat, let them glisten,
Saturate them with yourself all ashamed and wet,
Glow upon all I have written or shall write, bleeding
drops,
Let it all be seen in your light, blushing drops.

## *City of Orgies*

City of orgies, walks and joys,
City whom that I have lived and sung in your midst
will one day make you illustrious,
Not the pageants of you, not your shifting tableaus,
your spectacles, repay me,

Not the interminable rows of your houses, nor the ships
at the wharves,
Nor the processions in the streets, nor the bright
windows with goods in them,
Nor to converse with learn'd persons, or bear my
share in the soiree or feast;
Not those, but as I pass O Manhattan, your frequent
and swift flash of eyes offering me love,
Offering response to my own – these repay me,
Lovers, continual lovers, only repay me.

## *Behold This Swarthy Face*

Behold this swarthy face, these gray eyes,
This beard, the white wool unclipt upon my neck,
My brown hands and the silent manner of me
without charm;
Yet comes one a Manhattanese and ever at parting
kisses me lightly on the lips with robust love,
And I on the crossing of the street or on the ship's
deck give a kiss in return,
We observe that salute of American comrades land
and sea,
We are those two natural and nonchalant persons.

## *I Saw in Louisiana a Live-Oak Growing*

I saw in Louisiana a live-oak growing,
All alone stood it and the moss hung down from the
branches,
Without any companion it grew there uttering
joyous leaves of dark green,
And its look, rude, unbending, lusty, made me think
of myself,

But I wonder'd how it could utter joyous leaves
standing alone there without its friend near, for I
knew I could not,
And I broke off a twig with a certain number of
leaves upon it, and twined around it a little moss,
And brought it away, and I have placed it in sight, in
my room,
It is not needed to remind me as of my own dear friends,
(For I believe lately I think of little else than of them,)
Yet it remains to me a curious token, it makes me
think of manly love;
For all that, and though the live-oak glistens there in
Louisiana solitary in a wide flat space,
Uttering joyous leaves all its life without a friend a
lover near,
I know very well I could not.

## *To a Stranger*

Passing stranger! you do not know how longingly I
look upon you,
You must be he I was seeking, or she I was seeking,
(it comes to me as of a dream,)
I have somewhere surely lived a life of joy with you,
All is recall'd as we flit by each other, fluid,
affectionate, chaste, matured,
You grew up with me, were a boy with me or a girl
with me,
I ate with you and slept with you, your body has
become not yours only nor left my body mine only,
You give me the pleasure of your eyes, face, flesh, as
we pass, you take of my beard, breast, hands, in
return,

I am not to speak to you, I am to think of you when
    I sit alone or wake at night alone,
I am to wait, I do not doubt I am to meet you again,
I am to see to it that I do not lose you.

## *This Moment Yearning and Thoughtful*

This moment yearning and thoughtful sitting alone,
It seems to me there are other men in other lands
    yearning and thoughtful,
It seems to me I can look over and behold them in
    Germany, Italy, France, Spain,
Or far, far away, in China, or in Russia or Japan,
    talking other dialects,
And it seems to me if I could know those men I
    should become attached to them as I do to men
    in my own lands,
O I know we should be brethren and lovers,
I know I should be happy with them.

## *I Hear It was Charged against Me*

I hear it was charged against me that I sought to
    destroy institutions,
But really I am neither for nor against institutions,
(What indeed have I in common with them? or what
    with the destruction of them?)
Only I will establish in the Mannahatta and in every
    city of these States inland and seaboard,
And in the fields and woods, and above every keel
    little or large that dents the water,
Without edifices or rules or trustees or any
    argument,
The institution of the dear love of comrades.

## *The Prairie-Grass Dividing*

The prairie-grass dividing, its special odor breathing,
I demand of it the spiritual corresponding,
Demand the most copious and close companionship of men,
Demand the blades to rise of words, acts, beings,
Those of the open atmosphere, coarse, sunlit, fresh, nutritious,
Those that go their own gait, erect, stepping with freedom and command, leading not following,
Those with a never-quell'd audacity, those with sweet and lusty flesh clear of taint,
Those that look carelessly in the faces of Presidents and governors, as to say *Who are you?*
Those of earth-born passion, simple, never constrain'd, never obedient,
Those of inland America.

## *When I Peruse the Conquer'd Fame*

When I peruse the conquer'd fame of heroes and the victories of mighty generals, I do not envy the generals,
Nor the President in his Presidency, nor the rich in his great house,
But when I hear of the brotherhood of lovers, how it was with them,
How together through life, through dangers, odium, unchanging, long and long,
Through youth and through middle and old age, how unfaltering, how affectionate and faithful they were,
Then I am pensive – I hastily walk away fill'd with the bitterest envy.

## *We Two Boys together Clinging*

We two boys together clinging,
One the other never leaving,
Up and down the roads going, North and South
excursions making,
Power enjoying, elbows stretching, fingers clutching,
Arm'd and fearless, eating, drinking, sleeping, loving,
No law less than ourselves owning, sailing,
soldiering, thieving, threatening,
Misers, menials, priests alarming, air breathing, water
drinking, on the turf or the sea-beach dancing,
Cities wrenching, ease scorning, statutes mocking,
feebleness chasing,
Fulfilling our foray.

## *A Promise to California*

A promise to California,
Or inland to the great pastoral Plains, and on to
Puget sound and Oregon;
Sojourning east a while longer, soon I travel toward
you, to remain, to teach robust American love,
For I know very well that I and robust love belong
among you, inland, and along the Western sea;
For these States tend inland and toward the Western
sea, and I will also.

## *Here the Frailest Leaves of Me*

Here the frailest leaves of me and yet my strongest
lasting,
Here I shade and hide my thoughts, I myself do not
expose them,
And yet they expose me more than all my other poems.

## *No Labor-saving Machine*

No labor-saving machine,
Nor discovery have I made,
Nor will I be able to leave behind me any wealthy
bequest to found a hospital or library,
Nor reminiscence of any deed of courage for America,
Nor literary success nor intellect, nor book for the
book-shelf,
But a few carols vibrating through the air I leave,
For comrades and lovers.

## *A Glimpse*

A glimpse through an interstice caught,
Of a crowd of workmen and drivers in a bar-room
around the stove late of a winter night, and I
unremark'd seated in a corner,
Of a youth who loves me and whom I love, silently
approaching and seating himself near, that he
may hold me by the hand,
A long while amid the noises of coming and going,
of drinking and oath and smutty jest,
There we two, content, happy in being together,
speaking little, perhaps not a word.

## *A Leaf for Hand in Hand*

A leaf for hand in hand;
You natural persons old and young!
You on the Mississippi and on all the branches and bayous of the Mississippi!
You friendly boatmen and mechanics! you roughs!
You twain! and all processions moving along the streets!
I wish to infuse myself among you till I see it common for you to walk hand in hand.

## *Earth, My Likeness*

Earth, my likeness,
Though you look so impassive, ample and spheric there,
I now suspect that is not all;
I now suspect there is something fierce in you eligible to burst forth,
For an athlete is enamour'd of me, and I of him,
But toward him there is something fierce and terrible in me eligible to burst forth,
I dare not tell it in words, not even in these songs.

## *I Dream'd in a Dream*

I dream'd in a dream I saw a city invincible to the attacks of the whole of the rest of the earth,
I dream'd that was the new city of Friends,
Nothing was greater there than the quality of robust love, it led the rest,
It was seen every hour in the actions of the men of that city,
And in all their looks and words.

## *What Think You I Take My Pen in Hand?*

What think you I take my pen in hand to record?
The battle-ship, perfect-model'd, majestic, that I
saw pass the offing to-day under full sail?
The splendors of the past day? or the splendor of the
night that envelops me?
Or the vaunted glory and growth of the great city
spread around me? – no;
But merely of two simple men I saw to-day on the
pier in the midst of the crowd, parting the
parting of dear friends,
The one to remain hung on the other's neck and
passionately kiss'd him,
While the one to depart tightly prest the one to
remain in his arms.

## *To the East and to the West*

To the East and to the West,
To the man of the Seaside State and of
Pennsylvania,
To the Kanadian of the north, to the Southerner I love,
These with perfect trust to depict you as myself, the
germs are in all men,
I believe the main purport of these States is to found
a superb friendship, exalté, previously unknown,
Because I perceive it waits, and has been always
waiting, latent in all men.

## *Sometimes with One I Love*

Sometimes with one I love I fill myself with rage for
fear I effuse unreturn'd love,
But now I think there is no unreturn'd love, the pay
is certain one way or another,
(I loved a certain person ardently and my love was
not return'd,
Yet out of that I have written these songs.)

## *To a Western Boy*

Many things to absorb I teach to help you become
eleve of mine;
Yet if blood like mine circle not in your veins,
If you be not silently selected by lovers and do not
silently select lovers,
Of what use is it that you seek to become eleve of mine?

## *Fast-Anchor'd Eternal O Love!*

Fast-anchor'd eternal O love! O woman I love!
O bride! O wife! more resistless than I can tell, the
thought of you!
Then separate, as disembodied or another born,
Ethereal, the last athletic reality, my consolation,
I ascend, I float in the regions of your love O man,
O sharer of my roving life.

## *Among the Multitude*

Among the men and women the multitude,
I perceive one picking me out by secret and divine signs,
Acknowledging none else, not parent, wife,
husband, brother, child, any nearer than I am,
Some are baffled, but that one is not – that one
knows me.

Ah lover and perfect equal,
I meant that you should discover me so by faint
indirections,
And I when I meet you mean to discover you by the
like in you.

## *O You whom I Often and Silently Come*

O you whom I often and silently come where you
are that I may be with you,
As I walk by your side or sit near, or remain in the
same room with you,
Little you know the subtle electric fire that for your
sake is playing within me.

## *That Shadow My Likeness*

That shadow my likeness that goes to and fro
seeking a livelihood, chattering, chaffering,
How often I find myself standing and looking at it
where it flits,
How often I question and doubt whether that is
really me;
But among my lovers and caroling these songs,
O I never doubt whether that is really me.

## *Full of Life Now*

Full of life now, compact, visible,
I, forty years old the eighty-third year of the States,
To one a century hence or any number of centuries
hence,
To you yet unborn these, seeking you.

When you read these I that was visible am become
invisible,
Now it is you, compact, visible, realizing my poems,
seeking me,
Fancying how happy you were if I could be with you
and become your comrade;
Be it as if I were with you. (Be not too certain but I
am now with you.)

## *Salut Au Monde!*

1

O take my hand Walt Whitman!
Such gliding wonders! such sights and sounds!
Such join'd unended links, each hook'd to the next,
Each answering all, each sharing the earth with all.

What widens within you Walt Whitman?
What waves and soils exuding?
What climes? what persons and cities are here?
Who are the infants, some playing, some
    slumbering?
Who are the girls? who are the married women?
Who are the groups of old men going slowly with
    their arms about each other's necks?
What rivers are these? what forests and fruits are these?
What are the mountains call'd that rise so high in
    the mists?
What myriads of dwellings are they fill'd with dwellers?

2

Within me latitude widens, longitude lengthens,
Asia, Africa, Europe, are to the east – America is
    provided for in the west,
Banding the bulge of the earth winds the hot equator,
Curiously north and south turn the axis-ends,
Within me is the longest day, the sun wheels in
    slanting rings, it does not set for months,
Stretch'd in due time within me the midnight sun
    just rises above the horizon and sinks again,
Within me zones, seas, cataracts, forests, volcanoes,
    groups,
Malaysia, Polynesia, and the great West Indian
    islands.

3

What do you hear Walt Whitman?

I hear the workman singing and the farmer's wife
singing,
I hear in the distance the sounds of children and of
animals early in the day,
I hear emulous shouts of Australians pursuing the
wild horse,
I hear the Spanish dance with castanets in the
chestnut shade, to the rebeck and guitar,
I hear continual echoes from the Thames,
I hear fierce French liberty songs,
I hear of the Italian boat-sculler the musical
recitative of old poems,
I hear the locusts in Syria as they strike the grain and
grass with the showers of their terrible clouds,
I hear the Coptic refrain toward sundown, pensively
falling on the breast of the black venerable vast
mother the Nile,
I hear the chirp of the Mexican muleteer, and the
bells of the mule,
I hear the Arab muezzin calling from the top of the
mosque,
I hear the Christian priests at the altars of their
churches, I hear the responsive base and
soprano,
I hear the cry of the Cossack, and the sailor's voice
putting to sea at Okotsk,
I hear the wheeze of the slave-coffle as the slaves
march on, as the husky gangs pass on by twos
and threes, fasten'd together with wrist-chains
and ankle-chains,
I hear the Hebrew reading his records and psalms,

I hear the rhythmic myths of the Greeks, and the
strong legends of the Romans,
I hear the tale of the divine life and bloody death of
the beautiful God the Christ,
I hear the Hindoo teaching his favorite pupil the
loves, wars, adages, transmitted safely to this day
from poets who wrote three thousand years ago.

4

What do you see Walt Whitman?
Who are they you salute, and that one after another
salute you?

I see a great round wonder rolling through space,
I see diminute farms, hamlets, ruins, graveyards,
jails, factories, palaces, hovels, huts of
barbarians, tents of nomads upon the surface,
I see the shaded part on one side where the sleepers are
sleeping, and the sunlit part on the other side,
I see the curious rapid change of the light and shade,
I see distant lands, as real and near to the
inhabitants of them as my land is to me.
I see plenteous waters,
I see mountain peaks, I see the sierras of Andes
where they range,
I see plainly the Himalayas, Chian Shahs, Altays,
Ghauts,
I see the giant pinnacles of Elbruz, Kazbek,
Bazardjusi,
I see the Styrian Alps, and the Karnac Alps,
I see the Pyrenees, Balks, Carpathians, and to the
north the Dofrafields, and off at sea mount Hecla,
I see Vesuvius and Etna, the mountains of the
Moon, and the Red mountains of Madagascar,

I see the Lybian, Arabian, and Asiatic deserts,
I see huge dreadful Arctic and Antarctic icebergs,
I see the superior oceans and the interior ones, the
    Atlantic and Pacific, the sea of Mexico, the
    Brazilian sea, and the sea of Peru,
The waters of Hindustan, the China sea, and the
    gulf of Guinea,
The Japan waters, the beautiful bay of Nagasaki
    land-lock'd in its mountains,
The spread of the Baltic, Caspian, Bothnia, the
    British shores, and the bay of Biscay,
The clear-sunn'd Mediterranean, and from one to
    another of its islands,
The White sea, and the sea around Greenland.

I behold the mariners of the world,
Some are in storms, some in the night with the
    watch on the lookout,
Some drifting helplessly, some with contagious
    diseases.

I behold the sail and steamships of the world, some
    in clusters in port, some on their voyages,
Some double the cape of Storms, some cape Verde,
    others capes Guardafui, Bon, or Bajadore,
Others Dondra head, others pass the straits of
    Sunda, others cape Lopatka, others Behring's
    straits,
Others cape Horn, others sail the gulf of Mexico or
    along Cuba or Hayti, others Hudson's bay or
    Baffin's bay,
Others pass the straits of Dover, others enter the
    Wash, others the Firth of Solway, others round
    Cape Clear, others the Land's End,
Others traverse the Zuyder Zee or the Scheld,

Others as comers and goers at Gibraltar or the
Dardanelles,
Others sternly push their way through the northern
winterpacks,
Others descend or ascend the Obi or the Lena,
Others the Niger or the Congo, others the Indus, the
Burampooter and Cambodia,
Others wait steam'd up ready to start in the ports of
Australia,
Wait at Liverpool, Glasgow, Dublin, Marseilles,
Lisbon, Naples, Hamburg, Bremen, Bordeaux,
the Hague, Copenhagen,
Wait at Valparaiso, Rio Janeiro, Panama.

5

I see the tracks of the railroads of the earth,
I see them in Great Britain, I see them in Europe,
I see them in Asia and in Africa.

I see the electric telegraphs of the earth,
I see the filaments of the news of the wars, deaths,
losses, gains, passions, of my race.

I see the long river-stripes of the earth,
I see the Amazon and the Paraguay,
I see the four great rivers of China, the Amour, the
Yellow River, the Yiang-tse, and the Pearl,
I see where the Seine flows, and where the Danube, the
Loire, the Rhone, and the Guadalquiver flow,
I see the windings of the Volga, the Dnieper, the Oder,
I see the Tuscan going down the Arno, and the
Venetian along the Po,
I see the Greek seaman sailing out of Egina bay.

6

I see the sight of the old empire of Assyria, and that of Persia, and that of India,
I see the falling of the Ganges over the high rim of Saukara.
I see the place of the idea of the Deity incarnated by avatars in human forms,
I see the spots of the successions of priests on the earth, oracles, sacrificers, brahmins, sabians, llamas, monks, muftis, exhorters,
I see where druids walk'd the groves of Mona, I see the mistletoe and vervain,
I see the temples of the deaths of the bodies of Gods, I see the old signifiers.

I see Christ eating the bread of his last supper in the midst of youths and old persons,
I see where the strong divine young man the Hercules toil'd faithfully and long and then died,
I see the place of the innocent rich life and hapless fate of the beautiful nocturnal son, the full-limb'd Bacchus,
I see Kneph, blooming, drest in blue, with the crown of feathers on his head,
I see Hermes, unsuspected, dying, well-belov'd, saying to the people *Do not weep for me,*
*This is not my true country, I have lived banish'd from my true country, I now go back there,*
*I return to the celestial sphere where every one goes in his turn.*

7

I see the battle-fields of the earth, grass grows upon them and blossoms and corn,
I see the tracks of ancient and modern expeditions.
I see the nameless masonries, venerable messages of the unknown events, heroes, records of the earth.

I see the places of the sagas,
I see pine-trees and fir-trees torn by northern blasts,
I see granite bowlders and cliffs, I see green meadows and lakes,
I see the burial-cairns of Scandinavian warriors,
I see them raised high with stones by the marge of restless oceans, that the dead men's spirits when they wearied of their quiet graves might rise up through the mounds and gaze on the tossing billows, and be refresh'd by storms, immensity, liberty, action.

I see the steppes of Asia,
I see the tumuli of Mongolia, I see the tents of Kalmucks and Baskirs,
I see the nomadic tribes with herds of oxen and cows,
I see the table-lands notch'd with ravines, I see the jungles and deserts,
I see the camel, the wild steed, the bustard, the fat-tail'd sheep, the antelope, and the burrowing wolf.
I see the highlands of Abyssinia,
I see flocks of goats feeding, and see the fig-tree, tamarind, date,
And see fields of teff-wheat and places of verdure and gold.

I see the Brazilian vaquero,
I see the Bolivian ascending mount Sorata,
I see the Wacho crossing the plains, I see the incomparable rider of horses with his lasso on his arm,
I see over the pampas the pursuit of wild cattle for their hides.

8, (9)

I see the regions of snow and ice,
I see the sharp-eyed Samoiede and the Finn,
I see the seal-seeker in his boat poising his lance,
I see the Siberian on his slight-built sledge drawn by dogs,
I see the porpoise-hunters, I see the whale-crews of the south Pacific and the north Atlantic,
I see the cliffs, glaciers, torrents, valleys, of Switzerland – I mark the long winters and the isolation.

I see the cities of the earth and make myself at random a part of them,
I am a real Parisian,
I am a habitan of Vienna, St. Petersburg, Berlin, Constantinople,
I am of Adelaide, Sidney, Melbourne,
I am of London, Manchester, Bristol, Edinburgh, Limerick,
I am of Madrid, Cadiz, Barcelona, Oporto, Lyons, Brussels, Berne, Frankfort, Stuttgart, Turin, Florence,
I belong in Moscow, Cracow, Warsaw, or northward in Christiania or Stockholm, or in Siberian Irkutsk, or in some street in Iceland,
I descend upon all those cities, and rise from them again.

10

I see vapors exhaling from unexplored countries,
I see the savage types, the bow and arrow, the poison'd splint, the fetich, and the obi.

I see African and Asiatic towns,
I see Algiers, Tripoli, Derne, Mogadore, Timbuctoo, Monrovia,
I see the swarms of Pekin, Canton, Benares, Delhi, Calcutta, Tokio,
I see the Kruman in his hut, and the Dahoman and Ashanteeman in their huts,
I see the Turk smoking opium in Aleppo,
I see the picturesque crowds at the fairs of Khiva and those of Herat,
I see Teheran, I see Muscat and Medina and the intervening sands, I see the caravans toiling onward,
I see Egypt and the Egyptians, I see the pyramids and obelisks,
I look on chisell'd histories, records of conquering kings, dynasties, cut in slabs of sand-stone, or on granite-blocks,
I see at Memphis mummy-pits containing mummies embalm'd, swathed in linen-cloth, lying there many centuries,
I look on the fall'n Theban, the large-ball'd eyes, the side-drooping neck, the hands folded across the breast.

I see all the menials of the earth, laboring,
I see all the prisoners in the prisons,
I see the defective human bodies of the earth,
The blind, the deaf and dumb, idiots, hunchbacks, lunatics,

The pirates, thieves, betrayers, murderers, slave-makers of the earth,
The helpless infants, and the helpless old men and women.

I see male and female everywhere,
I see the serene brotherhood of philosophs,
I see the constructiveness of my race,
I see the results of the perseverance and industry of my race,
I see ranks, colors, barbarisms, civilizations, I go among them, I mix indiscriminately,
And I salute all the inhabitants of the earth.

11

You whoever you are!
You daughter or son of England!
You of the mighty Slavic tribes and empires! you Russ in Russia!
You dim-descended, black, divine-soul'd African, large, fine-headed, nobly-form'd, superbly destin'd, on equal terms with me!
You Norwegian! Swede! Dane! Icelander! you Prussian!
You Spaniard of Spain! you Portuguese!
You Frenchwoman and Frenchman of France!
You Belge! you liberty-lover of the Netherlands! (you stock whence I myself have descended;)
You sturdy Austrian! you Lombard! Hun! Bohemian! farmer of Styria!
You neighbor of the Danube!
You working-man of the Rhine, the Elbe, or the Weser! you working-woman too!

You Sardinian! you Bavarian! Swabian! Saxon!
 Wallachian! Bulgarian!
You Roman! Neapolitan! you Greek!
You lithe matador in the arena at Seville!
You mountaineer living lawlessly on the Taurus or
 Caucasus!
You Bokh horse-herd watching your mares and
 stallions feeding!
You beautiful-bodied Persian at full speed in the
 saddle shooting arrows to the mark!
You Chinaman and Chinawoman of China! you
 Tartar of Tartary!
You women of the earth subordinated at your tasks!
You Jew journeying in your old age through every
 risk to stand once on Syrian ground!
You other Jews waiting in all lands for your Messiah!
You thoughtful Armenian pondering by some
 stream of the Euphrates! you peering amid the
 ruins of Nineveh! you ascending mount Ararat!
You foot-worn pilgrim welcoming the far-away
 sparkle of the minarets of Mecca!
You sheiks along the stretch from Suez to Bab-el-
 mandeb ruling your families and tribes!
You olive-grower tending your fruit on fields of
 Nazareth, Damascus, or lake Tiberias!
You Thibet trader on the wide inland or bargaining
 in the shops of Lassa!
You Japanese man or woman! you liver in
 Madagascar, Ceylon, Sumatra, Borneo!
All you continentals of Asia, Africa, Europe,
 Australia, indifferent of place!
All you on the numberless islands of the
 archipelagoes of the sea!

And you of centuries hence when you listen to me!
And you each and everywhere whom I specify not,
but include just the same!
Health to you! good will to you all, from me and
America sent!
Each of us inevitable,
Each of us limitless – each of us with his or her right
upon the earth,
Each of us allow'd the eternal purports of the earth,
Each of us here as divinely as any is here.

12

You Hottentot with clicking palate! you woolly-
hair'd hordes!
You own'd persons dropping sweat-drops or blood-
drops!
You human forms with the fathomless ever-
impressive countenances of brutes!
You poor koboo whom the meanest of the rest look
down upon for all your glimmering language and
spirituality!
You dwarf'd Kamtschatkan, Greenlander, Lapp!
You Austral negro, naked, red, sooty, with
protrusive lip, groveling, seeking your food!
You Caffre, Berber, Soudanese!
You haggard, uncouth, untutor'd Bedowee!
You plague-swarms in Madras, Nankin, Kaubul,
Cairo!
You benighted roamer of Amazonia! you
Patagonian! you Feejee-man!
I do not prefer others so very much before you either,
I do not say one word against you, away back there
where you stand,
(You will come forward in due time to my side.)

## 13

My spirit has pass'd in compassion and
determination around the whole earth,
I have look'd for equals and lovers and found them
ready for me in all lands,
I think some divine rapport has equalized me with them.

You vapors, I think I have risen with you, moved
away to distant continents, and fallen down
there, for reasons,
I think I have blown with you you winds;
You waters I have finger'd every shore with you,
I have run through what any river or strait of the
globe has run through,
I have taken my stand on the bases of peninsulas
and on the high embedded rocks, to cry thence:
*Salut au monde!*
What cities the light or warmth penetrates I
penetrate those cities myself,
All islands to which birds wing their way I wing my
way myself.

Toward you all, in America's name,
I raise high the perpendicular hand, I make the signal,
To remain after me in sight forever,
For all the haunts and homes of men.

## *Song of the Open Road*

I

Afoot and light-hearted I take to the open road,
Healthy, free, the world before me,
The long brown path before me leading wherever I choose.

Henceforth I ask not good-fortune, I myself am good-for-tune,
Henceforth I whimper no more, postpone no more, need nothing,
Done with indoor complaints, libraries, querulous criticisms,
Strong and content I travel the open road.

The earth, that is sufficient,
I do not want the constellations any nearer,
I know they are very well where they are,
I know they suffice for those who belong to them.

(Still here I carry my old delicious burdens,
I carry them, men and women, I carry them with me wherever I go,
I swear it is impossible for me to get rid of them,
I am fill'd with them; and I will fill them in return.)

2

You road I enter upon and look around, I believe you are not all that is here,
I believe that much unseen is also here.

Here the profound lesson of reception, nor preference nor denial,
The black with his woolly head, the felon, the diseas'd, the illiterate person, are not denied;

The birth, the hasting after the physician, the
beggar's tramp, the drunkard's stagger, the
laughing party of mechanics,
The escaped youth, the rich person's carriage, the
fop, the eloping couple,
The early market-man, the hearse, the moving of
furniture into the town, the return back from the
town,
They pass, I also pass, any thing passes, none can be
interdicted,
None but are accepted, none but shall be dear to me.

3

You air that serves me with breath to speak!
You objects that call from diffusion my meanings
and give them shape!
You light that wraps me and all things in delicate
equable showers!
You paths worn in the irregular hollows by the
roadsides!
I believe you are latent with unseen existences, you
are so dear to me.

You flagg'd walks of the cities! you strong curbs at
the edges!
You ferries! you planks and posts of wharves! you
timberlined sides! you distant ships!
You rows of houses! you window-pierc'd façades!
you roofs!
You porches and entrances! you copings and iron
guards!
You windows whose transparent shells might expose
so much!
You doors and ascending steps! you arches!

You gray stones of interminable pavements! you trodden crossings!
From all that has touch'd you I believe you have imparted to yourselves, and now would impart the same secretly to me,
From the living and the dead you have peopled your impassive surfaces, and the spirits thereof would be evident and amicable with me.

4

The earth expanding right hand and left hand,
The picture alive, every part in its best light,
The music falling in where it is wanted, and stopping where it is not wanted,
The cheerful voice of the public road, the gay fresh sentiment of the road.

O highway I travel, do you say to me *Do not leave me?*
Do you say *Venture not – if you leave me you are lost?*
Do you say *I am already prepared, I am well-beaten and undenied, adhere to me?*

O public road, I say back I am not afraid to leave you, yet I love you,
You express me better than I can express myself,
You shall be more to me than my poem.

I think heroic deeds were all conceiv'd in the open air, and all free poems also,
I think I could stop here myself and do miracles,
I think whatever I shall meet on the road I shall like, and whoever beholds me shall like me,
I think whoever I see must be happy.

5

From this hour I ordain myself loos'd of limits and
imaginary lines,
Going where I list, my own master total and absolute,
Listening to others, considering well what they say,
Pausing, searching, receiving, contemplating,
Gently, but with undeniable will, divesting myself of
the holds that would hold me.

I inhale great draughts of space,
The east and the west are mine, and the north and
the south are mine.

I am larger, better than I thought,
I did not know I held so much goodness.

All seems beautiful to me,
I can repeat over to men and women You have done
such good to me I would do the same to you,
I will recruit for myself and you as I go,
I will scatter myself among men and women as I go,
I will toss a new gladness and roughness among them,
Whoever denies me it shall not trouble me,
Whoever accepts me he or she shall be blessed and
shall bless me.

6

Now if a thousand perfect men were to appear it
would not amaze me,
Now if a thousand beautiful forms of women
appear'd it would not astonish me.

Now I see the secret of the making of the best persons,
It is to grow in the open air and to eat and sleep with
the earth.

Here a great personal deed has room,
(Such a deed seizes upon the hearts of the whole race of men,
Its effusion of strength and will overwhelms law and mocks all authority and all argument against it.)

Here is the test of wisdom,
Wisdom is not finally tested in schools,
Wisdom cannot be pass'd from one having it to another not having it,
Wisdom is of the soul, is not susceptible of proof, is its own proof,
Applies to all stages and objects and qualities and is content,
Is the certainty of the reality and immortality of things, and the excellence of things;
Something there is in the float of the sight of things that provokes it out of the soul.

Now I re-examine philosophies and religions,
They may prove well in lecture-rooms, yet not prove at all under the spacious clouds and along the landscape and flowing currents.

Here is realization,
Here is a man tallied – he realizes here what he has in him,
The past, the future, majesty, love – if they are vacant of you, you are vacant of them.

Only the kernel of every object nourishes;
Where is he who tears off the husks for you and me?
Where is he that undoes stratagems and envelopes for you and me?

Here is adhesiveness, it is not previously fashion'd, it
is apropos;
Do you know what it is as you pass to be loved by
strangers?
Do you know the talk of those turning eye-balls?

7

Here is the efflux of the soul,
The efflux of the soul comes from within through
embower'd gates, ever provoking questions,
These yearnings why are they? these thoughts in the
darkness why are they?
Why are there men and women that while they are
nigh me the sunlight expands my blood?
Why when they leave me do my pennants of joy sink
flat and lank?
Why are there trees I never walk under but large and
melodious thoughts descend upon me?
(I think they hang there winter and summer on those
trees and always drop fruit as I pass;)
What is it I interchange so suddenly with strangers?
What with some driver as I ride on the seat by his side?
What with some fisherman drawing his seine by the
shore as I walk by and pause?
What gives me to be free to a woman's and man's
good-will? what gives them to be free to mine?

8

The efflux of the soul is happiness, here is happiness,
I think it pervades the open air, waiting at all times,
Now it flows unto us, we are rightly charged.

Here rises the fluid and attaching character,
The fluid and attaching character is the freshness
and sweetness of man and woman,

(The herbs of the morning sprout no fresher and
sweeter every day out of the roots of themselves,
than it sprouts fresh and sweet continually out of
itself.)
Toward the fluid and attaching character exudes the
sweat of the love of young and old,
From it falls distill'd the charm that mocks beauty
and attainments,
Toward it heaves the shuddering longing ache of
contact.

9

Allons! whoever you are come travel with me!
Traveling with me you find what never tires.

The earth never tires,
The earth is rude, silent, incomprehensible at first,
Nature is rude and incomprehensible at first,
Be not discouraged, keep on, there are divine things
well envelop'd,
I swear to you there are divine things more beautiful
than words can tell.

Allons! we must not stop here,
However sweet these laid-up stores, however
convenient this dwelling we cannot remain here,
However shelter'd this port and however calm these
waters we must not anchor here,
However welcome the hospitality that surrounds us
we are permitted to receive it but a little while.

10

Allons! the inducements shall be greater,
We will sail pathless and wild seas,

We will go where winds blow, waves dash, and the
    Yankee clipper speeds by under full sail.

Allons! with power, liberty, the earth, the elements,
Health, defiance, gayety, self-esteem, curiosity;
Allons! from all formules!
From your formules, O bat-eyed and materialistic
    priests.

The stale cadaver blocks up the passage – the burial
    waits no longer.

Allons! yet take warning!
He traveling with me needs the best blood, thews,
    endurance,
None may come to the trial till he or she bring
    courage and health,
Come not here if you have already spent the best of
    yourself,
Only those may come who come in sweet and
    determin'd bodies,
No diseas'd person, no rum-drinker or venereal taint
    is permitted here.

(I and mine do not convince by arguments, similes,
    rhymes,
We convince by our presence.)

11

Listen! I will be honest with you,
I do not offer the old smooth prizes, but offer rough
    new prizes,
These are the days that must happen to you:
You shall not heap up what is call'd riches,
You shall scatter with lavish hand all that you earn
    or achieve,

You but arrive at the city to which you were destin'd, you hardly settle yourself to satisfaction before you are call'd by an irresistible call to depart,
You shall be treated to the ironical smiles and mockings of those who remain behind you,
What beckonings of love you receive you shall only answer with passionate kisses of parting,
You shall not allow the hold of those who spread their reach'd hands toward you.

12

Allons! after the great Companions, and to belong to them!
They too are on the road – they are the swift and majestic men – they are the greatest women,
Enjoyers of calms of seas and storms of seas,
Sailors of many a ship, walkers of many a mile of land,
Habitués of many distant countries, habitués of far-distant dwellings,
Trusters of men and women, observers of cities, solitary toilers,
Pausers and contemplators of tufts, blossoms, shells of the shore,
Dancers at wedding-dances, kissers of brides, tender helpers of children, bearers of children,
Soldiers of revolts, standers by gaping graves, lowerers-down of coffins,
Journeyers over consecutive seasons, over the years, the curious years each emerging from that which preceded it,
Journeyers as with companions, namely their own diverse phases,
Forth-steppers from the latent unrealized baby-days,

Journeyers gayly with their own youth, journeyers
with their bearded and well-grain'd manhood,
Journeyers with their womanhood, ample,
unsurpass'd, content,
Journeyers with their own sublime old age of
manhood or womanhood,
Old age, calm, expanded, broad with the haughty
breadth of the universe,
Old age, flowing free with the delicious near-by
freedom of death.

13

Allons! to that which is endless as it was
beginningless,
To undergo much, tramps of days, rests of nights,
To merge all in the travel they tend to, and the days
and nights they tend to,
Again to merge them in the start of superior journeys,
To see nothing anywhere but what you may reach it
and pass it,
To conceive no time, however distant, but what you
may reach it and pass it,
To look up or down no road but it stretches and
waits for you, however long but it stretches and
waits for you,
To see no being, not God's or any, but you also go
thither,
To see no possession but you may possess it, enjoying
all without labor or purchase, abstracting the feast
yet not abstracting one particle of it,
To take the best of the farmer's farm and the rich
man's elegant villa, and the chaste blessings of the
well-married couple, and the fruits of orchards and
flowers of gardens,

To take to your use out of the compact cities as you pass through,
To carry buildings and streets with you afterward wherever you go,
To gather the minds of men out of their brains as you encounter them, to gather the love out of their hearts,
To take your lovers on the road with you, for all that you leave them behind you,
To know the universe itself as a road, as many roads, as roads for traveling souls.
All parts away for the progress of souls,
All religion, all solid things, arts, governments – all that was or is apparent upon this globe or any globe, falls into niches and corners before the procession of souls along the grand roads of the universe.

Of the progress of the souls of men and women along the grand roads of the universe, all other progress is the needed emblem and sustenance.

Forever alive, forever forward,
Stately, solemn, sad, withdrawn, baffled, mad, turbulent, feeble, dissatisfied,
Desperate, proud, fond, sick, accepted by men, rejected by men,
They go! they go! I know that they go, but I know not where they go,
But I know that they go toward the best – toward something great.

Whoever you are, come forth! or man or woman come forth!
You must not stay sleeping and dallying there in the house, though you built it, or though it has been built for you.

Out of the dark confinement! out from behind the screen!
It is useless to protest, I know all and expose it.

Behold through you as bad as the rest,
Through the laughter, dancing, dining, supping, of people,
Inside of dresses and ornaments, inside of those wash'd and trimm'd faces,
Behold a secret silent loathing and despair.

No husband, no wife, no friend, trusted to hear the confession,
Another self, a duplicate of every one, skulking and hiding it goes,
Formless and wordless through the streets of the cities, polite and bland in the parlors,
In the cars of railroads, in steamboats, in the public assembly,
Home to the houses of men and women, at the table, in the bedroom, everywhere,
Smartly attired, countenance smiling, form upright, death under the breast-bones, hell under the skull-bones,
Under the broadcloth and gloves, under the ribbons and artificial flowers,
Keeping fair with the customs, speaking not a syllable of itself,
Speaking of any thing else but never of itself.

14

Allons! through struggles and wars!
The goal that was named cannot be countermanded.

Have the past struggles succeeded?

What has succeeded? yourself? your nation? Nature?
Now understand me well – it is provided in the essence of things that from any fruition of success, no matter what, shall come forth something to make a greater struggle necessary.

My call is the call of battle, I nourish active rebellion,
He going with me must go well arm'd,
He going with me goes often with spare diet, poverty, angry enemies, desertions.

15

Allons! the road is before us!
It is safe – I have tried it – my own feet have tried it well – be not detain'd!
Let the paper remain on the desk unwritten, and the book on the shelf unopen'd!
Let the tools remain in the workshop! let the money remain unearn'd!
Let the school stand! mind not the cry of the teacher!
Let the preacher preach in his pulpit! let the lawyer plead in the court, and the judge expound the law.

Camerado, I give you my hand!
I give you my love more precise than money,
I give you myself before preaching or law;
Will you give me yourself? will you come travel with me?
Shall we stick by each other as long as we live?

## *Crossing Brooklyn Ferry*

1

Flood-tide below me! I see you face to face!
Clouds of the west – sun there half an hour high – I
see you also face to face.

Crowds of men and women attired in the usual
costumes, how curious you are to me!
On the ferry-boats the hundreds and hundreds that
cross, returning home, are more curious to me
than you suppose,
And you that shall cross from shore to shore years
hence are more to me, and more in my
meditations, than you might suppose.

2

The impalpable sustenance of me from all things at
all hours of the day,
The simple, compact, well-join'd scheme, myself
disintegrated, every one disintegrated yet part of
the scheme,
The similitudes of the past and those of the future,
The glories strung like beads on my smallest sights
and hearings, on the walk in the street and the
passage over the river,
The current rushing so swiftly and swimming with
me far away,
The others that are to follow me, the ties between
me and them,
The certainty of others, the life, love, sight, hearing
of others.

Others will enter the gates of the ferry and cross
from shore to shore,
Others will watch the run of the flood-tide,
Others will see the shipping of Manhattan north and
west, and the heights of Brooklyn to the south
and east,
Others will see the islands large and small;
Fifty years hence, others will see them as they cross,
the sun half an hour high,
A hundred years hence, or ever so many hundred
years hence, others will see them,
Will enjoy the sunset, the pouring-in of the flood-
tide, the falling-back to the sea of the ebb-tide.

3

It avails not, time nor place – distance avails not,
I am with you, you men and women of a generation,
or ever so many generations hence,
Just as you feel when you look on the river and sky,
so I felt,
Just as any of you is one of a living crowd, I was one
of a crowd,
Just as you are refresh'd by the gladness of the river
and the bright flow, I was refresh'd,
Just as you stand and lean on the rail, yet hurry with
the swift current, I stood yet was hurried,
Just as you look on the numberless masts of ships
and the thick-stemm'd pipes of steamboats, I
look'd.

I too many and many a time cross'd the river of old,
Watched the Twelfth-month sea-gulls, saw them
high in the air floating with motionless wings,
oscillating their bodies,

Saw how the glistening yellow lit up parts of their
bodies and left the rest in strong shadow,
Saw the slow-wheeling circles and the gradual
edging toward the south,
Saw the reflection of the summer sky in the water,
Had my eyes dazzled by the shimmering track of beams,
Look'd at the fine centrifugal spokes of light round
the shape of my head in the sunlit water,
Look'd on the haze on the hills southward and
south-west-ward,
Look'd on the vapor as it flew in fleeces tinged with
violet,
Look'd toward the lower bay to notice the vessels
arriving,
Saw their approach, saw aboard those that were near
me,
Saw the white sails of schooners and sloops, saw the
ships at anchor,
The sailors at work in the rigging or out astride the
spars,
The round masts, the swinging motion of the hulls,
the slender serpentine pennants,
The large and small steamers in motion, the pilots in
their pilot houses,
The white wake left by the passage, the quick
tremulous whirl of the wheels,
The flags of all nations, the falling of them at sunset,
The scallop-edged waves in the twilight, the ladled
cups, the frolicsome crests and glistening,
The stretch afar growing dimmer and dimmer, the
gray walls of the granite storehouses by the docks,
On the river the shadowy group, the big steam-tug
closely flank'd on each side by the barges, the
hay-boat, the belated lighter,

On the neighboring shore the fires from the foundry chimneys burning high and glaringly into the night,
Casting their flicker of black contrasted with wild red and yellow light over the tops of houses, and down into the clefts of streets.

4

These and all else were to me the same as they are to you,
I loved well those cities, loved well the stately and rapid river,
The men and women I saw were all near to me,
Others the same – others who look back on me because I look'd forward to them,
(The time will come, though I stop here to-day, and to-night.)

5

What is it then between us?
What is the count of the scores or hundreds of years between us?

Whatever it is, it avails not – distance avails not, and place avails not,
I too lived, Brooklyn of ample hills was mine,
I too walk'd the streets of Manhattan island, and bathed in the waters around it,
I too felt the curious abrupt questionings stir within me.
In the day among crowds of people sometimes they came upon me.
In my walks home late at night or as I lay in my bed they came upon me,
I too had been struck from the float forever held in solution,

I too had receiv'd identity by my body,
That I was I knew was of my body, and what I
should be I knew I should be of my body.

6

It is not upon you alone the dark patches fall,
The dark threw its patches down upon me also,
The best I had done seem'd to me blank and
suspicious,
My great thoughts as I supposed them, were they
not in reality meagre?
Nor is it you alone who know what it is to be evil,
I am he who knew what it was to be evil,
I too knitted the old knot of contrariety,
Blabb'd, blush'd, resented, lied, stole, grudg'd,
Had guile, anger, lust, hot wishes I dared not speak,
Was wayward, vain, greedy, shallow, sly, cowardly,
malignant,
The wolf, the snake, the hog, not wanting in me,
The cheating look, the frivolous word, the
adulterous wish, not wanting,
Refusals, hates, postponements, meanness, laziness,
none of these wanting,
Was one with the rest, the days and haps of the rest,
Was call'd by my nighest name by clear loud voices of
young men as they saw me approaching or passing,
Felt their arms on my neck as I stood, or the negligent
leaning of their flesh against me as I sat,
Saw many I loved in the street or ferry-boat or
public assembly, yet never told them a word,
Lived the same life with the rest, the same old
laughing, gnawing, sleeping,
Play'd the part that still looks back on the actor or
actress,

The same old role, the role that is what we make it,
as great as we like,
Or as small as we like, or both great and small.

7

Closer yet I approach you,
What thought you have of me now, I had as much of
you – I laid in my stores in advance,
I consider'd long and seriously of you before you
were born.

Who was to know what should come home to me?
Who knows but I am enjoying this?
Who knows, for all the distance, but I am as good as
looking at you now, for all you cannot see me?

8

Ah, what can ever be more stately and admirable to
me than mast-hemm'd Manhattan?
River and sunset and scallop-edg'd waves of flood-tide?
The sea-gulls oscillating their bodies, the hay-boat in
the twilight, and the belated lighter?
What gods can exceed these that clasp me by the
hand, and with voices I love call me promptly
and loudly by my nighest name as I approach?
What is more subtle than this which ties me to the
woman or man that looks in my face?
Which fuses me into you now, and pours my
meaning into you?

We understand then do we not?
What I promis'd without mentioning it, have you
not accepted?
What the study could not teach – what the preaching
could not accomplish is accomplish'd, is it not?

9

Flow on, river! flow with the flood-tide, and ebb
with the ebb-tide!
Frolic on, crested and scallop-edg'd waves!
Gorgeous clouds of the sunset! drench with your
splendor me, or the men and women generations
after me!
Cross from shore to shore, countless crowds of
passengers!
Stand up, tall masts of Mannahatta! stand up,
beautiful hills of Brooklyn!
Throb, baffled and curious brain! throw out
questions and answers!
Suspend here and everywhere, eternal float of solution!
Gaze, loving and thirsting eyes, in the house or street
or public assembly!
Sound out, voices of young men! loudly and
musically call me by my nighest name!
Live, old life! play the part that looks back on the
actor or actress!
Play the old role, the role that is great or small
according as one makes it!
Consider, you who peruse me, whether I may not in
unknown ways be looking upon you;
Be firm, rail over the river, to support those who
lean idly, yet haste with the hasting current;
Fly on, sea-birds! fly sideways, or wheel in large
circles high in the air;
Receive the summer sky, you water, and faithfully
hold it till all downcast eyes have time to take it
from you!
Diverge, fine spokes of light, from the shape of my
head, or any one's head, in the sunlit water!

Come on, ships from the lower bay! pass up or
down, whitesail'd schooners, sloops, lighters!
Flaunt away, flags of all nations! be duly lower'd at
sunset!
Burn high your fires, foundry chimneys! cast black
shadows at nightfall! cast red and yellow light
over the tops of the houses!
Appearances, now or henceforth, indicate what you are,
You necessary film, continue to envelop the soul,
About my body for me, and your body for you, be
hung our divinest aromas,
Thrive, cities – bring your freight, bring your shows,
ample and sufficient rivers,
Expand, being than which none else is perhaps more
spiritual,
Keep your places, objects than which none else is
more lasting.
You have waited, you always wait, you dumb,
beautiful ministers,
We receive you with free sense at last, and are
insatiate henceforward,
Not you any more shall be able to foil us, or
withhold yourselves from us,
We use you, and do not cast you aside – we plant
you permanently within us,
We fathom you not – we love you – there is
perfection in you also,
You furnish your parts toward eternity,
Great or small, you furnish your parts toward the soul.

## *Song of the Answerer*

### 1

Now list to my morning's romanza, I tell the signs of the Answerer,
To the cities and farms I sing as they spread in the sunshine before me.

A young man comes to me bearing a message from his brother,
How shall the young man know the whether and when of his brother?
Tell him to send me the signs.
And I stand before the young man face to face, and take his right hand in my left hand and his left hand in my right hand,
And I answer for his brother and for men, and I answer for him that answers for all, and send these signs.

Him all wait for, him all yield up to, his word is decisive and final,
Him they accept, in him lave, in him perceive themselves as amid light,
Him they immerse and he immerses them.
Beautiful women, the haughtiest nations, laws, the landscape, people, animals,
The profound earth and its attributes and the unquiet ocean, (so tell I my morning's romanza,)
All enjoyments and properties and money, and whatever money will buy,
The best farms, others toiling and planting and he unavoidably reaps,
The nobliest and costliest cities, others grading and building and he domiciles there,

Nothing for any one but what is for him, near and
far are for him, the ships in the offing,
The perpetual shows and marches on land are for
him if they are for anybody.

He puts things in their attitudes,
He puts to-day out of himself with plasticity and
love,
He places his own times, reminiscences, parents,
brothers and sisters, associations, employment,
politics, so that the rest never shame them
afterward, nor assume to command them.

He is the Answerer,
What can be answer'd he answers, and what cannot be
answer'd he shows how it cannot be answer'd.

A man is a summons and challenge,
(It is vain to skulk – do you hear that mocking and
laughter? do you hear the ironical echoes?)

Books, friendships, philosophers, priests, action,
pleasure, pride, beat up and down seeking to
give satisfaction,
He indicates the satisfaction, and indicates them that
beat up and down also.

Whichever the sex, whatever the season or place, he
may go freshly and gently and safely by day or by
night,
He has the pass-key of hearts, to him the response of
the prying of hands on the knobs.

His welcome is universal, the flow of beauty is not
more welcome or universal than he is,
The person he favors by day or sleeps with at night is
blessed.

Every existence has its idiom, every thing has an
idiom and tongue,
He resolves all tongues into his own and bestows it
upon men, and any man translates, and any man
translates himself also,
One part does not counteract another part, he is the
joiner, he sees how they join.

He says indifferently and alike *How are you friend?* to
the President at his levee,
And he says *Good-day my brother*, to Cudge that hoes
in the sugar-field,
And both understand him and know that his speech
is right.

He walks with perfect ease in the capitol,
He walks among the Congress, and one
Representative says to another, *Here is our equal
appearing and new.*

Then the mechanics take him for a mechanic,
And the soldiers suppose him to be a soldier, and
the sailors that he has follow'd the sea,
And the authors take him for an author, and the
artists for an artist,
And the laborers perceive he could labor with them
and love them,
No matter what the work is, that he is the one to
follow it or has follow'd it,
No matter what the nation, that he might find his
brothers and sisters there.

The English believe he comes of their English stock,
A Jew to the Jew he seems, a Russ to the Russ, usual
and near, removed from none.

Whoever he looks at in the traveler's coffee-house
claims him,
The Italian or Frenchman is sure, the German is sure,
the Spaniard is sure, and the island Cuban is sure,

The engineer, the deck-hand on the great lakes, or on
the Mississippi or St. Lawrence or Sacramento, or
Hudson or Paumanok sound, claims him.

The gentleman of perfect blood acknowledges his
perfect blood,
The insulter, the prostitute, the angry person, the
beggar, see themselves in the ways of him, he
strangely transmutes them,
They are not vile any more, they hardly know
themselves they are so grown.

2

The indications and tally of time,
Perfect sanity shows the master among philosophs,
Time, always without break, indicates itself in parts,
What always indicates the poet is the crowd of the
pleasant company of singers, and their words,
The words of the singers are the hours or minutes of
the light or dark, but the words of the maker of
poems are the general light and dark,
The maker of poems settles justice, reality,
immortality,
His insight and power encircle things and the human
race,
He is the glory and extract thus far of things and of
the human race.

The singers do not beget, only the Poet begets,
The singers are welcom'd, understood, appear often
  enough, but rare has the day been, likewise the
  spot, of the birth of the maker of poems, the
  Answerer,
(Not every century nor every five centuries has
  contain'd such a day, for all its names.)

The singers of successive hours of centuries may
  have ostensible names, but the name of each of
  them is one of the singers,
The name of each is, eye-singer, ear-singer, head-
  singer, sweet-singer, night-singer, parlor-singer,
  love-singer, weird-singer, or something else.

All this time and at all times wait the words of true
  poems,
The words of true poems do not merely please,
The true poets are not followers of beauty but the
  august masters of beauty;
The greatness of sons is the exuding of the greatness
  of mothers and fathers,
The words of true poems are the tuft and final
  applause of science.

Divine instinct, breadth of vision, the law of reason,
  health, rudeness of body, withdrawnness,
Gayety, sun-tan, air-sweetness, such are some of the
  words of poems.
The sailor and traveler underlie the maker of poems,
  the Answerer,
The builder, geometer, chemist, anatomist,
  phrenologist, artist, all these underlie the maker
  of poems, the Answerer.

The words of the true poems give you more than poems,
They give you to form for yourself poems, religions,
 politics, war, peace, behavior, histories, essays,
 daily life, and every thing else,
They balance ranks, colors, races, creeds, and the sexes,
They do not seek beauty, they are sought,
Forever touching them or close upon them follows
 beauty, longing, fain, love-sick.

They prepare for death, yet they are not the finish,
 but rather the outset,
They bring none to his or her terminus or to be
 content and full,
Whom they take they take into space to behold the
 birth of stars, to learn one of the meanings,
To launch off with absolute faith, to sweep through
 the ceaseless rings and never be quiet again.

## *Our Old Feuillage*

Always our old feuillage!
Always Florida's green peninsula – always the
 priceless delta of Louisiana – always the cotton-
 fields of Alabama and Texas,
Always California's golden hills and hollows, and the
 silver mountains of New Mexico – always soft-
 breath'd Cuba,
Always the vast slope drain'd by the Southern sea,
 inseparable with the slopes drain'd by the
 Eastern and Western seas,
The area the eighty-third year of these States, the
 three and a half millions of square miles,
The eighteen thousand miles of sea-coast and bay-
 coast on the main, the thirty thousand miles of
 river navigation,

The seven millions of distinct families and the same
number of dwellings – always these, and more,
branching forth into numberless branches,
Always the free range and diversity – always the
continent of Democracy;
Always the prairies, pastures, forests, vast cities,
travelers, Kanada, the snows;
Always these compact lands tied at the hips with the
belt stringing the huge oval lakes;
Always the West with strong native persons, the
increasing density there, the habitans, friendly,
threatening, ironical, scorning invaders;
All sights, South, North, East – all deeds
promiscuously done at all times,
All characters, movements, growths, a few noticed,
myriads unnoticed,
Through Mannahatta's streets I walking, these
things gathering,
On interior rivers by night in the glare of pine knots,
steamboats wooding up.
Sunlight by day on the valley of the Susquehanna,
and on the valleys of the Potomac and
Rappahannock, and the valleys of the Roanoke
and Delaware,
In their northerly wilds beasts of prey haunting the
Adirondacks the hills, or lapping the Saginaw
waters to drink,
In a lonesome inlet a sheldrake lost from the flock,
sitting on the water rocking silently,
In farmer's barns oxen in the stable, their harvest
labor done, they rest standing, they are too tired,
Afar on arctic ice the she-walrus lying drowsily while
her cubs play around,

The hawk sailing where men have not yet sail'd, the
farthest polar sea, ripply, crystalline, open,
beyond the floes,
White drift spooning ahead where the ship in the
tempest dashes,
On solid land what is done in cities as the bells strike
mid-night together,
In primitive woods the sounds there also sounding,
the howl of the wolf, the scream of the panther,
and the hoarse bellow of the elk,
In winter beneath the hard blue ice of Moosehead
lake, in summer visible through the clear waters,
the great trout swimming,
In lower latitudes in warmer air in the Carolinas the
large black buzzard floating slowly high beyond
the tree tops,
Below, the red cedar festoon'd with tylandria, the
pines and cypresses growing out of the white
sand that spreads far and flat,
Rude boats descending the big Pedee, climbing
plants, parasites with color'd flowers and berries
enveloping huge trees,
The waving drapery on the live-oak trailing long and
low, noiselessly waved by the wind.
The camp of Georgia wagoners just after dark, the
supperfires and the cooking and eating by whites
and negroes,
Thirty or forty great wagons, the mules, cattle,
horses, feeding from troughs,
The shadows, gleams, up under the leaves of the old
sycamore-trees, the flames with the black smoke
from the pitch-pine curling and rising;

Southern fishermen fishing, the sounds and inlets of North Carolina's coast, the shad-fishery and the herring-fishery, the large sweep-seines, the windlasses on shore work'd by horses, the clearing, curing, and packing-houses;
Deep in the forest in piney woods turpentine dropping from the incisions in the trees, there are the turpentine works,
There are the negroes at work in good health, the ground in all directions is cover'd with pine straw;
In Tennessee and Kentucky slaves busy in the coalings, at the forge, by the furnace-blaze, or at the corn-shucking,
In Virginia, the planter's son returning after a long absence, joyfully welcom'd and kiss'd by the aged mulatto nurse,
On rivers boatmen safely moor'd at nightfall in their boats under shelter of high banks,
Some of the younger men dance to the sound of the banjo or fiddle, others sit on the gunwale smoking and talking;
Late in the afternoon the mocking-bird, the American mimic, singing in the Great Dismal Swamp,
There are the greenish waters, the resinous odor, the plenteous moss, the cypress-tree, and the juniper-tree;
Northward, young men of Mannahatta, the target company from an excursion returning home at evening, the musket-muzzles all bear bunches of flowers presented by women;
Children at play, or on his father's lap a young boy fallen asleep, (how his lips move! how he smiles in his sleep!)

The scout riding on horseback over the plains west
of the Mississippi, he ascends a knoll and sweeps
his eyes around;
California life, the miner, bearded, dress'd in his
rude costume, the stanch California friendship,
the sweet air, the graves one in passing meets
solitary just aside the horsepath;
Down in Texas the cotton-field, the negro-cabins,
drivers driving mules or oxen before rude carts,
cotton bales piled on banks and wharves;
Encircling all, vast-darting up and wide, the
American Soul, with equal hemispheres, one
Love, one Dilation or Pride;
In arriere the peace-talk with the Iroquois the
aborigines, the calumet, the pipe of good-will,
arbitration, and indorsement,
The sachem blowing the smoke first toward the sun
and then toward the earth,
The drama of the scalp-dance enacted with painted
faces and guttural exclamations,
The setting out of the war-party, the long and
stealthy march,
The single file, the swinging hatchets, the surprise
and slaughter of enemies;
All the acts, scenes, ways, persons, attitudes of these
States, reminiscences, institutions,
All these States compact, every square mile of these
States without excepting a particle;
Me pleas'd, rambling in lanes and country fields,
Paumanok's fields,
Observing the spiral flight of two little yellow
butterflies shuffling between each other,
ascending high in the air,

The darting swallow, the destroyer of insects, the fall
traveler southward but returning northward early
in the spring,
The country boy at the close of the day driving the
herd of cows and shouting to them as they loiter
to browse by the roadside,
The city wharf, Boston, Philadelphia, Baltimore,
Charleston, New Orleans, San Francisco,
The departing ships when the sailors heave at the
capstan;
Evening – me in my room – the setting sun,
The setting summer sun shining in my open window,
showing the swarm of flies, suspended, balancing in
the air in the centre of the room, darting athwart, up
and down, casting swift shadows in specks on the
opposite wall where the shine is;
The athletic American matron speaking in public to
crowds of listeners,
Males, females, immigrants, combinations, the
copiousness, the individuality of the States, each
for itself – the money-makers,
Factories, machinery, the mechanical forces, the
windlass, lever, pulley, all certainties,
The certainty of space, increase, freedom, futurity,
In space the sporades, the scatter'd islands, the stars
– on the firm earth, the lands, my lands,
O lands! all so dear to me – what you are, (whatever
it is,) I putting it at random in these songs,
become a part of that, whatever it is,
Southward there, I screaming, with wings slow
flapping, with the myriads of gulls wintering
along the coasts of Florida,

Otherways there atwixt the banks of the Arkansas,
the Rio Grande, the Nueces, the Brazos, the
Tombigbee, the Red River, the Saskatchewan or
the Osage, I with the spring waters laughing and
skipping and running,
Northward, on the sands, on some shallow bay of
Paumanok, I with parties of snowy herons wading
in the wet to seek worms and aquatic plants,
Retreating, triumphantly twittering, the king-bird,
from piercing the crow with its bill, for
amusement – and I triumphantly twittering,
The migrating flock of wild geese alighting in
autumn to refresh themselves, the body of the
flock feed, the sentinels outside move around
with erect heads watching, and are from time to
time reliev'd by other sentinels – and I feeding
and taking turns with the rest,
In Kanadian forests the moose, large as an ox,
corner'd by hunters, rising desperately on his
hind-feet, and plunging with his fore-feet, the
hoofs as sharp as knives – and I, plunging at the
hunters, corner'd and desperate,
In the Mannahatta, streets, piers, shipping, storehouses, and the countless workmen working in
the shops,
And I too of the Mannahatta, singing thereof – and
no less in myself than the whole of the
Mannahatta in itself,
Singing the song of These, my ever-united lands –
my body no more inevitably united, part to part,
and made out of a thousand diverse
contributions one identity, any more than my
lands are inevitably united and made One
identity;

Nativities, climates, the grass of the great pastoral
Plains,
Cities, labors, death, animals, products, war, good
and evil – these me,
These affording, in all their particulars, the old
feuillage to me and to America, how can I do
less than pass the clew of the union of them, to
afford the like to you?
Whoever you are! how can I but offer you divine
leaves, that you also be eligible as I am?
How can I but as here chanting, invite you for
yourself to collect bouquets of the incomparable
feuillage of these States?

## *A Song of Joys*

O to make the most jubilant song!
Full of music – full of manhood, womanhood, infancy!
Full of common employments – full of grain and trees.

O for the voices of animals – O for the swiftness and
balance of fishes!
O for the dropping of raindrops in a song!
O for the sunshine and motion of waves in a song!

O the joy of my spirit – it is uncaged – it darts like
lightning!
It is not enough to have this globe or a certain time,
I will have thousands of globes and all time.

O the engineer's joys! to go with a locomotive!
To hear the hiss of steam, the merry shriek, the
steam-whistle, the laughing locomotive!
To push with resistless way and speed off in the
distance.

O the gleesome saunter over fields and hillsides!
The leaves and flowers of the commonest weeds, the moist fresh stillness of the woods,
The exquisite smell of the earth at daybreak, and all through the forenoon.

O the horseman's and horsewoman's joys!
The saddle, the gallop, the pressure upon the seat, the cool gurgling by the ears and hair.

O the fireman's joys!
I hear the alarm at dead of night,
I hear bells, shouts! I pass the crowd, I run!
The sight of the flames maddens me with pleasure.

O the joy of the strong-brawn'd fighter, towering in the arena in perfect condition, conscious of power, thirsting to meet his opponent.

O the joy of that vast elemental sympathy which only the human soul is capable of generating and emitting in steady and limitless floods.

O the mother's joys!
The watching, the endurance, the precious love, the anguish, the patiently yielded life.

O the joy of increase, growth, recuperation,
The joy of soothing and pacifying, the joy of concord and harmony.

O to go back to the place where I was born,
To hear the birds sing once more,
To ramble about the house and barn and over the fields once more,
And through the orchard and along the old lanes once more.

O to have been brought up on bays, lagoons, creeks,
or along the coast,
To continue and be employ'd there all my life,
The briny and damp smell, the shore, the salt weeds
exposed at low water,
The work of fishermen, the work of the eel-fisher
and clam-fisher;
I come with my clam-rake and spade, I come with
my eel-spear,
Is the tide out? I join the group of clam-diggers on
the flats,
I laugh and work with them, I joke at my work like a
mettle-some young man;
In winter I take my eel-basket and eel-spear and
travel out on foot on the ice – I have a small axe
to cut holes in the ice,
Behold me well-clothed going gayly or returning in
the afternoon, my brood of tough boys
accompanying me,
My brood of grown and part-grown boys, who love
to be with no one else so well as they love to be
with me,
By day to work with me, and by night to sleep with me.

Another time in warm weather out in a boat, to lift
the lobster-pots where they are sunk with heavy
stones, (I know the buoys,)
O the sweetness of the Fifth-month morning upon the
water as I row just before sunrise toward the buoys,
I pull the wicker pots up slantingly, the dark green
lobsters are desperate with their claws as I take
them out, I insert wooden pegs in the joints of
their pincers,

I go to all the places one after another, and then row back to the shore,
There in a huge kettle of boiling water the lobsters shall be boil'd till their color becomes scarlet.
Another time mackerel-taking,
Voracious, mad for the hook, near the surface, they seem to fill the water for miles;
Another time fishing for rock-fish in Chesapeake Bay, I one of the brown-faced crew;
Another time trailing for blue-fish off Paumanok, I stand with braced body,
My left foot is on the gunwale, my right arm throws far out the coils of slender rope,
In sight around me the quick veering and darting of fifty skiffs, my companions.

O boating on the rivers,
The voyage down the St. Lawrence, the superb scenery, the steamers,
The ships sailing, the Thousand Islands, the occasional timber-raft and the raftsmen with long-reaching sweep-oars,
The little huts on the rafts, and the stream of smoke when they cook supper at evening.

(O something pernicious and dread!
Something far away from a puny and pious life!
Something unproved! something in a trance!
Something escaped from the anchorage and driving free.)

O to work in mines, or forging iron,
Foundry casting, the foundry itself, the rude high roof, the ample and shadow'd space,
The furnace, the hot liquid pour'd out and running.

O to resume the joys of the soldier!
To feel the presence of a brave commanding officer
– to feel his sympathy!
To behold his calmness – to be warm'd in the rays of
his smile!
To go to battle – to hear the bugles play and the
drums beat!
To hear the crash of artillery – to see the glittering of
the bayonets and musket-barrels in the sun!
To see men fall and die and not complain!
To taste the savage taste of blood – to be so devilish!
To gloat so over the wounds and deaths of the
enemy.

O the whaleman's joys! O I cruise my old cruise again!
I feel the ship's motion under me, I feel the Atlantic
breezes fanning me,
I hear the cry again sent down from the mast-head,
*There – she blows!*

Again I spring up the rigging to look with the rest –
we descend, wild with excitement,
I leap in the lower'd boat, we row toward our prey
where he lies,
We approach stealthy and silent, I see the
mountainous mass, lethargic, basking,
I see the harpooner standing up, I see the weapon
dart from his vigorous arm;
O swift again far out in the ocean the wounded
whale, settling, running to windward, tows me,
Again I see him rise to breathe, we row close again,
I see a lance driven through his side, press'd deep,
turn'd in the wound,
Again we back off, I see him settle again, the life is
leaving him fast,

As he rises he spouts blood, I see him swim in circles
narrower and narrower, swiftly cutting the water
– I see him die,
He gives one convulsive leap in the centre of the circle,
and then falls flat and still in the bloody foam.

O the old manhood of me, my noblest joy of all!
My children and grand-children, my white hair and
beard,
My largeness, calmness, majesty, out of the long
stretch of my life.

O ripen'd joy of womanhood! O happiness at last!
I am more than eighty years of age, I am the most
venerable mother,
How clear is my mind – how all people draw nigh to me!
What attractions are these beyond any before? what
bloom more than the bloom of youth?
What beauty is this that descends upon me and rises
out of me?

O the orator's joys!
To inflate the chest, to roll the thunder of the voice
out from the ribs and throat,
To make the people rage, weep, hate, desire, with
yourself,
To lead America – to quell America with a great tongue.

O the joy of my soul leaning pois'd on itself,
receiving identity through materials and loving
them, observing characters and absorbing them,
My soul vibrated back to me from them, from sight,
hearing, touch, reason, articulation, comparison,
memory, and the like,
The real life of my senses and flesh transcending my
senses and flesh,

My body done with materials, my sight done with
my material eyes,
Proved to me this day beyond cavil that it is not my
material eyes which finally see,
Nor my material body which finally loves, walks,
laughs, shouts, embraces, procreates.

O the farmer's joys!
Ohioan's, Illinoisian's, Wisconsinese', Kanadian's,
Iowan's, Kansian's, Missourian's, Oregonese' joys!
To rise at peep of day and pass forth nimbly to work,
To plough land in the fall for winter-sown crops,
To plough land in the spring for maize,
To train orchards, to graft the trees, to gather apples
in the fall.

O to bathe in the swimming-bath, or in a good place
along shore,
To splash the water! to walk ankle-deep, or race
naked along the shore.

O to realize space!
The plenteousness of all, that there are no bounds,
To emerge and be of the sky, of the sun and moon
and flying clouds, as one with them.

O the joy of a manly self-hood!
To be servile to none, to defer to none, not to any
tyrant known or unknown,
To walk with erect carriage, a step springy and elastic,
To look with calm gaze or with a flashing eye,
To speak with a full and sonorous voice out of a
broad chest,
To confront with your personality all the other
personalities of the earth.

Know'st thou the excellent joys of youth?
Joys of the dear companions and of the merry word and laughing face?
Joy of the glad light-beaming day, joy of the wide-breath'd games?
Joy of sweet music, joy of the lighted ball-room and the dancers?
Joy of the plenteous dinner, strong carouse and drinking?
Yet O my soul supreme!
Know'st thou the joys of pensive thought?
Joys of the free and lonesome heart, the tender, gloomy heart?
Joys of the solitary walk, the spirit bow'd yet proud, the suffering and the struggle?
The agonistic throes, the ecstasies, joys of the solemn musings day or night?
Joys of the thought of Death, the great spheres Time and Space?
Prophetic joys of better, loftier love's ideals, the divine wife, the sweet, eternal, perfect comrade?
Joys all thine own undying one, joys worthy thee O soul.

O while I live to be the ruler of life, not a slave,
To meet life as a powerful conqueror,
No fumes, no ennui, no more complaints or scornful criticisms,
To these proud laws of the air, the water and the ground, proving my interior soul impregnable,
And nothing exterior shall ever take command of me.

For not life's joys alone I sing, repeating – the joy of death!
The beautiful touch of Death, soothing and benumbing a few moments, for reasons,

Myself discharging my excrementitious body to be
burn'd, or render'd to powder, or buried,
My real body doubtless left to me for other spheres,
My voided body nothing more to me, returning to
the purifications, further offices, eternal uses of
the earth.

O to attract by more than attraction!
How it is I know not – yet behold! the something
which obeys none of the rest,
It is offensive, never defensive – yet how magnetic it
draws.

O to struggle against great odds, to meet enemies
undaunted!
To be entirely alone with them, to find how much
one can stand!
To look strife, torture, prison, popular odium, face
to face!
To mount the scaffold, to advance to the muzzles of
guns with perfect nonchalance!
To be indeed a God!

O to sail to sea in a ship!
To leave this steady unendurable land,
To leave the tiresome sameness of the streets, the
sidewalks and the houses,
To leave you O you solid motionless land, and
entering a ship,
To sail and sail and sail!

O to have life henceforth a poem of new joys!
To dance, clap hands, exult, shout, skip, leap, roll
on, float on!
To be a sailor of the world bound for all ports,

A ship itself, (see indeed these sails I spread to the
sun and air,)
A swift and swelling ship full of rich words, full of joys.

## *Song of the Broad-Axe*

I

Weapon shapely, naked, wan,
Head from the mother's bowels drawn,
Wooded flesh and metal bone, limb only one and lip
only one,
Gray-blue leaf by red-heat grown, helve produced
from a little seed sown,
Resting the grass amid and upon,
To be lean'd and to lean on.

Strong shapes and attributes of strong shapes,
masculine trades, sights and sounds,
Long varied train of an emblem, dabs of music,
Fingers of the organist skipping staccato over the
keys of the great organ.

2

Welcome are all earth's lands, each for its kind,
Welcome are lands of pine and oak,
Welcome are lands of the lemon and fig,
Welcome are lands of gold,
Welcome are lands of wheat and maize, welcome
those of the grape,
Welcome are lands of sugar and rice,
Welcome the cotton-lands, welcome those of the
white potato and sweet potato,
Welcome are mountains, flats, sands, forests,
prairies,

Welcome the rich borders of rivers, table-lands,
openings,
Welcome the measureless grazing-lands, welcome
the teeming soil of orchards, flax, honey, hemp;
Welcome just as much the other more hard-faced lands,
Lands rich as lands of gold or wheat and fruit lands,
Lands of mines, lands of the manly and rugged ores,
Lands of coal, copper, lead, tin, zinc.
Lands of iron – lands of the make of the axe.

3

The log at the wood-pile, the axe supported by it,
The sylvan hut, the vine over the doorway, the space
clear'd for a garden,
The irregular tapping of rain down on the leaves
after the storm is lull'd,
The wailing and moaning at intervals, the thought of
the sea,
The thought of ships struck in the storm and put on
their beam ends, and the cutting away of masts,
The sentiment of the huge timbers of old-fashion'd
houses and barns,
The remember'd print or narrative, the voyage at a
venture of men, families, goods,
The disembarkation, the founding of a new city,
The voyage of those who sought a New England and
found it, the outset anywhere,
The settlements of the Arkansas, Colorado, Ottawa,
Willamette,
The slow progress, the scant fare, the axe, rifle,
saddle-bags;
The beauty of all adventurous and daring persons,
The beauty of wood-boys and wood-men with their
clear untrimm'd faces,

The beauty of independence, departure, actions that rely on themselves,
The American contempt for statutes and ceremonies, the boundless impatience of restraint,
The loose drift of character, the inkling through random types, the solidification;
The butcher in the slaughter-house, the hands aboard schooners and sloops, the raftsmen, the pioneer,
Lumbermen in their winter camp, daybreak in the woods, stripes of snow on the limbs of trees, the occasional snapping,
The glad clear sound of one's own voice, the merry song, the natural life of the woods, the strong day's work,
The blazing fire at night, the sweet taste of supper, the talk, the bed of hemlock-boughs and the bear-skin;
The house-builder at work in cities or anywhere,
The preparatory jointing, squaring, sawing, mortising,
The hoist-up of beams, the push of them in their places, laying them regular,
Setting the studs by their tenons in the mortices according as they were prepared,
The blows of mallets and hammers, the attitudes of the men, their curv'd limbs,
Bending, standing, astride the beams, driving in pins, holding on by posts and braces,
The hook'd arm over the plate, the other arm wielding the axe,
The floor-men forcing the planks close to be nail'd,
Their postures bringing their weapons downward on the bearers,

The echoes resounding through the vacant building;
The huge storehouse carried up in the city well
under way,
The six framing-men, two in the middle and two at
each end, carefully bearing on their shoulders a
heavy stick for a cross-beam,
The crowded line of masons with trowels in their
right hands rapidly laying the long side-wall, two
hundred feet from front to rear,
The flexible rise and fall of backs, the continual click
of the trowels striking the bricks,
The bricks one after another each laid so
workmanlike in its place, and set with a knock of
the trowel-handle,
The piles of materials, the mortar on the mortar-
boards, and the steady replenishing by the
hod-men;
Spar-makers in the spar-yard, the swarming row of
well-grown apprentices,
The swing of their axes on the square-hew'd log
shaping it toward the shape of a mast,
The brisk short crackle of the steel driven slantingly
into the pine,
The butter-color'd chips flying off in great flakes and
slivers,
The limber motion of brawny young arms and hips
in easy costumes,
The constructor of wharves, bridges, piers, bulk-
heads, floats, stays against the sea;
The city fireman, the fire that suddenly bursts forth
in the close-pack'd square,
The arriving engines, the hoarse shouts, the nimble
stepping and daring,

The strong command through the fire-trumpets, the
    falling in line, the rise and fall of the arms forcing
    the water,
The slender, spasmic, blue-white jets, the bringing to
    bear of the hooks and ladders and their execution,
The crash and cut away of connecting wood-work, or
    through floors if the fire smoulders under them,
The crowd with their lit faces watching, the glare
    and dense shadows;
The forger at his forge-furnace and the user of iron
    after him,
The maker of the axe large and small, and the
    welder and temperer,
The chooser breathing his breath on the cold steel
    and trying the edge with his thumb,
The one who clean-shapes the handle and sets it
    firmly in the socket;
The shadowy processions of the portraits of the past
    users also,
The primal patient mechanics, the architects and
    engineers,
The far-off Assyrian edifice and Mizra edifice,
The Roman lictors preceding the consuls,
The antique European warrior with his axe in combat,
The uplifted arm, the clatter of blows on the
    helmeted head,
The death-howl, the limpsy tumbling body, the rush
    of friend and foe thither,
The siege of revolted lieges determin'd for liberty,
The summons to surrender, the battering at castle
    gates, the truce and parley,
The sack of an old city in its time,
The bursting in of mercenaries and bigots
    tumultuously and disorderly,

Roar, flames, blood, drunkenness, madness,
Goods freely rifled from houses and temples,
    screams of women in the gripe of brigands,
Craft and thievery of camp-followers, men running,
    old persons despairing,
The hell of war, the cruelties of creeds,
The list of all executive deeds and words just or unjust,
The power of personality just or unjust.

4

Muscle and pluck forever!
What invigorates life invigorates death,
And the dead advance as much as the living advance,
And the future is no more uncertain than the present,
For the roughness of the earth and of man encloses as
    much as the delicatesse of the earth and of man,
And nothing endures but personal qualities.

What do you think endures?
Do you think a great city endures?
Or a teeming manufacturing state? or a prepared
    constitution? or the best built steamships?
Or hotels of granite and iron? or any chef-d'œuvres
    of engineering, forts, armaments?

Away! these are not to be cherish'd for themselves,
They fill their hour, the dancers dance, the
    musicians play for them,
The show passes, all does well enough of course,
All does very well till one flash of defiance.

A great city is that which has the greatest men and
    women,
If it be a few ragged huts it is still the greatest city in
    the whole world.

5

The place where a great city stands is not the place
of stretch'd wharves, docks, manufactures,
deposits of produce merely,
Nor the place of ceaseless salutes of new-comers or
the anchor-lifters of the departing,
Nor the place of the tallest and costliest buildings or
shops selling goods from the rest of the earth,
Nor the place of the best libraries and schools, nor
the place where money is plentiest,
Nor the place of the most numerous population.

Where the city stands with the brawniest breed of
orators and bards,
Where the city stands that is belov'd by these, and
loves them in return and understands them,
Where no monuments exist to heroes but in the
common words and deeds,
Where thrift is in its place, and prudence is in its place,
Where the men and women think lightly of the laws,
Where the slave ceases, and the master of slaves ceases,
Where the populace rise at once against the never-
ending audacity of elected persons,
Where fierce men and women pour forth as the sea
to the whistle of death pours its sweeping and
unript waves,
Where outside authority enters always after the
precedence of inside authority,
Where the citizen is always the head and ideal, and
President, Mayor, Governor and what not, are
agents for pay,
Where children are taught to be laws to themselves,
and to depend on themselves,
Where equanimity is illustrated in affairs,

Where speculations on the soul are encouraged,
Where women walk in public processions in the
 streets the same as the men,
Where they enter the public assembly and take
 places the same as the men;
Where the city of the faithfulest friends stands,
Where the city of the cleanliness of the sexes stands,
Where the city of the healthiest fathers stands,
Where the city of the best-bodied mothers stands,
There the great city stands.

6

How beggarly appear arguments before a defiant deed!
How the floridness of the materials of cities shrivels
 before a man's or woman's look!

All waits or goes by default till a strong being appears;
A strong being is the proof of the race and of the
 ability of the universe,
When he or she appears materials are overaw'd,
The dispute on the soul stops,
The old customs and phrases are confronted, turn'd
 back, or laid away.

What is your money-making now? what can it do now?
What is your respectability now?
What are your theology, tuition, society, traditions,
 statute-books, now?
Where are your jibes of being now?
Where are your cavils about the soul now?

7

A sterile landscape covers the ore, there is as good as
 the best for all the forbidding appearance,
There is the mine, there are the miners,

The forge-furnace is there, the melt is accomplish'd,
the hammers-men are at hand with their tongs
and hammers,
What always served and always serves is at hand.

Than this nothing has better served, it has served all,
Served the fluent-tongued and subtle-sensed Greek,
and long ere the Greek,
Served in building the buildings that last longer than
any,
Served the Hebrew, the Persian, the most ancient
Hindustanee,
Served the mound-raiser on the Mississippi, served
those whose relics remain in Central America,
Served Albic temples in woods or on plains, with
unhewn pillars and the druids,
Served the artificial clefts, vast, high, silent, on the
snow-cover'd hills of Scandinavia,
Served those who time out of mind made on the
granite walls rough sketches of the sun, moon,
stars, ships, ocean waves,
Served the paths of the irruption of the Goths,
served the pastoral tribes and nomads,
Served the long distant Kelt, served the hardy pirates
of the Baltic,
Served before any of those the venerable and
harmless men of Ethiopia,
Served the making of helms for the galleys of
pleasure and the making of those for war,
Served all great works on land and all great works on
the sea,
For the mediaeval ages and before the mediaeval ages,
Served not the living only then as now, but served
the dead.

## 8

I see the European headsman,
He stands mask'd, clothed in red, with huge legs
and strong naked arms,
And leans on a ponderous axe.

(Whom have you slaughter'd lately European
headsman?
Whose is that blood upon you so wet and sticky?)

I see the clear sunsets of the martyrs,
I see from the scaffolds the descending ghosts,
Ghosts of dead lords, uncrown'd ladies, impeach'd
ministers, rejected kings,
Rivals, traitors, poisoners, disgraced chieftains and
the rest.

I see those who in any land have died for the good cause,
The seed is spare, nevertheless the crop shall never
run out,
(Mind you O foreign kings, O priests, the crop shall
never run out.)

I see the blood wash'd entirely away from the axe,
Both blade and helve are clean,
They spirt no more the blood of European nobles,
they clasp no more the necks of queens.

I see the headsman withdraw and become useless,
I see the scaffold untrodden and mouldy, I see no
longer any axe upon it,
I see the mighty and friendly emblem of the power
of my own race, the newest, largest race.

9

(America! I do not vaunt my love for you,
I have what I have.)

The axe leaps!
The solid forest gives fluid utterances,
They tumble forth, they rise and form,
Hut, tent, landing, survey,
Flail, plough, pick, crowbar, spade,
Shingle, rail, prop, wainscot, jamb, lath, panel, gable,
Citadel, ceiling, saloon, academy, organ, exhibition-house, library,
Cornice, trellis, pilaster, balcony, window, turret, porch,
Hoe, rake, pitchfork, pencil, wagon, staff, saw, jack-plane, mallet, wedge, rounce,
Chair, tub, hoop, table, wicket, vane, sash, floor,
Work-box, chest, string'd instrument, boat, frame, and what not,
Capitols of States, and capitol of the nation of States,
Long stately rows in avenues, hospitals for orphans or for the poor or sick,
Manhattan steamboats and clippers taking the measure of all seas.

The shapes arise!
Shapes of the using of axes anyhow, and the users and all that neighbors them,
Cutters down of wood and haulers of it to the Penobscot or Kennebec,
Dwellers in cabins among the Californian mountains or by the little lakes, or on the Columbia,
Dwellers south on the banks of the Gila or Rio Grande, friendly gatherings, the characters and fun,

Dwellers along the St. Lawrence, or north in Kanada, or down by the Yellowstone, dwellers on coasts and off coasts,
Seal-fishers, whalers, arctic seamen breaking passages through the ice.

The shapes arise!
Shapes of factories, arsenals, foundries, markets,
Shapes of the two-threaded tracks of railroads,
Shapes of the sleepers of bridges, vast frameworks, girders, arches,
Shapes of the fleets of barges, tows, lake and canal craft, river craft,
Ship-yards and dry-docks along the Eastern and Western seas, and in many a bay and by-place,
The live-oak kelsons, the pine planks, the spars, the hackmatack-roots for knees,
The ships themselves on their ways, the tiers of scaffolds, the workmen busy outside and inside,
The tools lying around, the great auger and little auger, the adze, bolt, line, square, gouge, and bead-plane.

10

The shapes arise!
The shape measur'd, saw'd, jack'd, join'd, stain'd,
The coffin-shape for the dead to lie within in his shroud,
The shape got out in posts, in the bedstead posts, in the posts of the bride's bed,
The shape of the little trough, the shape of the rockers beneath, the shape of the babe's cradle,
The shape of the floor-planks, the floor-planks for dancer's feet,
The shape of the planks of the family home, the home of the friendly parents and children,

The shape of the roof of the home of the happy
young man and woman, the roof over the well-
married young man and woman,
The roof over the supper joyously cook'd by the
chaste wife, and joyously eaten by the chaste
husband, content after his day's work.

The shapes arise!
The shape of the prisoner's place in the court-room,
and of him or her seated in the place.
The shape of the liquor-bar lean'd against by the
young rum-drinker and the old rum-drinker,
The shape of the shamed and angry stairs trod by
sneaking footsteps,
The shape of the sly settee, and the adulterous
unwholesome couple,
The shape of the gambling-board with its devilish
winnings and losings,
The shape of the step-ladder for the convicted and
sentenced murderer, the murderer with haggard
face and pinion'd arms,
The sheriff at hand with his deputies, the silent and
whitelipp'd crowd, the dangling of the rope.

The shapes arise!
Shapes of doors giving many exits and entrances,
The door passing the dissever'd friend flush'd and in
haste,
The door that admits good news and bad news,
The door whence the son left home confident and
puff'd up,
The door he enter'd again from a long and
scandalous absence, diseas'd, broken down,
without innocence, without means.

11

Her shape arises,
She less guarded than ever, yet more guarded than ever,
The gross and soil'd she moves among do not make
her gross and soil'd,
She knows the thoughts as she passes, nothing is
conceal'd from her,
She is none the less considerate or friendly therefor,
She is the best belov'd, it is without exception, she
has no reason to fear and she does not fear,
Oaths, quarrels, hiccupp'd songs, smutty expressions
are idle to her as she passes,
She is silent, she is possess'd of herself, they do not
offend her,
She receives them as the laws of Nature receive
them, she is strong,
She too is a law of Nature – there is no law stronger
than she is.
The main shapes arise!
Shapes of Democracy total, result of centuries,
Shapes ever projecting other shapes,
Shapes of turbulent manly cities,
Shapes of the friends and home-givers of the whole
earth,
Shapes bracing the earth and braced with the whole
earth.

## *Song of the Exposition*

1

(Ah little recks the laborer,
How near his work is holding him to God,
The loving Laborer through space and time.)

After all not to create only, or found only,
But to bring perhaps from afar what is already
founded,
To give it our own identity, average, limitless, free,
To fill the gross the torpid bulk with vital religious fire,
Not to repel or destroy so much as accept, fuse,
rehabilitate,
To obey as well as command, to follow more than to
lead,
These also are the lessons of our New World;
While how little the New after all, how much the
Old, Old World!
Long and long has the grass been growing,
Long and long has the rain been falling,
Long has the globe been rolling round.

2

Come Muse migrate from Greece and Ionia,
Cross out please those immensely overpaid accounts,
That matter of Troy and Achilles' wrath, and
Aeneas', Odysseus' wanderings,
Placard 'Removed' and 'To Let' on the rocks of
your snowy Parnassus,
Repeat at Jerusalem, place the notice high on Jaffa's
gate and on Mount Moriah,
The same on the walls of your German, French and
Spanish castles, and Italian collections,

For know a better, fresher, busier sphere, a wide,
untried domain awaits, demands you.

3

Responsive to our summons,
Or rather to her long-nurs'd inclination,
Join'd with an irresistible, natural gravitation,
She comes! I hear the rustling of her gown,
I scent the odor of her breath's delicious fragrance,
I mark her step divine, her curious eyes a-turning,
rolling,
Upon this very scene.

The dame of dames! can I believe then,
Those ancient temples, sculptures classic, could
none of them retain her?
Nor shades of Virgil and Dante, nor myriad
memories, poems, old associations, magnetize
and hold on to her?
But that she's left them all – and here?

Yes, if you will allow me to say so,
I, my friends, if you do not, can plainly see her,
The same undying soul of earth's, activity's,
beauty's, heroism's expression,
Out from her evolutions hither come, ended the
strata of her former themes,
Hidden and cover'd by to-day's, foundation of
to-day's,
Ended, deceas'd through time, her voice by
Castaly's fountain,
Silent the broken-lipp'd Sphynx in Egypt, silent all
those century-baffling tombs,
Ended for aye the epics of Asia's, Europe's helmeted
warriors, ended the primitive call of the muses,

Calliope's call forever closed, Clio, Melpomene, Thalia
  dead,
Ended the stately rhythmus of Una and Oriana,
  ended the quest of the Holy Graal,
Jerusalem a handful of ashes blown by the wind, extinct,
The Crusaders' streams of shadowy midnight troops
  sped with the sunrise,
Amadis, Tancred, utterly gone, Charlemagne,
  Roland, Oliver gone,
Palmerin, ogre, departed, vanish'd the turrets that
  Usk from its waters reflected,
Arthur vanish'd with all his knights, Merlin and
  Lancelot and Galahad, all gone, dissolv'd utterly
  like an exhalation;
Pass'd! pass'd! for us, forever pass'd, that once so
  mighty world, now void, inanimate, phantom
  world,
Embroider'd, dazzling, foreign world, with all its
  gorgeous legends, myths,
Its kings and castles proud, its priests and warlike
  lords and courtly dames,
Pass'd to its charnel vault, coffin'd with crown and
  armor on,
Blazon'd with Shakspere's purple page,
And dirged by Tennyson's sweet sad rhyme.

I say I see, my friends, if you do not, the illustrious
  emigré, (having it is true in her day, although the
  same, changed, journey'd considerable,)
Making directly for this rendezvous, vigorously
  clearing a path for herself, striding through the
  confusion,
By thud of machinery and shrill steam-whistle
  undismay'd,

Bluff'd not a bit by drain-pipe, gasometers, artificial
fertilizers,
Smiling and pleas'd with palpable intent to stay,
She's here, install'd amid the kitchen ware!

4

But hold – don't I forget my manners?
To introduce the stranger, (what else indeed do I
live to chant for?) to thee Columbia;
In liberty's name welcome immortal! clasp hands,
And ever henceforth sisters dear be both.

Fear not O Muse! truly new ways and days receive,
surround you,
I candidly confess a queer, queer race, of novel fashion,
And yet the same old human race, the same within,
without,
Faces and hearts the same, feelings the same,
yearnings the same,
The same old love, beauty and use the same.

5

We do not blame thee elder World, nor really
separate ourselves from thee,
(Would the son separate himself from the father?)
Looking back on thee, seeing thee to thy duties,
grandeurs, through past ages bending, building,
We build to ours to-day.
Mightier than Egypt's tombs,
Fairer than Grecia's, Roma's temples,
Prouder then Milan's statued, spired, cathedral,
More picturesque than Rhenish castle-keeps,
We plan even now to raise, beyond them all,

Thy great cathedral sacred industry, no tomb,
A keep for life for practical invention.

As in a waking vision,
E'en while I chant I see it rise, I scan and prophesy
outside and in,
Its manifold ensemble.

Around a palace, loftier, fairer, ampler than any yet,
Earth's modern wonder, history's seven outstripping,
High rising tier on tier with glass and iron façades,
Gladdening the sun and sky, enhued in cheerfulest
hues,
Bronze, lilac, robin's-egg, marine and crimson,
Over whose golden roof shall flaunt, beneath thy
banner Freedom,
The banners of the States and flags of every land,
A brood of lofty, fair, but lesser palaces shall cluster.

Somewhere within their walls shall all that forwards
perfect human life be started,
Tried, taught, advanced, visibly exhibited.

Not only all the world of works, trade, products,
But all the workmen of the world here to be represented.

Here shall you trace in flowing operation,
In every state of practical, busy movement, the rills
of civilization,
Materials here under your eye shall change their
shape as if my magic,
The cotton shall be pick'd almost in the very field,
Shall be dried, clean'd, ginn'd, baled, spun into
thread and cloth before you,
You shall see hands at work at all the old processes
and all the new ones,

You shall see the various grains and how flour is
made and then bread baked by the bakers,
You shall see the crude ores of California and
Nevada passing on and on till they become
bullion,
You shall watch how the printer sets type, and learn
what a composing-stick is,
You shall mark in amazement the Hoe press
whirling its cylinders, shedding the printed leaves
steady and fast,
The photograph, model, watch, pin, nail, shall be
created before you.

In large calm halls, a stately museum shall teach you
the infinite lessons of minerals,
In another, woods, plants, vegetation shall be
illustrated – in another animals, animal life and
development.

One stately house shall be the music house,
Others for other arts – learning, the sciences, shall all
be here,
None shall be slighted, none but shall here be
honor'd, help'd, exampled.

6

(This, this and these, America, shall be *your*
pyramids and obelisks,
Your Alexandrian Pharos, gardens of Babylon,
Your temple at Olympia.)

The male and female many laboring not,
Shall ever here confront the laboring many,
With precious benefits to both, glory to all,
To thee America, and thee eternal Muse.

And here shall ye inhabit powerful Matrons!
In your vast state vaster than all the old,
Echoed through long, long centuries to come,
To sound of different, prouder songs, with stronger
themes,
Practical, peaceful life, the people's life, the People
themselves,
Lifted, illumin'd, bathed in peace – elate, secure in
peace.

7

Away with themes of war! away with war itself!
Hence from my shuddering sight to never more
return that show of blacken'd, mutilated corpses!
That hell unpent and raid of blood, fit for wild tigers
or for lop-tongued wolves, not reasoning men,
And in its stead speed industry's campaigns,
With thy undaunted armies, engineering,
Thy pennants labor, loosen'd to the breeze,
Thy bugles sounding loud and clear.
Away with old romance!
Away with novels, plots and plays of foreign courts,
Away with love-verses, sugar'd in rhyme, the
intrigues, amours of idlers,
Fitted for only banquets of the night where dancers
to late music slide,
The unhealthy pleasures, extravagant dissipation of
the few,
With perfumes, heat and wine, beneath the dazzling
chandeliers.

To you ye reverent sane sisters,
I raise a voice for far superber themes for poets and
for art,

To exalt the present and the real,
To teach the average man the glory of his daily walk
    and trade,
To sing in songs how exercise and chemical life are
    never to be baffled,
To manual work for each and all, to plough, hoe, dig,
To plant and tend the tree, the berry, vegetables,
    flowers,
For every man to see to it that he really do
    something, for every woman too;
To use the hammer and the saw, (rip, or cross-cut,)
To cultivate a turn for carpentering, plastering,
    painting,
To work as tailor, tailoress, nurse, hostler, porter,
To invent a little, something ingenious, to aid the
    washing, cooking, cleaning,
And hold it no disgrace to take a hand at them
    themselves.

I say I bring thee Muse to-day and here,
All occupations, duties broad and close,
Toil, healthy toil and sweat, endless, without cessation,
The old, old practical burdens, interests, joys,
The family, parentage, childhood, husband and wife,
The house-comforts, the house itself and all its
    belongings,
Food and its preservation, chemistry applied to it,
Whatever forms the average, strong, complete,
    sweet-blooded man or woman, the perfect
    longeve personality,
And helps its present life to health and happiness,
    and shapes its soul,
For the eternal real life to come.

With latest connections, works, the inter-transportation
 of the world,
Steam-power, the great express lines, gas, petroleum,
These triumphs of our time, the Atlantic's delicate
 cable,
The Pacific railroad, the Suez canal, the Mont Cenis
 and Gothard and Hoosac tunnels, the Brooklyn
 bridge,
The earth all spann'd with iron rails, with lines of
 steamships threading every sea,
Our own rondure, the current globe I bring.

8

And thou America,
Thy offspring towering e'er so high, yet higher
 These above all towering,
With Victory on thy left, and at thy right hand Law;
Thou Union holding all, fusing, absorbing,
 tolerating all,
Thee, ever thee, I sing.

Thou, also thou, a World,
With all thy wide geographies, manifold, different,
 distant,
Rounded by thee in one – one common orbic language,
One common indivisible destiny for All.

And by the spells which ye vouchsafe to those your
 ministers in earnest,
I here personify and call my themes, to make them
 pass before ye.
Behold, America! (and thou, ineffable guest and
 sister!)
For thee come trooping up thy waters and thy lands;

Behold! thy fields and farms, thy far-off woods and
    mountains,
As in procession coming.

Behold, the sea itself,
And on its limitless, heaving breast, the ships;
See, where their white sails, bellying in the wind,
    speckle the green and blue,
See, the steamers coming and going, steaming in or
    out of port,
See, dusky and undulating, the long pennants of smoke.

Behold, in Oregon, far in the north and west,
Or in Maine, far in the north and east, thy cheerful
    axemen,
Wielding all day their axes.

Behold, on the lakes, thy pilots at their wheels, thy
    oarsmen,
How the ash writhes under those muscular arms!

There by the furnace, and there by the anvil,
Behold thy sturdy blacksmiths swinging their sledges,
Overhand so steady, overhand they turn and fall
    with joyous clank,
Like a tumult of laughter.

Mark the spirit of invention everywhere, thy rapid
    patents,
Thy continual workshops, foundries, risen or rising,
See, from their chimneys how the tall flame-fires
    stream.

Mark, thy interminable farms, North, South,
Thy wealthy daughter-states, Eastern and Western,
The varied products of Ohio, Pennsylvania,
    Missouri, Georgia, Texas, and the rest,

Thy limitless crops, grass, wheat, sugar, oil, corn, rice, hemp, hops,
Thy barns all fill'd, the endless freight-train and the bulging storehouse,
The grapes that ripen on thy vines, the apples in thy orchards,
Thy incalculable lumber, beef, pork, potatoes, thy coal, thy gold and silver,
The inexhaustible iron in thy mines.

All thine, O sacred Union!
Ships, farms, shops, barns, factories, mines,
City and State, North, South, item and aggregate,
We dedicate, dread Mother, all to thee!

Protectress absolute, thou! bulwark of all!
For well we know that while thou givest each and all, (generous as God,)
Without thee neither all nor each, nor land, home,
Nor ship, nor mine, nor any here this day secure,
Nor aught, nor any day secure.

9

And thou, the Emblem waving over all!
Delicate beauty, a word to thee, (it may be salutary,)
Remember thou hast not always been as here to-day so comfortably ensovereign'd,
In other scenes than these have I observ'd thee flag,
Not quite so trim and whole and freshly blooming in folds of stainless silk,
But I have seen thee bunting, to tatters torn upon thy splinter'd staff,
Or clutch'd to some young color-bearer's breast with desperate hands,

Savagely struggled for, for life or death, fought over
long,
'Mid cannons' thunder-crash and many a curse and
groan and yell, and rifle-volleys cracking sharp,
And moving masses as wild demons surging, and
lives as nothing risk'd,
For thy mere remnant grimed with dirt and smoke
and sopp'd in blood,
For sake of that, my beauty, and that thou might'st
dally as now secure up there,
Many a good man have I seen go under.

Now here and these and hence in peace, all thine, O
flag!
And here and hence for thee, O universal Muse! and
thou for them!
And here and hence O Union, all the work and
workmen thine!
None separate from thee – henceforth One only, we
and thou,
(For the blood of the children, what is it, only the
blood maternal?
And lives and works, what are they all at last, except
the roads to faith and death?)

While we rehearse our measureless wealth, it is for
thee, dear Mother,
We own it all and several to-day indissoluble in thee;
Think not our chant, our show, merely for products
gross or lucre – it is for thee, the soul in thee,
electric, spiritual!
Our farms, inventions, crops, we own in thee! cities
and States in thee!
Our freedom all in thee! our very lives in thee!

## *Song of the Redwood-Tree*

I

A California song,
A prophecy and indirection, a thought impalpable to breathe as air,
A chorus of dryads, fading, departing, or hamadryads departing,
A murmuring, fateful, giant voice, out of the earth and sky,
Voice of a mighty dying tree in the redwood forest dense.

*Farewell my brethren,*
*Farewell O earth and sky, farewell ye neighboring waters,*
*My time has ended, my term has come.*

Along the northern coast,
Just back from the rock-bound shore and the caves,
In the saline air from the sea in the Mendocino country,
With the surge for base and accompaniment low and hoarse,
With crackling blows of axes sounding musically driven by strong arms,
Riven deep by the sharp tongues of the axes, there in the red-wood forest dense,
I heard the mighty tree its death-chant chanting.

The choppers heard not, the camp shanties echoed not,
The quick-ear'd teamsters and chain and jack-screw men heard not,
As the wood-spirits came from their haunts of a thousand years to join the refrain,
But in my soul I plainly heard.

Murmuring out of its myriad leaves,
Down from its lofty top rising two hundred feet high,
Out of its stalwart trunk and limbs, out of its foot-thick bark,
That chant of the seasons and time, chant not of the past only but the future.

*You untold life of me,*
*And all you venerable and innocent joys,*
*Perennial hardy life of me with joys 'mid rain and many a summer sun,*
*And the white snows and night and the wild winds;*
*O the great patient rugged joys my soul's strong joys unreck'd by man,*
*(For know I bear the soul befitting me, I too have consciousness, identity,*
*And all the rocks and mountains have, and all the earth,)*
*Joys of the life befitting me and brothers mine,*
*Our time, our term has come.*

*Nor yield we mournfully majestic brothers,*
*We who have grandly fill'd our time;*
*With Nature's calm content, with tacit huge delight,*
*We welcome what we wrought for through the past,*
*And leave the field for them.*
*For them predicted long,*
*For a superber race, they too to grandly fill their time,*
*For them we abdicate, in them ourselves ye forest kings!*
*In them these skies and airs, these mountain peaks, Shasta, Nevadas,*
*These huge precipitous cliffs, this amplitude, these valleys, far Yosemite,*
*To be in them absorb'd, assimilated.*

Then to a loftier strain,
Still prouder, more ecstatic rose the chant,
As if the heirs, the deities of the West,
Joining with master-tongue bore part.

*Not wan from Asia's fetiches,*
*Nor red from Europe's old dynastic slaughter-house,*
*(Area of murder-plots of thrones, with scent left yet of wars and scaffolds everywhere,)*
*But come from Nature's long and harmless throes, peacefully builded thence,*
*These virgin lands, lands of the Western shore,*
*To the new culminating man, to you, the empire new,*
*You promis'd long, we pledge, we dedicate.*

*You occult deep volitions,*
*You average spiritual manhood, purpose of all, pois'd on yourself, giving not taking law,*
*You womanhood divine, mistress and source of all, whence life and love and aught that comes from life and love,*
*You unseen moral essence of all the vast materials of America, (age upon age working in death the same as life,)*
*You that, sometimes known, oftener unknown, really shape and mould the New World, adjusting it to Time and Space,*
*You hidden national will lying in your abysms, conceal'd but ever alert,*
*You past and present purposes tenaciously pursued, may-be unconscious of yourselves,*
*Unswerv'd by all the passing errors, perturbations of the surface;*
*You vital, universal, deathless germs, beneath all creeds, arts, statutes, literatures,*

*Here build your homes for good, establish here, these*
*areas entire, lands of the Western shore,*
*We pledge, we dedicate to you.*

*For man of you, your characteristic race,*
*Here may he hardy, sweet, gigantic grow, here tower*
*proportionate to Nature,*
*Here climb the vast pure spaces unconfined, uncheck'd*
*by wall or roof,*
*Here laugh with storm or sun, here joy, here patiently inure,*
*Here heed himself, unfold himself, (not others' formulas*
*heed,) here fill his time,*
*To duly fall, to aid, unreck'd at last,*
*To disappear, to serve,*

Thus on the northern coast,
In the echo of teamsters' calls and the clinking
chains, and the music of choppers' axes,
The falling trunk and limbs, the crash, the muffled
shriek, the groan,
Such words combined from the redwood-tree, as of
voices ecstatic, ancient and rustling,
The century-lasting, unseen dryads, singing,
withdrawing,
All their recesses of forests and mountains leaving,
From the Cascade range to the Wasatch, or Idaho
far, or Utah,
To the deities of the modern henceforth yielding,
The chorus and indications, the vistas of coming
humanity, the settlements, features all,
In the Mendocino woods I caught.

2

The flashing and golden pageant of California,
The sudden and gorgeous drama, the sunny and ample lands
The long and varied stretch from Puget sound to Colorado south,
Lands bathed in sweeter, rarer, healthier air, valleys and mountain cliffs,
The fields of Nature long prepared and fallow, the silent, cyclic chemistry,
The slow and steady ages plodding, the unoccupied surface ripening, the rich ores forming beneath;
At last the New arriving, assuming, taking possession,
A swarming and busy race settling and organizing everywhere,
Ships coming in from the whole round world, and going out to the whole world,
To India and China and Australia and the thousand island paradises of the Pacific,
Populous cities, the latest inventions, the steamers on the rivers, the railroads, with many a thrifty farm, with machinery,
And wood and wheat and the grape, and diggings of yellow gold.

3

But more in you than these, lands of the Western shore,
(These but the means, the implements, the standing-ground,)
I see in you, certain to come, the promise of thousands of years, till now deferr'd,

Promis'd to be fulfill'd, our common kind, the race.
The new society at last, proportionate to Nature,
In man of you, more than your mountain peaks or
stalwart trees imperial.
In woman more, far more, than all your gold or
vines, or even vital air.
Fresh come, to a new world indeed, yet long
prepared,
I see the genius of the modern, child of the real and
ideal,
Clearing the ground for broad humanity, the true
America, heir of the past so grand,
To build a grander future.

## *A Song for Occupations*

I

A song for occupations!
In the labor of engines and trades and the labor of
fields I find the developments,
And find the eternal meanings.

Workmen and Workwomen!
Were all educations practical and ornamental well
display'd out of me, what would it amount to?
Were I as the head teacher, charitable proprietor,
wise statesman, what would it amount to?
Were I to you as the boss employing and paying you,
would that satisfy you?

The learn'd, virtuous, benevolent, and the usual terms,
A man like me and never the usual terms.

Neither a servant nor a master I,
I take no sooner a large price than a small price, I
will have my own whoever enjoys me,
I will be even with you and you shall be even with me.

If you stand at work in a shop I stand as nigh as the
nighest in the same shop,
If you bestow gifts on your brother or dearest friend I
demand as good as your brother or dearest friend,
If your lover, husband, wife, is welcome by day or
night, I must be personally as welcome,
If you become degraded, criminal, ill, then I become
so for your sake,
If you remember your foolish and outlaw'd deeds,
do you think I cannot remember my own foolish
and outlaw'd deeds?
If you carouse at the table I carouse at the opposite
side of the table,
If you meet some stranger in the streets and love him
or her, why I often meet strangers in the street
and love them.

Why what have you thought of yourself?
Is it you then that thought yourself less?
Is it you that thought the President greater than you?
Or the rich better off than you? or the educated
wiser than you?
(Because you are greasy or pimpled, or were once
drunk, or a thief,
Or that you are diseas'd, or rheumatic, or a
prostitute,
Or from frivolity or impotence, or that you are no
scholar and never saw your name in print,
Do you give in that you are any less immortal?)

2

Souls of men and women! it is not you I call unseen,
unheard, untouchable and untouching,
It is not you I go argue pro and con about, and to
settle whether you are alive or no,
I own publicly who you are, if nobody else owns.

Grown, half-grown and babe, of this country and
every country, indoors and out-doors, one just as
much as the other, I see,
And all else behind or through them.

The wife, and she is not one jot less than the
husband,
The daughter, and she is just as good as the son,
The mother, and she is every bit as much as the father.

Offspring of ignorant and poor, boys apprenticed to
trades,
Young fellows working on farms and old fellows
working on farms,
Sailor-men, merchant-men, coasters, immigrants,
All these I see, but nigher and farther the same I see,
None shall escape me and none shall wish to escape me.

I bring what you much need yet always have,
Not money, amours, dress, eating, erudition, but as
good,
I send no agent or medium, offer no representative
of value, but offer the value itself.

There is something that comes to one now and
perpetually,
It is not what is printed, preach'd, discussed, it
eludes discussion and print,
It is not to be put in a book, it is not in this book,

It is for you whoever you are, it is no farther from
you than your hearing and sight are from you,
It is hinted by nearest, commonest, readiest, it is
ever provoked by them.
You may read in many languages, yet read nothing
about it,
You may read the President's message and read
nothing about it there,
Nothing in the reports from the State department or
Treasury department, or in the daily papers or
weekly papers,
Or in the census or revenue returns, prices current,
or any accounts of stock.

3

The sun and stars that float in the open air,
The apple-shaped earth and we upon it, surely the
drift of them is something grand,
I do not know what it is except that it is grand, and
that it is happiness,
And that the enclosing purport of us here is not a
speculation or bon-mot or reconnoissance,
And that it is not something which by luck may turn out
well for us, and without luck must be a failure for us,
And not something which may yet be retracted in a
certain contingency.

The light and shade, the curious sense of body and
identity, the greed that with perfect
complaisance devours all things,
The endless pride and outstretching of man,
unspeakable joys and sorrows,
The wonder every one sees in every one else he sees, and
the wonders that fill each minute of time forever,

What have you reckon'd them for, camerado?
Have you reckon'd them for your trade or farm-work? or for the profits of your store?
Or to achieve yourself a position? or to fill a gentleman's leisure, or a lady's leisure?

Have you reckon'd that the landscape took substance and form that it might be painted in a picture?
Or men and women that they might be written of, and songs sung?
Or the attraction of gravity, and the great laws and harmonious combinations and the fluids of the air, as subjects for the savans?
Or the brown land and the blue sea for maps and charts?
Or the stars to be put in constellations and named fancy names?
Or that the growth of seeds is for agricultural tables, or agriculture itself?

Old institutions, these arts, libraries, legends, collections, and the practice handed along in manufactures, will we rate them so high?
Will we rate our cash and business high? I have no objection,
I rate them as high as the highest – then a child born of a woman and man I rate beyond all rate.

We thought our Union grand, and our Constitution grand,
I do not say they are not grand and good, for they are,
I am this day just as much in love with them as you,
Then I am in love with You, and with all my fellows upon the earth.

We consider bibles and religions divine – I do not say they are not divine,

I say they have all grown out of you, and may grow
out of you still,
It is not they who give the life, it is you who give the life,
Leaves are not more shed from the trees, or trees
from the earth, than they are shed out of you.

4

The sum of all known reverence I add up in you
whoever you are,
The President is there in the White House for you, it
is not you who are here for him,
The Secretaries act in their bureaus for you, not you
here for them,
The Congress convenes every Twelfth-month for
you,
Laws, courts, the forming of States, the charters of
cities, the going and coming of commerce and
mails, are all for you.

List close my scholars dear,
Doctrines, politics and civilization exurge from you,
Sculpture and monuments and any thing inscribed
anywhere are tallied in you,
The gist of histories and statistics as far back as the
records reach is in you this hour, and myths and
tales the same,
If you were not breathing and walking here, where
would they all be?
The most renown'd poems would be ashes, orations
and plays would be vacuums.

All architecture is what you do to it when you look
upon it,
(Did you think it was in the white or gray stone? or
the lines of the arches and cornices?)

All music is what awakes from you when you are
  reminded by the instruments,
It is not the violins and the cornets, it is not the oboe
  nor the beating drums, nor the score of the
  baritone singer singing his sweet romanza, nor
  that of the men's chorus, nor that of the
  women's chorus,
It is nearer and farther than they.

5

Will the whole come back then?
Can each see signs of the best by a look in the
  looking-glass? is there nothing greater or more?
Does all sit there with you, with the mystic unseen
  soul?

Strange and hard that paradox true I give,
Objects gross and the unseen soul are one.

House-building, measuring, sawing the boards,
Blacksmithing, glass-blowing, nail-making,
  coopering, tinroofing, shingle-dressing,
Ship-joining, dock-building, fish-curing, flagging of
  sidewalks by flaggers,
The pump, the pile driver, the great derrick, the
  coal-kiln and brick-kiln,
Coal-mines and all that is down there, the lamps in
  the darkness, echoes, songs, what meditations,
  what vast native thoughts looking through
  smutch'd faces,
Iron works, forge-fires in the mountains or by river-
  banks, men around feeling the melt with huge
  crowbars, lumps of ore, the due combining of
  ore, limestone, coal,

The blast-furnace and the pudding-furnace, the
 loup-lump at the bottom of the melt at last, the
 rolling-mill, the stumpy bars of pig-iron, the
 strong, clean-shaped T-rail for railroads,
Oil-works, silk-works, white-lead-works, the sugar-
 house, steam-saws, the great mills and factories,
Stone-cutting, shapely trimmings for façades or
 window or door-lintels, the mallet, the tooth-
 chisel, the jib to protect the thumb,
The calking-iron, the kettle of boiling vault-cement,
 and the fire under the kettle,
The cotton-bale, the stevedore's hook, the saw and
 buck of the sawyer, the mould of the moulder,
 the working-knife of the butcher, the ice-saw,
 and all the work with ice,
The work and tools of the rigger, grappler, sail-
 maker, blockmaker,
Goods of gutta-percha, papier-maché, colors,
 brushes, brushmaking, glazier's implements,
The veneer and glue-pot, the confectioner's ornaments,
 the decanter and glasses, the shears and flat-iron,
The awl and knee-strap, the pint measure and quart
 measure, the counter and stool, the writing-pen of
 quill or metal, the making of all sorts of edged tools,
The brewery, brewing, the malt, the vats, everything
 that is done by brewers, wine-makers, vinegar-
 makers,
Leather-dressing, coach-making, boiler-making,
 rope-twisting, distilling, sign-painting, lime-
 burning, cotton-picking, electroplating,
 electrotyping, stereotyping,
Stave -machines, planing -machines, reaping -
 machines, ploughing-machines,
 thrashing-machines, steam wagons,

The cart of the carman, the omnibus, the ponderous
dray,
Pyrotechny, letting off color'd fireworks at night,
fancy figures and jets;
Beef on the butcher's stall, the slaughter-house of
the butcher, the butcher in his killing-clothes,
The pens of live pork, the killing-hammer, the hog-
hook, the scalder's tub, gutting, the cutter's
cleaver, the packer's maul, and the plenteous
winterwork of pork-packing,
Flour-works, grinding of wheat, rye, maize, rice, the
barrels and the half and quarter barrels, the loaded
barges, the high piles on wharves and levees,
The men and the work of the men on ferries,
railroad, coasters, ash-boats, canals;
The hourly routine of your own or any man's life,
the shop, yard, store, or factory,
These shows all near you by day and night –
workman! whoever you are, your daily life!
In that and them the heft of the heaviest – in that
and them far more than you estimated, (and far
less also,)
In them realities for you and me, in them poems for
you and me,
In them, not yourself – you and your soul enclose all
things, regardless of estimation,
In them the development good – in them all themes,
hints, possibilities.

I do not affirm that what you see beyond is futile, I
do not advise you to stop,
I do not say leadings you thought great are not great,
But I say that none lead to greater than these lead to.

6

Will you seek afar off? you surely come back at last,
In things best known to you finding the best, or as
good as the best,
In folks nearest to you finding the sweetest,
strongest, lovingest,
Happiness, knowledge, not in another place but this
place, not for another hour but this hour,
Man in the first you see or touch, always in friend,
brother, nighest neighbor – woman in mother,
sister, wife,
The popular tastes and employments taking
precedence in poems or anywhere,
You workwomen and workmen of these States
having your own divine and strong life,
And all else giving place to men and women like you.

When the psalm sings instead of the singer,
When the script preaches instead of the preacher,
When the pulpit descends and goes instead of the
carver that carved the supporting desk,
When I can touch the body of books by night or by
day, and when they touch my body back again,
When a university course convinces like a
slumbering woman and child convince,
When the minted gold in the vault smiles like the
nightwatchman's daughter,
When warrantee deeds loafe in chairs opposite and
are my friendly companions,
I intend to reach them my hand, and make as much
of them as I do of men and women like you.

## *A Song of the Rolling Earth*

I

A song of the rolling earth, and of words according,
Were you thinking that those were the words, those
    upright lines? those curves, angles, dots?
No, those are not the words, the substantial words
    are in the ground and sea,
They are in the air, they are in you.

Were you thinking that those were the words, those
    delicious sounds out of your friends' mouths?
No, the real words are more delicious than they.

Human bodies are words, myriads of words,
(In the best poems re-appears the body, man's or
    woman's, well-shaped, natural, gay,
Every part able, active, receptive, without shame or
    the need of shame.)

Air, soil, water, fire – those are words,
I myself am a word with them – my qualities
    interpenetrate with theirs – my name is nothing
    to them,
Though it were told in the three thousand
    languages, what would air, soil, water, fire, know
    of my name?

A healthy presence, a friendly or commanding
    gesture, are words, sayings, meanings,
The charms that go with the mere looks of some
    men and women, are sayings and meanings also.

The workmanship of souls is by those inaudible
    words of the earth,
The masters know the earth's words and use them
    more than audible words.

Amelioration is one of the earth's words,
The earth neither lags nor hastens,
It has all attributes, growths, effects, latent in itself
from the jump,
It is not half beautiful only, defects and excrescences
show just as much as perfections show.

The earth does not withhold, it is generous enough,
The truths of the earth continually wait, they are not
so conceal'd either,
They are calm, subtle, untransmissible by print,
They are imbued through all things conveying
themselves willingly,
Conveying a sentiment and invitation, I utter and utter,
I speak not, yet if you hear me not of what avail am I
to you?

To bear, to better, lacking these of what avail am I?
(Accouche! accouchez!
Will you rot your own fruit in yourself there?
Will you squat and stifle there?)

The earth does not argue,
Is not pathetic, has no arrangements,
Does not scream, haste, persuade, threaten,
promise,
Makes no discriminations, has no conceivable
failures,
Closes nothing, refuses nothing, shuts none out,
Of all the powers, objects, states, it notifies, shuts
none out.

The earth does not exhibit itself nor refuse to exhibit
itself, possesses still underneath,
Underneath the ostensible sounds, the august
chorus of heroes, the wail of slaves,

Persuasions of lovers, curses, gasps of the dying,
laughter of young people, accents of bargainers,
Underneath these possessing words that never fail.

To her children the words of the eloquent dumb
great mother never fail,
The true words do not fail, for motion does not fail
and reflection does not fail,
Also the day and night do not fail, and the voyage
we pursue does not fail.

Of the interminable sisters,
Of the ceaseless cotillions of sisters,
Of the centripetal and centrifugal sisters, the elder
and younger sisters,
The beautiful sister we know dances on with the rest.

With her ample back towards every beholder,
With the fascinations of youth and the equal
fascinations of age,
Sits she whom I too love like the rest, sits undisturb'd,
Holding up in her hand what has the character of a
mirror, while her eyes glance back from it,
Glance as she sits, inviting none, denying none,
Holding a mirror day and night tirelessly before her
own face.

Seen at hand or seen at a distance,
Duly the twenty-four appear in public every day,
Duly approach and pass with their companions or a
companion,
Looking from no countenances of their own, but from
the countenances of those who are with them,
From the countenances of children or women or the
manly countenance,

From the open countenances of animals or from
inanimate things,
From the landscape or waters or from the exquisite
apparition of the sky,
From our countenances, mine and yours, faithfully
returning them,
Every day in public appearing without fail, but never
twice with the same companions.

Embracing man, embracing all, proceed the three
hundred and sixty-five resistlessly round the sun;
Embracing all, soothing, supporting, follow close
three hundred and sixty-five offsets of the first,
sure and necessary as they.

Tumbling on steadily, nothing dreading,
Sunshine, storm, cold, heat, forever withstanding,
passing, carrying,
The soul's realization and determination still
inheriting,
The fluid vacuum around and ahead still entering
and dividing,
No balk retarding, no anchor anchoring, on no rock
striking,
Swift, glad, content, unbereav'd, nothing losing,
Of all able and ready at any time to give strict
account,
The divine ship sails the divine sea.

2

Whoever you are! motion and reflection are
especially for you,
The divine ship sails the divine sea for you.
Whoever you are! you are he or she for whom the
earth is solid and liquid,

You are he or she for whom the sun and moon hang in
the sky,
For none more than you are the present and the past,
For none more than you is immortality.

Each man to himself and each woman to herself, is
the word of the past and present, and the true
word of immortality;
No one can acquire for another – not one,
Not one can grow for another – not one.

The song is to the singer, and comes back most to him,
The teaching is to the teacher, and comes back most
to him,
The murder is to the murderer, and comes back
most to him,
The theft is to the thief, and comes back most to him,
The love is to the lover, and comes back most to him,
The gift is to the giver, and comes back most to him –
it cannot fail,
The oration is to the orator, the acting is to the actor
and actress not to the audience,
And no man understands any greatness or goodness
but his own, or the indication of his own.

3

I swear the earth shall surely be complete to him or
her who shall be complete,
The earth remains jagged and broken only to him or
her who remains jagged and broken.

I swear there is no greatness or power that does not
emulate those of the earth,
There can be no theory of any account unless it
corroborate the theory of the earth,

No politics, song, religion, behavior, or what not, is
of account, unless it compare with the amplitude
of the earth,

Unless it face the exactness, vitality, impartiality,
rectitude of the earth.

I swear I begin to see love with sweeter spasms than
that which responds love,

It is that which contains itself, which never invites
and never refuses.

I swear I begin to see little or nothing in audible words,

All merges toward the presentation of the unspoken
meanings of the earth.

Toward him who sings the songs of the body and of
the truths of the earth,

Toward him who makes the dictionaries of words
that print cannot touch.

I swear I see what is better than to tell the best,

It is always to leave the best untold.

When I undertake to tell the best I find I cannot,

My tongue is ineffectual on its pivots,

My breath will not be obedient to its organs,

I become a dumb man.

The best of the earth cannot be told anyhow, all or
any is best,

It is not what you anticipated, it is cheaper, easier,
nearer,

Things are not dismiss'd from the places they held
before,

The earth is just as positive and direct as it was before,

Facts, religions, improvements, politics, trades, are
as real as before,

But the soul is also real, it too is positive and direct,
No reasoning, no proof has establish'd it,
Undeniable growth has establish'd it.

4

These to echo the tones of souls and the phrases of souls,
(If they did not echo the phrases of souls what were they then?
If they had not reference to you in especial what were they then?)

I swear I will never henceforth have to do with the faith that tells the best,
I will have to do only with that faith that leaves the best untold.

Say on, sayers! sing on, singers!
Delve! mould! pile the words of the earth!
Work on, age after age, nothing is to be lost,
It may have to wait long, but it will certainly come in use,
When the materials are all prepared and ready. the architects shall appear.

I swear to you the architects shall appear without fail,
I swear to you they will understand you and justify you,
The greatest among them shall be he who best knows you, and encloses all and is faithful to all,
He and the rest shall not forget you, they shall perceive that you are not an iota less than they,
You shall be fully glorified in them.

## *Youth, Day, Old Age and Night*

Youth, large, lusty, loving – youth full of grace, force, fascination,
Do you know that Old Age may come after you with equal grace, force, fascination?
Day full-blown and splendid – day of the immense sun, action, ambition, laughter,
The Night follows close with millions of suns, and sleep and restoring darkness.

# BIRDS OF PASSAGE

## *Song of the Universal*

I

Come said the Muse,
Sing me a song no poet yet has chanted,
Sing me the universal.

In this broad earth of ours,
Amid the measureless grossness and the slag,
Enclosed and safe within its central heart,
Nestles the seed perfection.

By every life a share or more or less,
None born but it is born, conceal'd or unconceal'd
the seed is waiting.

2

Lo! keen-eyed towering science,
As from tall peaks the modern overlooking,
Successive absolute fiats issuing.

Yet again, lo! the soul, above all science,
For it has history gather'd like husks around the globe,
For it the entire star-myriads roll through the sky.

In spiral routes by long detours,
(As a much-tacking ship upon the sea,)
For it the partial to the permanent flowing,
For it the real to the ideal tends.

For it the mystic evolution,
Not the right only justified, what we call evil also
justified.
Forth from their masks, no matter what,
From the huge festering trunk, from craft and guile
and tears,
Health to emerge and joy, joy universal.

Out of the bulk, the morbid and the shallow,
Out of the bad majority, the varied countless frauds
  of men and states,
Electric, antiseptic yet, cleaving, suffusing all,
Only the good is universal.

3

Over the mountain-growths disease and sorrow,
An uncaught bird is ever hovering, hovering,
High in the purer, happier air.

From imperfection's murkiest cloud,
Darts always forth one ray of perfect light,
One flash of heaven's glory.

To fashion's, custom's discord,
To the mad Babel-din, the deafening orgies,
Soothing each lull a strain is heard, just heard,
From some far shore the final chorus sounding.

O the blest eyes, the happy hearts,
That see, that know the guiding thread so fine,
Along the mighty labyrinth.

4

And thou America,
For the scheme's culmination, its thought and its
  reality,
For these (not for thyself) thou hast arrived.

Thou too surroundest all,
Embracing carrying welcoming all, thou too by
  pathways broad and new,
To the ideal tendest.

The measur'd faiths of other lands, the grandeurs of the
  past,

Are not for thee, but grandeurs of thine own,
Deific faiths and amplitudes, absorbing,
comprehending all,
All eligible to all.

All, all for immortality,
Love like the light silently wrapping all,
Nature's amelioration blessing all,
The blossoms, fruits of ages, orchards divine and
certain,
Forms, objects, growths, humanities, to spiritual
images ripening.

Give me O God to sing that thought,
Give me, give him or her I love this quenchless faith
In Thy ensemble, whatever else withheld withhold
not from us,
Belief in plan of Thee enclosed in Time and Space,
Health, peace, salvation universal.

Is it a dream?
Nay but the lack of it the dream,
And failing it life's lore and wealth a dream,
And all the world a dream.

## *Pioneers! O Pioneers!*

Come my tan-faced children,
Follow well in order, get your weapons ready,
Have you your pistols? have you your sharp-edged axes?
Pioneers! O pioneers!

For we cannot tarry here,
We must march my darlings, we must bear the
brunt of danger,

We the youthful sinewy races, all the rest on us depend,
Pioneers! O pioneers!

O you youths, Western youths,
So impatient, full of action, full of manly pride and friendship,
Plain I see you Western youths, see you tramping with the foremost,
Pioneers! O pioneers!

Have the elder races halted?
Do they droop and end their lesson, wearied over there beyond the seas?
We take up the task eternal, and the burden and the lesson,
Pioneers! O pioneers!

All the past we leave behind,
We debouch upon a newer mightier world, varied world,
Fresh and strong the world we seize, world of labor and the march,
Pioneers! O pioneers!

We detachments steady throwing,
Down the edges, through the passes, up the mountains steep,
Conquering, holding, daring, venturing as we go the unknown ways,
Pioneers! O pioneers!

We primeval forests felling,
We the rivers stemming, vexing we and piercing deep the mines within,
We the surface broad surveying, we the virgin soil upheaving,
Pioneers! O pioneers!

Colorado men are we,
From the peaks gigantic, from the great sierras and the high plateaus,
From the mine and from the gully, from the hunting trail we come,
Pioneers! O pioneers!

From Nebraska, from Arkansas,
Central inland race are we, from Missouri, with the continental blood intervein'd,
All the hands of comrades clasping, all the Southern, all the Northern,
Pioneers! O pioneers!

O resistless restless race!
O beloved race in all! O my breast aches with tender love for all!
O I mourn and yet exult, I am rapt with love for all,
Pioneers! O pioneers!

Raise the mighty mother mistress,
Waving high the delicate mistress, over all the starry mistress, (bend your heads all,)
Raise the fang'd and warlike mistress, stern, impassive, weapon'd mistress,
Pioneers! O pioneers!

See my children, resolute children,
By those swarms upon our rear we must never yield or falter,
Ages back in ghostly millions frowning there behind us urging,
Pioneers! O pioneers!

On and on the compact ranks,
With accessions ever waiting, with the places of the dead quickly fill'd,
Through the battle, through defeat, moving yet and never stopping,
Pioneers! O pioneers!

O to die advancing on!
Are there some of us to droop and die? has the hour come?
Then upon the march we fittest die, soon and sure the gap is fill'd,
Pioneers! O pioneers!

All the pulses of the world,
Falling in they beat for us, with the Western movement beat,
Holding single or together, steady moving to the front, all for us,
Pioneers! O pioneers!

Life's involv'd and varied pageants,
All the forms and shows, all the workmen at their work,
All the seamen and the landsmen, all the masters with their slaves,
Pioneers! O pioneers!

All the hapless silent lovers,
All the prisoners in the prisons, all the righteous and the wicked,
All the joyous, all the sorrowing, all the living, all the dying,
Pioneers! O pioneers!

I too with my soul and body,
We, a curious trio, picking, wandering on our way,

Through these shores amid the shadows, with the
  apparitions pressing,
Pioneers! O pioneers!

Lo, the darting bowling orb!
Lo, the brother orbs around, all the clustering suns
  and planets,
All the dazzling days, all the mystic nights with
  dreams,
Pioneers! O pioneers!

These are of us, they are with us,
All for primal needed work, while the followers there
  in embryo wait behind,
We to-day's procession heading, we the route for
  travel clearing,
Pioneers! O pioneers!

O you daughters of the West!
O you young and elder daughters! O you mothers
  and you wives!
Never must you be divided, in our ranks you move
  united,
Pioneers! O pioneers!

Minstrels latent on the prairies!
(Shrouded bards of other lands, you may rest, you
  have, done your work,)
Soon I hear you coming warbling, soon you rise and
  tramp amid us,
Pioneers! O pioneers!

Not for delectations sweet,
Not the cushion and the slipper, not the peaceful
  and the studious,

Not the riches safe and palling, not for us the tame
enjoyment,
Pioneers! O pioneers!

Do the feasters gluttonous feast?
Do the corpulent sleepers sleep? have they lock'd
and bolted doors?
Still be ours the diet hard, and the blanket on the
ground,
Pioneers! O pioneers!

Has the night descended?
Was the road of late so toilsome? did we stop
discouraged nodding on our way?
Yet a passing hour I yield you in your tracks to pause
oblivious,
Pioneers! O pioneers!

Till with sound of trumpet,
Far, far off the daybreak call – hark! how loud and
clear I hear it wind,
Swift! to the head of the army! – swift! spring to your
places,
Pioneers! O pioneers!

## *To You*

Whoever you are, I fear you are walking the walks of
dreams,
I fear these supposed realities are to melt from under
your feet and hands,
Even now your features, joys, speech, house, trade,
manners, troubles, follies, costume, crimes,
dissipate away from you,
Your true soul and body appear before me,

They stand forth out of affairs, out of commerce,
shops, work, farms, clothes, the house, buying,
selling, eating, drinking, suffering, dying.

Whoever you are, now I place my hand upon you,
that you be my poem,
I whisper with my lips close to your ear,
I have loved many women and men, but I love none
better than you.

O I have been dilatory and dumb,
I should have made my way straight to you long ago,
I should have blabb'd nothing but you, I should
have chanted nothing but you.

I will leave all and come and make the hymns of you,
None has understood you, but I understand you,
None has done justice to you, you have not done
justice to yourself,
None but has found you imperfect, I only find no
imperfection in you,
None but would subordinate you, I only am he who
will never consent to subordinate you,
I only am he who places over you no master, owner,
better, God, beyond what waits intrinsically in
yourself.

Painters have painted their swarming groups and the
centre-figure of all,
From the head of the centre-figure spreading a
nimbus of gold-color'd light,
But I paint myriads of heads, but paint no head
without its nimbus of gold color'd light,
From my hand from the brain of every man and
woman it streams, effulgently flowing forever.

O I could sing such grandeurs and glories about you!
You have not known what you are, you have
slumber'd upon yourself all your life,
Your eyelids have been the same as closed most of
the time,
What you have done returns already in mockeries,
(Your thrift, knowledge, prayers, if they do not
return in mockeries, what is their return?)

The mockeries are not you,
Underneath them and within them I see you lurk,
I pursue you where none else has pursued you,
Silence, the desk, the flippant expression, the night,
the accustom'd routine, if these conceal you
from others or from yourself, they do not conceal
you from me,
The shaved face, the unsteady eye, the impure
complexion, if these balk others they do not balk
me,
The pert apparel, the deform'd attitude, drunkenness,
greed, premature death, all these I part aside.

There is no endowment in man or woman that is
not tallied in you,
There is no virtue, no beauty in man or woman, but
as good is in you,
No pluck, no endurance in others, but as good is in you,
No pleasure waiting for others, but an equal pleasure
waits for you.

As for me, I give nothing to any one except I give the
like carefully to you,
I sing the songs of the glory of none, not God,
sooner than I sing the songs of the glory of you.

Whoever you are! claim your own at any hazard!
These shows of the East and West are tame
compared to you,
These immense meadows, these interminable rivers,
you are immense and interminable as they,
These furies, elements, storms, motions of Nature,
throes of apparent dissolution, you are he or she
who is master or mistress over them,
Master or mistress in your own right over Nature,
elements, pain, passion, dissolution.

The hopples fall from your ankles, you find an
unfailing sufficiency,
Old or young, male or female, rude, low, rejected by
the rest, whatever you are promulges itself,
Through birth, life, death, burial, the means are
provided, nothing is scanted,
Through angers, losses, ambition, ignorance, ennui,
what you are picks its way.

## *France:*
## *the 18th Year of these States*

A great year and place,
A harsh discordant natal scream out-sounding, to
  touch the mother's heart closer than any yet.

I walk'd the shores of my Eastern sea,
Heard over the waves the little voice,
Saw the divine infant where she woke mournfully
  wailing, amid the roar of cannon, curses, shouts,
  crush of falling buildings,
Was not so sick from the blood in the gutters
  running, nor from the single corpses, nor those
  in heaps, nor those borne away in the tumbrils,
Was not so desperate at the battues of death – was not
  so shock'd at the repeated fusillades of the guns.
Pale, silent, stern, what could I say to that
  long-accrued retribution?
Could I wish humanity different?
Could I wish the people made of wood and stone?
Or that there be no justice in destiny or time?

O liberty! O mate for me!
Here too the blaze, the grape-shot and the axe, in
  reserve, to fetch them out in case of need,
Here too, though long represt, can never be destroy'd,
Here too could rise at last murdering and ecstatic,
Here too demanding full arrears of vengeance.

Hence I sign this salute over the sea,
And I do not deny that terrible red birth and baptism,
But remember the little voice that I heard wailing,
  and wait with perfect trust, no matter how long,
And from to-day sad and cogent I maintain the
  bequeath'd cause, as for all lands,

And I send these words to Paris with my love,
And I guess some chansonniers there will
understand them,
For I guess there is latent music yet in France, floods
of it,
O I hear already the bustle of instruments, they will
soon be drowning all that would interrupt them,
O I think the east wind brings a triumphal and free
march,
It reaches hither, it swells me to joyful madness,
I will run transpose it in words, to justify it,
I will yet sing a song for you ma femme.

## *Myself and Mine*

Myself and mine gymnastic ever,
To stand the cold or heat, to make good aim with a
gun, to sail a boat, to manage horses, to beget
superb children,
To speak readily and clearly, to feel at home among
common people,
And to hold our own in terrible positions on land
and sea.

Not for an embroiderer,
(There will always be plenty of embroiderers, I
welcome them also,)
But for the fibre of things and for inherent men and
women.

Not to chisel ornaments,
But to chisel with free stroke the heads and limbs of
plenteous supreme Gods, that the States may
realize them walking and talking.

Let me have my own way,
Let others promulge the laws, I will make no
account of the laws,
Let others praise eminent men and hold up peace, I
hold up agitation and conflict,
I praise no eminent man, I rebuke to his face the one
that was thought most worthy.

(Who are you? and what are you secretly guilty of all
your life?
Will you turn aside all your life? will you grub and
chatter all your life?
And who are you, blabbing by rote, years, pages,
languages, reminiscences,
Unwitting to-day that you do not know how to
speak properly a single word?)

Let others finish specimens, I never finish specimens,
I start them by exhaustless laws as Nature does,
fresh and modern continually.

I give nothing as duties,
What others give as duties I give as living impulses,
(Shall I give the heart's action as a duty?)

Let others dispose of questions, I dispose of nothing,
I arouse unanswerable questions,
Who are they I see and touch, and what about them?
What about these likes of myself that draw me so
close by tender directions and indirections?

I call to the world to distrust the accounts of my
friends, but listen to my enemies, as I myself do,
I charge you forever reject those who would
expound me, for I cannot expound myself,

I charge that there be no theory or school founded
out of me,
I charge you to leave all free, as I have left all free.

After me, vista!
O I see life is not short, but immeasurably long,
I henceforth tread the world chaste, temperate, an
early riser, a steady grower,
Every hour the semen of centuries, and still of centuries.

I must follow up these continual lessons of the air,
water, earth,
I perceive I have no time to lose.

## *Year of Meteors (1859–60)*

Year of meteors! brooding year!
I would bind in words retrospective some of your
deeds and signs,
I would sing your contest for the 19th Presidentiad,
I would sing how an old man, tall, with white hair,
mounted the scaffold in Virginia,
(I was at hand, silent I stood with teeth shut close, I
watch'd,
I stood very near you old man when cool and
indifferent, but trembling with age and your
unheal'd wounds, you mounted the scaffold;)
I would sing in my copious song your census returns
of the States,
The tables of population and products, I would sing
of your ships and their cargoes,
The proud black ships of Manhattan arriving, some
fil'd with immigrants, some from the isthmus
with cargoes of gold,

Songs thereof would I sing, to all that hitherward
comes would I welcome give,
And you would I sing, fair stripling! welcome to you
from me, young prince of England!
(Remember you surging Manhattan's crowds as you
pass'd with your cortege of nobles?
There in the crowds stood I, and singled you out
with attachment;)
Nor forget I to sing of the wonder, the ship as she
swam up my bay,
Well-shaped and stately the Great Eastern swam up
my bay, she was 600 feet long,
Her moving swiftly surrounded by myriads of small
craft I forget not to sing;
Nor the comet that came unannounced out of the
north flaring in heaven,
Nor the strange huge meteor-procession dazzling
and clear shooting over our heads,
(A moment, a moment long it sail'd its balls of
unearthly light over our heads,
Then departed, dropt in the night, and was gone;)
Of such, and fitful as they, I sing – with gleams from
them would I gleam and patch these chants,
Your chants, O year all mottled with evil and good –
year of forebodings!
Year of comets and meteors transient and strange –
lo! even here one equally transient and strange!
As I flit through you hastily, soon to fall and be
gone, what is this chant,
What am I myself but one of your meteors?

## *With Antecedents*

### 1

With antecedents,
With my fathers and mothers and the accumulations
of past ages,
With all which, had it not been, I would not now be
here, as I am,
With Egypt, India, Phenicia, Greece and Rome,
With the Kelt, the Scandinavian, the Alb and the Saxon,
With antique maritime ventures, laws, artisanship,
wars and journeys,
With the poet, the skald, the saga, the myth, and the
oracle,
With the sale of slaves, with enthusiasts, with the
troubadour, the crusader, and the monk,
With those old continents whence we have come to
this new continent,
With the fading kingdoms and kings over there,
With the fading religions and priests,
With the small shores we look back to from our own
large and present shores,
With countless years drawing themselves onward
and arrived at these years,
You and me arrived – America arrived and making
this year,
This year! sending itself ahead countless years to come.

### 2

O but it is not the years – it is I, it is You,
We touch all laws and tally all antecedents,
We are the skald, the oracle, the monk and the
knight, we easily include them and more,

We stand amid time beginningless and endless, we
stand amid evil and good,
All swings around us, there is as much darkness as light,
The very sun swings itself and its system of planets
around us,
Its sun, and its again, all swing around us.

As for me, (torn, stormy, amid these vehement days,)
I have the idea of all, and am all and believe in all,
I believe materialism is true and spiritualism is true,
I reject no part.

(Have I forgotten any part? any thing in the past?
Come to me whoever and whatever, till I give you
recognition.)

I respect Assyria, China, Teutonia, and the Hebrews,
I adopt each theory, myth, god, and demi-god,
I see that the old accounts, bibles, genealogies, are
true, without exception,
I assert that all past days were what they must have
been,
And that they could no-how have been better than
they were,
And that to-day is what it must be, and that America is,
And that to-day and America could no-how be
better than they are.

3

In the name of these States and in your and my
name, the Past,
And in the name of these States and in your and my
name, the Present time.
I know that the past was great and the future will be
great,

And I know that both curiously conjoint in the
present time,
(For the sake of him I typify, for the common
average man's sake, your sake if you are he,)
And that where I am or you are this present day,
there is the centre of all days, all races,
And there is the meaning to us of all that has ever
come of races and days, or ever will come.

## *A Broadway Pageant*

### I

Over the Western sea hither from Niphon come,
Courteous, the swart-cheek'd two-sworded envoys,
Leaning back in their open barouches, bare-headed,
impassive,
Ride to-day through Manhattan.

Libertad! I do not know whether others behold what
I behold,
In the procession along with the nobles of Niphon,
the errand-bearers,
Bringing up the rear, hovering above, around, or in
the ranks marching,
But I will sing you a song of what I behold Libertad.
When million-footed Manhattan unpent descends to
her pavements,
When the thunder-cracking guns arouse me with the
proud roar I love,
When the round-mouth'd guns out of the smoke
and smell I love spit their salutes,

When the fire-flashing guns have fully alerted me,
 and heaven clouds canopy my city with a
 delicate thin haze,
When gorgeous the countless straight stems, the
 forests at the wharves, thicken with colors,
When every ship richly drest carries her flag at the peak,
When pennants trail and street-festoons hang from
 the windows,
When Broadway is entirely given up to foot-passengers
 and foot-standers, when the mass is densest,
When the façades of the houses are alive with people,
 when eyes gaze riveted tens of thousands at a time,
When the guests from the islands advance, when the
 pageant moves forward visible,
When the summons is made, when the answer that
 waited thousands of years answers,
I too arising, answering, descend to the pavements,
 merge with the crowd, and gaze with them.

2

Superb-faced Manhattan!
Comrade Americanos! to us, then at last the Orient
 comes.

To us, my city,
Where our tall-topt marble and iron beauties range
 on opposite sides, to walk in the space between,
To-day our Antipodes comes.

The Originatress comes,
The nest of languages, the bequeather of poems, the
 race of eld,
Florid with blood, pensive, rapt with musings, hot
 with passion,
Sultry with perfume, with ample and flowing garments,

With sunburnt visage, with intense soul and
 glittering eyes,
The race of Brahma comes.

See my cantabile! these and more are flashing to us
 from the procession,
As it moves changing, a kaleidoscope divine it moves
 changing before us.

For not the envoys nor the tann'd Japanee from his
 island only,
Lithe and silent the Hindoo appears, the Asiatic
 continent itself appears, the past, the dead,
The murky night-morning of wonder and fable
 inscrutable,
The envelop'd mysteries, the old and unknown
 hive-bees,
The north, the sweltering south, eastern Assyria, the
 Hebrews, the ancient of ancients,
Vast desolated cities, the gliding present, all of these
 and more are in the pageant-procession.

Geography, the world, is in it,
The Great Sea, the brood of islands, Polynesia, the
 coast beyond,
The coast you henceforth are facing – you, Libertad!
 from your Western golden shores,
The countries there with their populations, the
 millions enmasse are curiously here,
The swarming market-places, the temples with idols
 ranged along the sides or at the end, bonze,
 brahmin, and llama,
Mandarin, farmer, merchant, mechanic, and
 fisherman,
The singing-girl and the dancing-girl, the ecstatic
 persons, the secluded emperors,

Confucius himself, the great poets and heroes, the
warriors, the castes, all,
Trooping up, crowding from all directions, from the
Altay mountains,
From Thibet, from the four winding and far-flowing
rivers of China,
From the southern peninsulas and the demi-
continental islands, from Malaysia,
These and whatever belongs to them palpable show
forth to me, and are seiz'd by me,
And I am seiz'd by them, and friendlily held by them,
Till as here them all I chant, Libertad! for
themselves and for you.

For I too raising my voice join the ranks of this pageant,
I am the chanter, I chant aloud over the pageant,
I chant the world on my Western sea,
I chant copious the islands beyond, thick as stars in
the sky,
I chant the new empire grander than any before, as
in a vision it comes to me,
I chant America the mistress, I chant a greater
supremacy,
I chant projected a thousand blooming cities yet in
time on those groups of sea-islands,
My sail-ships and steam-ships threading the
archipelagoes,
My stars and stripes fluttering in the wind,
Commerce opening, the sleep of ages having done
its work, races reborn, refresh'd,
Lives, works resumed – the object I know not – but
the old, the Asiatic renew'd as it must be,
Commencing from this day surrounded by the world.

3

And you Libertad of the world!
You shall sit in the middle well-pois'd thousands
and thousands of years,
As to-day from one side the nobles of Asia come to you,
As to-morrow from the other side the queen of
England sends her eldest son to you.

The sign is reversing, the orb is enclosed,
The ring is circled, the journey is done,
The box-lid is but perceptibly open'd, nevertheless the
perfume pours copiously out of the whole box.

Young Libertad! with the venerable Asia, the all-
mother,
Be considerate with her now and ever hot Libertad,
for you are all,
Bend your proud neck to the long-off mother now
sending messages over the archipelagoes to you,
Bend your proud neck low for once, young Libertad.

Were the children straying westward so long? so
wide the tramping?
Were the precedent dim ages debouching westward
from Paradise so long?
Were the centuries steadily footing it that way, all
the while unknown, for you, for reasons?

They are justified, they are accomplish'd, they shall
now be turn'd the other way also, to travel
toward you thence,
They shall now also march obediently eastward for
your sake Libertad.

# SEA-DRIFT

## *Out of the Cradle Endlessly Rocking*

Out of the cradle endlessly rocking,
Out of the mocking-bird's throat, the musical shuttle,
Out of the Ninth-month midnight,
Over the sterile sands and the fields beyond, where
 the child leaving his bed wander'd alone,
 bareheaded, barefoot,
Down from the shower'd halo,
Up from the mystic play of shadows twining and
 twisting as if they were alive,
Out from the patches of briers and blackberries,
From the memories of the bird that chanted to me,
From your memories sad brother, from the fitful
 risings and fallings I heard,
From under that yellow half-moon late-risen and
 swollen as if with tears,
From those beginning notes of yearning and love
 there in the mist,
From the thousand responses of my heart never to
 cease,
From the myriad thence-arous'd words,
From the word stronger and more delicious than any,
From such as now they start the scene revisiting,
As a flock, twittering, rising, or overhead passing,
Borne hither, ere all eludes me, hurriedly,
A man, yet by these tears a little boy again,
Throwing myself on the sand, confronting the waves,
I, chanter of pains and joys, uniter of her and hereafter,
Taking all hints to use them, but swiftly leaping
 beyond them,
A reminiscence sing.

Once Paumanok,
When the lilac-scent was in the air and Fifth-month
grass was growing,
Up this seashore in some briers,
Two feather'd guests from Alabama, two together,
And their nest, and four light-green eggs spotted
with brown,
And every day the he-bird to and fro near at hand,
And every day the she-bird crouch'd on her nest,
silent, with bright eyes,
And every day I, a curious boy, never too close,
never disturbing them,
Cautiously peering, absorbing, translating.

*Shine! shine! shine!*
*Pour down your warmth, great sun!*
*While we bask, we two together.*

*Two together!*
*Winds blow south, or winds blow north,*
*Day come white, or night come black,*
*Home, or rivers and mountains from home,*
*Singing all time, minding no time,*
*While we two keep together.*

Till of a sudden,
May-be kill'd, unknown to her mate,
One forenoon the she-bird crouch'd not on the nest,
Nor return'd that afternoon, nor the next,
Nor ever appear'd again.

And thenceforward all summer in the sound of the sea,
And at night under the full of the moon in calmer
weather,
Over the hoarse surging of the sea,
Or flitting from brier to brier by day,

I saw, I heard at intervals the remaining one, the
    he-bird,
The solitary guest from Alabama.

*Blow! blow! blow!*
*Blow up sea-winds along Paumanok's shore;*
*I wait and I wait till you blow my mate to me.*

Yes, when the stars glisten'd,
All night long on the prong of a moss-scallop'd stake,
Down almost amid the slapping waves,
Sat the lone singer wonderful causing tears.

He call'd on his mate,
He pour'd forth the meanings which I of all men know.

Yes my brother I know,
The rest might not, but I have treasur'd every note,
For more than once dimly down to the beach gliding,
Silent, avoiding the moonbeams, blending myself
    with the shadows,
Recalling now the obscure shapes, the echoes, the
    sounds and sights after their sorts,
The white arms out in the breakers tirelessly tossing,
I, with bare feet, a child, the wind wafting my hair,
Listen'd long and long.

Listen'd to keep, to sing, now translating the notes,
Following you my brother.

*Soothe! soothe! soothe!*
*Close on its wave soothes the wave behind,*
*And again another behind embracing and lapping, every*
    *one close,*
*But my love soothes not me, not me.*

*Low hangs the moon, it rose late,*
*It is lagging – O I think it is heavy with love, with love.*

*O madly the sea pushes upon the land,*
*With love, with love.*

*O night! do I not see my love fluttering out among the breakers?*
*What is that little black thing I see there in the white?*

*Loud! loud! loud!*
*Loud I call to you, my love!*
*High and clear I shoot my voice over the waves,*
*Surely you must know who is here, is here,*
*You must know who I am, my love.*

*Low-hanging moon!*
*What is that dusky spot in your brown yellow?*
*O it is the shape, the shape of my mate!*
*O moon do not keep her from me any longer.*

*Land! land! O land!*
*Whichever way I turn, O I think you could give me my mate back again if you only would,*
*For I am almost sure I see her dimly whichever way I look.*

*O rising stars!*
*Perhaps the one I want so much will rise, will rise with some of you.*

*O throat! O trembling throat!*
*Sound clearer through the atmosphere!*
*Pierce the woods, the earth,*
*Somewhere listening to catch you must be the one I want.*

*Shake out carols!*
*Solitary here, the night's carols!*
*Carols of lonesome love! death's carols!*

*Carols under that lagging, yellow, waning moon!*
*O under that moon where she droops almost down into the sea!*
*O reckless despairing carols.*

*But soft! sink low!*
*Soft! let me just murmur,*
*And do you wait a moment you husky-nois'd sea,*
*For somewhere I believe I heard my mate responding to me,*
*So faint, I must be still, be still to listen,*
*But not altogether still, for then she might not come immediately to me.*

*Hither my love!*
*Here I am! here!*
*With this just-sustain'd note I announce myself to you,*
*This gentle call is for you my love, for you.*

*Do not be decoy'd elsewhere,*
*That is the whistle of the wind, it is not my voice,*
*That is the fluttering, the fluttering of the spray,*
*Those are the shadows of leaves.*

*O darkness! O in vain!*
*O I am very sick and sorrowful.*

*O brown halo in the sky near the moon, drooping upon the sea!*
*O troubled reflection in the sea!*
*O throat! O throbbing heart!*
*And I singing uselessly, uselessly all the night.*

*O past! O happy life! O songs of joy!*
*In the air, in the woods, over fields,*
*Loved! loved! loved! loved! loved!*
*But my mate no more, no more with me!*
*We two together no more.*

The aria sinking,
All else continuing, the stars shining,
The winds blowing, the notes of the bird continuous echoing,
With angry moans the fierce old mother incessantly moaning,
On the sands of Paumanok's shore gray and rustling,
The yellow half-moon enlarged, sagging down, drooping, the face of the sea almost touching,
The boy ecstatic, with his bare feet the waves, with his hair the atmosphere dallying,
The love in the heart long pent, now loose, now at last tumultuously bursting,
The aria's meaning, the ears, the soul, swiftly depositing,
The strange tears down the cheeks coursing,
The colloquy there, the trio, each uttering,
The undertone, the savage old mother incessantly crying,
To the boy's soul's questions sullenly timing, some drown'd secret hissing.
To the outsetting bard.

Demon or bird! (said the boy's soul,)
Is it indeed toward your mate you sing? or is it really to me?
For I, that was a child, my tongue's use sleeping, now I have heard you,
Now in a moment I know what I am for, I awake,
And already a thousand singers, a thousand songs, clearer, louder and more sorrowful than yours,
A thousand warbling echoes have started to life within me, never to die.

O you singer solitary, singing by yourself, projecting me,

O solitary me listening, never more shall I cease
perpetuating you,
Never more shall I escape, never more the
reverberations,
Never more the cries of unsatisfied love be absent
from me,
Never again leave me to be the peaceful child I was
before what there in the night,
By the sea under the yellow and sagging moon,
The messenger there arous'd, the fire, the sweet hell
within,
The unknown want, the destiny of me.

O give me the clew! (it lurks in the night here
somewhere,)
O if I am to have so much, let me have more!

A word then, (for I will conquer it,)
The word final, superior to all,
Subtle, sent up – what is it? – I listen;
Are you whispering it, and have been all the time,
you sea waves?
Is that it from your liquid rims and wet sands?
Whereto answering, the sea,
Delaying not, hurrying not,
Whisper'd me through the night, and very plainly
before daybreak,
Lisp'd to me the low and delicious word death,
And again death, death, death, death,
Hissing melodious, neither like the bird nor like my
arous'd child's heart,
But edging near as privately for me rustling at my feet,
Creeping thence steadily up to my ears and laving
me softly all over,
Death, death, death, death, death.

Which I do not forget,
But fuse the song of my dusky demon and brother,
That he sang to me in the moonlight on Paumanok's gray beach,
With the thousand responsive songs at random,
My own songs awaked from that hour,
And with them the key, the word up from the waves,
The word of the sweetest song and all songs,
That strong and delicious word which, creeping to my feet,
(Or like some old crone rocking the cradle, swathed in sweet garments, bending aside,)
The sea whisper'd me.

## *As I Ebb'd with the Ocean of Life*

### 1

As I ebb'd with the ocean of life,
As I wended the shores I know,
As I walk'd where the ripples continually wash you Paumanok,
Where they rustle up hoarse and sibilant,
Where the fierce old mother endlessly cries for her castaways,
I musing late in the autumn day, gazing off southward,
Held by this electric self out of the pride of which I utter poems,
Was seiz'd by the spirit that trails in the lines underfoot,
The rim, the sediment that stands for all the water and all the land of the globe.

Fascinated, my eyes reverting from the south, dropt, to follow those slender windrows,

Chaff, straw, splinters of wood, weeds, and the
sea-gluten,
Scum, scales from shining rocks, leaves of
salt-lettuce, left by the tide,
Miles walking, the sound of breaking waves the
other side of me,
Paumanok there and then as I thought the old
thought of likenesses,
These you presented to me you fish-shaped island,
As I wended the shores I know,
As I walk'd with that electric self seeking types.

2

As I wend to the shores I know not,
As I list to the dirge, the voices of men and women
wreck'd,
As I inhale the impalpable breezes that set in upon me,
As the ocean so mysterious rolls toward me closer
and closer,
I too but signify at the utmost a little wash'd-up drift,
A few sands and dead leaves to gather,
Gather, and merge myself as part of the sands and drift.

O baffled, balk'd, bent to the very earth,
Oppress'd with myself that I have dared to open my
mouth,
Aware now that amid all that blab whose echoes
recoil upon me I have not once had the least idea
who or what I am,
But that before all my arrogant poems the real Me
stands yet touch'd, untold, altogether unreach'd,
Withdrawn far, mocking me with
mock-congratulatory signs and bows,

With peals of distant ironical laughter at every word
I have written,
Pointing in silence to these songs, and then to the
sand beneath.
I perceive I have not really understood any thing,
not a single object, and that no man ever can,
Nature here in sight of the sea taking advantage of
me to dart upon me and sting me,
Because I have dared to open my mouth to sing at all.

3

You oceans both, I close with you,
We murmur alike reproachfully rolling sands and
drift, knowing not why,
These little shreds indeed standing for you and me
and all.
You friable shore with trails of debris,
You fish-shaped island, I take what is underfoot,
What is yours is mine my father.

I too Paumanok,
I too have bubbled up, floated the measureless float,
and been wash'd on your shores,
I too am but a trail of drift and debris,
I too leave little wrecks upon you, you fish-shaped
island.

I throw myself upon your breast my father,
I cling to you so that you cannot unloose me,
I hold you so firm till you answer me something.

Kiss me my father,
Touch me with your lips as I touch those I love,
Breathe to me while I hold you close the secret of
the murmuring I envy.

4

Ebb, ocean of life, (the flow will return,)
Cease not your moaning you fierce old mother,
Endlessly cry for your castaways, but fear not, deny
not me,
Rustle not up so hoarse and angry against my feet as
I touch you or gather from you.

I mean tenderly by you and all,
I gather for myself and for this phantom looking down
where we lead, and following me and mine.

Me and mine, loose windrows, little corpses,
Froth, snowy white, and bubbles,
(See, from my dead lips the ooze exuding at last,
See, the prismatic colors glistening and rolling,)
Tufts of straw, sands, fragments,
Buoy'd hither from many moods, one contradicting
another,
From the storm, the long calm, the darkness, the swell,
Musing, pondering, a breath, a briny tear, a dab of
liquid or soil,
Up just as much out of fathomless workings
fermented and thrown,
A limp blossom or two, torn, just as much over
waves floating, drifted at random,
Just as much for us that sobbing dirge of Nature,
Just as much whence we come that blare of the
cloud-trumpets,
We, capricious, brought hither we know not whence,
spread out before you,
You up there walking or sitting,
Whoever you are, we too lie in drifts at your feet.

*Tears*

Tears! tears! tears!
In the night, in solitude, tears,
On the white shore dripping, dripping, suck'd in by the sand,
Tears, not a star shining, all dark and desolate,
Moist tears from the eyes of a muffled head;
O who is that ghost? that form in the dark, with tears?
What shapeless lump is that, bent, crouch'd there on the sand?
Streaming tears, sobbing tears, throes, choked with wild cries;
O storm, embodied, rising, careering with swift steps along the beach!
O wild and dismal night storm, with wind – O belching and desperate!
O shade so sedate and decorous by day, with calm countenance and regulated pace,
But away at night as you fly, none looking – O then the unloosen'd ocean,
Of tears! tears! tears!

## *To the Man-of-War-Bird*

Thou who hast slept all night upon the storm,
Waking renew'd on thy prodigious pinions,
(Burst the wild storm? above it thou ascended'st,
And rested on the sky, thy slave that cradled thee,)
Now a blue point, far, far in heaven floating,
As to the light emerging here on deck I watch thee,
(Myself a speck, a point on the world's floating vast.)
Far, far at sea,
After the night's fierce drifts have strewn the shore
 with wrecks,
With re-appearing day as now so happy and serene,
The rosy and elastic dawn, the flashing sun,
The limpid spread of air cerulean,
Thou also re-appearest.

Thou born to match the gale, (thou art all wings,)
To cope with heaven and earth and sea and hurricane,
Thou ship of air that never furl'st thy sails,
Days, even weeks untired and onward, through
 spaces, realms gyrating,
At dusk that look'st on Senegal, at morn America,
That sport'st amid the lightning-flash and
 thunder-cloud,
In them, in thy experiences, had'st thou my soul,
What joys! what joys were thine!

## *Aboard at a Ship's Helm*

Aboard at a ship's helm,
A young steersman steering with care.

Through fog on a sea-coast dolefully ringing,
An ocean-bell – O a warning bell, rock'd by the waves.

O you give good notice indeed, you bell by the sea-reefs ringing,
Ringing, ringing, to warn the ship from its wreck-place.

For as on the alert O steersman, you mind the loud admonition,
The bows turn, the freighted ship tacking speeds away under her gray sails,
The beautiful and noble ship with all her precious wealth speeds away gayly and safe.

But O the ship, the immortal ship! O ship aboard the ship!
Ship of the body, ship of the soul, voyaging, voyaging, voyaging.

## *On the Beach at Night*

On the beach at night,
Stands a child with her father,
Watching the east, the autumn sky.

Up through the darkness,
While ravening clouds, the burial clouds, in black masses spreading,
Lower sullen and fast athwart and down the sky,
Amid a transparent clear belt of ether yet left in the east,
Ascends large and calm the lord-star Jupiter,
And nigh at hand, only a very little above,
Swim the delicate sisters the Pleiades.

From the beach the child holding the hand of her father,
Those burial clouds that lower victorious soon to devour all,
Watching, silently weeps.

Weep not, child,
Weep not, my darling,
With these kisses let me remove your tears,
The ravening clouds shall not long be victorious,
They shall not long possess the sky, they devour the
    stars only in apparition,
Jupiter shall emerge, be patient, watch again another
    night, the Pleiades shall emerge,
They are immortal, all those stars both silvery and
    golden shall shine out again,
The great stars and the little ones shall shine out
    again, they endure,
The vast immortal suns and the long-enduring
    pensive moons shall again shine.

Then dearest child mournest thou only for Jupiter?
Considerest thou alone the burial of the stars?

Something there is,
(With my lips soothing thee, adding I whisper,
I give thee the first suggestion, the problem and
    indirection,)
Something there is more immortal even than the stars,
(Many the burials, many the days and nights,
    passing away,)
Something that shall endure longer even than
    lustrous Jupiter,
Longer than sun or any revolving satellite,
Or the radiant sisters the Pleiades.

## *The World Below the Brine*

The world below the brine,
Forests at the bottom of the sea, the branches and
 leaves,
Sea-lettuce, vast lichens, strange flowers and seeds,
 the thick tangle, openings, and pink turf,
Different colors, pale gray and green, purple, white,
 and gold, the play of light through the water,
Dumb swimmers there among the rocks, coral, gluten,
 grass, rushes, and the aliment of the swimmers,
Sluggish existences grazing there suspended, or
 slowly crawling close to the bottom,
The sperm-whale at the surface blowing air and
 spray, or disporting with his flukes,
The leaden-eyed shark, the walrus, the turtle, the
 hairy sea-leopard, and the sting-ray,
Passions there, wars, pursuits, tribes, sight in those
 oceandepths, breathing that thick-breathing air,
 as so many do,
The change thence to the sight here, and to the subtle
 air breathed by beings like us who walk this sphere,
The change onward from ours to that of beings who
 walk other spheres.

## *On the Beach at Night Alone*

On the beach at night alone,
As the old mother sways her to and fro singing her
 husky song,
As I watch the bright stars shining, I think a thought
 of the clef of the universes and of the future.

A vast similitude interlocks all,
All spheres, grown, ungrown, small, large, suns,
moons, planets,
All distances of place however wide,
All distances of time, all inanimate forms,
All souls, all living bodies though they be ever so
different, or in different worlds,
All gaseous, watery, vegetable, mineral processes,
the fishes, the brutes,
All nations, colors, barbarisms, civilizations,
languages,
All identities that have existed or may exist on this
globe, or any globe,
All lives and deaths, all of the past, present, future,
This vast similitude spans them, and always has
spann'd,
And shall forever span them and compactly hold and
enclose them.

## *Song for All Seas, All Ships*

### I

To-day a rude brief recitative,
Of ships sailing the seas, each with its special flag or
ship-signal,
Of unnamed heroes in the ships – of waves
spreading and spreading far as the eye can reach,
Of dashing spray, and the winds piping and blowing,
And out of these a chant for the sailors of all nations,
Fitful, like a surge.

Of sea-captains young or old, and the mates, and of
all intrepid sailors,

Of the few, very choice, taciturn, whom fate can never surprise nor death dismay,
Pick'd sparingly without noise by thee old ocean, chosen by thee,
Thou sea that pickest and cullest the race in time, and unitest nations,
Suckled by thee, old husky nurse, embodying thee,
Indomitable, untamed as thee.
(Ever the heroes on water or on land, by ones or twos appearing,
Ever the stock preserv'd and never lost, though rare, enough for seed preserv'd.)

2

Flaunt out O sea your separate flags of nations!
Flaunt out visible as ever the various ship-signals!
But do you reserve especially for yourself and for the soul of man one flag above all the rest,
A spiritual woven signal for all nations, emblem of man elate above death,
Token of all brave captains and all intrepid sailors and mates,
And all that went down doing their duty,
Reminiscent of them, twined from all intrepid captains young or old,
A pennant universal, subtly waving all time, o'er all brave sailors,
All seas, all ships.

## *Patroling Barnegat*

Wild, wild the storm, and the sea high running,
Steady the roar of the gale, with incessant undertone muttering,
Shouts of demoniac laughter fitfully piercing and pealing,
Waves, air, midnight, their savagest trinity lashing,
Out in the shadows there milk-white combs careering,
On beachy slush and sand spirts of snow fierce slanting,
Where through the murk the easterly death-wind breasting,
Through cutting swirl and spray watchful and firm advancing,
(That in the distance! is that a wreck? is the red signal flaring?)
Slush and sand of the beach tireless till daylight wending,
Steadily, slowly, through hoarse roar never remitting,
Along the midnight edge by those milk-white combs careering,
A group of dim, weird forms, struggling, the night confronting,
That savage trinity warily watching.

## *After the Sea-Ship*

After the sea-ship, after the whistling winds,
After the white-gray sails taut to their spars and ropes,
Below, a myriad myriad waves hastening, lifting up their necks,
Tending in ceaseless flow toward the track of the ship,
Waves of the ocean bubbling and gurgling, blithely prying,

Waves, undulating waves, liquid, uneven, emulous
    waves,
Toward that whirling current, laughing and
    buoyant, with curves,
Where the great vessel sailing and tacking displaced
    the surface,
Larger and smaller waves in the spread of the ocean
    yearnfully flowing,
The wake of the sea-ship after she passes, flashing
    and frolicsome under the sun,
A motley procession with many a fleck of foam and
    many fragments,
Following the stately and rapid ship, in the wake
    following.

# BY THE ROADSIDE

## *A Boston Ballad (1854)*

To get betimes in Boston town I rose this morning early,
Here's a good place at the corner, I must stand and see the show.

Clear the way there Jonathan!
Way for the President's marshal – way for the government cannon!
Way for the Federal foot and dragoons, (and the apparitions copiously tumbling.)

I love to look on the Stars and Stripes, I hope the fifes will play Yankee Doodle.

How bright shine the cutlasses of the foremost troops!
Every man holds his revolver, marching stiff through Boston town.

A fog follows, antiques of the same come limping,
Some appear wooden-legged, and some appear bandaged and bloodless.

Why this is indeed a show – it has called the dead out of the earth!
The old graveyards of the hills have hurried to see!
Phantoms! phantoms countless by flank and rear!
Cock'd hats of mothy mould – crutches made of mist!
Arms in slings – old men leaning on young men's shoulders.

What troubles you Yankee phantoms? what is all this chattering of bare gums?
Does the ague convulse your limbs? do you mistake your crutches for firelocks and level them?

If you blind your eyes with tears you will not see the President's marshal,

If you groan such groans you might balk the
government cannon.
For shame old maniacs – bring down those toss'd
arms, and let your white hair be,
Here gape your great-grandsons, their wives gaze at
them from the windows,
See how well dress'd, see how orderly they conduct
themselves.

Worse and worse – can't you stand it? are you
retreating?
Is this hour with the living too dead for you?

Retreat then – pell-mell!
To your graves – back – back to the hills old limpers!
I do not think you belong here anyhow.

But there is one thing that belongs here – shall I tell
you what it is, gentlemen of Boston?

I will whisper it to the Mayor, he shall send a
committee to England,
They shall get a grant from the Parliament, go with a
cart to the royal vault,
Dig out King George's coffin, unwrap him quick from
the grave-clothes, box up his bones for a journey,
Find a swift Yankee clipper – here is freight for you,
black-bellied clipper,
Up with your anchor – shake out your sails – steer
straight toward Boston bay.

Now call for the President's marshal again, bring out
the government cannon,
Fetch home the roarers from Congress, make another
procession, guard it with foot and dragoons.

This centre-piece for them;
Look, all orderly citizens – look from the windows,
women!
The committee open the box, set up the regal ribs,
glue those that will not stay,
Clap the skull on top of the ribs, and clap a crown
on top of the skull.

You have got your revenge, old buster – the crown is
come to its own, and more than its own.

Stick your hands in your pockets, Jonathan – you are
a made man from this day,
You are mighty cute – and here is one of your bargains.

## *Europe: the 72nd and 73rd Years of These States*

Suddenly out of its stale and drowsy lair, the lair of slaves,
Like lightning it le'pt forth half startled at itself,
Its feet upon the ashes and the rags, its hand tight to the throats of kings.

O hope and faith!
O aching close of exiled patriots' lives!
O many a sicken'd heart!
Turn back unto this day and make yourselves afresh.

And you, paid to defile the People – you hars, mark!
Not for numberless agonies, murders, lusts,
For court thieving in its manifold mean forms, worming from his simplicity the poor man's wages,
For many a promise sworn by royal lips and broken and laugh'd at in the breaking,
Then in their power not for all these did the blows strike revenge, or the heads of the nobles fall;
The People scorn'd the ferocity of kings.

But the sweetness of mercy brew'd bitter destruction, and the frighten'd monarchs come back,
Each comes in state with his train, hangman, priest, taxgatherer,
Soldier, lawyer, lord, jailer, and sycophant.

Yet behind all lowering stealing, lo, a shape,
Vague as the night, draped interminably, head, front and form, in scarlet folds,
Whose face and eyes none may see,
Out of its robes only this, the red robes lifted by the arm,

One finger crook'd pointed high over the top, like
the head of a snake appears.

Meanwhile corpses lie in new-made graves, bloody
corpses of young men,
The rope of the gibbet hangs heavily, the bullets of
princes are flying, the creatures of power laugh
aloud,
And all these things bear fruits, and they are good.

Those corpses of young men,
Those martyrs that hang from the gibbets, those
hearts pierc'd by the gray lead,
Cold and motionless as they seem live elsewhere
with unslaughter'd vitality.

They live in other young men O kings!
They live in brothers again ready to defy you,
They were purified by death, they were taught and
exalted.

Not a grave of the murder'd for freedom but grows
seed for freedom, in its turn to bear seed,
Which the winds carry afar and re-sow, and the rains
and the snows nourish.

Not a disembodied spirit can the weapons of tyrants
let loose,
But it stalks invisibly over the earth, whispering,
counseling, cautioning.
Liberty, let others despair of you – I never despair of
you.
Is the house shut? is the master away?
Nevertheless, be ready, be not weary of watching,
He will soon return, his messengers come anon.

## *A Hand-Mirror*

Hold it up sternly – see this it sends back, (who is it?
is it you?)
Outside fair costume, within ashes and filth,
No more a flashing eye, no more a sonorous voice or
springy step,
Now some slave's eye, voice, hands, step,
A drunkard's breath, unwholesome eater's face,
venerealee's flesh,
Lungs rotting away piecemeal, stomach sour and
cankerous,
Joints rheumatic, bowels clogged with abomination,
Blood circulating dark and poisonous streams,
Words babble, hearing and touch callous,
No brain, no heart left, no magnetism of sex;
Such from one look in this looking-glass ere you go
hence,
Such a result so soon – and from such a beginning!

## *Gods*

Lover divine and perfect Comrade,
Waiting content, invisible yet, but certain,
Be thou my God.

Thou, thou, the Ideal Man,
Fair, able, beautiful, content, and loving,
Complete in body and dilate in spirit,
Be thou my God.

O Death, (for Life has served its turn,)
Opener and usher to the heavenly mansion,
Be thou my God.

Aught, aught of mightiest, best I see, conceive, or know,
(To break the stagnant tie – thee, thee to free, O soul,)
Be thou my God.

All great ideas, the races' aspirations,
All heroisms, deeds of rapt enthusiasts,
Be ye my Gods.

Or Time and Space,
Or shape of Earth divine and wondrous,
Or some fair shape I viewing, worship,
Or lustrous orb of sun or star by night,
Be ye my Gods.

## *Germs*

Forms, qualities, lives, humanity, language, thoughts,
The ones known, and the ones unknown, the ones
 on the stars,
The stars themselves, some shaped, others unshaped,
Wonders as of those countries, the soil, trees, cities,
 inhabitants, whatever they may be,
Splendid suns, the moons and rings, the countless
 combinations and effects,
Such-like, and as good as such-like, visible here or
 anywhere, stand provided for in a handful of
 space, which I extend my arm and half enclose
 with my hand,
That containing the start of each and all, the virtue,
 the germs of all.

## *Thoughts*

Of ownership – as if one fit to own things could not at pleasure enter upon all, and incorporate them into himself or herself;
Of vista – suppose some sight in arriere through the formative chaos, presuming the growth, fulness, life, now attain'd on the journey,
(But I see the road continued, and the journey ever continued;)
Of what was once lacking on earth, and in due time has become supplied – and of what will yet be supplied,
Because all I see and know I believe to have its main purport in what will yet be supplied.

## *When I Heard the Learn'd Astronomer*

When I heard the learn'd astronomer,
When the proofs, the figures, were ranged in columns before me,
When I was shown the charts and diagrams, to add, divide, and measure them,
When I sitting heard the astronomer where he lectured with much applause in the lecture-room,
How soon unaccountable I became tired and sick,
Till rising and gliding out I wander'd off by myself,
In the mystical moist night-air, and from time to time,
Look'd up in perfect silence at the stars.

## *Perfections*

Only themselves understand themselves and the like of themselves,
As souls only understand souls.

## *O Me! O Life!*

O me! O life! of the questions of these recurring,
Of the endless trains of the faithless, of cities fill'd
with the foolish,
Of myself forever reproaching myself, (for who more
foolish than I, and who more faithless?)
Of eyes that vainly crave the light, of the objects
mean, of the struggle ever renew'd,
Of the poor results of all, of the plodding and sordid
crowds I see around me,
Of the empty and useless years of the rest, with the
rest me intertwined,
The question, O me! so sad, recurring – What good
amid these, O me, O life?

*Answer*

That you are here – that life exists and identity,
That the powerful play goes on, and you may
contribute a verse.

## *To a President*

All you are doing and saying is to America dangled
mirages,
You have not learn'd of Nature – of the politics of
Nature you have not learn'd the great amplitude,
rectitude, impartiality,
You have not seen that only such as they are for
these States,
And that what is less than they must sooner or later
lift off from these States.

## *I Sit and Look Out*

I sit and look out upon all the sorrows of the world,
 and upon all oppression and shame,
I hear secret convulsive sobs from young men at anguish
 with themselves, remorseful after deeds done,
I see in low life the mother misused by her children,
 dying, neglected, gaunt, desperate,
I see the wife misused by her husband, I see the
 treacherous seducer of young women,
I mark the ranklings of jealousy and unrequited love
 attempted to be hid, I see these sights on the earth,
I see the workings of battle, pestilence, tyranny, I see
 martyrs and prisoners,
I observe a famine at sea, I observe the sailors
 casting lots who shall be kill'd to preserve the
 lives of the rest,
I observe the slights and degradations cast by
 arrogant persons upon laborers, the poor, and
 upon negroes, and the like;
All these – all the meanness and agony without end I
 sitting look out upon,
See, hear, and am silent.

## *To Rich Givers*

What you give me I cheerfully accept,
A little sustenance, a hut and garden, a little money, as I rendezvous with my poems,
A traveler's lodging and breakfast as I journey through the States, – why should I be ashamed to own such gifts? why to advertise for them?
For I myself am not one who bestows nothing upon man and woman,
For I bestow upon any man or woman the entrance to all the gifts of the universe.

## *The Dalliance of the Eagles*

Skirting the river road, (my forenoon walk, my rest,)
Skyward in air a sudden muffled sound, the dalliance of the eagles,
The rushing amorous contact high in space together,
The clinching interlocking claws, a living, fierce, gyrating wheel,
Four beating wings, two beaks, a swirling mass tight grappling,
In tumbling turning clustering loops, straight downward falling,
Till o'er the river pois'd, the twain yet one, a moment's lull,
A motionless still balance in the air, then parting, talons loosing,
Upward again on slow-firm pinions slanting, their separate diverse flight,
She hers, he his, pursuing.

## *Roaming in Thought*

(*After reading* Hegel)

Roaming in thought over the Universe, I saw the little that is Good steadily hastening towards immortality,
And the vast all that is call'd Evil I saw hastening to merge itself and become lost and dead.

## *A Farm Picture*

Through the ample open door of the peaceful country barn,
A sunlit pasture field with cattle and horses feeding,
And haze and vista, and the far horizon fading away.

## *A Child's Amaze*

Silent and amazed even when a little boy,
I remember I heard the preacher every Sunday put God in his statements,
As contending against some being or influence.

## *The Runner*

On a flat road runs the well-train'd runner,
He is lean and sinewy with muscular legs,
He is thinly clothed, he leans forward as he runs,
With lightly closed fists and arms partially rais'd.

## *Beautiful Women*

Women sit or move to and fro, some old, some young,
The young are beautiful – but the old are more
    beautiful than the young.

## *Mother and Babe*

I see the sleeping babe nestling the breast of its mother,
The sleeping mother and babe – hush'd, I study
    them long and long.

## *Thought*

Of obedience, faith, adhesiveness;
As I stand aloof and look there is to me something
    profoundly affecting in large masses of men
    following the lead of those who do not believe in
    men.

## *Visor'd*

A mask, a perpetual natural disguiser of herself,
Concealing her face, concealing her form,
Changes and transformations every hour, every
    moment,
Falling upon her even when she sleeps.

## *Thought*

Of Justice – as if Justice could be any thing but the same ample law, expounded by natural judges and saviors,
As if it might be this thing or that thing, according to decisions.

## *Gliding o'er All*

Gliding o'er all, through all,
Through Nature, Time, and Space,
As a ship on the waters advancing,
The voyage of the soul – not life alone,
Death, many deaths I'll sing.

## *Hast Never Come to Thee an Hour*

Hast never come to thee an hour,
A sudden gleam divine, precipitating, bursting all these bubbles, fashions, wealth?
These eager business aims – books, politics, art, amours,
To utter nothingness?

## *Thought*

Of Equality – as if it harm'd me, giving others the same chances and rights as myself – as if it were not indispensable to my own rights that others possess the same.

### *To Old Age*

I see in you the estuary that enlarges and spreads
itself grandly as it pours in the great sea.

### *Locations and Times*

Locations and times – what is it in me that meets
them all, whenever and wherever, and makes me
at home?
Forms, colors, densities, odors – what is it in me that
corresponds with them?

### *Offerings*

A thousand perfect men and women appear,
Around each gathers a cluster of friends, and gay
children and youths, with offerings.

### *To the States*

*To Identify the 16th, 17th, or 18th Presidentiad*

Why reclining, interrogating? why myself and all
drowsing?
What deepening twilight – scum floating atop of the
waters,
Who are they as bats and night-dogs askant in the
capitol?
What a filthy Presidentiad! (O South, your torrid
suns! O North, your arctic freezings!)
Are those really Congressmen? are those the great
Judges? is that the President?

Then I will sleep awhile yet, for I see that these
States sleep, for reasons;
(With gathering murk, with muttering thunder and
lambent shoots we all duly awake,
South, North, East, West, inland and seaboard, we
will surely awake.)

# DRUM-TAPS

## *First O Songs for a Prelude*

First O songs for a prelude,
Lightly strike on the stretch'd tympanum pride and
joy in my city,
How she led the rest to arms, how she gave the cue,
How at once with lithe limbs unwaiting a moment
she sprang,
(O superb! O Manhattan, my own, my peerless!
O strongest you in the hour of danger, in crisis! O
truer than steel!)
How you sprang – how you threw off the costumes
of peace with indifferent hand,
How your soft opera-music changed, and the drum
and fife were heard in their stead,
How you led to the war, (that shall serve for our
prelude, songs of soldiers,)
How Manhattan drum-taps led.

Forty years had I in my city seen soldiers parading,
Forty years as a pageant, till unawares the lady of
this teeming and turbulent city,
Sleepless amid her ships, her houses, her
incalculable wealth,
With her million children around her, suddenly,
At dead of night, at news from the south,
Incens'd struck with clinch'd hand the pavement.

A shock electric, the night sustain'd it,
Till with ominous hum our hive at daybreak pour'd
out its myriads.

From the houses then and the workshops, and
through all the doorways,
Leapt they tumultuous, and lo! Manhattan arming.

To the drum-taps prompt,
The young men falling in and arming,
The mechanics arming, (the trowel, the jack-plane, the black-smith's hammer, tost aside with precipitation,)
The lawyer leaving his office and arming, the judge leaving the court,
The driver deserting his wagon in the street, jumping down, throwing the reins abruptly down on the horses' backs,
The salesman leaving the store, the boss, book-keeper, porter, all leaving;
Squads gather everywhere by common consent and arm,
The new recruits, even boys, the old men show them how to wear their accoutrements, they buckle the straps carefully,
Outdoors, arming, indoors arming, the flash of the musket-barrels,
The white tents cluster in camps, the arm'd sentries around, the sunrise cannon and again at sunset,
Arm'd regiments arrive every day, pass through the city, and embark from the wharves,
(How good they look as they tramp down to the river, sweaty, with their guns on their shoulders!
How I love them! how I could hug them, with their brown faces and their clothes and knapsacks cover'd with dust!)
The blood of the city up – arm'd! arm'd! the cry everywhere,
The flags flung out from the steeples of churches and from all the public buildings and stores,
The tearful parting, the mother kisses her son, the son kisses his mother,

(Loth is the mother to part, yet not a word does she
speak to detain him,)
The tumultuous escort, the ranks of policemen
preceding, clearing the way,
The unpent enthusiasm, the wild cheers of the
crowd for their favorites,
The artillery, the silent cannons bright as gold,
drawn along, rumble lightly over the stones,
(Silent cannons, soon to cease your silence,
Soon unlimber'd to begin the red business;)
All the mutter of preparation, all the determin'd arming,
The hospital service, the lint, bandages and medicines,
The women volunteering for nurses, the work begun
for in earnest, no mere parade now;
War! an arm'd race is advancing! the welcome for
battle, no turning away;
War! be it weeks, months, or years, an arm'd race is
advancing to welcome it.

Mannahatta a-march – and it's O to sing it well!
It's O for a manly life in the camp.

And the sturdy artillery,
The guns bright as gold, the work for giants, to serve
well the guns,
Unlimber them! (no more as the past forty years for
salute or courtesies merely,
Put in something now besides powder and wadding.)

And you lady of ships, you Mannahatta,
Old matron of this proud, friendly, turbulent city,
Often in peace and wealth you were pensive or
covertly frown'd amid all your children,
But now you smile with joy exulting old Mannahatta.

## *Eighteen Sixty-One*

Arm'd year – year of the struggle,
No dainty rhymes or sentimental love verses for you
 terrible year,
Not you as some pale poetling seated at a desk
 lisping cadenzas piano,
But as a strong man erect, clothed in blue clothes,
 advancing, carrying a rifle on your shoulder,
With well-gristled body and sunburnt face and
 hands, with a knife in the belt at your side,
As I heard you shouting loud, your sonorous voice
 ringing across the continent,
Your masculine voice O year, as rising amid the
 great cities,
Amid the men of Manhattan I saw you as one of the
 workmen, the dwellers in Manhattan,
Or with large steps crossing the prairies out of
 Illinois and Indiana,
Rapidly crossing the West with springy gait and
 descending the Alleghanies,
Or down from the great lakes or in Pennsylvania, or
 on deck along the Ohio river,
Or southward along the Tennessee or Cumberland
 rivers, or at Chattanooga on the mountain top,
Saw I your gait and saw I your sinewy limbs clothed
 in blue, bearing weapons, robust year,
Heard your determin'd voice launch'd forth again
 and again,
Year that suddenly sang by the mouths of the round-
 lipp'd cannon,
I repeat you, hurrying, crashing, sad, distracted year.

## *Beat! Beat! Drums!*

Beat! beat! drums! – blow! bugles! blow!
Through the windows – through doors – burst like a
  ruthless force,
Into the solemn church, and scatter the congregation,
Into the school where the scholar is studying;
Leave not the bridegroom quiet – no happiness must
  he have now with his bride,
Nor the peaceful farmer any peace, ploughing his
  field or gathering his grain,
So fierce you whirr and pound you drums – so shrill
  you bugles blow.

Beat! beat! drums! – blow! bugles! blow!
Over the traffic of cities – over the rumble of wheels
  in the streets;
Are beds prepared for sleepers at night in the
  houses? no sleepers must sleep in those beds,
No bargainers' bargains by day – no brokers or
  speculators – would they continue?
Would the talkers be talking? would the singer
  attempt to sing?
Would the lawyer rise in the court to state his case
  before the judge?
Then rattle quicker, heavier drums – you bugles
  wilder blow.

Beat! beat! drums! – blow! bugles! blow!
Make no parley – stop for no expostulation,
Mind not the timid – mind not the weeper or prayer,
Mind not the old man beseeching the young man,
Let not the child's voice be heard, nor the mother's
  entreaties,

Make even the trestles to shake the dead where they
lie awaiting the hearses,
So strong you thump O terrible drums – so loud you
bugles blow.

## *From Paumanok Starting I Fly like a Bird*

From Paumanok starting I fly like a bird,
Around and around to soar to sing the idea of all,
To the north betaking myself to sing there arctic songs,
To Kanada till I absorb Kanada in myself, to
Michigan then,
To Wisconsin, Iowa, Minnesota, to sing their songs,
(they are inimitable;)
Then to Ohio and Indiana to sing theirs, to Missouri
and Kansas and Arkansas to sing theirs,
To Tennessee and Kentucky, to the Carolinas and
Georgia to sing theirs,
To Texas and so along up toward California, to
roam accepted everywhere;
To sing first, (to the tap of the war-drum if need be,)
The idea of all, of the Western world one and
inseparable,
And then the song of each member of these States.

## *Song of the Banner at Daybreak*

*Poet*

O a new song, a free song,
Flapping, flapping, flapping, flapping, by sounds, by
voices clearer,
By the wind's voice and that of the drum,

By the banner's voice and child's voice and sea's
    voice and father's voice,
Low on the ground and high in the air,
On the ground where father and child stand,
In the upward air where their eyes turn,
Where the banner at daybreak is flapping.

Words! book-words! what are you?
Words no more, for hearken and see,
My song is there in the open air, and I must sing,
With the banner and pennant a-flapping.

I'll weave the chord and twine in,
Man's desire and babe's desire, I'll twine them in,
    I'll put in life,
I'll put the bayonet's flashing point, I'll let bullets
    and slugs whizz,
(As one carrying a symbol and menace far into the
    future,
Crying with trumpet voice, *Arouse and beware!*
    *Beware and arouse!*)
I'll pour the verse with streams of blood, full of
    volition, full of joy,
Then loosen, launch forth, to go and compete,
With the banner and pennant a-flapping.

*Pennant*

Come up here, bard, bard,
Come up here, soul, soul,
Come up here, dear little child,
To fly in the clouds and winds with me, and play
    with the measureless light.

*Child*

Father what is that in the sky beckoning to me with long finger?
And what does it say to me all the while?

*Father*

Nothing my babe you see in the sky,
And nothing at all to you it says – but look you my babe,
Look at these dazzling things in the houses, and see you the money-shops opening,
And see you the vehicles preparing to crawl along the streets with goods;
These, ah these, how valued and toil'd for these!
How envied by all the earth!

*Poet*

Fresh and rosy red the sun is mounting high,
On floats the sea in distant blue careering through its channels,
On floats the wind over the breast of the sea setting in toward land,
The great steady wind from west or west-by-south,
Floating so buoyant with milk-white foam on the waters.
But I am not the sea nor the red sun,
I am not the wind with girlish laughter,
Not the immense wind which strengthens, not the wind which lashes,
Not the spirit that ever lashes its own body to terror and death,
But I am that which unseen comes and sings, sings, sings,
Which babbles in brooks and scoots in showers on the land,

Which the birds know in the woods mornings and
evenings,
And the shore-sands know and the hissing wave, and
that banner and pennant,
Aloft there flapping and flapping.

*Child*

O father it is alive – it is full of people – it has children,
O now it seems to me it is talking to its children,
I hear it – it talks to me – O it is wonderful!
O it stretches – it spreads and runs so fast – O my father,
It is so broad it covers the whole sky.

*Father*

Cease, cease, my foolish babe,
What you are saying is sorrowful to me, much it
displeases me;
Behold with the rest again I say, behold not banners
and pennants aloft,
But the well-prepared pavements behold, and mark
the solid-wall'd houses.

*Banner and Pennant*

Speak to the child O bard out of Manhattan,
To our children all, or north or south of Manhattan,
Point this day, leaving all the rest, to us over all –
and yet we know not why,
For what are we, mere strips of cloth profiting nothing,
Only flapping in the wind?

I hear and see not strips of cloth alone,
I hear the tramp of armies, I hear the challenging sentry,
I hear the jubilant shouts of millions of men, I hear
 Liberty!
I hear the drums beat and the trumpets blowing,
I myself move abroad swift-rising flying then,
I use the wings of the land-bird and use the wings of
 the sea-bird, and look down as from a height,
I do not deny the precious results of peace, I see
 populous cities with wealth incalculable,
I see numberless farms, I see the farmers working in
 their fields or barns,
I see mechanics working, I see buildings everywhere
 founded, going up, or finish'd,
I see trains of cars swiftly speeding along railroad
 tracks drawn by the locomotives,
I see the stores, depots, of Boston, Baltimore,
 Charleston, New Orleans,
I see far in the West the immense area of grain, I
 dwell awhile hovering,
I pass to the lumber forests of the North, and again to
 the Southern plantation, and again to California;
Sweeping the whole I see the countless profit, the
 busy gatherings, earn'd wages,
See the Identity formed out of thirty-eight spacious
 and haughty States, (and many more to come,)
See forts on the shores of harbors, see ships sailing in
 and out;
Then over all, (aye! aye!) my little and lengthen'd
 pennant shaped like a sword,
Runs swiftly up indicating war and defiance – and
 now the halyards have rais'd it,

Side of my banner broad and blue, side of my starry
banner,
Discarding peace over all the sea and land.

*Banner and Pennant*

Yet louder, higher, stronger, bard! yet ſarther, wider
cleave!
No longer let our children deem us riches and peace
alone,
We may be terror and carnage, and are so now,
Not now are we any one of these spacious and
haughty States, (nor any five, nor ten,)
Nor market nor depot we, nor money-bank in the city,
But these and all, and the brown and spreading
land, and the mines below, are ours,
And the shores of the sea are ours, and the rivers
great and small,
And the fields they moisten, and the crops and the fruits
are ours,
Bays and channels and ships sailing in and out are
ours – while we over all,
Over the area spread below, the three or four
millions of square miles, the capitals,
The forty millions of people, – O bard! in life and
death supreme,
We, even we, henceforth flaunt out masterful, high
up above,
Not for the present alone, for a thousand years
chanting through you,
This song to the soul of one poor little child.

*Child*

O my father I like not the houses,
They will never to me be anything, nor do I like money,

But to mount up there I would like, O father dear,
that banner I like,
That pennant I would be and must be.

*Father*

Child of mine you fill me with anguish,
To be that pennant would be too fearful,
Little you know what it is this day, and after this
day, forever,
It is to gain nothing, but risk and defy everything,
Forward to stand in front of wars – and O, such
wars! – what have you to do with them?
With passions of demons, slaughter, premature death?

*Banner*

Demons and death then I sing,
Put in all, aye all will I, sword-shaped pennant for war,
And a pleasure new and ecstatic, and the prattled
yearning of children,
Blent with the sounds of the peaceful land and the
liquid wash of the sea,
And the black ships fighting on the sea envelop'd in
smoke,
And the icy cool of the far, far north, with rustling
cedars and pines,
And the whirr of drums and the sound of soldiers
marching, and the hot sun shining south,
And the beach-waves combing over the beach on my
Eastern shore, and my Western shore the same,
And all between those shores, and my ever running
Mississippi with bends and chutes,
And my Illinois fields, and my Kansas fields, and my
fields of Missouri,

The Continent, devoting the whole identity without
reserving an atom,
Pour in! whelm that which asks, which sings, with all
and the yield of all,
Fusing and holding, claiming, devouring the whole,
No more with tender lip, nor musical labial sound,
But out of the night emerging for good, our voice
persuasive no more,
Croaking like crows here in the wind.

*Poet*

My limbs, my veins dilate, my theme is clear at last,
Banner so broad advancing out of the night, I sing
you haughty and resolute,
I burst through where I waited long, too long,
deafen'd and blinded,
My hearing and tongue are come to me, (a little
child taught me,)
I hear from above O pennant of war your ironical
call and demand,
Insensate! insensate (yet I at any rate chant you,)
O banner!
Not houses of peace indeed are you, nor any nor all
their prosperity, (if need be, you shall again have
every one of those houses to destroy them,
You thought not to destroy those valuable houses,
standing fast, full of comfort, built with money,
May they stand fast, then? not an hour except you
above them and all stand fast;)
O banner, not money so precious are you, not farm
produce you, nor the material good nutriment,
Nor excellent stores, nor landed on wharves from
the ships,

Not the superb ships with sail-power or steam-
power, fetching and carrying cargoes,
Nor machinery, vehicles, trade, nor revenues – but
you as henceforth I see you,
Running up out of the night, bringing your cluster of
stars, (ever-enlarging stars,)
Divider of daybreak you, cutting the air, touch'd by
the sun, measuring the sky,
(Passionately seen and yearn'd for by one poor little
child,
While others remain busy or smartly talking, forever
teaching thrift, thrift;)
O you up there! O pennant! where you undulate like
a snake hissing so curious,
Out of reach, an idea only, yet furiously fought for,
risking bloody death, loved by me,
So loved – O you banner leading the day with stars
brought from the night!
Valueless, object of eyes, over all and demanding all
– (absolute owner of all) – O banner and
pennant!
I too leave the rest – great as it is, it is nothing –
houses, machines are nothing – I see them not,
I see but you, O warlike pennant! O banner so
broad, with stripes, I sing you only,
Flapping up there in the wind.

## *Rise O Days from Your Fathomless Deeps*

1

Rise O days from your fathomless deeps, till you
loftier, fiercer sweep,
Long for my soul hungering gymnastic I devour'd
what the earth gave me,
Long I roam'd the woods of the north, long I
watch'd Niagara pouring,
I travel'd the prairies over and slept on their breast, I
cross'd the Nevadas, I cross'd the plateaus,
I ascended the towering rocks along the Pacific, I
sail'd out to sea,
I sail'd through the storm, I was refresh'd by the storm,
I watch'd with joy the threatening maws of the waves,
I mark'd the white combs where they career'd so
high, curling over,
I heard the wind piping, I saw the black clouds,
Saw from below what arose and mounted, (O
superb! O wild as my heart, and powerful!)
Heard the continuous thunder as it bellow'd after
the lightning,
Noted the slender and jagged threads of lightning as
sudden and fast amid the din they chased each
other across the sky;
These, and such as these, I, elate, saw – saw with
wonder, yet pensive and masterful,
All the menacing might of the globe uprisen around me,
Yet there with my soul I fed, I fed content, supercilious.

2

'Twas well, O soul – 'twas a good preparation you
gave me,
Now we advance our latent and ampler hunger to fill,

Now we go forth to receive what the earth and the sea never gave us,
Not through the mighty woods we go, but through the mightier cities,
Something for us is pouring now more than Niagara pouring,
Torrents of men, (sources and rills of the Northwest are you indeed inexhaustible?)
What, to pavements and homesteads here, what were those storms of the mountains and sea?
What, to passions I witness around me to-day? was the sea risen?
Was the wind piping the pipe of death under the black clouds?
Lo! from deeps more unfathomable, something more deadly and savage,
Manhattan rising, advancing with menacing front – Cincinnati, Chicago, unchain'd;
What was that swell I saw on the ocean? behold what comes here,
How it climbs with daring feet and hands – how it dashes!
How the true thunder bellows after the lightning – how bright the flashes of lightning!
How Democracy with desperate vengeful port strides on, shown through the dark by those flashes of lightning!
(Yet a mournful wail and low sob I fancied I heard through the dark,
In a lull of the deafening confusion.)

3

Thunder on! stride on, Democracy! strike with
vengeful stroke!
And do you rise higher than ever yet O days, O cities!
Crash heavier, heavier yet O storms! you have done
me good,
My soul prepared in the mountains absorbs your
immortal strong nutriment,
Long had I walk'd my cities, my country roads
through farms, only half satisfied,
One doubt nauseous undulating like a snake,
crawl'd on the ground before me,
Continually preceding my steps, turning upon me
oft, ironically hissing low;
The cities I love so well I abandon'd and left, I sped
to the certainties suitable to me,
Hungering, hungering, hungering, for primal
energies and Nature's dauntlessness,
I refresh'd myself with it only, I could relish it only,
I waited the bursting forth of the pent fire – on the
water and air I waited long;
But now I no longer wait, I am fully satisfied, I am
glutted,
I have witness'd the true lightning, I have witness'd
my cities electric,
I have lived to behold man burst forth and warlike
America rise,
Hence I will seek no more the food of the northern
solitary wilds,
No more the mountains roam or sail the stormy sea.

## *Virginia – the West*

The noble sire fallen on evil days,
I saw with hand uplifted, menacing, brandishing,
(Memories of old in abeyance, love and faith in
  abeyance,)
The insane knife toward the Mother of All.
The noble son on sinewy feet advancing,
I saw, out of the land of prairies, land of Ohio's
  waters and Indiana,
To the rescue the stalwart giant hurry his plenteous
  offspring.
Drest in blue, bearing their trusty rifles on their
  shoulders.
Then the Mother of All with calm voice speaking,
As to you Rebellious, (I seemed to hear her say,)
  why strive against me, and why seek my life?
When you yourself forever provide to defend me?
For you provided me Washington – and now these also.

## *City of Ships*

City of Ships!
(O the black ships! O the fierce ships!
O the beautiful sharp-bow'd steam-ships and
  sail-ships!)
City of the world! (for all races are here,
All the lands of the earth make contributions here;)
City of the sea! city of hurried and glittering tides!
City whose gleeful tides continually rush or recede,
  whirling in and out with eddies and foam!
City of wharves and stores – city of tall façades of
  marble and iron!
Proud and passionate city – mettlesome, mad,
  extravagant city!

Spring up O city – not for peace alone, but be
indeed yourself, warlike!
Fear not – submit to no models but your own O city!
Behold me – incarnate me as I have incarnated you!
I have rejected nothing you offer'd me – whom you
adopted I have adopted,
Good or bad I never question you – I love all – I do
not condemn anything,
I chant and celebrate all that is yours – yet peace no
more,
In peace I chanted peace, but now the drum of war
is mine,
War, red war is my song through your streets, O city!

## *The Centenarian's Story*

*Volunteer of* 1861–2, (*at Washington Park, Brooklyn, assisting the Centenarian*)

Give me your hand old Revolutionary,
The hill-top is nigh, but a few steps, (make room
gentlemen,)
Up the path you have follow'd me well, spite of your
hundred and extra years,
You can walk old man, though your eyes are almost
done,
Your faculties serve you, and presently I must have
them serve me.

Rest, while I tell what the crowd around us means,
On the plain below recruits are drilling and exercising,
There is the camp, one regiment departs to-morrow,
Do you hear the officers giving their orders?
Do you hear the clank of the muskets?

Why what comes over you now old man?
Why do you tremble and clutch my hand so convulsively?
The troops are but drilling, they are yet surrounded with smiles,
Around them at hand the well-drest friends and the women,
While splendid and warm the afternoon sun shines down,
Green the midsummer verdure and fresh blows the dallying breeze,
O'er proud and peaceful cities and arm of the sea between.

But drill and parade are over, they march back to quarters,
Only hear that approval of hands! hear what a clapping!
As wending the crowds now part and disperse – but we old man,
Not for nothing have I brought you hither – we must remain,
You to speak in your turn, and I to listen and tell.

*The Centenarian*

When I clutch'd your hand it was not with terror,
But suddenly pouring about me here on every side,
And below there where the boys were drilling, and up the slopes they ran,
And where tents are pitch'd, and wherever you see south and south-east and south-west,
Over hills, across lowlands and in the skirts of woods,

And along the shores in mire (now fill'd over) came
again and suddenly raged,
As eighty-five years a-gone no mere parade receiv'd
with applause of friends,
But a battle which I took part in myself – aye, long
ago as it is, I took part in it,
Walking then this hilltop, this same ground.

Aye, this is the ground,
My blind eyes even as I speak behold it re-peopled
from graves,
The years recede, pavements and stately houses
disappear,
Rude forts appear again, the old hoop'd guns are
mounted,
I see the lines of rais'd earth stretching from river to bay,
I mark the vista of waters, I mark the uplands and
slopes;
Here we lay encamp'd, it was this time in summer also.

As I talk I remember all, I remember the Declaration,
It was read here, the whole army paraded, it was
read to us here,
By his staff surrounded the General stood in the
middle, he held up his unsheath'd sword,
It glitter'd in the sun in full sight of the army.

'Twas a bold act then – the English war-ships had
just arrived,
We could watch down the lower bay where they lay
at anchor,
And the transports swarming with soldiers.

A few days more and they landed and then the battle.

Twenty thousand were brought against us,
A veteran force furnish'd with good artillery.

I tell not now the whole of the battle,
But one brigade early in the forenoon order'd forward to engage the red-coats,
Of that brigade I tell, and how steadily it march'd,
And how long and well it stood confronting death.

Who do you think that was marching steadily sternly confronting death?
It was the brigade of the youngest men, two thousand strong,
Rais'd in Virginia and Maryland, and most of them known personally to the General.

Jauntily forward they went with quick step toward Gowanus' waters,
Till of a sudden unlook'd for by defiles through the woods, gain'd at night,
The British advancing, rounding in from the east, fiercely playing their guns,
That brigade of the youngest was cut off and at the enemy's mercy.

The General watch'd them from this hill,
They made repeated desperate attempts to burst their environment,
Then drew close together, very compact, their flag flying in the middle,
But O from the hills how the cannon were thinning and thinning them!

It sickens me yet, that slaughter!
I saw the moisture gather in drops on the face of the General.

I saw how he wrung his hands in anguish.

Meanwhile the British manœuvr'd to draw us out for
    a pitch'd battle,
But we dared not trust the chances of a pitch'd battle.

We fought the fight in detachments,
Sallying forth we fought at several points, but in
    each the luck was against us,
Our foe advancing, steadily getting the best of it,
    push'd us back to the works on this hill,
Till we turn'd menacing here, and then he left us.

That was the going out of the brigade of the
    youngest men, two thousand strong,
Few return'd, nearly all remain in Brooklyn.
That and here my General's first battle,
No women looking on nor sunshine to bask in, it did
    not conclude with applause,
Nobody clapp'd hands here then.

But in darkness in mist on the ground under a chill rain,
Wearied that night we lay foil'd and sullen,
While scornfully laugh'd many an arrogant lord off
    against us encamp'd,
Quite within hearing, feasting, clinking wineglasses
    together over their victory.

So dull and damp and another day,
But the night of that, mist lifting, rain ceasing,
Silent as a ghost while they thought they were sure
    of him, my General retreated.

I saw him at the river-side,
Down by the ferry lit by torches, hastening the
    embarcation;

My General waited till the soldiers and wounded
were all pass'd over,
And then, (it was just ere sunrise,) these eyes rested
on him for the last time.

Every one else seem'd fill'd with gloom,
Many no doubt thought of capitulation.

But when my General pass'd me,
As he stood in his boat and look'd toward the
coming sun,
I saw something different from capitulation.

*Terminus*

Enough, the Centenarian's story ends,
The two, the past and present, have interchanged,
I myself as connecter, a chansonnier of a great
future, am now speaking.

And is this the ground Washington trod?
And these waters I listlessly daily cross, are these the
waters he cross'd,
As resolute in defeat as other generals in their
proudest triumphs?

I must copy the story, and send it eastward and
westward,
I must preserve that look as it beam'd on you rivers
of Brooklyn.

See – as the annual round returns the phantoms
return,
It is the 27th of August and the British have landed,
The battle begins and goes against us, behold
through the smoke Washington's face,
The brigade of Virginia and Maryland have march'd
forth to intercept the enemy,

They are cut off, murderous artillery from the hills
plays upon them,
Rank after rank falls, while over them silently droops
the flag,
Baptized that day in many a young man's bloody
wounds,
In death, defeat, and sisters', mothers' tears.

Ah, hills and slopes of Brooklyn! I perceive you are
more valuable than your owners supposed;
In the midst of you stands an encampment very old,
Stands forever the camp of that dead brigade.

## *Cavalry Crossing a Ford*

A line in long array where they wind betwixt green
islands,
They take a serpentine course, their arms flash in the
sun – hark to the musical clank,
Behold the silvery river, in it the splashing horses
loitering stop to drink,
Behold the brown-faced men, each group, each
person a picture, the negligent rest on the saddles,
Some emerge on the opposite bank, others are just
entering the ford – while,
Scarlet and blue and snowy white,
The guidon flags flutter gayly in the wind.

## *Bivouac on a Mountain Side*

I see before me now a traveling army halting,
Below a fertile valley spread, with barns and the
orchards of summer,

Behind, the terraced sides of a mountain, abrupt, in
places rising high,
Broken, with rocks, with clinging cedars, with tall
shapes dingily seen,
The numerous camp-fires scatter'd near and far,
some away up on the mountain,
The shadowy forms of men and horses, looming,
large-sized, flickering,
And over all the sky – the sky! far, far out of reach,
studded, breaking out, the eternal stars.

## *An Army Corps on the March*

With its cloud of skirmishers in advance,
With now the sound of a single shot snapping like a
whip, and now an irregular volley,
The swarming ranks press on and on, the dense
brigades press on,
Glittering dimly, toiling under the sun – the dust-
cover'd men,
In columns rise and fall to the undulations of the
ground,
With artillery interspers'd – the wheels rumble, the
horses sweat,
As the army corps advances.

## *By the Bivouac's Fitful Flame*

By the bivouac's fitful flame,
A procession winding around me, solemn and sweet
and slow – but first I note,
The tents of the sleeping army, the fields' and
woods' dim outline,

The darkness lit by spots of kindled fire, the silence,
Like a phantom far or near an occasional figure moving,
The shrubs and trees, (as I lift my eyes they seem to
    be stealthily watching me,)
While wind in procession thoughts, O tender and
    wondrous thoughts,
Of life and death, of home and the past and loved,
    and of those that are far away;
A solemn and slow procession there as I sit on the
    ground,
By the bivouac's fitful flame.

*Come up from the Fields Father*

Come up from the fields father, here's a letter from
    our Pete,
And come to the front door mother, here's a letter
    from thy dear son.

Lo, 'tis autumn,
Lo, where the trees, deeper green, yellower and redder,
Cool and sweeten Ohio's villages with leaves
    fluttering in the moderate wind,
Where apples ripe in the orchards hang and grapes
    on the trellis'd vines,
(Smell you the smell of the grapes on the vines?
Smell you the buckwheat where the bees were lately
    buzzing?)

Above all, lo, the sky so calm, so transparent after
    the rain, and with wondrous clouds,
Below too, all calm, all vital and beautiful, and the
    farm prospers well.

Down in the fields all prospers well,

But now from the fields come father, come at the daughter's call,
And come to the entry mother, to the front door come right away.

Fast as she can she hurries, something ominous, her steps trembling,
She does not tarry to smooth her hair nor adjust her cap.

Open the envelope quickly,
O this is not our son's writing, yet his name is sign'd,
O a strange hand writes for our dear son, O stricken mother's soul!
All swims before her eyes, flashes with black, she catches the main words only,
Sentences broken, *gunshot wound in the breast, cavalry skirmish, taken to hospital,*
*At present low, but will soon be better.*

Ah now the single figure to me,
Amid all teeming and wealthy Ohio with all its cities and farms,
Sickly white in the face and dull in the head, very faint,
By the jamb of a door leans.

*Grieve not so, dear mother,* (the just-grown daughter speaks through her sobs,
The little sisters huddle around speechless and dismay'd,)
*See, dearest mother, the letter says Pete will soon be better.*

Alas poor boy, he will never be better, (nor may-be needs to be better, that brave and simple soul,)
While they stand at home at the door he is dead already,
The only son is dead.

But the mother needs to be better,
She with thin form presently drest in black,
By day her meals untouch'd, then at night fitfully
  sleeping, often waking,
In the midnight waking, weeping, longing with one
  deep longing,
O that she might withdraw unnoticed, silent from
  life escape and withdraw,
To follow, to seek, to be with her dear dead son.

## *Vigil Strange I Kept on the Field One Night*

Vigil strange I kept on the field one night;
When you my son and my comrade dropt at my side
  that day,
One look I but gave which your dear eyes return'd
  with a look I shall never forget,
One touch of your hand to mine O boy, reach'd up
  as you lay on the ground,
Then onward I sped in the battle, the even-
  contested battle,
Till late in the night reliev'd to the place at last again
  I made my way,
Found you in death so cold dear comrade, found
  your body son of responding kisses, (never again
  on earth responding,)
Bared your face in the starlight, curious the scene,
  cool blew the moderate night-wind,
Long there and then in vigil I stood, dimly around
  me the battlefield spreading,
Vigil wondrous and vigil sweet there in the fragrant
  silent night,

But not a tear fell, not even a long-drawn sigh, long, long I gazed,
Then on the earth partially reclining sat by your side leaning my chin in my hands,
Passing sweet hours, immortal and mystic hours with you dearest comrade – not a tear, not a word,
Vigil of silence, love and death, vigil for you my son and my soldier,
As onward silently stars aloft, eastward new ones upward stole,
Vigil final for you brave boy, (I could not save you, swift was your death,
I faithfully loved you and cared for you living, I think we shall surely meet again,)
Till at latest lingering of the night, indeed just as the dawn appear'd,
My comrade I wrapt in his blanket, envelop'd well his form,
Folded the blanket well, tucking it carefully over head and carefully under feet,
And there and then and bathed by the rising sun, my son in his grave, in his rude-dug grave I deposited,
Ending my vigil strange with that, vigil of night and battle-field dim,
Vigil for boy of responding kisses, (never again on earth responding,)
Vigil for comrade swiftly slain, vigil I never forget, how as day brighten'd,
I rose from the chill ground and folded my soldier well in his blanket,
And buried him where he fell.

## *A March in the Ranks Hard-Prest, and the Road Unknown*

A march in the ranks hard-prest, and the road unknown,
A route through a heavy wood with muffled steps in the darkness,
Our army foil'd with loss severe, and the sullen remnant retreating,
Till after midnight glimmer upon us the lights of a dimlighted building,
We come to an open space in the woods, and halt by the dim-lighted building,
'Tis a large old church at the crossing roads, now an impromptu hospital,
Entering but for a minute I see a sight beyond all the pictures and poems ever made,
Shadows of deepest, deepest black, just lit by moving candles and lamps,
And by one great pitchy torch stationary with wild red flame and clouds of smoke,
By these, crowds, groups of forms vaguely I see on the floor, some in the pews laid down,
At my feet more distinctly a soldier, a mere lad, in danger of bleeding to death, (he is shot in the abdomen,)
I staunch the blood temporarily, (the youngster's face is white as a lily,)
Then before I depart I sweep my eyes o'er the scene fain to absorb it all,
Faces, varieties, postures beyond description, most in obscurity, some of them dead,
Surgeons operating, attendants holding lights, the smell of ether, the odor of blood,

The crowd, O the crowd of the bloody forms, the
yard outside also fill'd,
Some on the bare ground, some on planks or
stretchers, some in the death-spasm sweating,
An occasional scream or cry, the doctor's shouted
orders or calls,
The glisten of the little steel instruments catching
the glint of the torches,
These I resume as I chant, I see again the forms, I
smell the odor,
Then hear outside the orders given, *Fall in, my men,
fall in*;
But first I bend to the dying lad, his eyes open, a
half-smile gives he me,
Then the eyes close, calmly close, and I speed forth
to the darkness,
Resuming, marching, ever in darkness marching, on
in the ranks,
The unknown road still marching.

## *A Sight in Camp in the Daybreak Gray and Dim*

A sight in camp in the daybreak gray and dim,
As from my tent I emerge so early sleepless,
As slow I walk in the cool fresh air the path near by
the hospital tent,
Three forms I see on stretchers lying, brought out
there untended lying,
Over each the blanket spread, ample brownish
woolen blanket,
Gray and heavy blanket, folding, covering all.

Curious I halt and silent stand,
Then with light fingers I from the face of the nearest
the first just lift the blanket;
Who are you elderly man so gaunt and grim, with well-
gray'd hair, and flesh all sunken about the eyes?
Who are you my dear comrade?

Then to the second I step – and who are you my
child and darling?
Who are you sweet boy with cheeks yet blooming?

Then to the third – a face nor child nor old, very
calm, as of beautiful yellow-white ivory;
Young man I think I know you – I think this face is
the face of the Christ himself,
Dead and divine and brother of all, and here again
he lies.

## *As Toilsome I Wander'd Virginia's Woods*

As toilsome I wander'd Virginia's woods,
To the music of rustling leaves kick'd by my feet,
(for 'twas autumn,)
I mark'd at the foot of a tree the grave of a soldier;
Mortally wounded he and buried on the retreat,
(easily all could I understand,)
The halt of a mid-day hour, when up! no time to
lose – yet this sign left,
On a tablet scrawl'd and nail'd on the tree by the grave,
*Bold, cautious, true, and my loving comrade.*

Long, long I muse, then on my way go wandering,
Many a changeful season to follow, and many a
scene of life,

Yet at times through changeful season and scene,
abrupt, alone, or in the crowded street,
Comes before me the unknown soldier's grave,
comes the inscription rude in Virginia's woods,
*Bold, cautious, true, and my loving comrade.*

## *Not the Pilot*

Not the pilot has charged himself to bring his ship into
port, though beaten back and many times baffled;
Not the pathfinder penetrating inland weary and long,
By deserts parch'd, snows chill'd, rivers wet,
perseveres till he reaches his destination,
More than I have charged myself, heeded or
unheeded, to compose a march for these States,
For a battle-call, rousing to arms if need be, years,
centuries hence.

## *Year that Trembled and Reel'd Beneath Me*

Year that trembled and reel'd beneath me!
Your summer wind was warm enough, yet the air I
breathed froze me,
A thick gloom fell through the sunshine and
darken'd me,
Must I change my triumphant songs? said I to myself,
Must I indeed learn to chant the cold dirges of the
baffled?
And sullen hymns of defeat?

## *The Wound-Dresser*

1

An old man bending I come among new faces,
Years looking backward resuming in answer to children,
Come tell us old man, as from young men and maidens that love me,
(Arous'd and angry, I'd thought to beat the alarum, and urge relentless war,
But soon my fingers fail'd me, my face droop'd and I resign'd myself,
To sit by the wounded and soothe them, or silently watch the dead;)
Years hence of these scenes, of these furious passions, these chances,
Of unsurpass'd heroes, (was one side so brave? the other was equally brave;)
Now be witness again, paint the mightiest armies of earth,
Of those armies so rapid so wondrous what saw you to tell us?
What stays with you latest and deepest? of curious panics,
Of hard-fought engagements or sieges tremendous what deepest remains?

2

O maidens and young men I love and that love me,
What you ask of my days those the strangest and sudden your talking recalls,
Soldier alert I arrive after a long march cover'd with sweat and dust,

In the nick of time I come, plunge in the fight,
loudly shout in the rush of successful charge,
Enter the captur'd works – yet lo, like a swift
running river they fade,
Pass and are gone they fade – I dwell not on soldiers'
perils or soldiers' joys,
(Both I remember well – many of the hardships, few
the joys, yet I was content.)

But in silence, in dreams' projections,
While the world of gain and appearance and mirth
goes on,
So soon what is over forgotten, and waves wash the
imprints off the sand,
With hinged knees returning I enter the doors,
(while for you up there,
Whoever you are, follow without noise and be of
strong heart.)

Bearing the bandages, water and sponge,
Straight and swift to my wounded I go,
Where they lie on the ground after the battle
brought in,
Where their priceless blood reddens the grass the
ground,
Or to the rows of the hospital tent, or under the
roof'd hospital,
To the long rows of cots up and down each side I
return,
To each and all one after another I draw near, not
one do I miss,
An attendant follows holding a tray, he carries a
refuse pail,
Soon to be fill'd with clotted rags and blood,
emptied, and fill'd again.

I onward go, I stop,
With hinged knees and steady hand to dress wounds,
I am firm with each, the pangs are sharp yet
unavoidable,
One turns to me his appealing eyes – poor boy! I
never knew you,
Yet I think I could not refuse this moment to die for
you, if that would save you.

3

On, on I go, (open doors of time! open hospital doors!)
The crush'd head I dress, (poor crazed hand tear not
the bandage away,)
The neck of the cavalry-man with the bullet through
and through I examine,
Hard the breathing rattles, quite glazed already the
eye, yet life struggles hard,
(Come sweet death! be persuaded O beautiful death!
In mercy come quickly.)

From the stump of the arm, the amputated hand,
I undo the clotted lint, remove the slough, wash off
the matter and blood,
Back on his pillow the soldier bends with curv'd
neck and side falling head,
His eyes are closed, his face is pale, he dares not look
on the bloody stump,
And has not yet look'd on it.

I dress a wound in the side, deep, deep,
But a day or two more, for see the frame all wasted
and sinking,
And the yellow-blue countenance see.

I dress the perforated shoulder, the foot with the
 bullet-wound,
Cleanse the one with a gnawing and putrid
 gangrene, so sickening, so offensive,
While the attendant stands behind aside me holding
 the tray and pail.

I am faithful, I do not give out,
The fractur'd thigh, the knee, the wound in the
 abdomen,
These and more I dress with impassive hand, (yet
 deep in my breast a fire, a burning flame.)

4

Thus in silence in dreams' projections,
Returning, resuming, I thread my way through the
 hospitals,
The hurt and wounded I pacify with soothing hand,
I sit by the restless all the dark night, some are so young,
Some suffer so much, I recall the experience sweet
 and sad,
(Many a soldier's loving arms about this neck have
 cross'd and rested,
Many a soldier's kiss dwells on these bearded lips.)

## *Long, too Long America*

Long, too long America,
Traveling roads all even and peaceful you learn'd
from joys and prosperity only,
But now, ah now, to learn from crises of anguish,
advancing, grappling with direst fate and
recoiling not,
And now to conceive and show to the world what
your children en-masse really are,
(For who except myself has yet conceiv'd what your
children en-masse really are?)

## *Give Me the Splendid Silent Sun*

### 1

Give me the splendid silent sun with all his beams
full-dazzling,
Give me juicy autumnal fruit ripe and red from the
orchard,
Give me a field where the unmow'd grass grows,
Give me an arbor, give me the trellis'd grape,
Give me fresh corn and wheat, give me serene-
moving animals teaching content,
Give me nights perfectly quiet as on high plateaus west
of the Mississippi, and I looking up at the stars,
Give me odorous at sunrise a garden of beautiful
flowers where I can walk undisturb'd,
Give me for marriage a sweet-breath'd woman of
whom I should never tire,
Give me a perfect child, give me away aside from the
noise of the world a rural domestic life,
Give me to warble spontaneous songs recluse by
myself, for my own ears only,

Give me solitude, give me Nature, give me again O
Nature your primal sanities!
These demanding to have them, (tired with ceaseless
excitement, and rack'd by the war-strife,)
These to procure incessantly asking, rising in cries
from my heart,
While yet incessantly asking still I adhere to my city,
Day upon day and year upon year O city, walking
your streets,
Where you hold me enchain'd a certain time
refusing to give me up,
Yet giving to make me glutted, enrich'd of soul, you
give me forever faces;
(O I see what I sought to escape, confronting,
reversing my cries,
I see my own soul trampling down what it ask'd for.)

2

Keep your splendid silent sun,
Keep your woods O Nature, and the quiet places by
the woods,
Keep your fields of clover and timothy, and your
corn-fields and orchards,
Keep the blossoming buckwheat fields where the
Ninth-month bees hum;
Give me faces and streets – give me these phantoms
incessant and endless along the trottoirs!
Give me interminable eyes – give me women – give
me comrades and lovers by the thousand!
Let me see new ones every day – let me hold new
ones by the hand every day!
Give me such shows – give me the streets of Manhattan!
Give me Broadway, with the soldiers marching –
give me the sound of the trumpets and drums!

(The soldiers in companies or regiments – some starting away, flush'd and reckless,
Some, their time up, returning with thinn'd ranks, young, yet very old, worn, marching, noticing nothing;)
Give me the shores and wharves heavy-fringed with black ships!
O such for me! O an intense life, full to repletion and varied!
The life of the theatre, bar-room, huge hotel, for me!
The saloon of the steamer! the crowded excursion for me! the torchlight procession!
The dense brigade bound for the war, with high piled military wagons following;
People, endless, streaming, with strong voices, passions, pageants,
Manhattan streets with their powerful throbs, with beating drums as now,
The endless and noisy chorus, the rustle and clank of muskets, (even the sight of the wounded,)
Manhattan crowds, with their turbulent musical chorus!
Manhattan faces and eyes forever for me.

## *Dirge for Two Veterans*

The last sunbeam
Lightly falls from the finish'd Sabbath,
On the pavement here, and there beyond it is looking,
Down a new-made double grave.

Lo, the moon ascending,
Up from the east the silvery round moon,
Beautiful over the house-tops, ghastly, phantom moon,
Immense and silent moon.

I see a sad procession,
And I hear the sound of coming full-key'd bugles,
All the channels of the city streets they're flooding,
As with voices and with tears.

I hear the great drums pounding,
And the small drums steady whirring,
And every blow of the great convulsive drums,
Strikes me through and through.

For the son is brought with the father,
(In the foremost ranks of the fierce assault they fell,
Two veterans son and father dropt together,
And the double grave awaits them.)

Now nearer blow the bugles,
And the drums strike more convulsive,
And the daylight o'er the pavement quite has faded,
And the strong dead-march enwraps me.

In the eastern sky up-buoying,
The sorrowful vast phantom moves illumin'd,
('Tis some mother's large transparent face,
In heaven brighter growing.)

O strong dead-march you please me!
O moon immense with your silvery face you soothe me!
O my soldiers twain! O my veterans passing to burial!
What I have I also give you.

The moon gives you light,
And the bugles and the drums give you music,
And my heart, O my soldiers, my veterans,
My heart gives you love.

### *Over the Carnage Rose Prophetic a Voice*

Over the carnage rose prophetic a voice,
Be not dishearten'd, affection shall solve the
  problems of freedom yet,
Those who love each other shall become invincible,
They shall yet make Columbia victorious.

Sons of the Mother of All, you shall yet be victorious,
You shall yet laugh to scorn the attacks of all the
  remainder of the earth.

No danger shall balk Columbia's lovers,
If need be a thousand shall sternly immolate
  themselves for one.

One from Massachusetts shall be a Missourian's
  comrade,
From Maine and from hot Carolina, and another an
  Oregonese, shall be friends triune,
More precious to each other than all the riches of
  the earth.

To Michigan, Florida perfumes shall tenderly come,
Not the perfumes of flowers, but sweeter, and
  wafted beyond death.

It shall be customary in the houses and streets to see
  manly affection,
The most dauntless and rude shall touch face to face
  lightly,
The dependence of Liberty shall be lovers,
The continuance of Equality shall be comrades.

These shall tie you and band you stronger than
  hoops of iron,

I, ecstatic, O partners! O lands, with the love of
lovers tie you.
(Were you looking to be held together by lawyers?
Or by an agreement on a paper? or by arms?
Nay, nor the world, nor any living thing, will so
cohere.)

## *I Saw Old General at Bay*

I saw old General at bay,
(Old as he was, his gray eyes yet shone out in battle
like stars,)
His small force was now completely hemm'd in, in
his works,
He call'd for volunteers to run the enemy's lines, a
desperate emergency,
I saw a hundred and more step forth from the ranks,
but two or three were selected,
I saw them receive their orders aside, they listen'd
with care, the adjutant was very grave,
I saw them depart with cheerfulness, freely risking
their lives.

## *The Artilleryman's Vision*

While my wife at my side lies slumbering, and the
wars are over long,
And my head on the pillow rests at home, and the
vacant midnight passes,
And through the stillness, through the dark, I hear,
just hear, the breath of my infant,
There in the room as I wake from sleep this vision
presses upon me;

The engagement opens there and then in fantasy
unreal,
The skirmishers begin, they crawl cautiously ahead,
I hear the irregular snap! snap!
I hear the sounds of the different missiles, the short
*t-h-t! t-h-t!* of the rifle-balls,
I see the shells exploding leaving small white clouds,
I hear the great shells shrieking as they pass,
The grape like the hum and whirr of wind through
the trees, (tumultuous now the contest rages,)
All the scenes at the batteries rise in detail before me
again,
The crashing and smoking, the pride of the men in
their pieces,
The chief-gunner ranges and sights his piece and
selects a fuse of the right time,
After firing I see him lean aside and look eagerly off
to note the effect;
Elsewhere I hear the cry of a regiment charging, (the
young colonel leads himself this time with
brandish'd sword,)
I see the gaps cut by the enemy's volleys, (quickly
fill'd up, no delay,)
I breathe the suffocating smoke, then the flat clouds
hover low concealing all;
Now a strange lull for a few seconds, not a shot fired
on either side,
Then resumed the chaos louder than ever, with
eager calls and orders of officers,
While from some distant part of the field the wind
wafts to my ears a shout of applause, (some
special success,)

And ever the sound of the cannon far or near,
(rousing even in dreams a devilish exultation and all the old mad joy in the depths of my soul,)
And ever the hastening of infantry shifting positions, batteries, cavalry, moving hither and thither,
(The falling, dying, I heed not, the wounded dripping and red I heed not, some to the rear are hobbling,)
Grime, heat, rush, aides-de-camp galloping by or on a full run,
With the patter of small arms, the warning *s-s-t* of the rifles, (these in my vision I hear or see,)
And bombs bursting in air, and at night the vari-color'd rockets.

## *Ethiopia Saluting the Colors*

Who are you dusky woman, so ancient hardly human,
With your woolly-white and turban'd head, and bare bony feet?
Why rising by the roadside here, do you the colors greet?

('Tis while our army lines Carolina's sands and pines,
Forth from thy hovel door thou Ethiopia com'st to me,
As under doughty Sherman I march toward the sea.)

*Me master years a hundred since from my parents sunder'd,*
*A little child, they caught me as the savage beast is caught,*
*Then hither me across the sea the cruel slaver brought.*

No further does she say, but lingering all the day,
Her high-borne turban'd head she wags, and rolls her darkling eye,
And courtesies to the regiments, the guidons moving by.

What is it fateful woman, so blear, hardly human?
Why wag your head with turban bound, yellow, red and green?
Are the things so strange and marvelous you see or have seen?

## *Not Youth Pertains to Me*

Not youth pertains to me,
Nor delicatesse, I cannot beguile the time with talk,
Awkward in the parlor, neither a dancer nor elegant,
In the learn'd coterie sitting constrain'd and still, for learning inures not to me,
Beauty, knowledge, inure not to me – yet there are two or three things inure to me,
I have nourish'd the wounded and sooth'd many a dying soldier,
And at intervals waiting or in the midst of camp,
Composed these songs.

## *Race of Veterans*

Race of veterans – race of victors!
Race of the soil, ready for conflict – race of the conquering march!
(No more credulity's race, abiding-temper'd race,)
Race henceforth owning no law but the law of itself,
Race of passion and the storm.

## *World Take Good Notice*

World take good notice, silver stars fading,
Milky hue ript, weft of white detaching,
Coals thirty-eight, baleful and burning,
Scarlet, significant, hands off warning,
Now and henceforth flaunt from these shores.

## *O Tan-Faced Prairie-Boy*

O tan-faced prairie-boy,
Before you came to camp came many a welcome gift,
Praises and presents came and nourishing food, till
at last among the recruits,
You came, taciturn, with nothing to give – we but
look'd on each other,
When lo! more than all the gifts of the world you
gave me.

## *Look Down Fair Moon*

Look down fair moon and bathe this scene,
Pour softly down night's nimbus floods on faces
ghastly, swollen, purple,
On the dead on their backs with arms toss'd wide,
Pour down your unstinted nimbus sacred moon.

## *Reconciliation*

Word over all, beautiful as the sky,
Beautiful that war and all its deeds of carnage must
in time be utterly lost,

That the hands of the sisters Death and Night
    incessantly softly wash again, and ever again, this
    soil'd world;
For my enemy is dead, a man divine as myself is dead,
I look where he lies white-faced and still in the coffin
    – I draw near,
Bend down and touch lightly with my lips the white
    face in the coffin.

## *How Solemn as One by One*

(*Washington City*, 1865)

How solemn as one by one,
As the ranks returning worn and sweaty, as the men
    file by where I stand,
As the faces the masks appear, as I glance at the
    faces studying the masks,
As I glance upward out of this page studying you,
    dear friend, whoever you are,)
How solemn the thought of my whispering soul to
    each in the ranks, and to *you*!
I see behind each mask that wonder a kindred soul,
O the bullet could never kill what you really are,
    dear friend,
Nor the bayonet stab what you really are;
The soul! yourself I see, great as any, good as the best,
Waiting secure and content, which the bullet could
    never kill,
Nor the bayonet stab O friend.

## *As I Lay with My Head in Your Lap Camerado*

As I lay with my head in your lap camerado,
The confession I made I resume, what I said to you
and the open air I resume,
I know I am restless and make others so,
I know my words are weapons full of danger, full of
death,
For I confront peace, security, and all the settled
laws, to unsettle them,
I am more resolute because all have denied me than
I could ever have been had all accepted me,
I heed not and have never heeded either experience,
cautions, majorities, nor ridicule,
And the threat of what is call'd hell is little or
nothing to me,
And the lure of what is call'd heaven is little or
nothing to me;
Dear camerado! I confess I have urged you onward
with me, and still urge you, without the least
idea what is our destination,
Or whether we shall be victorious, or utterly quell'd
and defeated.

## *Delicate Cluster*

Delicate cluster! flag of teeming life!
Covering all my lands – all my seashores lining!
Flag of death! (how I watch'd you through the
smoke of battle pressing!
How I heard you flap and rustle, cloth defiant!)
Flag cerulean – sunny flag, with the orbs of night
dappled!
Ah my silvery beauty – ah my woolly white and crimson!

Ah to sing the song of you, my matron mighty!
My sacred one, my mother!

## *To a Certain Civilian*

Did you ask dulcet rhymes from me?
Did you seek the civilian's peaceful and languishing rhymes?
Did you find what I sang erewhile so hard to follow?
Why I was not singing erewhile for you to follow, to understand – nor am I now;
(I have been born of the same as the war was born,
The drum-corps' rattle is ever to me sweet music, I love well the martial dirge,
With slow wail and convulsive throb leading the officer's funeral;)
What to such as you anyhow such a poet as I? therefore leave my works,
And go lull yourself with what you can understand, and with piano-tunes,
For I lull nobody, and you will never understand me.

## *Lo, Victress on the Peaks*

Lo, Victress on the peaks,
Where thou with mighty brow regarding the world,
(The world O Libertad, that vainly conspired against thee,)
Out of its countless beleaguering toils, after thwarting them all,
Dominant, with the dazzling sun around thee,
Flauntest now unharm'd in immortal soundness and bloom – lo, in these hours supreme,

No poem proud, I chanting bring to thee, nor
mastery's rapturous verse,
But a cluster containing night's darkness and blood-
dripping wounds,
And psalms of the dead.

## *Spirit Whose Work is Done*

(*Washington City*, 1865)

Spirit whose work is done – spirit of dreadful hours!
Ere departing fade from my eyes your forests of
bayonets;
Spirit of gloomiest fears and doubts, (yet onward
ever unfaltering pressing,)
Spirit of many a solemn day and many a savage
scene – electric spirit,
That with muttering voice through the war now
closed, like a tireless phantom flitted,
Rousing the land with breath of flame, while you
beat and beat the drum,
Now as the sound of the drum, hollow and harsh to
the last, reverberates round me,
As your ranks, your immortal ranks, return, return
from the battles,
As the muskets of the young men yet lean over their
shoulders,
As I look on the bayonets bristling over their
shoulders,
As those slanted bayonets, whole forests of them
appearing in the distance, approach and pass on,
returning homeward,
Moving with steady motion, swaying to and fro to
the right and left,

Evenly, lightly rising and falling while the steps keep
time;
Spirit of hours I knew, all hectic red one day, but
pale as death next day,
Touch my mouth ere you depart, press my lips close,
Leave me your pulses of rage – bequeath them to me
– fill me with currents convulsive,
Let them scorch and blister out of my chants when
you are gone,
Let them identify you to the future in these songs.

## *Adieu to a Soldier*

Adieu O soldier,
You of the rude campaigning, (which we shared,)
The rapid march, the life of the camp,
The hot contention of opposing fronts, the long
manœuvre,
Red battles with their slaughter, the stimulus, the
strong terrific game,
Spell of all brave and manly hearts, the trains of time
through you and like of you all fill'd,
With war and war's expression.

Adieu dear comrade,
Your mission is fulfill'd – but I, more warlike,
Myself and this contentious soul of mine,
Still on our own campaigning bound,
Through untried roads with ambushes opponents
lined,
Through many a sharp defeat and many a crisis,
often baffled,
Here marching, ever marching on, a war fight out –
aye here,
To fiercer, weightier battles give expression.

## *Turn O Libertad*

Turn O Libertad, for the war is over,
From it and all henceforth expanding, doubting no
 more, resolute, sweeping the world,
Turn from lands retrospective recording proofs of
 the past,
From the singers that sing the trailing glories of the past,
From the chants of the feudal world, the triumphs of
 kings, slavery, caste,
Turn to the world, the triumphs reserv'd and to
 come – give up that backward world,
Leave to the singers of hitherto, give them the
 trailing past,
But what remains remains for singers for you – wars
 to come are for you,
(Lo, how the wars of the past have duly inured to
 you, and the wars of the present also inure;)
Then turn, and be not alarm'd O Libertad – turn
 your undying face,
To where the future, greater than all the past,
Is swiftly, surely preparing for you.

### *To the Leaven'd Soil They Trod*

To the leaven'd soil they trod calling I sing for the last,
(Forth from my tent emerging for good, loosing,
untying the tent-ropes,)
In the freshness the forenoon air, in the far-stretching
circuits and vistas again to peace restored,
To the fiery fields emanative and the endless vistas
beyond, to the South and the North,
To the leaven'd soil of the general Western world to
attest my songs,
To the Alleghanian hills and the tireless Mississippi,
To the rocks I calling sing, and all the trees in the
woods,
To the plains of the poems of heroes, to the prairies
spreading wide,
To the far-off sea and the unseen winds, and the
sane impalpable air;
And responding they answer all, (but not in words,)
The average earth, the witness of war and peace,
acknowledges mutely,
The prairie draws me close, as the father to bosom
broad the son,
The Northern ice and rain that began me nourish
me to the end,
But the hot sun of the South is to fully ripen my
songs.

# MEMORIES OF PRESIDENT LINCOLN

## *When Lilacs Last in the Dooryard Bloom'd*

1

When lilacs last in the dooryard bloom'd,
And the great star early droop'd in the western sky
    in the night,
I mourn'd, and yet shall mourn with ever-returning
    spring.

Ever-returning spring, trinity sure to me you bring,
Lilac blooming perennial and drooping star in the west,
And thought of him I love.

2

O powerful western fallen star!
O shades of night – O moody, tearful night!
O great star disappear'd – O the black murk that
    hides the star!
O cruel hands that hold me powerless – O helpless
    soul of me!
O harsh surrounding cloud that will not free my soul.

3

In the dooryard fronting an old farm-house near the
    white-wash'd palings,
Stands the lilac-bush tall-growing with heart-shaped
    leaves of rich green,
With many a pointed blossom rising delicate, with
    the perfume strong I love,
With every leaf a miracle – and from this bush in the
    dooryard,
With delicate-color'd blossoms and heart-shaped
    leaves of rich green,
A sprig with its flower I break.

4

In the swamp in secluded recesses,
A shy and hidden bird is warbling a song.

Solitary the thrush,
The hermit withdrawn to himself, avoiding the settlements,
Sings by himself a song.

Song of the bleeding throat,
Death's outlet song of life, (for well dear brother I know,
If thou wast not granted to sing thou would'st surely die.)

5

Over the breast of the spring, the land, amid cities,
Amid lanes and through old woods, where lately the violets peep'd from the ground, spotting the gray debris,
Amid the grass in the fields each side of the lanes, passing the endless grass,
Passing the yellow-spear'd wheat, every grain from its shroud in the dark-brown fields uprisen,
Passing the apple-tree blows of white and pink in the orchards,
Carrying a corpse to where it shall rest in the grave,
Night and day journeys a coffin.

6

Coffin that passes through lanes and streets,
Through day and night with the great cloud darkening the land,

With the pomp of the inloop'd flags with the cities
    draped in black,
With the show of the States themselves as of crape-
    veil'd women standing,
With processions long and winding and the
    flambeaus of the night,
With the countless torches lit, with the silent sea of
    faces and the unbared heads,
With the waiting depot, the arriving coffin, and the
    sombre faces,
With dirges through the night, with the thousand
    voices rising strong and solemn,
With all the mournful voices of the dirges pour'd
    around the coffin,
The dim-lit churches and the shuddering organs –
    where amid these you journey,
With the tolling bells' perpetual clang,
Here, coffin that slowly passes,
I give you my sprig of lilac.

7

(Nor for you, for one alone,
Blossoms and branches green to coffins all I bring,
For fresh as the morning, thus would I chant a song
    for you O sane and sacred death.

All over bouquets of roses,
O death, I cover you over with roses and early lilies,
But mostly and now the lilac that blooms the first,
Copious I break, I break the sprigs from the bushes,
With loaded arms I come, pouring for you,
For you and the coffins all of you O death.)

8

O western orb sailing the heaven,
Now I know what you must have meant as a month since I walk'd,
As I walk'd in silence the transparent shadowy night,
As I saw you had something to tell as you bent to me night after night,
As you droop'd from the sky low down as if to my side, (while the other stars all look'd on,)
As we wander'd together the solemn night, (for something I know not what kept me from sleep,)
As the night advanced, and I saw on the rim of the west how full you were of woe,
As I stood on the rising ground in the breeze in the cool transparent night,
As I watch'd where you pass'd and was lost in the netherward black of the night,
As my soul in its trouble dissatisfied sank, as where you sad orb,
Concluded, dropt in the night, and was gone.

9

Sing on there in the swamp,
O singer bashful and tender, I hear your notes, I hear your call,
I hear, I come presently, I understand you,
But a moment I linger, for the lustrous star has detain'd me,
The star my departing comrade holds and detains me.

10

O how shall I warble myself for the dead one there I loved?

And how shall I deck my song for the large sweet
soul that has gone?
And what shall my perfume be for the grave of him I
love?
Sea-winds blown from east and west,
Blown from the Eastern sea and blown from the
Western sea, till there on the prairies meeting,
These and with these and the breath of my chant,
I'll perfume the grave of him I love.

11

O what shall I hang on the chamber walls?
And what shall the pictures be that I hang on the walls,
To adorn the burial-house of him I love?
Pictures of growing spring and farms and homes,
With the Fourth-month eve at sundown, and the
gray smoke lucid and bright,
With floods of the yellow gold of the gorgeous,
indolent, sinking sun, burning, expanding the air,
With the fresh sweet herbage under foot, and the
pale green leaves of the trees prolific,
In the distance the flowing glaze, the breast of the
river, with a wind-dapple here and there,
With ranging hills on the banks, with many a line
against the sky, and shadows,
And the city at hand with dwellings so dense, and
stacks of chimneys,
And all the scenes of life and the workshops, and the
workmen homeward returning.

12

Lo, body and soul – this land,
My own Manhattan with spires, and the sparkling
and hurrying tides, and the ships,

The varied and ample land, the South and the
North in the light, Ohio's shores and flashing
Missouri,
And ever the far-spreading prairies cover'd with
grass and corn.

Lo, the most excellent sun so calm and haughty,
The violet and purple morn with just-felt breezes,
The gentle soft-born measureless light,
The miracle spreading bathing all, the fulfill'd noon,
The coming eve delicious, the welcome night and
the stars,
Over my cities shining all, enveloping man and land.

13

Sing on, sing on you gray-brown bird,
Sing from the swamps, the recesses, pour your chant
from the bushes,
Limitless out of the dusk, out of the cedars and pines.
Sing on dearest brother, warble your reedy song,
Loud human song, with voice of uttermost woe.

O liquid and free and tender!
O wild and loose to my soul – O wondrous singer!
You only I hear – yet the star holds me, (but will
soon depart,)
Yet the lilac with mastering odor holds me.

14

Now while I sat in the day and look'd forth,
In the close of the day with its light and the fields of
spring, and the farmers preparing their crops,
In the large unconscious scenery of my land with its
lakes and forests,

In the heavenly aerial beauty, (after the perturb'd
    winds and the storms,)
Under the arching heavens of the afternoon swift
    passing, and the voices of children and women,
The many-moving sea-tides, and I saw the ships
    how they sail'd,
And the summer approaching with richness, and the
    fields all busy with labor,
And the infinite separate houses, how they all went on,
    each with its meals and minutia of daily usages,
And the streets how their throbbings throbb'd, and
    the cities pent – lo, then and there,
Falling upon them all and among them all,
    enveloping me with the rest,
Appear'd the cloud, appear'd the long black trail,
And I knew death, its thought, and the sacred
    knowledge of death.

Then with the knowledge of death as walking one
    side of me,
And the thought of death close-walking the other
    side of me,
And I in the middle as with companions, and as
    holding the hands of companions,
I fled forth to the hiding receiving night that talks not,
Down to the shores of the water, the path by the
    swamp in the dimness,
To the solemn shadowy cedars and ghostly pines so still.

And the singer so shy to the rest receiv'd me,
The gray-brown bird I know receiv'd us comrades
    three,
And he sang the carol of death, and a verse for him I
    love.

From deep secluded recesses,
From the fragrant cedars and the ghostly pines so still,
Came the carol of the bird.

And the charm of the carol rapt me,
As I held as if by their hands my comrades in the night,
And the voice of my spirit tallied the song of the bird.

*Come lovely and soothing death,*
*Undulate round the world, serenely arriving, arriving,*
*In the day, in the night, to all, to each,*
*Sooner or later delicate death.*

*Prais'd be the fathomless universe,*
*For life and joy, and for objects and knowledge curious,*
*And for love, sweet love – but praise! praise! praise!*
*For the sure-enwinding arms of cool-enfolding death.*

*Dark mother always gliding near with soft feet,*
*Have none chanted for thee a chant of fullest welcome?*
*Then I chant it for thee, I glorify thee above all,*
*I bring thee a song that when thou must indeed come,*
*come unfalteringly.*

*Approach strong deliveress,*
*When it is so, when thou hast taken them I joyously sing*
*the dead,*
*Lost in the loving floating ocean of thee,*
*Laved in the flood of thy bliss O death.*

*From me to thee glad serenades,*
*Dances for thee I propose saluting thee, adornments and*
*feastings for thee,*
*And the sights of the open landscape and the high-spread*
*sky are fitting,*
*And life and the fields, and the huge and thoughtful night.*

*The night in silence under many a star,*
*The ocean shore and the husky whispering wave whose voice I know,*
*And the soul turning to thee O vast and well-veil'd death,*
*And the body gratefully nestling close to thee.*

*Over the tree-tops I float thee a song,*
*Over the rising and sinking waves, over the myriad fields and the prairies wide,*
*Over the dense-pack'd cities all and the teeming wharves and ways,*
*I float this carol with joy, with joy to thee O death.*

15

To the tally of my soul,
Loud and strong kept up the gray-brown bird,
With pure deliberate notes spreading filling the night.

Loud in the pines and cedars dim,
Clear in the freshness moist and the swamp-perfume,
And I with my comrades there in the night.

While my sight that was bound in my eyes unclosed,
As to long panoramas of visions.

And I saw askant the armies,
I saw as in noiseless dreams hundreds of battle-flags,
Borne through the smoke of the battles and pierc'd with missiles I saw them,
And carried hither and yon through the smoke, and torn and bloody,
And at last but a few shreds left on the staffs, (and all in silence,)
And the staffs all splinter'd and broken.

I saw battle-corpses, myriads of them,
And the white skeletons of young men, I saw them,
I saw the debris and debris of all the slain soldiers of the war,
But I saw they were not as was thought,
They themselves were fully at rest, they suffer'd not,
The living remain'd and suffer'd, the mother suffer'd,
And the wife and the child and the musing comrade suffer'd,
And the armies that remain'd suffer'd.

16

Passing the visions, passing the night,
Passing, unloosing the hold of my comrades' hands,
Passing the song of the hermit bird and the tallying song of my soul,
Victorious song, death's outlet song, yet varying ever-altering song,
As low and wailing, yet clear the notes, rising and falling, flooding the night,
Sadly sinking and fainting, as warning and warning, and yet again bursting with joy,
Covering the earth and filling the spread of the heaven,
As that powerful psalm in the night I heard from recesses,
Passing, I leave thee lilac with heart-shaped leaves,
I leave thee there in the door-yard, blooming, returning with spring.

I cease from my song for thee,
From my gaze on thee in the west, fronting the west, communing with thee,
O comrade lustrous with silver face in the night.

Yet each to keep and all, retrievements out of the night,
The song, the wondrous chant of the gray-brown bird,
And the tallying chant, the echo arous'd in my soul,
With the lustrous and drooping star with the
countenace full of woe,
With the holders holding my hand nearing the call of
the bird,
Comrades mine and I in the midst, and their memory
ever to keep, for the dead I loved so well,
For the sweetest, wisest soul of all my days and lands
– and this for his dear sake,
Lilac and star and bird twined with the chant of my
soul,
There in the fragrant pines and the cedars dusk and
dim.

## *O Captain! My Captain!*

O Captain! my Captain! our fearful trip is done,
The ship has weather'd every rack, the prize we
sought is won,
The port is near, the bells I hear, the people all exulting,
While follow eyes the steady keel, the vessel grim
and daring;
But O heart! heart! heart!
O the bleeding drops of red,
Where on the deck my Captain lies,
Fallen cold and dead.

O Captain! my Captain! rise up and hear the bells;
Rise up – for you the flag is flung – for you the bugle
trills,
For you bouquets and ribbon'd wreaths – for you
the shores a-crowding,

For you they call, the swaying mass, their eager faces
turning;
Here Captain! dear father!
The arm beneath your head!
It is some dream that on the deck,
You 've fallen cold and dead.

My Captain does not answer, his lips are pale and still,
My father does not feel my arm, he has no pulse nor will,
The ship is anchor'd safe and sound, its voyage
closed and done,
From fearful trip the victor ship comes in with object
won:
Exult O shores, and ring O bells!
But I with mournful tread,
Walk the deck my Captain lies,
Fallen cold and dead.

## *Hush'd be the Camps To-day*

(*May* 4, 1865)

Hush'd be the camps to-day,
And soldiers let us drape our war-worn weapons,
And each with musing soul retire to celebrate,
Our dear commander's death.

No more for him life's stormy conflicts,
Nor victory, nor defeat – no more time's dark events,
Charging like ceaseless clouds across the sky.

But sing poet in our name,
Sing of the love we bore him – because you – dweller
in camps, know it truly.

As they invault the coffin there,
Sing – as they close the doors of earth upon him – one verse,
For the heavy hearts of soldiers.

### *This Dust Was Once the Man*

This dust was once the man,
Gentle, plain, just and resolute, under whose cautious hand,
Against the foulest crime in history known in any land or age,
Was saved the Union of these States.

## *By Blue Ontario's Shore*

I

By blue Ontario's shore,
As I mused of these warlike days and of peace
return'd, and the dead that return no more,
A Phantom gigantic superb, with stern visage
accosted me,
*Chant me the poem,* it said, *that comes from the soul of*
*America, chant me the carol of victory,*
*And strike up the marches of Libertad, marches more*
*powerful yet,*
*And sing me before you go the song of the throes of*
*Democracy.*

(Democracy, the destin'd conqueror, yet treacherous
lip-smiles everywhere,
And death and infidelity at every step.)

2

A Nation announcing itself,
I myself make the only growth by which I can be
appreciated,
I reject none, accept all, then reproduce all in my
own forms.

A breed whose proof is in time and deeds,
What we are we are, nativity is answer enough to
objections,
We wield ourselves as a weapon is wielded,
We are powerful and tremendous in ourselves,
We are executive in ourselves, we are sufficient in
the variety of ourselves,
We are the most beautiful to ourselves and in
ourselves,

We stand self-pois'd in the middle, branching thence
over the world,
From Missouri, Nebraska, or Kansas, laughing
attacks to scorn.
Nothing is sinful to us outside of ourselves,
Whatever appears, whatever does not appear, we are
beautiful or sinful in ourselves only.

(O Mother – O Sisters dear!
If we are lost, no victor else has destroy'd us,
It is by ourselves we go down to eternal night.)

3

Have you thought there could be but a single
supreme?
There can be any number of supremes – one does
not countervail another any more than one
eyesight countervails another, or one life
countervails another.

All is eligible to all,
All is for individuals, all is for you,
No condition is prohibited, not God's or any.
All comes by the body, only health puts you rapport
with the universe.

Produce great Persons, the rest follows.

4

Piety and conformity to them that like,
Peace, obesity, allegiance, to them that like,
I am he who tauntingly compels men, women, nations,
Crying, Leap from your seats and contend for your
lives!

I am he who walks the States with a barb'd tongue, questioning every one I meet,
Who are you that wanted only to be told what you knew before?
Who are you that wanted only a book to join you in your nonsense?

(With pangs and cries as thine own O bearer of many children,
These clamors wild to a race of pride I give.)

O lands, would you be freer than all that has ever been before?
If you would be freer than all that has been before, come listen to me.

Fear grace, elegance, civilization, delicatesse,
Fear the mellow sweet, the sucking of honey-juice,
Beware the advancing mortal ripening of Nature,
Beware what precedes the decay of the ruggedness of states and men.

5

Ages, precedents, have long been accumulating undirected materials,
America brings builders, and brings its own styles.

The immortal poets of Asia and Europe have done their work and pass'd to other spheres,
A work remains, the work of surpassing all they have done.

America, curious toward foreign characters, stands by its own at all hazards,
Stands removed, spacious, composite, sound, initiates the true use of precedents,

Does not repel them or the past or what they have
  produced under their forms,
Takes the lesson with calmness, perceives the corpse
  slowly borne from the house,
Perceives that it waits a little while in the door, that
  it was fittest for its days,
That its life has descended to the stalwart and
  well-shaped heir who approaches,
And that he shall be fittest for his days.

Any period one nation must lead,
One land must be the promise and reliance of the
  future.
These States are the amplest poem,
Here is not merely a nation but a teeming Nation of
  nations,
Here the doings of men correspond with the
  broadcast doings of the day and night,
Here is what moves in magnificent masses careless
  of particulars,
Here are the roughs, beards, friendliness,
  combativeness, the soul loves,
Here the flowing trains, here the crowds, equality,
  diversity, the soul loves.

6

Land of lands and bards to corroborate!
Of them standing among them, one lifts to the light
  a westbred face,
To him the hereditary countenance bequeath'd both
  mother's and father's,
His first parts substances, earth, water, animals, trees,
Built of the common stock, having room for far and
  near,

Used to dispense with other lands, incarnating this
land,
Attracting it body and soul to himself, hanging on its
neck with incomparable love,
Plunging his seminal muscle into its merits and
demerits,
Making its cities, beginnings, events, diversities,
wars, vocal in him,
Making its rivers, lakes, bays, embouchure in him,
Mississippi with yearly freshets and changing chutes,
Columbia, Niagara, Hudson, spending
themselves lovingly in him,
If the Atlantic coast stretch or the Pacific coast
stretch, he stretching with them North or South,
Spanning between them East and West, and
touching whatever is between them,
Growths growing from him to offset the growths of
pine, cedar, hemlock, live-oak, locust, chestnut,
hickory, cottonwood, orange, magnolia,
Tangles as tangled in him as any cranebake or
swamp,
He likening sides and peaks of mountains, forests
coated with northern transparent ice,
Off him pasturage sweet and natural as savanna,
upland, prairie,
Through him flights, whirls, screams, answering
those of the fish-hawk, mocking-bird, night-
heron, and eagle,
His spirit surrounding his country's spirit, unclosed
to good and evil,
Surrounding the essences of real things, old times
and present times,
Surrounding just found shores, islands, tribes of red
aborigines,

Weather-beaten vessels, landings, settlements,
embryo stature and muscle,
The haughty defiance of the Year One, war, peace,
the formation of the Constitution,
The separate States, the simple elastic scheme, the
immigrants,
The Union always swarming with blatherers and
always sure and impregnable,
The unsurvey'd interior, log-houses, clearings, wild
animals, hunters, trappers,
Surrounding the multiform agriculture, mines,
temperature, the gestation of new States,
Congress convening every Twelfth-month, the
members duly coming up from the uttermost
parts,
Surrounding the noble character of mechanics and
farmers, especially the young men,
Responding their manners, speech, dress,
friendships, the gait they have of persons who
never knew how it felt to stand in the presence of
superiors,
The freshness and candor of their physiognomy, the
copiousness and decision of their phrenology,
The picturesque looseness of their carriage, their
fierceness when wrong'd,
The fluency of their speech, their delight in music,
their curiosity, good temper and open-
handedness, the whole composite make,
The prevailing ardor and enterprise, the large
amativeness,
The perfect equality of the female with the male, the
fluid movement of the population,
The superior marine, free commerce, fisheries,
whaling, gold-digging,

Wharf-hemm'd cities, railroad and steamboat lines
intersecting all points,
Factories, mercantile life, labor-saving machinery,
the Northeast, Northwest, Southwest,
Manhattan firemen, the Yankee swap, southern
plantation life,
Slavery – the murderous, treacherous conspiracy to
raise it upon the ruins of all the rest,
On and on to the grapple with it – Assassin! then your
life or ours be the stake, and respite no more.

7

(Lo, high toward heaven, this day,
Liberated, from the conqueress' field return'd,
I mark the new aureola around your head,
No more of soft astral, but dazzling and fierce,
With war's flames and the lambent lightnings playing,
And your port immovable where you stand,
With still the inextinguishable glance and the
clinch'd and lifted fist,
And your foot on the neck of the menacing one, the
scorner utterly crush'd beneath you,
The menacing arrogant one that strode and
advanced with his senseless scorn, bearing the
murderous knife,
The wide-swelling one, the braggart that would
yesterday do so much,
To-day a carrion dead and damn'd, the despised of
all the earth,
An offal rank, to the dunghill maggots spurn'd.)

8

Others take finish, but the Republic is ever
constructive and ever keeps vista,

Others adorn the past, but you O days of the present, I adorn you,
O days of the future I believe in you – I isolate myself for your sake,
O America because you build for mankind I build for you,
O well-beloved stone-cutters, I lead them who plan with decision and science,
Lead the present with friendly hand toward the future.

(Bravas to all impulses sending sane children to the next age!
But damn that which spends itself with no thought of the stain, pains, dismay, feebleness, it is bequeathing.)

9

I listened to the Phantom by Ontario's shore,
I heard the voice arising demanding bards,
By them all native and grand, by them alone can these States be fused into the compact organism of a Nation.

To hold men together by paper and seal or by compulsion is no account,
That only holds men together which aggregates all in a living principle, as the hold of the limbs of the body or the fibres of plants.

Of all races and eras these States with veins full of poetical stuff most need poets, and are to have the greatest, and use them the greatest,
Their Presidents shall not be their common referee so much as their poets shall.

(Soul of love and tongue of fire!
Eye to pierce the deepest deeps and sweep the world!
Ah Mother, prolific and full in all besides, yet how
    long barren, barren?)

10

Of these States the poet is the equable man,
Not in him but off from him things are grotesque,
    eccentric, fail of their full returns,
Nothing out of its place is good, nothing in its place
    is bad,
He bestows on every object or quality its fit
    proportion, neither more nor less,
He is the arbiter of the diverse, he is the key,
He is the equalizer of his age and land,
He supplies what wants supplying, he checks what
    wants checking,
In peace out of him speaks the spirit of peace, large,
    rich, thrifty, building populous towns,
    encouraging agriculture, arts, commerce, lighting
    the study of man, the soul, health, immortality,
    government,
In war he is the best backer of the war, he fetches
    artillery as good as the engineer's, he can make
    every word he speaks draw blood,
The years straying toward infidelity he withholds by
    his steady faith,
He is no arguer, he is judgment, (Nature accepts
    him absolutely,)
He judges not as the judge judges but as the sun
    falling round a helpless thing,
As he sees the farthest he has the most faith,
His thoughts are the hymns of the praise of things,
In the dispute on God and eternity he is silent,

He sees eternity less like a play with a prologue and
denouement,
He sees eternity in men and women, he does not see
men and women as dreams or dots.

For the great Idea, the idea of perfect and free
individuals,
For that, the bard walks in advance, leader of leaders,
The attitude of him cheers up slaves and horrifies
foreign despots.

Without extinction is Liberty, without retrograde is
Equality,
They live in the feelings of young men and the best
women,
(Not for nothing have the indomitable heads of the
earth been always ready to fall for Liberty.)

II

For the great Idea,
That, O my brethren, that is the mission of poets.

Songs of stern defiance ever ready,
Songs of the rapid arming and the march,
The flag of peace quick-folded, and instead the flag
we know,
Warlike flag of the great Idea.

(Angry cloth I saw there leaping!
I stand again in leaden rain your flapping folds saluting,
I sing you over all, flying beckoning through the fight
– O the hard-contested fight!
The cannons ope their rosy-flashing muzzles – the
hurtled balls scream,
The battle-front forms amid the smoke – the volleys
pour incessant from the line,

Hark, the ringing word *Charge!* – now the tussle and
the furious maddening yells,
Now the corpses tumble curl'd upon the ground,
Cold, cold in death, for precious life of you,
Angry cloth I saw there leaping.)

12

Are you he who would assume a place to teach or be
a poet here in the States?
The place is august, the terms obdurate.

Who would assume to teach here may well prepare
himself body and mind,
He may well survey, ponder, arm, fortify, harden,
make lithe himself,
He shall surely be question'd beforehand by me with
many and stern questions.

Who are you indeed who would talk or sing to America?
Have you studied out the land, its idioms and men?
Have you learn'd the physiology, phrenology,
politics, geography, pride, freedom, friendship of
the land? its substratums and objects?
Have you consider'd the organic compact of the first
day of the first year of Independence, sign'd by
the Commissioners, ratified by the States, and
read by Washington at the head of the army?
Have you possess'd yourself of the Federal
Constitution?
Do you see who have left all feudal processes and
poems behind them, and assumed the poems
and processes of Democracy?
Are you faithful to things? do you teach what the
land and sea, the bodies of men, womanhood,
amativeness, heroic angers, teach?

Have you sped through fleeting customs, popularities?
Can you hold your hand against all seductions, follies, whirls, fierce contentions? are you very strong? are you really of the whole People?
Are you not of some coterie? some school or mere religion?
Are you done with reviews and criticisms of life? animating now to life itself?
Have you vivified yourself from the maternity of these States?
Have you too the old ever-fresh forbearance and impartiality?
Do you hold the like love for those hardening to maturity? for the last-born? little and big? and for the errant?

What is this you bring my America?
Is it uniform with my country?
Is it not something that has been better told or done before?
Have you not imported this or the spirit of it in some ship?
Is it not a mere tale? a rhyme? a prettiness? – is the good old cause in it?
Has it not dangled long at the heels of the poets, politicians, literats, of enemies' lands?
Does it not assume that what is notoriously gone is still here?
Does it answer universal needs? will it improve manners?
Does it sound with trumpet-voice the proud victory of the Union in that secession war?
Can your performance face the open fields and the seaside?

Will it absorb into me as I absorb food, air, to
appear again in my strength, gait, face?
Have real employments contributed to it? original
makers, not mere amanuenses?
Does it meet modern discoveries, calibres, facts, face
to face?
What does it mean to American persons, progresses,
cities? Chicago, Kanada, Arkansas?
Does it see behind the apparent custodians the real
custodians standing, menacing, silent, the
mechanics, Manhattanese, Western men,
Southerners, significant alike in their apathy, and
in the promptness of their love?
Does it see what finally befalls, and has always finally
befallen, each temporizer, patcher, outsider,
partialist, alarmist, infidel, who has ever ask'd
any thing of America?
What mocking and scornful negligence?
The track strew'd with the dust of skeletons,
By the roadside others disdainfully toss'd.

13

Rhymes and rhymers pass away, poems distill'd
from poems pass away,
The swarms of reflectors and the polite pass, and
leave ashes,
Admirers, importers, obedient persons, make but
the soil of literature,
America justifies itself, give it time, no disguise can
deceive it or conceal from it, it is impassive enough,
Only toward the likes of itself will it advance to meet
them,
If its poets appear it will in due time advance to meet
them, there is no fear of mistake,

(The proof of a poet shall be sternly deferr'd till his
country absorbs him as affectionately as he has
absorb'd it.)

He masters whose spirit masters, he tastes sweetest
who results sweetest in the long run,
The blood of the brawn beloved of time is
unconstraint;
In the need of songs, philosophy, an appropriate
native grand-opera, shipcraft, any craft,
He or she is greatest who contributes the greatest
original practical example.

Already a nonchalant breed, silently emerging,
appears on the streets,
People's lips salute only doers, lovers, satisfiers,
positive knowers,
There will shortly be no more priests, I say their
work is done,
Death is without emergencies here, but life is
perpetual emergencies here,
Are your body, days, manners, superb? after death
you shall be superb,
Justice, health, self-esteem, clear the way with
irresistible power;
How dare you place any thing before a man?

14

Fall behind me States!
A man before all – myself, typical, before all.

Give me the pay I have served for,
Give to sing the songs of the great Idea, take all the rest,
I have loved the earth, sun, animals, I have despised
riches,

I have given alms to every one that ask'd, stood up for the stupid and crazy, devoted my income and labor to others,
Hated tyrants, argued not concerning God, had patience and indulgence toward the people, taken off my hat to nothing known or unknown,
Gone freely with powerful uneducated persons and with the young, and with the mothers of families,
Read these leaves to myself in the open air, tried them by trees, stars, rivers,
Dismiss'd whatever insulted my own soul or defiled my body,
Claim'd nothing to myself which I have not carefully claim'd for others on the same terms,
Sped to the camps, and comrades found and accepted from every State,
(Upon this breast has many a dying soldier lean'd to breathe his last,
This arm, this hand, this voice, have nourish'd, rais'd, restored,
To life recalling many a prostrate form;)
I am willing to wait to be understood by the growth of the taste of myself,
Rejecting none, permitting all.
(Say O Mother, have I not to your thought been faithful?
Have I not through life kept you and yours before me?)

15

I swear I begin to see the meaning of these things,
It is not the earth, it is not America who is so great,
It is I who am great or to be great, it is You up there, or any one,

It is to walk rapidly through civilizations,
governments, theories,
Through poems, pageants, shows, to form individuals.

Underneath all, individuals,
I swear nothing is good to me now that ignores
individuals,
The American compact is altogether with individuals,
The only government is that which makes minute of
individuals,
The whole theory of the universe is directed unerringly
to one single individual – namely to You.

(Mother! with subtle sense severe, with the naked
sword in your hand,
I saw you at last refuse to treat but directly with
individuals.)

16

Underneath all, Nativity,
I swear I will stand by my own nativity, pious or
impious so be it;
I swear I am charm'd with nothing except nativity,
Men, women, cities, nations, are only beautiful from
nativity.
Underneath all is the Expression of love for men and
women,
(I swear I have seen enough of mean and impotent
modes of expressing love for men and women,
After this day I take my own modes of expressing
love for men and women.)

I swear I will have each quality of my race in myself,
(Talk as you like, he only suits these States whose
manners favor the audacity and sublime turbulence
of the States.)

Underneath the lessons of things, spirits, Nature, governments, ownerships, I swear I perceive other lessons,
Underneath all to me is myself, to you yourself, (the same monotonous old song.)

17

O I see flashing that this America is only you and me,
Its power, weapons, testimony, are you and me,
Its crimes, lies, thefts, defections, are you and me,
Its Congress is you and me, the officers, capitols, armies, ships, are you and me,
Its endless gestations of new States are you and me,
The war, (that war so bloody and grim, the war I will henceforth forget), was you and me,
Natural and artificial are you and me,
Freedom, language, poems, employments, are you and me,
Past, present, future, are you and me.

I dare not shirk any part of myself,
Not any part of America good or bad,
Not to build for that which builds for mankind,
Not to balance ranks, complexions, creeds, and the sexes,
Not to justify science nor the march of equality,
Nor to feed the arrogant blood of the brawn belov'd of time.

I am for those that have never been master'd,
For men and women whose tempers have never been master'd,
For those whom laws, theories, conventions, can never master.

I am for those who walk abreast with the whole earth,
Who inaugurate one to inaugurate all.

I will not be outfaced by irrational things,
I will penetrate what it is in them that is sarcastic upon me,
I will make cities and civilizations defer to me,
This is what I have learnt from America – it is the amount, and it I teach again.

(Democracy, while weapons were everywhere aim'd at your breast,
I saw you serenely give birth to immortal children, saw in dreams your dilating form,
Saw you with spreading mantle covering the world.)

18

I will confront these shows of the day and night,
I will know if I am to be less than they,
I will see if I am not as majestic as they,
I will see if I am not as subtle and real as they,
I will see if I am to be less generous than they,
I will see if I have no meaning, while the houses and ships have meaning,
I will see if the fishes and birds are to be enough for themselves, and I am not to be enough for myself.

I match my spirit against yours you orbs, growths, mountains, brutes,
Copious as you are I absorb you all in myself, and become the master myself,
America isolated yet embodying all, what is it finally except myself?
These States, what are they except myself?

I know now why the earth is gross, tantalizing,
    wicked, it is for my sake,
I take you specially to be mine, you terrible, rude forms.

(Mother, bend down, bend close to me your face,
I know not what these plots and wars and
    deferments are for,
I know not fruition's success, but I know that
    through war and crime your work goes on, and
    must yet go on.)

19

Thus by blue Ontario's shore,
While the winds fann'd me and the waves came
    trooping toward me,
I thrill'd with the power's pulsations, and the charm
    of my theme was upon me,
Till the tissues that held me parted their ties upon me.

And I saw the free souls of poets,
The loftiest bards of past ages strode before me,
Strange large men, long unwaked, undisclosed, were
    disclosed to me.

20

O my rapt verse, my call, mock me not!
Not for the bards of the past, not to invoke them
    have I launch'd you forth,
Not to call even those lofty bards here by Ontario's
    shores,
Have I sung so capricious and loud my savage song.

Bards for my own land only I invoke,
(For the war, the war is over, the field is clear'd,)

Till they strike up marches henceforth triumphant
and onward,
To cheer O Mother your boundless expectant soul.

Bards of the great Idea! bards of the peaceful
inventions! (for the war, the war is over!)
Yet bards of latent armies, a million soldiers waiting
ever-ready,
Bards with songs as from burning coals or the
lightning's fork'd stripes!
Ample Ohio's, Kanada's bards – bards of California!
inland bards – bards of the war!
You by my charm I invoke.

## *Reversals*

Let that which stood in front go behind,
Let that which was behind advance to the front,
Let bigots, fools, unclean persons, offer new
propositions,
Let the old propositions be postponed,
Let a man seek pleasure everywhere except in himself,
Let a woman seek happiness everywhere except in
herself.

# AUTUMN RIVULETS

## *As Consequent, etc.*

As consequent from store of summer rains,
Or wayward rivulets in autumn flowing,
Or many a herb-lined brook's reticulations,
Or subterranean sea-rills making for the sea,
Songs of continued years I sing.

Life's ever-modern rapids first, (soon, soon to blend,
With the old streams of death.)

Some threading Ohio's farm-fields or the woods,
Some down Colorado's cañons from sources of
perpetual snow,
Some half-hid in Oregon, or away southward in Texas,
Some in the north finding their way to Erie, Niagara,
Ottawa,
Some to Atlantica's bays, and so to the great salt brine.

In you whoe'er you are my book perusing,
In I myself, in all the world, these currents flowing,
All, all toward the mystic ocean tending.

Currents for starting a continent new,
Overtures sent to the solid out of the liquid,
Fusion of ocean and land, tender and pensive waves,
(Not safe and peaceful only, waves rous'd and
ominous too,
Out of the depths the storm's abysmic waves, who
knows whence?
Raging over the vast, with many a broken spar and
tatter'd sail.)

Or from the sea of Time, collecting vasting all, I bring,
A windrow-drift of weeds and shells.

O little shells, so curious-convolute, so limpid-cold
and voiceless,
Will you not little shells to the tympans of temples held,
Murmurs and echoes still call up, eternity's music
faint and far,
Wafted inland, sent from Atlantica's rim, strains for
the soul of the prairies,
Whisper'd reverberations, chords for the ear of the
West joyously sounding,
Your tidings old, yet ever new and untranslatable,
Infinitesimals out of my life, and many a life,
(For not my life and yours alone I give – all, all I give,)
These waifs from the deep, cast high and dry,
Wash'd on America's shores?

## *The Return of the Heroes*

### I

For the lands and for these passionate days and for
myself,
Now I awhile retire to thee O soil of autumn fields,
Reclining on thy breast, giving myself to thee,
Answering the pulses of thy sane and equable heart,
Tuning a verse for thee.

O earth that hast no voice, confide to me a voice,
O harvest of my lands – O boundless summer growths,
O lavish brown parturient earth – O infinite teeming
womb,
A song to narrate thee.

2

Over upon this stage,
Is acted God's calm annual drama,
Gorgeous procession, songs of birds,
Sunrise that fullest feeds and freshens most the soul,
The heaving sea, the waves upon the shore, the musical, strong waves,
The woods, the stalwart trees, the slender, tapering trees,
The liliput countless armies of the grass,
The heat, the showers, the measureless pasturages,
The scenery of the snows, the winds' free orchestra,
The stretching light-hung roof of clouds, the clear cerulean and the silvery fringes,
The high dilating stars, the placid beckoning stars,
The moving flocks and herds, the plains and emerald meadows,
The shows of all the varied lands and all the growths and products.

3

Fecund America – to-day,
Thou art over set in births and joys!
Thou groan'st with riches, thy wealth clothes thee as a swathing-garment,
Thou laughest loud with ache of great possessions,
A myriad-twining life like interlacing vines binds all thy vast demesne,
As some huge ship freighted to water's edge thou ridest into port,
As rain falls from the heaven and vapors rise from earth, so have the precious values fallen upon thee and risen out of thee;

Thou envy of the globe! thou miracle!
Thou, bathed, choked, swimming in plenty,
Thou lucky Mistress of the tranquil barns,
Thou Prairie Dame that sittest in the middle and lookest out upon thy world, and lookest East and lookest West,
Dispensatress, that by a word givest a thousand miles, a million farms, and missest nothing,
Thou all-acceptress – thou hospitable, (thou only art hospitable as God is hospitable.)

4

When late I sang sad was my voice,
Sad were the shows around me with deafening noises of hatred and smoke of war;
In the midst of the conflict, the heroes, I stood,
Or pass'd with slow step through the wounded and dying.

But now I sing not war,
Nor the measur'd march of soldiers, nor the tents of camps,
Nor the regiments hastily coming up deploying in line of battle;
No more the sad, unnatural shows of war.

Ask'd room those flush'd immortal ranks, the first forth-stepping armies?
Ask room alas the ghastly ranks, the armies dread that follow'd.

(Pass, pass, ye proud brigades, with your tramping sinewy legs,
With your shoulders young and strong, with your knapsacks and your muskets;

How elate I stood and watch'd you, where starting
    off you march'd.

Pass – then rattle drums again,
For an army heaves in sight, O another gathering army,
Swarming, trailing on the rear, O you dread
    accruing army,
O you regiments so piteous, with your mortal
    diarrhoea, with your fever,
O my land's maim'd darlings, with the plenteous
    bloody bandage and the crutch,
Lo, your pallid army follows.)

5

But on these days of brightness,
On the far-stretching beauteous landscape, the roads
    and lanes, the high-piled farm-wagons, and the
    fruits and barns,
Should the dead intrude?

Ah the dead to me mar not, they fit well in Nature,
They fit very well in the landscape under the trees
    and grass,
And along the edge of the sky in the horizon's far
    margin.

Nor do I forget you Departed,
Nor in winter or summer my lost ones,
But most in the open air as now when my soul is
    rapt and at peace, like pleasing phantoms,
Your memories rising glide silently by me.

6

I saw the day the return of the heroes,
(Yet the heroes never surpass'd shall never return,
Them that day I saw not.)

I saw the interminable corps, I saw the processions
 of armies,
I saw them approaching, defiling by with divisions,
Streaming northward, their work done, camping
 awhile in clusters of mighty camps.

No holiday soldiers – youthful, yet veterans,
Worn, swart, handsome, strong, of the stock of
 homestead and workshop,
Harden'd of many a long campaign and sweaty march,
Inured on many a hard-fought bloody field.

A pause – the armies wait,
A million flush'd embattled conquerors wait,
The world too waits, then soft as breaking night and
 sure as dawn,
They melt, they disappear.
Exult O lands! victorious lands!
Not there your victory on those red shuddering fields,
But here and hence your victory.

Melt, melt away ye armies – disperse ye blue-clad
 soldiers,
Resolve ye back again, give up for good your deadly
 arms,
Other the arms the fields henceforth for you, or
 South or North,
With saner wars, sweet wars, life-giving wars.

7

Loud O my throat, and clear O soul!
The season of thanks and the voice of full-yielding,
The chant of joy and power for boundless fertility.

All till'd and untill'd fields expand before me,
I see the true arenas of my race, or first or last,
Man's innocent and strong arenas.

I see the heroes at other toils,
I see well-wielded in their hands the better weapons.

I see where the Mother of All,
With full-spanning eye gazes forth, dwells long,
And counts the varied gathering of the products.

Busy the far, the sunlit panorama,
Prairie, orchard, and yellow grain of the North,
Cotton and rice of the South and Louisianian cane,
Open unseeded fallows, rich fields of clover and timothy,
Kine and horses feeding, and droves of sheep and swine,
And many a stately river flowing and many a jocund brook,
And healthy uplands with herby-perfumed breezes,
And the good green grass, that delicate miracle the ever-recurring grass.

8

Toil on heroes! harvest the products!
Not alone on those warlike fields the Mother of All,
With dilated form and lambent eyes watch'd you.
Toil on heroes! toil well! handle the weapons well!
The Mother of All, yet here as ever she watches you.

Well-pleased America thou beholdest,
Over the fields of the West those crawling monsters,
The human-divine inventions, the labor-saving implements;
Beholdest moving in every direction imbued as with life the revolving hay-rakes,

The steam-power reaping-machines and the horse-
    power machines,
The engines, thrashers of grain and cleaners of grain,
    well separating the straw, the nimble work of the
    patent pitchfork,
Beholdest the newer saw-mill, the southern cotton-
    gin, and the rice-cleanser.
Beneath thy look O Maternal,
With these and else and with their own strong hands
    the heroes harvest.

All gather and all harvest,
Yet but for thee O Powerful, not a scythe might
    swing as now in security,
Not a maize-stalk dangle as now its silken tassels in
    peace.

Under thee only they harvest, even but a wisp of hay
    under thy great face only,
Harvest the wheat of Ohio, Illinois, Wisconsin, every
    barbed spear under thee,
Harvest the maize of Missouri, Kentucky,
    Tennessee, each ear in its light-green sheath,
Gather the hay to its myriad mows in the odorous
    tranquil barns,
Oats to their bins, the white potato, the buckwheat
    of Michigan, to theirs;
Gather the cotton in Mississippi or Alabama, dig
    and hoard the golden the sweet potato of
    Georgia and the Carolinas,
Clip the wool of California or Pennsylvania,
Cut the flax in the Middle States, or hemp or
    tobacco in the Borders,
Pick the pea and the bean, or pull apples from the
    trees or bunches of grapes from the vines,

Or aught that ripens in all these States or North or
South,
Under the beaming sun and under thee.

## *There was a Child went Forth*

There was a child went forth every day,
And the first object he look'd upon, that object he
became,
And that object became part of him for the day
or a certain part of the day,
Or for many years or stretching cycles of years.

The early lilacs became part of this child,
And grass and white and red morning-glories, and white
and red clover, and the song of the phoebe-bird,
And the Third-month lambs and the sow's pink-faint
litter, and the mare's foal and the cow's calf,
And the noisy brood of the barnyard or by the mire
of the pond-side,
And the fish suspending themselves so curiously
below there, and the beautiful curious liquid,
And the water-plants with their graceful flat heads,
all became part of him.

The field-sprouts of Fourth-month and Fifth-month
became part of him,
Winter-grain sprouts and those of the light-yellow
corn, and the esculent roots of the garden,
And the apple-trees cover'd with blossoms and the
fruit afterward, and wood-berries, and the
commonest weeds by the road.
And the old drunkard staggering home from the
outhouse of the tavern whence he had lately risen,

And the schoolmistress that pass'd on her way to the school,
And the friendly boys that pass'd, and the quarrelsome boys,
And the tidy and fresh-cheek'd girls, and the barefoot negro boy and girl,
And all the changes of city and country wherever he went.

His own parents, he that had father'd him and she that had conceiv'd him in her womb and birth'd him,
They gave this child more of themselves than that,
They gave him afterward every day, they became part of him.

The mother at home quietly placing the dishes on the supper-table,
The mother with mild words, clean her cap and gown, a wholesome odor falling off her person and clothes as she walks by,
The father, strong, self-sufficient, manly, mean, anger'd, unjust,
The blow, the quick loud word, the tight, bargain, the crafty lure,
The family usages, the language, the company, the furniture, the yearning and swelling heart,
Affection that will not be gainsay'd, the sense of what is real, the thought if after all it should prove unreal,
The doubts of day-time and the doubts of night-time, the curious whether and how,
Whether that which appears so is so, or is it all flashes and specks?
Men and women crowding fast in the streets, if they are not flashes and specks what are they?

The streets themselves and the façades of houses, and
goods in the windows,
Vehicles, teams, the heavy-plank'd wharves, the
huge crossing at the ferries,
The village on the highland seen from afar at sunset,
the river between,
Shadows, aureola and mist, the light falling on roofs
and gables of white or brown two miles off,
The schooner near by sleepily dropping down the
tide, the little boat slack-tow'd astern,
The hurrying tumbling waves, quick-broken crests,
slapping,
The strata of color'd clouds, the long bar of maroon-
tint away solitary by itself, the spread of purity it
lies motionless in,
The horizon's edge, the flying sea-crow, the
fragrance of salt marsh and shore mud,
These became part of that child who went forth
every day, and who now goes, and will always go
forth every day.

## *Old Ireland*

Far hence amid an isle of wondrous beauty,
Crouching over a grave an ancient sorrowful mother,
Once a queen, now lean and tatter'd seated on the
ground,
Her old white hair drooping dishevel'd round her
shoulders,
At her feet fallen an unused royal harp,
Long silent, she too long silent, mourning her
shrouded hope and heir,

Of all the earth her heart most full of sorrow because
most full of love.

Yet a word ancient mother,
You need crouch there no longer on the cold ground
with forehead between your knees,
O you need not sit there veil'd in your old white hair
so dishevel'd,
For know you the one you mourn is not in that grave,
It was an illusion, the son you love was not really dead,
The Lord is not dead, he is risen again young and
strong in another country,
Even while you wept there by your fallen harp by the
grave,
What you wept for was translated, pass'd from the
grave,
The winds favor'd and the sea sail'd it,
And now with rosy and new blood,
Moves to-day in a new country.

## *The City Dead-House*

By the city dead-house by the gate,
As idly sauntering wending my way from the clangor,
I curious pause, for lo, an outcast form, a poor dead
prostitute brought,
Her corpse they deposit unclaim'd, it lies on the
damp brick pavement,
The divine woman, her body, I see the body, I look
on it alone,
That house once full of passion and beauty, all else I
notice not,
Nor stillness so cold, nor running water from faucet,
nor odors morbific impress me,

But the house alone – that wondrous house – that
 delicate fair house – that ruin!
That immortal house more than all the rows of
 dwellings ever built!
Or white-domed capitol with majestic figure
 surmounted, or all the old high-spired
 cathedrals,
That little house alone more than them all – poor,
 desperate house!
Fair, fearful wreck – tenement of a soul – itself a soul,
Unclaim'd, avoided house – take one breath from
 my tremulous lips,
Take one tear dropt aside as I go for thought of you,
Dead house of love – house of madness and sin,
 crumbled, crush'd,
House of life, erewhile talking and laughing – but ah,
 poor house, dead even then,
Months, years, an echoing, garnish'd house – but
 dead, dead, dead.

## *This Compost*

I

Something startles me where I thought I was safest,
I withdraw from the still woods I loved,
I will not go now on the pastures to walk,
I will not strip the clothes from my body to meet my
 lover the sea,
I will not touch my flesh to the earth as to other flesh
 to renew me.

O how can it be that the ground itself does not sicken?
How can you be alive you growths of spring?

How can you furnish health you blood of herbs, roots, orchards, grain?
Are they not continually putting distemper'd corpses within you?
Is not every continent work'd over and over with sour dead?

Where have you disposed of their carcasses?
Those drunkards and gluttons of so many generations?
Where have you drawn off all the foul liquid and meat?
I do not see any of it upon you to-day, or perhaps I am deceiv'd,
I will run a furrow with my plough, I will press my spade through the sod and turn it up underneath,
I am sure I shall expose some of the foul meat.

2

Behold this compost! behold it well!
Perhaps every mite has once form'd part of a sick person – yet behold!
The grass of spring covers the prairies,
The bean bursts noiselessly through the mould in the garden,
The delicate spear of the onion pierces upward,
The apple-buds cluster together on the apple-branches,
The resurrection of the wheat appears with pale visage out of its graves,
The tinge awakes over the willow-tree and the mulberry-tree,
The he-birds carol mornings and evenings while the she-birds sit on their nests,
The young of poultry break through the hatch'd eggs,

The new-born of animals appear, the calf is dropt
from the cow, the colt from the mare,
Out of its little hill faithfully rise the potato's dark
green leaves,
Out of its hill rises the yellow maize-stalk, the lilacs
bloom in the door-yards,
The summer growth is innocent and disdainful
above all those strata of sour dead.

What chemistry!
That the winds are really not infectious,
That this is no cheat, this transparent green-wash of
the sea which is so amorous after me,
That it is safe to allow it to lick my naked body all
over with its tongues,
That it will not endanger me with the fevers that
have deposited themselves in it,
That all is clean forever and forever,
That the cool drink from the well tastes so good,
That blackberries are so flavorous and juicy,
That the fruits of the apple-orchard and the orange-
orchard, that melons, grapes, peaches, plums,
will none of them poison me,
That when I recline on the grass I do not catch any
disease,
Though probably every spear of grass rises out of
what was once a catching disease.

Now I am terrified at the Earth, it is that calm and
patient,
It grows such sweet things out of such corruptions,
It turns harmless and stainless on its axis, with such
endless successions of diseas'd corpses,
It distills such exquisite winds out of such infused
fetor,

It renews with such unwitting looks its prodigal,
annual, sumptuous crops,
It gives such divine materials to men, and accepts
such leavings from them at last.

### *To a Foil'd European Revolutionaire*

Courage yet, my brother or my sister!
Keep on – Liberty is to be subserv'd whatever occurs;
That is nothing that is quell'd by one or two failures,
or any number of failures,
Or by the indifference or ingratitude of the people,
or by any unfaithfulness,
Or the show of the tushes of power, soldiers,
cannon, penal statutes.

What we believe in waits latent forever through all
the continents,
Invites no one, promises nothing, sits in calmness
and light, is positive and composed, knows no
discouragement,
Waiting patiently, waiting its time.

(Not songs of loyalty alone are these,
But songs of insurrection also,
For I am the sworn poet of every dauntless rebel the
world over,
And he going with me leaves peace and routine
behind him,
And stakes his life to be lost at any moment.)

The battle rages with many a loud alarm and
frequent advance and retreat,
The infidel triumphs, or supposes he triumphs,

The prison, scaffold, garrote, handcuffs, iron
    necklace and lead-balls do their work,
The named and unnamed heroes pass to other spheres,
The great speakers and writers are exiled, they lie
    sick in distant lands,
The cause is asleep, the strongest throats are choked
    with their own blood,
The young men droop their eyelashes toward the
    ground when they meet;
But for all this Liberty has not gone out of the place,
    nor the infidel enter'd into full possession.
When Liberty goes out of a place it is not the first to
    go, nor the second or third to go,
It waits for all the rest to go, it is the last.

When there are no more memories of heroes and
    martyrs,
And when all life and all the souls of men and women
    are discharged from any part of the earth,
Then only shall liberty or the idea of liberty be
    discharged from that part of the earth,
And the infidel come into full possession.

Then courage European revolter, revoltress!
For till all ceases neither must you cease.

I do not know what you are for, (I do not know what
    I am for myself, nor what any thing is for,)
But I will search carefully for it even in being foil'd,
In defeat, poverty, misconception, imprisonment –
    for they too are great.

Did we think victory great?
So it is – but now it seems to me, when it cannot be
    help'd, that defeat is great,
And that death and dismay are great.

## *Unnamed Lands*

Nations ten thousand years before these States, and many times ten thousand years before these States,
Garner'd clusters of ages that men and women like us grew up and travel'd their course and pass'd on,
What vast-built cities, what orderly republics, what pastoral tribes and nomads,
What histories, rulers, heroes, perhaps transcending all others,
What laws, customs, wealth, arts, traditions,
What sort of marriage, what costumes, what physiology and phrenology,
What of liberty and slavery among them, what they thought of death and the soul,
Who were witty and wise, who beautiful and poetic, who brutish and undevelop'd,
Not a mark, not a record remains – and yet all remains.
O I know that those men and women were not for nothing, any more than we are for nothing,
I know that they belong to the scheme of the world every bit as much as we now belong to it.

Afar they stand, yet near to me they stand,
Some with oval countenances learn'd and calm,
Some naked and savage, some like huge collections of insects,
Some in tents, herdsmen, patriarchs, tribes, horsemen,
Some prowling through woods, some living peaceably on farms, laboring, reaping, filling barns,
Some traversing paved avenues, amid temples, palaces, factories, libraries, shows, courts, theatres, wonderful monuments.

Are those billions of men really gone?
Are those women of the old experience of the earth gone?
Do their lives, cities, arts, rest only with us?
Did they achieve nothing for good for themselves?

I believe of all those men and women that fill'd the unnamed lands, every one exists this hour here or elsewhere, invisible to us,
In exact proportion to what he or she grew from in life, and out of what he or she did, felt, became, loved, sinn'd, in life.

I believe that was not the end of those nations or any person of them, any more than this shall be the end of my nation, or of me;
Of their languages, governments, marriage, literature, products, games, wars, manners, crimes, prisons, slaves, heroes, poets,
I suspect their results curiously await in the yet unseen world, counterparts of what accrued to them in the seen world,
I suspect I shall meet them there,
I suspect I shall there find each old particular of those unnamed lands.

## *Song of Prudence*

Manhattan's streets I saunter'd, pondering
On Time, Space, Reality – on such as these, and abreast with them Prudence.
The last explanation always remains to be made about prudence,
Little and large alike drop quietly aside from the prudence that suits immortality.

The soul is of itself,
All verges to it, all has reference to what ensues,
All that a person does, says, thinks, is of
consequence,
Not a move can a man or woman make, that affects
him or her in a day, month, any part of the direct
lifetime, or the hour of death,
But the same affects him or her onward afterward
through the indirect lifetime.

The indirect is just as much as the direct,
The spirit receives from the body just as much as it
gives to the body, if not more.

Not one word or deed, not venerea
l sore, discoloration, privacy of the onanist,
Putridity of gluttons or rum-drinkers, peculation,
cunning, betrayal, murder, seduction, prostitution,
But has results beyond death as really as before death.

Charity and personal force are the only investments
worth any thing.

No specification is necessary, all that a male or
female does, that is vigorous, benevolent, clean,
is so much profit to him or her,
In the unshakable order of the universe and through
the whole scope of it forever.

Who has been wise receives interest,
Savage, felon, President, judge, farmer, sailor,
mechanic, literat, young, old, it is the same,
The interest will come round – all will come round.

Singly, wholly, to affect now, affected their time, will
forever affect, all of the past and all of the
present and all of the future,

All the brave actions of war and peace,
All help given to relatives, strangers, the poor, old,
sorrowful, young children, widows, the sick, and
to shunn'd persons,
All self-denial that stood steady and aloof on wrecks,
and saw others fill the seats of the boats,
All offering of substance or life for the good old
cause, or for a friend's sake, or opinion's sake,
All pains of enthusiasts scoff'd at by their neighbors,
All the limitless sweet love and precious suffering of
mothers,
All honest men baffled in strifes recorded or
unrecorded,
All the grandeur and good of ancient nations whose
fragments we inherit,
All the good of the dozens of ancient nations
unknown to us by name, date, location,
All that was ever manfully begun, whether it
succeeded or no,
All suggestions of the divine mind of man or the divinity
of his mouth, or the shaping of his great hands,
All that is well thought or said this day on any part of
the globe, or on any of the wandering stars, or on
any of the fix'd stars, by those there as we are here,
All that is henceforth to be thought or done by you
whoever you are, or by any one,
These inure, have inured, shall inure, to the identities
from which they sprang, or shall spring.

Did you guess any thing lived only its moment?
The world does not so exist, no parts palpable or
impalpable so exist,
No consummation exists without being from some long
previous consummation, and that from some other,

Without the farthest conceivable one coming a bit
nearer the beginning than any.

Whatever satisfies souls is true;
Prudence entirely satisfies the craving and glut of souls,
Itself only finally satisfies the soul,
The soul has that measureless pride which revolts
from every lesson but its own.

Now I breathe the word of the prudence that walks
abreast with time, space, reality,
That answers the pride which refuses every lesson
but its own.

What is prudence is indivisible,
Declines to separate one part of life from every part,
Divides not the righteous from the unrighteous or
the living from the dead,
Matches every thought or act by its correlative,
Knows no possible forgiveness or deputed atonement,
Knows that the young man who composedly peril'd
his life
and lost it has done exceedingly well for himself
without doubt,
That he who never peril'd his life, but retains it to
old age in riches and ease, has probably achiev'd
nothing for himself worth mentioning,
Knows that only that person has really learn'd who
has learn'd to prefer results,
Who favors body and soul the same,
Who perceives the indirect assuredly following the
direct,
Who in his spirit in any emergency whatever neither
hurries nor avoids death.

## *The Singer in the Prison*

1

*O sight of pity, shame and dole!*
*O fearful thought – a convict soul.*

Rang the refrain along the hall, the prison,
Rose to the roof, the vaults of heaven above,
Pouring in floods of melody in tones so pensive sweet
 and strong the like whereof was never heard,
Reaching the far-off sentry and the armed guards,
 who ceas'd their pacing,
Making the hearer's pulses stop for ecstasy and awe.

2

The sun was low in the west one winter day,
When down a narrow aisle amid the thieves and
 outlaws of the land,
(There by the hundreds seated, sear-faced
 murderers, wily counterfeiters,
Gather'd to Sunday church in prison walls, the
 keepers round,
Plenteous, well-armed, watching with vigilant eyes,)
Calmly a lady walk'd holding a little innocent child
 by either hand,
Whom seating on their stools beside her on the
 platform,
She, first preluding with the instrument a low and
 musical prelude,
In voice surpassing all, sang forth a quaint old hymn.

A soul confined by bars and bands,
Cries, help! O help! and wrings her hands,
Blinded her eyes, bleeding her breast,
Nor pardon finds, nor balm of rest.

Ceaseless she paces to and fro,
O heart-sick days! O nights of woe!
Nor hand of friend, nor loving face,
Nor favor comes, nor word of grace.

It was not I that sinn'd the sin,
The ruthless body dragg'd me in;
Though long I strove courageously,
The body was too much for me.

Dear prison'd soul bear up a space,
For soon or late the certain grace;
To set thee free and bear thee home,
The heavenly pardoner death shall come.

*Convict no more, nor shame, nor dole!*
*Depart – a God-enfranchis'd soul!*

3

The singer ceas'd,
One glance swept from her clear calm eyes o'er all
those upturn'd faces,
Strange sea of prison faces, a thousand varied,
crafty, brutal, seam'd and beauteous faces,
Then rising, passing back along the narrow aisle
between them,
While her gown touch'd them rustling in the silence,
She vanish'd with her children in the dusk.
While upon all, convicts and armed keepers ere they
stirr'd,
(Convict forgetting prison, keeper his loaded pistol,)
A hush and pause fell down a wondrous minute,
With deep half-stifled sobs and sound of bad men
bow'd and moved to weeping,
And youth's convulsive breathings, memories of home,

The mother's voice in lullaby, the sister's care, the
happy childhood,
The long-pent spirit rous'd to reminiscence;
A wondrous minute then – but after in the solitary
night, to many, many there,
Years after, even in the hour of death, the sad
refrain, the tune, the voice, the words,
Resumed, the large calm lady walks the narrow aisle,
The wailing melody again, the singer in the prison sings,

*O sight of pity, shame and dole!*
*O fearful thought – a convict soul.*

## *Warble for Lilac-Time*

Warble me now for joy of lilac-time, (returning in
reminiscence,)
Sort me O tongue and lips for Nature's sake,
souvenirs of earliest summer,
Gather the welcome signs, (as children with pebbles
or stringing shells,)
Put in April and May, the hylas croaking in the
ponds, the elastic air,
Bees, butterflies, the sparrow with its simple notes,
Blue-bird and darting swallow, nor forget the
high-hole flashing his golden wings,
The tranquil sunny haze, the clinging smoke, the vapor,
Shimmer of waters with fish in them, the cerulean
above,
All that is jocund and sparkling, the brooks running,
The maple woods, the crisp February days and the
sugarmaking,
The robin where he hops, bright-eyed,
brown-breasted,

With musical clear call at sunrise, and again at sunset,
Or flitting among the trees of the apple-orchard,
  building the nest of his mate,
The melted snow of March, the willow sending forth
  its yellow-green sprouts,
For spring-time is here! the summer is here! and
  what is this in it and from it?
Thou, soul, unloosen'd – the restlessness after I
  know not what;
Come, let us lag here no longer, let us be up and away!
O if one could but fly like a bird!
O to escape, to sail forth as in a ship!
To glide with thee O soul, o'er all, in all, as a ship
  o'er the waters;
Gathering these hints, the preludes, the blue sky, the
  grass, the morning drops of dew,
The lilac-scent, the bushes with dark green heart-
  shaped leaves,
Wood-violets, the little delicate pale blossoms called
  innocence,
Samples and sorts not for themselves alone, but for
  their atmosphere,
To grace the bush I love – to sing with the birds,
A warble for joy of lilac-time, returning in reminiscence.

## *Outlines for a Tomb*

*(G. P., Buried* 1870)

1

What may we chant, O thou within this tomb?
What tablets, outlines, hang for thee, O millionaire?
The life thou lived'st we know not,
But that thou walk'dst thy years in barter, 'mid the haunts of brokers,
Nor heroism thine, nor war, nor glory.

2

Silent, my soul,
With drooping lids, as waiting, ponder'd,
Turning from all the samples, monuments of heroes.

While through the interior vistas,
Noiseless uprose, phantasmic, (as by night Auroras of the north,)
Lambent tableaus, prophetic, bodiless scenes,
Spiritual projections.

In one, among the city streets a laborer's home appear'd,
After his day's work done, cleanly, sweet-air'd, the gaslight burning,
The carpet swept and a fire in the cheerful stove.

In one, the sacred parturition scene,
A happy painless mother birth'd a perfect child

In one, at a bounteous morning meal,
Sat peaceful parents with contented sons.

In one, by twos and threes, young people,
Hundreds concentring, walk'd the paths and streets
    and roads,
Toward a tall-domed school.

In one a trio beautiful,
Grandmother, loving daughter, loving daughter's
    daughter, sat,
Chatting and sewing.

In one, along a suite of noble rooms,
'Mid plenteous books and journals, paintings on the
    walls, fine statuettes,
Were groups of friendly journeymen, mechanics
    young and old,
Reading, conversing.

All, all the shows of laboring life,
City and country, women's, men's and children's,
Their wants provided for, hued in the sun and
    tinged for once with joy,
Marriage, the street, the factory, farm, the house-
    room, lodging-room,
Labor and toil, the bath, gymnasium, playground,
    library, college,
The student, boy or girl, led forward to be taught,
The sick cared for, the shoeless shod, the orphan
    father'd and mother'd,
The hungry fed, the houseless housed;
(The intentions perfect and divine,
The workings, details, haply human.)

3

O thou within this tomb,
From thee such scenes, thou stintless, lavish giver,

Tallying the gifts of earth, large as the earth,
Thy name an earth, with mountains, fields and tides.

Nor by your streams alone, you rivers,
By you, your banks Connecticut,
By you and all your teeming life old Thames,
By you Potomac laving the ground Washington
 trod, by you Patapsco,
You Hudson, you endless Mississippi – nor you alone,
But to the high seas launch, my thought, his memory.

## *Out from Behind This Mask*

(*To Confront a Portrait*)

I

Out from behind this bending rough-cut mask,
These lights and shades, this drama of the whole,
This common curtain of the face contain'd in me for
 me, in you for you, in each for each,
(Tragedies, sorrows, laughter, tears – O heaven!
The passionate teeming plays this curtain hid!)
This glaze of God's serenest purest sky,
This film of Satan's seething pit,
This heart's geography's map, this limitless small
 continent, this soundless sea;
Out from the convolutions of this globe,
This subtler astronomic orb than sun or moon, than
 Jupiter, Venus, Mars,
This condensation of the universe, (nay here the
 only universe,
Here the idea, all in this mystic handful wrapt;)

These burin'd eyes, flashing to you to pass to future time,
To launch and spin through space revolving sideling, from these to emanate,
To you whoe'er you are – a look.

2

A traveler of thoughts and years, of peace and war,
Of youth long sped and middle age declining,
(As the first volume of a tale perused and laid away, and this the second,
Songs, ventures, speculations, presently to close,)
Lingering a moment here and now, to you I opposite turn,
As on the road or at some crevice door by chance, or open'd window,
Pausing, inclining, baring my head, you specially I greet,
To draw and clinch your soul for once inseparably with mine,
Then travel travel on.

## *Vocalism*

1

Vocalism, measure, concentration, determination, and the divine power to speak words;
Are you full-lung'd and limber-lipp'd from long trial? from vigorous practice? from physique?
Do you move in these broad lands as broad as they?
Come duly to the divine power to speak words?
For only at last after many years, after chastity, friendship, procreation, prudence, and nakedness,

After treading ground and breasting river and lake,
After a loosen'd throat, after absorbing eras, temperaments, races, after knowledge, freedom, crimes,
After complete faith, after clarifyings, elevations, and removing obstructions,
After these and more, it is just possible there comes to a man, a woman, the divine power to speak words;
Then toward that man or that woman swiftly hasten all – none refuse, all attend,
Armies, ships, antiquities, libraries, paintings, machines, cities, hate, despair, amity, pain, theft, murder, aspiration, form in close ranks,
They debouch as they are wanted to march obediently through the mouth of that man or that woman.

2

O what is it in me that makes me tremble so at voices?
Surely whoever speaks to me in the right voice, him or her I shall follow,
As the water follows the moon, silently, with fluid steps, anywhere around the globe.

All waits for the right voices;
Where is the practis'd and perfect organ? where is the develop'd soul?
For I see every word utter'd thence has deeper, sweeter, new sounds, impossible on less terms.

I see brains and lips closed, tympans and temples unstruck,
Until that comes which has the quality to strike and to unclose,
Until that comes which has the quality to bring forth what lies slumbering forever ready in all words.

## *To Him that was Crucified*

My spirit to yours dear brother,
Do not mind because many sounding your name do
not understand you,
I do not sound your name, but I understand you,
I specify you with joy O my comrade to salute you,
and to salute those who are with you, before and
since, and those to come also,
That we all labor together transmitting the same
charge and succession,
We few equals indifferent of lands, indifferent of times,
We, enclosers of all continents, all castes, allowers of
all theologies,
Compassionaters, perceivers, rapport of men,
We walk silent among disputes and assertions, but
reject not the disputers nor any thing that is
asserted,
We hear the bawling and din, we are reach'd at by
divisions, jealousies, recriminations on every side,
They close peremptorily upon us to surround us, my
comrade,
Yet we walk unheld, free, the whole earth over,
journeying up and down till we make our
ineffaceable mark upon time and the diverse eras,
Till we saturate time and eras, that the men and
women of races, ages to come, may prove
brethren and lovers as we are.

## *You Felons on Trial in Courts*

You felons on trial in courts,
You convicts in prison-cells, you sentenced assassins chain'd and hand-cuff'd with iron,
Who am I too that I am not on trial or in prison?
Me ruthless and devilish as any, that my wrists are not chain'd with iron, or my ankles with iron?

You prostitutes flaunting over the trottoirs or obscene in your rooms,
Who am I that I should call you more obscence than myself?
O culpable! I acknowledge – I exposé!
(O admirers, praise not me – compliment not me – you make me wince,
I see what you do not – I know what you do not.)

Inside these breast-bones I lie smutch'd and choked,
Beneath this face that appears so impassive hell's tides continually run,
Lusts and wickedness are acceptable to me,
I walk with delinquents with passionate love,
I feel I am of them – I belong to those convicts and prostitutes myself,
And henceforth I will not deny them – for how can I deny myself?

## *Laws for Creations*

Laws for creations,
For strong artists and leaders, for fresh broods of teachers and perfect literats for America,
For noble savans and coming musicians.

All must have reference to the ensemble of the
world, and the compact truth of the world,
There shall be no subject too pronounced – all works
shall illustrate the divine law of indirections.

What do you suppose creation is?
What do you suppose will satisfy the soul, except to
walk free and own no superior?
What do you suppose I would intimate to you in a
hundred ways, but that man or woman is as
good as God?
And that there is no God any more divine than
Yourself?
And that that is what the oldest and newest myths
finally mean?
And that you or any one must approach creations
through such laws?

## *To a Common Prostitute*

Be composed – be at ease with me – I am Walt
Whitman, liberal and lusty as Nature,
Not till the sun excludes you do I exclude you,
Not till the waters refuse to glisten for you and the
leaves to rustle for you, do my words refuse to
glisten and rustle for you.

My girl I appoint with you an appointment, and I
charge you that you make preparation to be
worthy to meet me,
And I charge you that you be patient and perfect till
I come.

Till then I salute you with a significant look that you
do not forget me.

## *I was Looking a Long While*

I was looking a long while for Intentions,
For a clew to the history of the past for myself, and
for these chants – and now I have found it,
It is not in those paged fables in the libraries, (them I
neither accept nor reject,)
It is no more in the legends than in all else,
It is in the present – it is this earth to-day,
It is in Democracy – (the purport and aim of all the
past,)
It is the life of one man or one woman to-day – the
average man of to-day,
It is in languages, social customs, literatures, arts,
It is in the broad show of artificial things, ships,
machinery, politics, creeds, modern
improvements, and the interchange of nations,
All for the modern – all for the average man of to-day.

## *Thought*

Of persons arrived at high positions, ceremonies,
wealth, scholarships, and the like;
(To me all that those persons have arrived at sinks
away from them, except as it results to their
bodies and souls,
So that often to me they appear gaunt and naked,
And often to me each one mocks the others, and
mocks himself or herself,
And of each one the core of life, namely happiness,
is full of the rotten excrement of maggots,
And often to me those men and women pass
unwittingly the true realities of life, and go
toward false realities,

And often to me they are alive after what custom has served them, but nothing more,
And often to me they are sad, hasty, unwaked sonnambules walking the dusk.)

## *Miracles*

Why, who makes much of a miracle?
As to me I know of nothing else but miracles,
Whether I walk the streets of Manhattan,
Or dart my sight over the roofs of houses toward the sky,
Or wade with naked feet along the beach just in the edge of the water,
Or stand under trees in the woods,
Or talk by day with any one I love, or sleep in the bed at night with any one I love,
Or sit at table at dinner with the rest,
Or look at strangers opposite me riding in the car,
Or watch honey-bees busy around the hive of a summer forenoon,
Or animals feeding in the fields,
Or birds, or the wonderfulness of insects in the air,
Or the wonderfulness of the sundown, or of stars shining so quiet and bright,
Or the exquisite delicate thin curve of the new moon in spring;
These with the rest, one and all, are to me miracles,
The whole referring, yet each distinct and in its place.

To me every hour of the light and dark is a miracle,
Every cubic inch of space is a miracle,
Every square yard of the surface of the earth is spread with the same,
Every foot of the interior swarms with the same.

To me the sea is a continual miracle,
The fishes that swim – the rocks – the motion of the waves – the ships with men in them,
What stranger miracles are there?

## *Sparkles from the Wheel*

Where the city's ceaseless crowd moves on the livelong day,
Withdrawn I join a group of children watching, I pause aside with them.

By the curb toward the edge of the flagging,
A knife-grinder works at his wheel sharpening a great knife,
Bending over he carefully holds it to the stone, by foot and knee,
With measur'd tread he turns rapidly, as he presses with light but firm hand,
Forth issue then in copious golden jets,
Sparkles from the wheel.
The scene and all its belongings, how they seize and affect me,
The sad sharp-chinn'd old man with worn clothes and broad shoulder-band of leather,
Myself effusing and fluid, a phantom curiously floating, now here absorb'd and arrested,
The group, (an unminded point set in a vast surrounding,)
The attentive, quiet children, the loud, proud, restive base of the streets,
The low hoarse purr of the whirling stone, the light-press'd blade,

Diffusing, dropping, sideways-darting, in tiny showers
of gold,
Sparkles from the wheel.

## *To a Pupil*

Is reform needed? is it through you?
The greater the reform needed, the greater the
Personality you need to accomplish it.

You! do you not see how it would serve to have eyes,
blood, complexion, clean and sweet?
Do you not see how it would serve to have such a
body and soul that when you enter the crowd an
atmosphere of desire and command enters with
you, and every one is impress'd with your
Personality?
O the magnet! the flesh over and over!
Go, dear friend, if need be give up all else, and
commence to-day to inure yourself to pluck,
reality, self-esteem, definiteness, elevatedness,
Rest not till you rivet and publish yourself of your
own Personality.

## *Unfolded Out of the Folds*

Unfolded out of the folds of the woman man comes
unfolded, and is always to come unfolded,
Unfolded only out of the superbest woman of the
earth is to come the superbest man of the earth,
Unfolded out of the friendliest woman is to come
the friendliest man,

Unfolded only out of the perfect body of a woman
can a man be form'd of perfect body,
Unfolded only out of the inimitable poems of
woman can come the poems of man, (only
thence have my poems come;)
Unfolded out of the strong and arrogant woman I
love, only thence can appear the strong and
arrogant man I love,
Unfolded by brawny embraces from the well-
muscled woman I love, only thence come the
brawny embraces of the man,
Unfolded out of the folds of the woman's brain come
all the folds of the man's brain, duly obedient,
Unfolded out of the justice of the woman all justice
is unfolded,
Unfolded out of the sympathy of the woman is all
sympathy;
A man is a great thing upon the earth and through
eternity, but every jot of the greatness of man is
unfolded out of woman;
First the man is shaped in the woman, he can then
be shaped in himself.

## *What am I After All*

What am I after all but a child, pleas'd with the sound
of my own name? repeating it over and over;
I stand apart to hear – it never tires me.

To you your name also;
Did you think there was nothing but two or three
pronunciations in the sound of your name?

## *Kosmos*

Who includes diversity and is Nature,
Who is the amplitude of the earth, and the coarseness
and sexuality of the earth, and the great charity of
the earth, and the equilibrium also,
Who has not look'd forth from the windows the eyes
for nothing, or whose brain held audience with
messengers for nothing,
Who contains believers and disbelievers, who is the
most majestic lover,
Who holds duly his or her triune proportion of realism,
spiritualism, and of the aesthetic or intellectual,
Who having consider'd the body finds all its organs
and parts good,
Who, out of the theory of the earth and of his or her
body understands by subtle analogies all other
theories,
The theory of a city, a poem, and of the large politics
of these States;
Who believes not only in our globe with its sun and
moon, but in other globes with their suns and
moons,
Who, constructing the house of himself or herself,
not for a day but for all time, sees races, eras,
dates, generations,
The past, the future, dwelling there, like space,
inseparable together.

## *Others may Praise What They Like*

Others may praise what they like;
But I, from the banks of the running Missouri,
    praise nothing in art or aught else,
Till it has well inhaled the atmosphere of this river,
    also the western prairie-scent,
And exudes it all again.

## *Who Learns My Lesson Complete?*

Who learns my lesson complete?
Boss, journeyman, apprentice, churchman and atheist,
The stupid and the wise thinker, parents and
    offspring, merchant, clerk, porter and customer,
Editor, author, artist, and schoolboy – draw nigh
    and commence;
It is no lesson – it lets down the bars to a good lesson,
And that to another, and every one to another still.

The great laws take and effuse without argument,
I am of the same style, for I am their friend,
I love them quits and quits, I do not halt and make
    salaams.

I lie abstracted and hear beautiful tales of things and
    the reasons of things,
They are so beautiful I nudge myself to listen.

I cannot say to any person what I hear – I cannot say
    it to myself – it is very wonderful.

It is no small matter, this round and delicious globe
    moving so exactly in its orbit for ever and ever,
    without one jolt or the untruth of a single
    second,

I do not think it was made in six days, nor in ten thousand years, nor ten billions of years,
Nor plann'd and built one thing after another as an architect plans and builds a house.

I do not think seventy years is the time of a man or woman,
Nor that seventy millions of years is the time of a man or woman,
Nor that years will ever stop the existence of me, or any one else.

Is it wonderful that I should be immortal? as every one is immortal;
I know it is wonderful, but my eyesight is equally wonderful, and how I was conceived in my mother's womb is equally wonderful,
And pass'd from a babe in the creeping trance of a couple of summers and winters to articulate and walk – all this is equally wonderful.

And that my soul embraces you this hour, and we affect each other without ever seeing each other, and never perhaps to see each other, is every bit as wonderful.

And that I can think such thoughts as these is just as wonderful,
And that I can remind you, and you think them and know them to be true, is just as wonderful.
And that the moon spins round the earth and on with the earth, is equally wonderful,
And that they balance themselves with the sun and stars is equally wonderful.

### *Tests*

All submit to them where they sit, inner, secure,
unapproachable to analysis in the soul,
Not traditions, not the outer authorities are the judges,
They are the judges of outer authorities and of all
traditions,
They corroborate as they go only whatever
corroborates themselves, and touches themselves;
For all that, they have it forever in themselves to
corroborate far and near without one exception.

### *The Torch*

On my Northwest coast in the midst of the night a
fishermen's group stands watching,
Out on the lake that expands before them, others are
spearing salmon,
The canoe, a dim shadowy thing, moves across the
black water,
Bearing a torch ablaze at the prow.

### *O Star of France*

*1870–1*

O star of France,
The brightness of thy hope and strength and fame,
Like some proud ship that led the fleet so long,
Beseems to-day a wreck driven by the gale, a
mastless hulk,
And 'mid its teeming madden'd half-drown'd
crowds,
Nor helm nor helmsman.

Dim smitten star,
Orb not of France alone, pale symbol of my soul, its
dearest hopes,
The struggle and the daring, rage divine for liberty,
Of aspirations toward the far ideal, enthusiast's
dreams of brotherhood,
Of terror to the tyrant and the priest.

Star crucified – by traitors sold,
Star panting o'er a land of death, heroic land,
Strange, passionate, mocking, frivolous land.
Miserable! yet for thy errors, vanities, sins, I will not
now rebuke thee,
Thy unexampled woes and pangs have quell'd them all,
And left thee sacred.

In that amid thy many faults thou ever aimedst highly,
In that thou wouldst not really sell thyself however
great the price,
In that thou surely wakedst weeping from thy
drugg'd sleep,
In that alone among thy sisters thou, giantess, didst
rend the ones that shamed thee,
In that thou couldst not, wouldst not, wear the usual
chains,
This cross, thy livid face, thy pierced hands and feet,
The spear thrust in thy side.

O star! O ship of France, beat back and baffled long!
Bear up O smitten orb! O ship continue on!

Sure as the ship of all, the Earth itself,
Product of deathly fire and turbulent chaos,
Forth from its spasms of fury and its poisons,
Issuing at last in perfect power and beauty,

Onward beneath the sun following its course,
So thee O ship of France!

Finish'd the days, the clouds dispel'd,
The travail o'er, the long-sought extrication,
When lo! reborn, high o'er the European world,
(In gladness answering thence, as face afar to face,
reflecting ours Columbia,)
Again thy star O France, fair lustrous star,
In heavenly peace, clearer, more bright than ever,
Shall beam immortal.

## *The Ox-Tamer*

In a far-away northern county in the placid pastoral
region,
Lives my farmer friend, the theme of my recitative, a
famous tamer of oxen,
There they bring him the three-year-olds and the
four-year-olds to break them,
He will take the wildest steer in the world and break
him and tame him,
He will go fearless without any whip where the
young bullock chafes up and down the yard,
The bullock's head tosses restless high in the air with
raging eyes,
Yet see you! how soon his rage subsides – how soon
this tamer tames him;
See you! on the farms hereabouts a hundred oxen
young and old, and he is the man who has tamed
them,
They all know him, all are affectionate to him;
See you! some are such beautiful animals, so lofty
looking;

Some are buff-color'd, some mottled, one has a white
line running along his back, some are brindled,
Some have wide flaring horns (a good sign) – see
you! the bright hides,
See, the two with stars on their foreheads – see, the
round bodies and broad backs,
How straight and square they stand on their legs –
what fine sagacious eyes!
How they watch their tamer – they wish him near
them – how they turn to look after him!
What yearning expression! how uneasy they are
when he moves away from them;
Now I marvel what it can be he appears to them,
(books, politics, poems, depart – all else departs,)
I confess I envy only his fascination – my silent,
illiterate friend,
Whom a hundred oxen love there in his life on farms,
In the northern country far, in the placid pastoral
region.

## *An Old Man's Thought of School*

*For the Inauguration of a Public School,*
*Camden, New Jersey,* 1874

An old man's thought of school,
An old man gathering youthful memories and
blooms that youth itself cannot.

Now only do I know you,
O fair auroral skies – O morning dew upon the grass!
And these I see, these sparkling eyes,
These stores of mystic meaning, these young lives,
Building, equipping like a fleet of ships, immortal ships,

Soon to sail out over the measureless seas,
On the soul's voyage.

Only a lot of boys and girls?
Only the tiresome spelling, writing, ciphering
classes?
Only a public school?

Ah more, infinitely more;
(As George Fox rais'd his warning cry, 'Is it this pile
of brick and mortar, these dead floors, windows,
rails, you call the church?
Why this is not the church at all – the church is
living, ever living souls.')

And you America,
Cast you the real reckoning for your present?
The lights and shadows of your future, good or evil?
To girlhood, boyhood look, the teacher and the school.

## *Wandering at Morn*

Wandering at morn,
Emerging from the night from gloomy thoughts,
thee in my thoughts,
Yearning for thee harmonious Union! thee, singing
bird divine!
Thee coil'd in evil times my country, with craft and
black dismay, with every meanness, treason
thrust upon thee,
This common marvel I beheld – the parent thrush I
watch'd feeding its young,
The singing thrush whose tones of joy and faith ecstatic,
Fail not to certify and cheer my soul.

There ponder'd, felt I,
If worms, snakes, loathsome grubs, may to sweet
spiritual songs be turn'd,
If vermin so transposed, so used and bless'd may be,
Then may I trust in you, your fortunes, days, my
country;
Who knows but these may be the lessons fit for you?
From these your future song may rise with joyous trills,
Destin'd to fill the world.

## *Italian Music in Dakota*

('*The Seventeenth – the finest
Regimental Band I ever heard.*')

Through the soft evening air enwinding all,
Rocks, woods, fort, cannon, pacing sentries, endless
wilds,
In dulcet streams, in flutes' and cornets' notes,
Electric, pensive, turbulent, artificial,
(Yet strangely fitting even here, meanings unknown
before,
Subtler than ever, more harmony, as if born here,
related here,
Not to the city's fresco'd rooms, not to the audience
of the opera house,
Sounds, echoes, wandering strains, as really here at
home,
*Sonnambula's* innocent love, trios with *Norma's*
anguish,
And thy ecstatic chorus *Poliuto;*)
Ray'd in the limpid yellow slanting sundown,
Music, Italian music in Dakota.

While Nature, sovereign of this gnarl'd realm,
Lurking in hidden barbaric grim recesses,
Acknowledging rapport however far remov'd,
(As some old root or soil of earth its last-born flower or fruit,)
Listens well pleas'd.

## *With all Thy Gifts*

With all thy gifts America,
Standing secure, rapidly tending, overlooking the world,
Power, wealth, extent, vouchsafed to thee – with these and like of these vouchsafed to thee,
What if one gift thou lackest? (the ultimate human problem never solving,)
The gift of perfect women fit for thee – what if that gift of gifts thou lackest?
The towering feminine of thee? the beauty, health, completion, fit for thee?
The mothers fit for thee?

## *My Picture-Gallery*

In a little house keep I pictures suspended, it is not a fix'd house,
It is round, it is only a few inches from one side to the other;
Yet behold, it has room for all the shows of the world, all memories!
Here the tableaus of life, and here the groupings of death;
Here, do you know this? this is cicerone himself,
With finger rais'd he points to the prodigal pictures.

## *The Prairie States*

A newer garden of creation, no primal solitude,
Dense, joyous, modern, populous millions, cities
and farms,
With iron interlaced, composite, tied, many in one,
By all the world contributed – freedom's and law's
and thrift's society,
The crown and teeming paradise, so far, of time's
accumulations,
To justify the past.

## *Proud Music of the Storm*

### 1

Proud music of the storm,
Blast that careers so free, whistling across the prairies,
Strong hum of forest tree-tops – wind of the mountains,
Personified dim shapes – you hidden orchestras,
You serenades of phantoms with instruments alert,
Bending with Nature's rhythmus all the tongues of
nations;
You chords left as by vast composers – you choruses,
You formless, free, religious dances – you from the
Orient,
You undertone of rivers, roar of pouring cataracts,
You sounds from distant guns with galloping cavalry,
Echoes of camps with all the different bugle-calls,
Trooping tumultuous, filling the midnight late,
bending me powerless,
Entering my lonesome slumber-chamber, why have
you seiz'd me?

2

Come forward O my soul, and let the rest retire,
Listen, lose not, it is toward thee they tend,
Parting the midnight, entering my slumber-chamber,
For thee they sing and dance O soul.

A festival song,
The duet of the bridegroom and the bride, a marriage-march,
With lips of love, and hearts of lovers fill'd to the brim with love,
The red-flush'd cheeks and perfumes, the cortege swarming full of friendly faces young and old,
To flutes' clear notes and sounding harps' cantabile.

Now loud approaching drums,
Victoria! see'st thou in powder-smoke the banners torn but flying? the rout of the baffled?
Hearest those shouts of a conquering army?

(Ah soul, the sobs of women, the wounded groaning in agony,
The hiss and crackle of flames, the blacken'd ruins, the embers of cities,
The dirge and desolation of mankind.)

Now airs antique and mediaeval fill me,
I see and hear old harpers with their harps at Welsh festivals,
I hear the minnesingers singing their lays of love,
I hear the minstrels, gleemen, troubadours, of the middle ages.

Now the great organ sounds,
Tremulous, while underneath, (as the hid footholds of the earth,

On which arising rest, and leaping forth depend,
All shapes of beauty, grace and strength, all hues we know,
Green blades of grass and warbling birds, children that gambol and play, the clouds of heaven above,)
The strong base stands, and its pulsations intermits not,
Bathing, supporting, merging all the rest, maternity of all the rest,
And with it every instrument in multitudes,
The players playing, all the world's musicians,
The solemn hymns and masses rousing adoration,
All passionate heart-chants, sorrowful appeals,
The measureless sweet vocalists of ages,
And for their solvent setting earth's own diapason,
Of winds and woods and mighty ocean waves,
A new composite orchestra, binder of years and climes, tenfold renewer,
As of the far-back days the poets tell, the Paradiso,
The straying thence, the separation long, but now the wandering done,
The journey done, the journeyman come home,
And man and art with Nature fused again.

Tutti! for earth and heaven;
(The Almighty leader now for once has signal'd with his wand.)

The manly strophe of the husbands of the world,
And all the wives responding.

The tongues of violins,
(I think O tongues ye tell this heart, that cannot tell itself,
This brooding yearning heart, that cannot tell itself.)

3

Ah from a little child,
Thou knowest soul how to me all sounds became
music,
My mother's voice in lullaby or hymn,
(The voice, O tender voices, memory's loving voices,
Last miracle of all, O dearest mother's, sister's, voices;)
The rain, the growing corn, the breeze among the
long-leav'd corn,
The measur'd sea-surf beating on the sand,
The twittering bird, the hawk's sharp scream,
The wild-fowl's notes at night as flying low
migrating north or south,
The psalm in the country church or mid the
clustering trees, the open air camp-meeting,
The fiddler in the tavern, the glee, the long-strung
sailor-song,
The lowing cattle, bleating sheep, the crowing cock
at dawn.

All songs of current lands come sounding round me,
The German airs of friendship, wine and love,
Irish ballads, merry jigs and dances, English warbles,
Chansons of France, Scotch tunes, and o'er the rest,
Italia's peerless compositions.]

Across the stage with pallor on her face, yet lurid
passion,
Stalks Norma brandishing the dagger in her hand.

I see poor crazed Lucia's eyes' unnatural gleam,
Her hair down her back falls loose and dishevel'd.

I see where Ernani walking the bridal garden,
Amid the scent of night-roses, radiant, holding his
bride by the hand,

Hears the infernal call, the death-pledge of the horn.

To crossing swords and gray hairs bared to heaven,
The clear electric base and baritone of the world,
The trombone duo, Libertad forever!

From Spanish chestnut trees' dense shade,
By old and heavy convent walls a wailing song,
Song of lost love, the torch of youth and life
quench'd in despair,
Song of the dying swan, Fernando's heart is breaking.

Awaking from her woes at last retriev'd Amina sings,
Copious as stars and glad as morning light the
torrents of her joy.

(The teeming lady comes,
The lustrous orb, Venus contralto, the blooming
mother,
Sister of loftiest gods, Alboni's self I hear.)

4

I hear those odes, symphonies, operas,
I hear in the *William Tell* the music of an arous'd and
angry people,
I hear Meyerbeer's *Huguenots*, the *Prophet*, or *Robert*,
Gounod's *Faust*, or Mozart's *Don Juan*.

I hear the dance-music of all nations,
The waltz, some delicious measure, lapsing, bathing
me in bliss,
The bolero to tinkling guitars and clattering castanets.

I see religious dances old and new,
I hear the sound of the Hebrew lyre,
I see the crusaders marching bearing the cross on
high, to the martial clang of cymbals,

I hear dervishes monotonously chanting, interspers'd
with frantic shouts, as they spin around turning
always towards Mecca,
I see the rapt religious dances of the Persians and the
Arabs,
Again, at Eleusis, home of Ceres, I see the modern
Greeks dancing,
I hear them clapping their hands as they bend their
bodies,
I hear the metrical shuffling of their feet.

I see again the wild old Corybantian dance, the
performers wounding each other,
I see the Roman youth to the shrill sound of
flageolets throwing and catching their weapons,
As they fall on their knees and rise again.

I hear from the Mussulman mosque the muezzin
calling,
I see the worshippers within, nor form nor sermon,
argument nor word,
But silent, strange, devout, rais'd glowing heads,
ecstatic faces.

I hear the Egyptian harp of many strings,
The primitive chants of the Nile boatmen,
The sacred imperial hymns of China,
To the delicate sounds of the king, (the stricken
wood and stone,)
Or to Hindu flutes and the fretting twang of the vina,
A band of bayaderes.

5

Now Asia, Africa leave me, Europe seizing inflates me,
To organs huge and bands I hear as from vast
    concourses of voices,
Luther's strong hymn *Eine feste Burg ist unser Gott*,
Rossini's *Stabat Mater dolorosa*,
Or floating in some high cathedral dim with
    gorgeous color'd windows,
The passionate *Agnus Dei* or *Gloria in Excelsis*.

Composers! mighty maestros!
And you, sweet singers of old lands, soprani, tenori,
    bassi!
To you a new bard caroling in the West,
Obeisant sends his love.
(Such led to thee O soul,
All senses, shows and objects, lead to thee,
But now it seems to me sound leads o'er all the rest.)

I hear the annual singing of the children in St. Paul's
    cathedral,
Or, under the high roof of some colossal hall, the
    symphonies, oratorios of Beethoven, Handel, or
    Haydn,
The *Creation* in billows of godhood laves me.

Give me to hold all sounds, (I madly struggling cry,)
Fill me with all the voices of the universe,
Endow me with their throbbings, Nature's also,
The tempests, waters, winds, operas and chants,
    marches and dances,
Utter, pour in, for I would take them all!

6

Then I woke softly,
And pausing, questioning awhile the music of my dream,
And questioning all those reminiscences, the tempest in its fury,
And all the songs of sopranos and tenors,
And those rapt oriental dances of religious fervor,
And the sweet varied instruments, and the diapason of organs,
And all the artless plaints of love and grief and death,
I said to my silent curious soul out of the bed of the slumber-chamber,
Come, for I have found the clew I sought so long,
Let us go forth refresh'd amid the day,
Cheerfully tallying life, walking the world, the real,
Nourish'd henceforth by our celestial dream.

And I said, moreover,
Haply what thou hast heard O soul was not the sound of winds,
Nor dream of raging storm, nor sea-hawk's flapping wings nor harsh scream,
Nor vocalism of sun-bright Italy,
Nor German organ majestic, nor vast concourse of voices, nor layers of harmonies,
Nor strophes of husbands and wives, nor sound of marching soldiers,
Nor flutes, nor harps, nor the bugle-calls of camps,
But to a new rhythmus fitted for thee,
Poems bridging the way from Life to Death, vaguely wafted in night air, uncaught, unwritten,
Which let us go forth in the bold day and write.

## *Passage to India*

### 1

Singing my days,
Singing the great achievements of the present,
Singing the strong light works of engineers,
Our modern wonders, (the antique ponderous
 Seven outvied,)
In the Old World the east the Suez canal,
The New by its mighty railroad spann'd,
The seas inland with eloquent gentle wires;
Yet first to sound, and ever sound, the cry with thee
 O soul,
The Past! the Past! the Past!

The Past – the dark unfathom'd retrospect!
The teeming gulf – the sleepers and the shadows!
The past – the infinite greatness of the past!
For what is the present after all but a growth out of
 the past?
(As a projectile form'd, impell'd, passing a certain
 line, still keeps on,
So the present, utterly form'd, impell'd by the past.)

### 2

Passage O soul to India!
Eclaircise the myths Asiatic, the primitive fables.

Not you alone proud truths of the world,
Nor you alone ye facts of modern science,
But myths and fables of eld, Asia's, Africa's fables,
The far-darting beams of the spirit, the unloos'd
 dreams,
The deep diving bibles and legends,
The daring plots of the poets, the elder religions;

O you temples fairer than lilies pour'd over by the
rising sun!
O you fables spurning the known, eluding the hold
of the known, mounting to heaven!
You lofty and dazzling towers, pinnacled, red as
roses, burnish'd with gold!
Towers of fables immortal fashion'd from mortal
dreams!
You too I welcome and fully the same as the rest!
You too with joy I sing.

Passage to India!
Lo, soul, seest thou not God's purpose from the first?
The earth to be spann'd, connected by network,
The races, neighbors, to marry and be given in
marriage,
The oceans to be cross'd, the distant brought near,
The lands to be welded together.

A worship new I sing,
You captains, voyagers, explorers, yours,
You engineers, you architects, machinists, yours,
You, not for trade or transportation only,
But in God's name, and for thy sake O soul.

3

Passage to India!
Lo soul for thee of tableaus twain,
I see in one the Suez canal initiated, open'd,
I see the procession of steamships, the Empress
Eugenie's leading the van,
I mark from on deck the strange landscape, the pure
sky, the level sand in the distance,
I pass swiftly the picturesque groups, the workmen
gather'd,

The gigantic dredging machines.

In one again, different, (yet thine, all thine, O soul, the same,)
I see over my own continent the Pacific railroad surmounting every barrier,
I see continual trains of cars winding along the Platte carrying freight and passengers,
I hear the locomotives rushing and roaring, and the shrill steam-whistle,
I hear the echoes reverberate through the grandest scenery in the world,
I cross the Laramie plains, I note the rocks in grotesque shapes, the buttes,
I see the plentiful larkspur and wild onions, the barren, colorless, sage-deserts,
I see in glimpses afar or towering immediately above me the great mountains, I see the Wind river and the Wahsatch mountains,
I see the Monument mountain and the Eagle's Nest, I pass the Promontory, I ascend the Nevadas,
I scan the noble Elk mountain and wind around its base,
I see the Humboldt range, I thread the valley and cross the river,
I see the clear waters of lake Tahoe, I see forests of majestic pines,
Or crossing the great desert, the alkaline plains, I behold enchanting mirages of waters and meadows,
Marking through these and after all, in duplicate slender lines,
Bridging the three or four thousand miles of land travel,

Tying the Eastern to the Western sea,
The road between Europe and Asia.

(Ah Genoese thy dream! thy dream!
Centuries after thou art laid in thy grave,
The shore thou foundest verifies thy dream.)

4

Passage to India!
Struggles of many a captain, tales of many a sailor
dead,
Over my mood stealing and spreading they come,
Like clouds and cloudlets in the unreach'd sky.

Along all history, down the slopes,
As a rivulet running, sinking now, and now again to
the surface rising,
A ceaseless thought, a varied train – lo, soul, to thee,
thy sight, they rise,
The plans, the voyages again, the expeditions;
Again Vasco de Gama sails forth,
Again the knowledge gain'd, the mariner's compass,
Lands found and nations born, thou born America,
For purpose vast, man's long probation fill'd,
Thou rondure of the world at last accomplish'd.

5

O vast Rondure, swimming in space,
Cover'd all over with visible power and beauty,
Alternate light and day and the teeming spiritual
darkness,
Unspeakable high processions of sun and moon and
countless stars above,
Below, the manifold grass and waters, animals,
mountains, trees,

With inscrutable purpose, some hidden prophetic
intention,
Now first it seems my thought begins to span thee.

Down from the gardens of Asia descending
radiating,
Adam and Eve appear, then their myriad progeny
after them,
Wandering, yearning, curious, with restless
explorations,
With questionings, baffled, formless, feverish, with
neverhappy hearts,
With that sad incessant refrain, *Wherefore unsatisfied
soul?* and *Whither O mocking life?*

Ah who shall soothe these feverish children?
Who justify these restless explorations?
Who speak the secret of impassive earth?
Who bind it to us? what is this separate Nature so
unnatural?
What is this earth to our affections? (unloving earth,
without a throb to answer ours,
Cold earth, the place of graves.)

Yet soul be sure the first intent remains, and shall be
carried out,
Perhaps even now the time has arrived.

After the seas are all cross'd, (as they seem already
cross'd,)
After the great captains and engineers have
accomplish'd their work,
After the noble inventors, after the scientists, the
chemist, the geologist, ethnologist,
Finally shall come the poet worthy that name,
The true son of God shall come singing his songs.

Then not your deeds only O voyagers, O scientists
and inventors, shall be justified,
All these hearts as of fretted children shall be sooth'd,
All affection shall be fully responded to, the secret
shall be told,
All these separations and gaps shall be taken up and
hook'd and link'd together,
The whole earth, this cold, impassive, voiceless
earth, shall be completely justified,
Trinitas divine shall be gloriously accomplish'd and
compacted by the true son of God, the poet,
(He shall indeed pass the straits and conquer the
mountains,
He shall double the cape of Good Hope to some
purpose,)
Nature and Man shall be disjoin'd and diffused no
more,
The true son of God shall absolutely fuse them.

6

Year at whose wide-flung door I sing!
Year of the purpose accomplish'd!
Year of the marriage of continents, climates and
oceans!
(No mere doge of Venice now wedding the Adriatic,)
I see O year in you the vast terraqueous globe given
and giving all,
Europe to Asia, Africa join'd, and they to the New
World,
The lands, geographies, dancing before you, holding
a festival garland,
As brides and bridegrooms hand in hand.

Passage to India!
Cooling airs from Caucasus, far, soothing cradle of
man,
The river Euphrates flowing, the past lit up again.

Lo soul, the retrospect brought forward,
The old, most populous, wealthiest of earth's lands,
The streams of the Indus and the Ganges and their
many affluents,
(I my shores of America walking to-day behold,
resuming all,)
The tale of Alexander on his warlike marches
suddenly dying,
On one side China and on the other side Persia and
Arabia,
To the south the great seas and the bay of Bengal,
The flowing literatures, tremendous epics, religions,
castes,
Old occult Brahma interminably far back, the tender
and junior Buddha,
Central and southern empires and all their
belongings, possessors,
The wars of Tamerlane, the reign of Aurungzebe,
The traders, rulers, explorers, Moslems, Venetians,
Byzantium, the Arabs, Portuguese,
The first travelers famous yet, Marco Polo, Batouta
the Moor,
Doubts to be solv'd, the map incognita, blanks to be
fill'd,
The foot of man unstay'd, the hands never at rest,
Thyself O soul that will not brook a challenge.

The mediaeval navigators rise before me,
The world of 1492, with its awaken'd enterprise,

Something swelling in humanity now like the sap of
the earth in spring,
The sunset splendor of chivalry declining.

And who art thou sad shade?
Gigantic, visionary, thyself a visionary,
With majestic limbs and pious beaming eyes,
Spreading around with every look of thine a golden
world,
Enhuing it with gorgeous hues.

As the chief histrion,
Down to the footlights walks in some great scena,
Dominating the rest I see the Admiral himself,
(History's type of courage, action, faith,)
Behold him sail from Palos leading his little fleet,
His voyage behold, his return, his great fame,
His misfortunes, calumniators, behold him a
prisoner, chain'd,
Behold his dejection, poverty, death.

(Curious in time I stand, noting the efforts of heroes,
Is the deferment long? bitter the slander, poverty,
death?
Lies the seed unreck'd for centuries in the ground?
lo, to God's due occasion,
Uprising in the night, it sprouts, blooms,
And fills the earth with use and beauty.)

7

Passage indeed O soul to primal thought,
Not lands and seas alone, thy own clear freshness,
The young maturity of brood and bloom,
To realms of budding bibles.

O soul, repressless, I with thee and thou with me,
Thy circumnavigation of the world begin,
Of man, the voyage of his mind's return,
To reason's early paradise,
Back, back to wisdom's birth, to innocent intuitions,
Again with fair creation.

8

O we can wait no longer,
We too take ship O soul,
Joyous we too launch out on trackless seas,
Fearless for unknown shores on waves of ecstasy to sail,
Amid the wafting winds, (thou pressing me to thee, I
thee to me, O soul,)
Caroling free, singing our song of God,
Chanting our chant of pleasant exploration.

With laugh and many a kiss,
(Let others deprecate, let others weep for sin,
remorse, humiliation,)
O soul thou pleasest me, I thee.

Ah more than any priest O soul we too believe in God,
But with the mystery of God we dare not dally.

O soul thou pleasest me, I thee,
Sailing these seas or on the hills, or waking in the night,
Thoughts, silent thoughts, of Time and Space and
Death, like waters flowing,
Bear me indeed as through the regions infinite,
Whose air I breathe, whose ripples hear, lave me all
over,
Bathe me O God in thee, mounting to thee,
I and my soul to range in range of thee.

O Thou transcendent,
Nameless, the fibre and the breath,
Light of the light, shedding forth universes, thou
centre of them,
Thou mightier centre of the true, the good, the loving,
Thou moral, spiritual fountain – affection's source –
thou reservoir,
(O pensive soul of me – O thirst unsatisfied – waitest
not there?
Waitest not haply for us somewhere there the
Comrade perfect?)
Thou pulse – thou motive of the stars, suns, systems,
That, circling, move in order, safe, harmonious,
Athwart the shapeless vastnesses of space,
How should I think, how breathe a single breath,
how speak, if, out of myself,
I could not launch, to those, superior universes?

Swiftly I shrivel at the thought of God,
At Nature and its wonders, Time and Space and Death,
But that I, turning, call to thee O soul, thou actual Me,
And lo, thou gently masterest the orbs,
Thou matest Time, smilest content at Death,
And fillest, swellest full the vastnesses of Space.

Greater than stars or suns,
Bounding O soul thou journeyest forth;
What love than thine and ours could wider amplify?
What aspirations, wishes, outvie thine and ours O soul?
What dreams of the ideal? what plans of purity,
perfection, strength,
What cheerful willingness for others' sake to give up all?
For others' sake to suffer all?

Reckoning ahead O soul, when thou, the time achiev'd,
The seas all cross'd, weather'd the capes, the voyage done,
Surrounded, copest, frontest God, yieldest, the aim attain'd,
As fill'd with friendship, love complete, the Elder Brother found,
The Younger melts in fondness in his arms.

9

Passage to more than India!
Are thy wings plumed indeed for such far flights?
O soul, voyagest thou indeed on voyages like those?
Disportest thou on waters such as those?
Soundest below the Sanscrit and the Vedas?
Then have thy bent unleash'd.

Passage to you, your shores, ye aged fierce enigmas!
Passage to you, to mastership of you, ye strangling problems!
You, strew'd with the wrecks of skeletons, that, living, never reach'd you.

Passage to more than India!
O secret of the earth and sky!
Of you O waters of the sea! O winding creeks and rivers!
Of you O woods and fields! of you strong mountains of my land!
Of you O prairies! of you gray rocks!
O morning red! O clouds! O rain and snows!
O day and night, passage to you!

O sun and moon and all you stars! Sirius and Jupiter!
Passage to you!

Passage, immediate passage! the blood burns in my veins!
Away O soul! hoist instantly the anchor!
Cut the hawsers – haul out – shake out every sail!
Have we not stood here like trees in the ground long enough?

Have we not grovel'd here long enough, eating and drinking like mere brutes?
Have we not darken'd and dazed ourselves with books long enough?
Sail forth – steer for the deep waters only,
Reckless O soul, exploring, I with thee, and thou with me,
For we are bound where mariner has not yet dared to go,
And we will risk the ship, ourselves and all.

O my brave soul!
O farther farther sail!
O daring joy, but safe! are they not all the seas of God?
O farther, farther, farther sail!

## *Prayer of Columbus*

A batter'd, wreck'd old man,
Thrown on this savage shore, far, far from home,
Pent by the sea and dark rebellious brows, twelve dreary months,
Sore, stiff with many toils, sicken'd and nigh to death,
I take my way along the island's edge,
Venting a heavy heart.

I am too full of woe!
Haply I may not live another day;

I cannot rest O God, I cannot eat or drink or sleep,
Till I put forth myself, my prayer, once more to Thee,
Breathe, bathe myself once more in Thee, commune
with Thee,
Report myself once more to Thee.

Thou knowest my years entire, my life,
My long and crowded life of active work, not
adoration merely;
Thou knowest the prayers and vigils of my youth,
Thou knowest my manhood's solemn and visionary
meditations,
Thou knowest how before I commenced I devoted
all to come to Thee,
Thou knowest I have in age ratified all those vows
and strictly kept them,
Thou knowest I have not once lost nor faith nor
ecstasy in Thee,
In shackles, prison'd, in disgrace, repining not,
Accepting all from Thee, as duly come from Thee.
All my emprises have been fill'd with Thee,
My speculations, plans, begun and carried on in
thought of Thee,
Sailing the deep or journeying the land for Thee;
Intentions, purports, aspirations mine, leaving
results to Thee.

O I am sure they really came from Thee,
The urge, the ardor, the unconquerable will,
The potent, felt, interior command, stronger than
words,
A message from the Heavens whispering to me even
in sleep,
These sped me on.

By me and these the work so far accomplish'd,
By me earth's elder cloy'd and stifled lands,
uncloy'd, unloos'd,
By me the hemispheres rounded and tied, the
unknown to the known.

The end I know not, it is all in Thee,
Or small or great I know not – haply what broad
fields, what lands,
Haply the brutish measureless human undergrowth
I know,
Transplanted there may rise to stature, knowledge
worthy Thee,
Haply the swords I know may there indeed be turn'd
to reaping-tools,
Haply the lifeless cross I know, Europe's dead cross,
may bud and blossom there.

One effort more, my altar this bleak sand;
That Thou O God my life hast lighted,
With ray of light, steady, ineffable, vouchsafed of
Thee,
Light rare untellable, lighting the very light,
Beyond all signs, descriptions, languages;
For that O God, be it my latest word, here on my
knees,
Old, poor, and paralyzed, I thank Thee.

My terminus near,
The clouds already closing in upon me,
The voyage balk'd, the course disputed, lost,
I yield my ships to Thee.

My hands, my limbs, grow nerveless,
My brain feels rack'd, bewilder'd,
Let the old timbers part, I will not part,

I will cling fast to Thee, O God, though the waves buffet me,
Thee, Thee at least I know.

Is it the prophet's thought I speak, or am I raving?
What do I know of life? what of myself?
I know not even my own work past or present,
Dim ever-shifting guesses of it spread before me,
Of newer better worlds, their mighty parturition,
Mocking, perplexing me.

And these things I see suddenly, what mean they?
As if some miracle, some hand divine unseal'd my eyes,
Shadowy vast shapes smile through the air and sky,
And on the distant waves sail countless ships,
And anthems in new tongues I hear saluting me.

## *The Sleepers*

### I

I wander all night in my vision,
Stepping with light feet, swiftly and noiselessly stepping and stopping,
Bending with open eyes over the shut eyes of sleepers,
Wandering and confused, lost to myself, ill-assorted, contradictory,
Pausing, gazing, bending, and stopping.
How solemn they look there, stretch'd and still,
How quiet they breathe, the little children in their cradles.

The wretched features of ennuyés, the white features of corpses, the livid faces of drunkards, the sick-gray faces of onanists,

The gash'd bodies on battle-fields, the insane in
 their strong-door'd rooms, the sacred idiots, the
 new-born emerging from gates, and the dying
 emerging from gates,
The night pervades them and infolds them.

The married couple sleep calmly in their bed, he
 with his palm on the hip of the wife, and she
 with her palm on the hip of the husband,
The sisters sleep lovingly side by side in their bed,
The men sleep lovingly side by side in theirs,
And the mother sleeps with her little child carefully
 wrapt.

The blind sleep, and the deaf and dumb sleep,
The prisoner sleeps well in the prison, the runaway
 son sleeps,
The murderer that is to be hung next day, how does
 he sleep?
And the murder'd person, how does he sleep?
The female that loves unrequited sleeps,
And the male that loves unrequited sleeps,
The head of the money-maker that plotted all day
 sleeps,
And the enraged and treacherous dispositions, all, all
 sleep.

I stand in the dark with drooping eyes by the worst-
 suffering and the most restless,
I pass my hands soothingly to and fro a few inches
 from them,
The restless sink in their beds, they fitfully sleep.

Now I pierce the darkness, new beings appear,
The earth recedes from me into the night,
I saw that it was beautiful, and I see that what is not
the earth is beautiful.

I go from bedside to bedside, I sleep close with the
other sleepers each in turn,
I dream in my dream all the dreams of the other
dreamers,
And I become the other dreamers.

I am a dance – play up there! the fit is whirling me fast!
I am the ever-laughing – it is new moon and twilight,
I see the hiding of douceurs, I see nimble ghosts
whichever way I look,
Cache and cache again deep in the ground and sea,
and where it is neither ground nor sea.

Well do they do their jobs those journeymen divine,
Only from me can they hide nothing, and would not
if they could,
I reckon I am their boss and they make me a pet
besides,
And surround me and lead me and run ahead when
I walk,
To lift their cunning covers to signify me with
stretch'd arms, and resume the way;
Onward we move, a gay gang of blackguards! with
mirth-shouting music and wild-flapping
pennants of joy!

I am the actor, the actress, the voter, the politician,
The emigrant and the exile, the criminal that stood
in the box,
He who has been famous and he who shall be
famous after to-day,

The stammerer, the well-formed person, the wasted
or feeble person.

I am she who adorn'd herself and folded her hair
expectantly,
My truant lover has come, and it is dark.

Double yourself and receive me darkness,
Receive me and my lover too, he will not let me go
without him.

I roll myself upon you as upon a bed, I resign myself
to the dusk.

He whom I call answers me and takes the place of
my lover,
He rises with me silently from the bed.

Darkness, you are gentler than my lover, his flesh
was sweaty and panting,
I feel the hot moisture yet that he left me.

My hands are spread forth, I pass them in all directions,
I would sound up the shadowy shore to which you
are journeying.

Be careful darkness! already what was it touch'd me?
I thought my lover had gone, else darkness and he
are one,
I hear the heart-beat, I follow, I fade away.

2

I descend my western course, my sinews are flaccid,
Perfume and youth course through me and I am
their wake.

It is my face yellow and wrinkled instead of the old
woman's,

I sit low in a straw-bottom chair and carefully darn
  my grandson's stockings.

It is I too, the sleepless widow looking out on the
  winter midnight,
I see the sparkles of starshine on the icy and pallid earth.

A shroud I see and I am the shroud, I wrap a body
  and lie in the coffin,
It is dark here under ground, it is not evil or pain
  here, it is blank here, for reasons.

(It seems to me that every thing in the light and air
  ought to be happy,
Whoever is not in his coffin and the dark grave let
  him know he has enough.)

3

I see a beautiful gigantic swimmer swimming naked
  through the eddies of the sea,
His brown hair lies close and even to his head, he
  strikes out with courageous arms, he urges
  himself with his legs,
I see his white body, I see his undaunted eyes,
I hate the swift-running eddies that would dash him
  head-foremost on the rocks.

What are you doing you ruffianly red-trickled waves?
Will you kill the courageous giant? will you kill him
  in the prime of his middle age?

Steady and long he struggles,
He is baffled, bang'd, bruis'd, he holds out while his
  strength holds out,
The slapping eddies are spotted with his blood, they
  bear him away, they roll him, swing him, turn him,

His beautiful body is borne in the circling eddies, it
is continually bruis'd on rocks,
Swiftly and out of sight is borne the brave corpse.

4

I turn but do not extricate myself,
Confused, a past-reading, another, but with
darkness yet.

The beach is cut by the razory ice-wind, the
wreck-guns sound,
The tempest lulls, the moon comes floundering
through the drifts.

I look where the ship helplessly heads end on, I hear
the burst as she strikes, I hear the howls of
dismay, they grow fainter and fainter.

I cannot aid with my wringing fingers,
I can but rush to the surf and let it drench me and
freeze upon me.

I search with the crowd, not one of the company is
wash'd to us alive,
In the morning I help pick up the dead and lay them
in rows in a barn.

5

Now of the older war-days, the defeat at Brookly,
Washington stands inside the lines, he stands on the
intrench'd hills amid a crowd of officers,
His face is cold and damp, he cannot repress the
weeping drops,
He lifts the glass perpetually to his eyes, the color is
blanch'd from his cheeks,

He sees the slaughter of the southern braves
confided to him by their parents.

The same at last and at last when peace is declared,
He stands in the room of the old tavern, the well-
belov'd soldiers all pass through,
The officers speechless and slow draw near in their
turns,
The chief encircles their necks with his arm and
kisses them on the cheek,
He kisses lightly the wet cheeks one after another, he
shakes hands and bids good-by to the army.

6

Now what my mother told me one day as we sat at
dinner together,
Of when she was a nearly grown girl living home
with her parents on the old homestead.

A red squaw came one breakfast-time to the old
homestead,
On her back she carried a bundle of rushes for rush-
bottoming chairs,
Her hair, straight, shiny, coarse, black, profuse, half-
envelop'd her face,
Her step was free and elastic, and her voice sounded
exquisitely as she spoke.

My mother looked in delight and amazement at the
stranger,
She look'd at the freshness of her tall-borne face and
full and pliant limbs,
The more she look'd upon her she loved her,
Never before had she seen such wonderful beauty
and purity.

She made her sit on a bench by the jamb of the
fireplace, she cook'd food for her,
She had no work to give her, but she gave her
remembrance and fondness.

The red squaw staid all the forenoon, and toward
the middle of the afternoon she went away,
O my mother was loth to have her go away,
All the week she thought of her, she watch'd for her
many a month,
She remember'd her many a winter and many a
summer,
But the red squaw never came nor was heard of
there again.

7

A show of the summer softness – a contact of
something unseen – an amour of the light and air,
I am jealous and overwhelm'd with friendliness,
And will go gallivant with the light and air myself.

O love and summer, you are in the dreams and in me,
Autumn and winter are in the dreams, the farmer
goes with his thrift,
The droves and crops increase, the barns are well-fill'd.
Elements merge in the night, ships make tacks in the
dreams,
The sailor sails; the exile returns home,
The fugitive returns unharm'd, the immigrant is
back beyond months and years,
The poor Irishman lives in the simple house of his
childhood with the well-known neighbors and
faces,
They warmly welcome him, he is barefoot again, he
forgets he is well off,

The Dutchman voyages home, and the Scotchman and Welshman voyage home, and the native of the Mediterranean voyages home,
To every port of England, France, Spain, enter well-fill'd ships,
The Swiss foots it toward his hills, the Prussian goes his way, the Hungarian his way, and the Pole his way,
The Swede returns, and the Dane and Norwegian return.

The homeward bound and the outward bound,
The beautiful lost swimmer, the ennuyé, the onanist, the female that loves unrequited, the money-maker,
The actor and actress, those through with their parts and those waiting to commence,
The affectionate boy, the husband and wife, the voter, the nominee that is chosen and the nominee that has fail'd,
The great already known and the great any time after to-day,
The stammerer, the sick, the perfect-form'd, the homely,
The criminal that stood in the box, the judge that sat and sentenced him, the fluent lawyers, the jury, the audience,
The laugher and weeper, the dancer, the midnight widow, the red squaw,
The consumptive, the erysipalite, the idiot, he that is wrong'd,
The antipodes, and every one between this and them in the dark,
I swear they are averaged now – one is no better than the other,

The night and sleep have liken'd them and restored
them.

I swear they are all beautiful,
Every one that sleeps is beautiful, every thing in the
dim light is beautiful,
The wildest and bloodiest is over, and all is peace.

Peace is always beautiful,
The myth of heaven indicates peace and night.
The myth of heaven indicates the soul,
The soul is always beautiful, it appears more or it
appears less, it comes or it lags behind,
It comes from its embower'd garden and looks
pleasantly on itself and encloses the world,
Perfect and clean the genitals previously jetting, and
perfect and clean the womb cohering,
The head well-grown proportion'd and plumb, and
the bowels and joints proportion'd and plumb.

The soul is always beautiful,
The universe is duly in order, every thing is in its place,
What has arrived is in its place and what waits shall
be in its place,
The twisted skull waits, the watery or rotten blood
waits,
The child of the glutton or venerealee waits long,
and the child of the drunkard waits long, and the
drunkard himself waits long,
The sleepers that lived and died wait, the far
advanced are to go on in their turns, and the far
behind are to come on in their turns,
The diverse shall be no less diverse, but they shall
flow and unite – they unite now.

8

The sleepers are very beautiful as they lie unclothed,
They flow hand in hand over the whole earth from east to west as they lie unclothed,
The Asiatic and African are hand in hand, the European and American are hand in hand,
Learn'd and unlearn'd are hand in hand, and male and female are hand in hand,
The bare arm of the girl crosses the bare breast of her lover, they press close without lust, his lips press her neck,
The father holds his grown or ungrown son in his arms with measureless love, and the son holds the father in his arms with measureless love,
The white hair of the mother shines on the white wrist of the daughter,
The breath of the boy goes with the breath of the man, friend is inarm'd by friend,
The scholar kisses the teacher and the teacher kisses the scholar, the wrong'd is made right,
The call of the slave is one with the master's call, and the master salutes the slave,
The felon steps forth from the prison, the insane becomes sane, the suffering of sick persons is reliev'd,
The sweatings and fevers stop, the throat that was unsound is sound, the lungs of the consumptive are resumed, the poor distress'd head is free,
The joints of the rheumatic move as smoothly as ever, and smoother than ever,
Stiflings and passages open, the paralyzed become supple,

They swell'd and convuls'd and congested awake to
themselves in condition,
They pass the invigoration of the night and the
chemistry of the night, and awake.

I too pass from the night,
I stay a while away O night, but I return to you again
and love you.

Why should I be afraid to trust myself to you?
I am not afraid, I have been well brought forward by
you,
I love the rich running day, but I do not desert her in
whom I lay so long,
I know not how I came of you and I know not where I go
with you, but I know I came well and shall go well.

I will stop only a time with the night, and rise betimes,
I will duly pass the day O my mother, and duly
return to you.

## *Transpositions*

Let the reformers descend from the stands where
they are forever bawling – let an idiot or insane
person appear on each of the stands;
Let judges and criminals be transposed – let the
prison-keepers be put in prison – let those that
were prisoners take the keys;
Let them that distrust birth and death lead the rest.

## *To Think of Time*

I

To think of time – of all that retrospection,
To think of to-day, and the ages continued henceforward.

Have you guess'd you yourself would not continue?
Have you dreaded these earth-beetles?
Have you fear'd the future would be nothing to you?

Is to-day nothing? is the beginningless past nothing?
If the future is nothing they are just as surely nothing.

To think that the sun rose in the east – that men and women were flexible, real, alive – that every thing was alive,
To think that you and I did not see, feel, think, nor bear our part,
To think that we are now here and bear our part.

2

Not a day passes, not a minute or second without an accouchement,
Not a day passes, not a minute or second without a corpse.

The dull nights go over and the dull days also,
The soreness of lying so much in bed goes over,
The physician after long putting off gives the silent and terrible look for an answer,
The children come hurried and weeping, and the brothers and sisters are sent for,
Medicines stand unused on the shelf, (the camphor-smell has long pervaded the rooms,)
The faithful hand of the living does not desert the hand of the dying,

The twitching lips press lightly on the forehead of
the dying,
The breath ceases and the pulse of the heart ceases,
The corpse stretches on the bed and the living look
upon it,
It is palpable as the living are palpable.

The living look upon the corpse with their eyesight,
But without eyesight lingers a different living and
looks curiously on the corpse.

3

To think the thought of death merged in the thought
of materials,
To think of all these wonders of city and country,
and others taking great interest in them, and we
taking no interest in them.
To think how eager we are in building our houses,
To think others shall be just as eager, and we quite
indifferent.
(I see one building the house that serves him a few
years, or seventy or eighty years at most,
I see one building the house that serves him longer
than that.)
Slow-moving and black lines creep over the whole
earth – they never cease – they are the burial lines,
He that was President was buried, and he that is
now President shall surely be buried.

4

A reminiscence of the vulgar fate,
A frequent sample of the life and death of workmen,
Each after his kind.

Cold dash of waves at the ferry-wharf, posh and ice
in the river, half-frozen mud in the streets,
A gray discouraged sky overhead, the short last
daylight of December,
A hearse and stages, the funeral of an old Broadway
stage-driver, the cortege mostly drivers.

Steady the trot to the cemetery, duly rattles the
death-bell,
The gate is pass'd, the new-dug grave is halted at,
the living alight, the hearse uncloses,
The coffin is pass'd out, lower'd and settled, the whip
is laid on the coffin, the earth is swiftly shovel'd in,
The mound above is flatted with the spades – silence,
A minute – no one moves or speaks – it is done,
He is decently put away – is there any thing more?

He was a good fellow, free-mouth'd, quick-temper'd,
not bad-looking,
Ready with life or death for a friend, fond of women,
gambled, ate hearty, drank hearty,
Had known what it was to be flush, grew low-
spirited toward the last, sicken'd, was help'd by a
contribution,
Died, aged forty-one years – and that was his funeral.

Thumb extended, finger uplifted, apron, cape, gloves,
strap, wet-weather clothes, whip carefully chosen,
Boss, spotter, starter, hostler, somebody loafing on
you, you loafing on somebody, headway, man
before and man behind,
Good day's work, bad day's work, pet stock, mean
stock, first out, last out, turning-in at night,
To think that these are so much and so nigh to other
drivers, and he there takes no interest in them.

5

The markets, the government, the working-man's
wages, to think what account they are through
our nights and days,
To think that other working-men will make just as great
account of them, yet we make little or no account.

The vulgar and the refined, what you call sin and what
you call goodness, to think how wide a difference,
To think the difference will still continue to others,
yet we lie beyond the difference.

To think how much pleasure there is,
Do you enjoy yourself in the city? or engaged in
business? or planning a nomination and election?
or with your wife and family?
Or with your mother and sisters? or in womanly
housework? or the beautiful maternal cares?
These also flow onward to others, you and I flow
onward,
But in due time you and I shall take less interest in them.

Your farm, profits, crops – to think how engross'd
you are,
To think there will still be farms, profits, crops, yet
for you of what avail?

6

What will be will be well, for what is is well,
To take interest is well, and not to take interest shall
be well.

The domestic joys, the daily housework or business,
the building of houses, are not phantasms, they
have weight, form, location,

Farms, profits, crops, markets, wages, government,
    are none of them phantasms,
The difference between sin and goodness is no
    delusion,
The earth is not an echo, man and his life and all the
    things of his life are well-consider'd.

You are not thrown to the winds, you gather
    certainly and safely around yourself,
Yourself! yourself! yourself, for ever and ever!

7

It is not to diffuse you that you were born of your
    mother and father, it is to identify you,
It is not that you should be undecided, but that you
    should be decided,
Something long preparing and formless is arrived
    and form'd in you,
You are henceforth secure, whatever comes or goes.

The threads that were spun are gather'd, the weft
    crosses the warp, the pattern is systematic.

The preparations have every one been justified,
The orchestra have sufficiently tuned their
    instruments, the baton has given the signal.

The guest that was coming, he waited long, he is
    now housed,
He is one of those who are beautiful and happy, he
    is one of those that to look upon and be with is
    enough.

The law of the past cannot be eluded,
The law of the present and future cannot be eluded,
The law of the living cannot be eluded, it is eternal,

The law of promotion and transformation cannot be
 eluded,
The law of heroes and good-doers cannot be eluded,
The law of drunkards, informers, mean persons, not
 one iota thereof can be eluded.

8

Slow moving and black lines go ceaselessly over the
 earth,
Northerner goes carried and Southerner goes carried,
 and they on the Atlantic side and they on the Pacific,
And they between, and all through the Mississippi
 country, and all over the earth.
The great masters and kosmos are well as they go,
 the heroes and good-doers are well,
The known leaders and inventors and the rich
 owners and pious and distinguish'd may be well,
But there is more account than that, there is strict
 account of all.

The interminable hordes of the ignorant and wicked
 are not nothing,
The barbarians of Africa and Asia are not nothing,
The perpetual successions of shallow people are not
 nothing as they go.

Of and in all these things,
I have dream'd that we are not to be changed so
 much, nor the law of us changed,
I have dream'd that heroes and good-doers shall be
 under the present and past law,
And that murderers, drunkards, liars, shall be under
 the present and past law,
For I have dream'd that the law they are under now
 is enough.

And I have dream'd that the purpose and essence of
the known life, the transient,
Is to form and decide identity for the unknown life,
the permanent.

If all came but to ashes of dung,
If maggots and rats ended us, then Alarum! for we
are betray'd,
Then indeed suspicion of death.

Do you suspect death? if I were to suspect death I
should die now,
Do you think I could walk pleasantly and well-suited
toward annihilation?

Pleasantly and well-suited I walk,
Whither I walk I cannot define, but I know it is good,

The whole universe indicates that it is good,
The past and the present indicate that it is good.
How beautiful and perfect are the animals!
How perfect the earth, and the minutest thing upon it!
What is called good is perfect, and what is called bad
is just as perfect,
The vegetables and minerals are all perfect, and the
imponderable fluids perfect;
Slowly and surely they have pass'd on to this, and
slowly and surely they yet pass on.

9

I swear I think now that every thing without
exception has an eternal soul!
The trees have, rooted in the ground! the weeds of
the sea have! the animals!

I swear I think there is nothing but immortality!
That the exquisite scheme is for it, and the nebulous
float is for it, and the cohering is for it!
And all preparation is for it – and identity is for it –
and life and materials are altogether for it!

# WHISPERS OF HEAVENLY DEATH

## *Darest Thou Now O Soul*

Darest thou now O soul,
Walk out with me toward the unknown region,
Where neither ground is for the feet nor any path to follow?

No map there, nor guide,
Nor voice sounding, nor touch of human hand,
Nor face with blooming flesh, nor lips, nor eyes, are in that land.

I know it not O soul,
Nor dost thou, all is a blank before us,
All waits undream'd of in that region, that inaccessible land.

Till when the ties loosen,
All but the ties eternal, Time and Space,
Nor darkness, gravitation, sense, nor any bounds bounding us.

Then we burst forth, we float,
In Time and Space O soul, prepared for them,
Equal, equipt at last, (O joy! O fruit of all!) them to fulfil O soul.

## *Whispers of Heavenly Death*

Whispers of heavenly death murmur'd I hear,
Labial gossip of night, sibilant chorals,
Footsteps gently ascending, mystical breezes wafted soft and low,
Ripples of unseen rivers, tides of a current flowing, forever flowing,

(Or is it the plashing of tears? the measureless waters
of human tears?)

I see, just see skyward, great cloud-masses,
Mournfully slowly they roll, silently swelling and
mixing,
With at times a half-dimm'd sadden'd far-off star,
Appearing and disappearing.

(Some parturition rather, some solemn immortal birth;
On the frontiers to eyes impenetrable,
Some soul is passing over.)

## *Chanting the Square Deific*

I

Chanting the square deific, out of the One
advancing, out of the sides,
Out of the old and new, out of the square entirely divine,
Solid, four-sided, (all the sides needed,) from this
side Jehovah am I,
Old Brahm I, and I Saturnius am;
Not Time affects me – I am Time, old, modern as any,
Unpersuadable, relentless, executing righteous
judgments,
As the Earth, the Father, the brown old Kronos,
with laws,
Aged beyond computation, yet ever new, ever with
those mighty laws rolling,
Relentless I forgive no man – whoever sins dies – I
will have that man's life;
Therefore let none expect mercy – have the seasons,
gravitation, the appointed days, mercy? no more
have I,

But as the seasons and gravitation, and as all the
appointed days that forgive not,
I dispense from this side judgments inexorable
without the least remorse.

2

Consolator most mild, the promis'd one advancing,
With gentle hand extended, the mightier God am I,
Foretold by prophets and poets in their most rapt
prophecies and poems,
From this side, lo! the Lord Christ gazes – lo!
Hermes I – lo! mine is Hercules' face,
All sorrow, labor, suffering, I, tallying it, absorb in
myself,
Many times have I been rejected, taunted, put in
prison, and crucified, and many times shall be
again,
All the world have I given up for my dear brothers'
and sisters' sake, for the soul's sake,
Wending my way through the homes of men, rich or
poor, with the kiss of affection,
For I am affection, I am the cheer-bringing God,
with hope and all-enclosing charity,
With indulgent words as to children, with fresh and
sane words, mine only,
Young and strong I pass knowing well I am destin'd
myself to an early death;
But my charity has no death – my wisdom dies not,
neither early nor late,
And my sweet love bequeath'd here and elsewhere
never dies.

3

Aloof, dissatisfied, plotting revolt,
Comrade of criminals, brother of slaves,
Crafty, despised, a drudge, ignorant,
With sudra face and worn brow, black, but in the depths of my heart, proud as any,
Lifted now and always against whoever scorning assumes to rule me,
Morose, full of guile, full of reminiscences, brooding, with many wiles,
(Though it was thought I was baffled and dispel'd, and my wiles done, but that will never be,)
Defiant, I, Satan, still live, still utter words, in new lands duly appearing, (and old ones also,)
Permanent here from my side, warlike, equal with any, real as any,
Nor time nor change shall ever change me or my words.

4

Santa Spirita, breather, life,
Beyond the light, lighter than light,
Beyond the flames of hell, joyous, leaping easily above hell,
Beyond Paradise, perfumed solely with mine own perfume,
Including all life on earth, touching, including God, including Saviour and Satan,
Ethereal, pervading all, (for without me what were all? what were God?)
Essence of forms, life of the real identities, permanent, positive, (namely the unseen,)
Life of the great round world, the sun and stars, and of man, I, the general soul,

Here the square finishing, the solid, I the most solid,
Breathe my breath also through these songs.

## *Of Him I Love Day and Night*

Of him I love day and night I dream'd I heard he
was dead,
And I dream'd I went where they had buried him I
love, but he was not in that place,
And I dream'd I wander'd searching among burial-
places to find him,
And I found that every place was a burial-place;
The houses full of life were equally full of death,
(this house is now,)
The streets, the shipping, the places of amusement, the
Chicago, Boston, Philadelphia, the Mannahatta,
were as full of the dead as of the living,
And fuller, O vastly fuller of the dead than of the living;
And what I dream'd I will henceforth tell to every
person and age,
And I stand henceforth bound to what I dream'd,
And now I am willing to disregard burial-places and
dispense with them,
And if the memorials of the dead were put up
indifferently everywhere, even in the room where
I eat or sleep, I should be satisfied,
And if the corpse of any one I love, or if my own
corpse, be duly render'd to powder and pour'd
in the sea, I shall be satisfied,
Or if it be distributed to the winds I shall be satisfied.

## *Yet, Yet, Ye Downcast Hours*

Yet, yet, ye downcast hours, I know ye also,
Weights of lead, how ye clog and cling at my ankles,
Earth to a chamber of mourning turns – I hear the
o'erweening, mocking voice,
*Matter is conqueror – matter, triumphant only, continues onward.*

Despairing cries float ceaselessly toward me,
The call of my nearest lover, putting forth, alarm'd, uncertain,
*The sea I am quickly to sail, come tell me,*
*Come tell me where I am speeding, tell me my destination.*

I understand your anguish, but I cannot help you,
I approach, hear, behold, the sad mouth, the look out of the eyes, your mute inquiry,
*Whither I go from the bed I recline on, come tell me;*
Old age, alarm'd, uncertain – a young woman's voice, appealing to me for comfort;
A young man's voice, *Shall I not escape?*

## *As if a Phantom Caress'd Me*

As if a phantom caress'd me,
I thought I was not alone walking here by the shore;
But the one I thought was with me as now I walk by the shore, the one I loved that caress'd me,
As I lean and look through the glimmering light, that one has utterly disappear'd,
And those appear that are hateful to me and mock me.

## *Assurances*

I need no assurances, I am a man who is
pre-occupied of his own soul;
I do not doubt that from under the feet and beside
the hands and face I am cognizant of, are now
looking faces I am not cognizant of, calm and
actual faces,
I do not doubt but the majesty and beauty of the
world are latent in any iota of the world,
I do not doubt I am limitless, and that the universes
are limitless, in vain I try to think how limitless,
I do not doubt that the orbs and the systems of orbs
play their swift sports through the air on
purpose, and that I shall one day be eligible to
do as much as they, and more than they,
I do not doubt that temporary affairs keep on and on
millions of years,
I do not doubt interiors have their interiors, and
exteriors have their exteriors, and that the
eyesight has another eyesight, and the hearing
another hearing, and the voice another voice,
I do not doubt that the passionately-wept deaths of
young men are provided for, and that the deaths
of young women and the deaths of little children
are provided for, (Did you think Life was so well
provided for, and Death, the purport of all Life,
is not well provided for?)
I do not doubt that wrecks at sea, no matter what
the horrors of them, no matter whose wife, child,
husband, father, lover, has gone down, are
provided for, to the minutest points,

I do not doubt that whatever can possibly happen
anywhere at any time, is provided for in the
inherences of things,
I do not think Life provides for all and for Time and
Space, but I believe Heavenly Death provides
for all.

## *Quicksand Years*

Quicksand years that whirl me I know not whither,
Your schemes, politics, fail, lines give way,
substances mock and elude me,
Only the theme I sing, the great and strong-
possess'd soul, eludes not,
One's-self must never give way – that is the final
substance – that out of all is sure,
Out of politics, triumphs, battles, life, what at last
finally remains?
When shows break up what but One's-Self is sure?

## *That Music Always Round Me*

That music always round me, unceasing,
unbeginning, yet long untaught I did not hear,
But now the chorus I hear and am elated,
A tenor, strong, ascending with power and health,
with glad notes of daybreak I hear,
A soprano at intervals sailing buoyantly over the tops
of immense waves,
A transparent base shuddering lusciously under and
through the universe,
The triumphant tutti, the funeral wailings with sweet
flutes and violins, all these I fill myself with,

I hear not the volumes of sound merely, I am moved by the exquisite meanings,
I listen to the different voices winding in and out, striving, contending with fiery vehemence to excel each other in emotion;
I do not think the performers know themselves – but now I think I begin to know them.

## *What Ship Puzzled at Sea*

What ship puzzled at sea, cons for the true reckoning?
Or coming in, to avoid the bars and follow the channel a perfect pilot needs?
Here, sailor! here, ship! take aboard the most perfect pilot,
Whom, in a little boat, putting off and rowing, I hailing you offer.

## *A Noiseless Patient Spider*

A noiseless patient spider,
I mark'd where on a little promontory it stood isolated,
Mark'd how to explore the vacant vast surrounding,
It launched forth filament, filament, filament, out of itself,
Ever unreeling them, ever tirelessly speeding them.
And you O my soul where you stand,
Surrounded, detached, in measureless oceans of space,
Ceaselessly musing, venturing, throwing, seeking the spheres to connect them,
Till the bridge you will need be form'd, till the ductile anchor hold,
Till the gossamer thread you fling catch somewhere, O my soul.

## *O Living Always, Always Dying*

O living always, always dying!
O the burials of me past and present,
O me while I stride ahead, material, visible,
  imperious as ever;
O me, what I was for years, now dead, (I lament not,
  I am content;)
O to disengage myself from those corpses of me,
  which I turn and look at where I cast them,
To pass on, (O living! always living!) and leave the
  corpses behind.

## *To One Shortly to Die*

From all the rest I single out you, having a message
  for you,
You are to die – let others tell you what they please,
  I cannot prevaricate,
I am exact and merciless, but I love you – there is no
  escape for you.

Softly I lay my right hand upon you, you just feel it,
I do not argue, I bend my head close and half
  envelop it,
I sit quietly by, I remain faithful,
I am more than nurse, more than parent or
  neighbor,
I absolve you from all except yourself spiritual bodily,
  that is eternal, you yourself will surely escape,
The corpse you will leave will be but
  excrementitious.

The sun bursts through in unlooked-for directions,
Strong thoughts fill you and confidence, you smile,

You forget you are sick, as I forget you are sick,
You do not see the medicines, you do not mind the
    weeping friends, I am with you,
I exclude others from you, there is nothing to be
    commiserated,
I do not commiserate, I congratulate you.

## *Night on the Prairies*

Night on the prairies,
The supper is over, the fire on the ground burns low,
The wearied emigrants sleep, wrapt in their blankets;
I walk by myself – I stand and look at the stars,
    which I think now I never realized before.

Now I absorb immortality and peace,
I admire death and test propositions.

How plenteous! how spiritual! how résumé!
The same old man and soul – the same old
    aspirations, and the same content.

I was thinking the day most splendid till I saw what
    the not-day exhibited,
I was thinking this globe enough till there sprang out
    so noiseless around me myriads of other globes.

Now while the great thoughts of space and eternity
    fill me I will measure myself by them,
And now touch'd with the lives of other globes
    arrived as far along as those of the earth,
Or waiting to arrive, or pass'd on farther than those
    of the earth,
I henceforth no more ignore them than I ignore my
    own life,

Or the lives of the earth arrived as far as mine, or
waiting to arrive.

O I see now that life cannot exhibit all to me, as the
day cannot,
I see that I am to wait for what will be exhibited by
death.

## *Thought*

As I sit with others at a great feast, suddenly while
the music is playing,
To my mind, (whence it comes I know not,) spectral
in mist of a wreck at sea,
Of certain ships, how they sail from port with flying
streamers and wafted kisses, and that is the last
of them,
Of the solemn and murky mystery about the fate of
the President,
Of the flower of the marine science of fifty generations
founder'd off the Northeast coast and going down
– of the steamship Arctic going down,
Of the veil'd tableau – women gather'd together on
deck, pale, heroic, waiting the moment that
draws so close – O the moment!
A huge sob – a few bubbles – the white foam spirting
up – and then the women gone,
Sinking there while the passionless wet flows on – and
I now pondering, Are those women indeed gone?
Are souls drown'd and destroy'd so?
Is only matter triumphant?

## *The Last Invocation*

At the last, tenderly,
From the walls of the powerful fortress'd house,
From the clasp of the knitted locks, from the keep of
the well-closed doors,
Let me be wafted.

Let me glide noiselessly forth;
With the key of softness unlock the locks – with a
whisper,
Set ope the doors O soul.

Tenderly – be not impatient,
(Strong is your hold O mortal flesh,
Strong is your hold O love.)

## *As I Watch'd the Ploughman Ploughing*

As I watch'd the ploughman ploughing,
Or the sower sowing in the fields, or the harvester
harvesting,
I saw there too, O life and death, your analogies;
(Life, life is the tillage, and Death is the harvest
according.)

## *Pensive and Faltering*

Pensive and faltering,
The words *the Dead* I write,
For living are the Dead,
(Haply the only living, only real,
And I the apparition, I the spectre.)

## *Thou Mother with Thy Equal Brood*

1

Thou Mother with thy equal brood,
Thou varied chain of different States, yet one
identity only,
A special song before I go I'd sing o'er all the rest,
For thee, the future.

I'd sow a seed for thee of endless Nationality,
I'd fashion thy ensemble including body and soul,
I'd show away ahead thy real Union, and how it may
be accomplish'd.

The paths to the house I seek to make,
But leave to those to come the house itself.

Belief I sing, and preparation;
As Life and Nature are not great with reference to
the present only,
But greater still from what is yet to come,
Out of that formula for thee I sing.

2

As a strong bird on pinions free,
Joyous, the amplest spaces heavenward cleaving,
Such be the thought I'd think of thee America,
Such be the recitative I'd bring for thee.

The conceits of the poets of other lands I'd bring
thee not,
Nor the compliments that have served their turn so
long,
Nor rhyme, nor the classics, nor perfume of foreign
court or indoor library;

But an odor I'd bring as from forests of pine in
Maine, or breath of an Illinois prairie,
With open airs of Virginia or Georgia or Tennessee,
or from Texas uplands, or Florida's glades,
Or the Saguenay's black stream, or the wide blue
spread of Huron,
With presentment of Yellowstone's scenes, or
Yosemite,
And murmuring under, pervading all, I'd bring the
rustling sea-sound,
That endlessly sounds from the two Great Seas of
the world.

And for thy subtler sense subtler refrains dread
Mother,
Preludes of intellect tallying these and thee,
mind-formulas fitted for thee, real and sane and
large as these and thee,
Thou! mounting higher, diving deeper than we
knew, thou transcendental Union!
By thee fact to be justified, blended with thought,
Thought of man justified, blended with God,
Through thy idea, lo, the immortal reality!
Through thy reality, lo, the immortal ideal!

3

Brain of the New World, what a task is thine,
To formulate the Modern – out of the peerless
grandeur of the modern,
Out of thyself, comprising science, to recast poems,
churches, art,
(Recast, maybe discard them, end them – maybe
their work is done, who knows?)

By vision, hand, conception, on the background of
    the mighty past, the dead,
To limn with absolute faith the mighty living present.

And yet thou living present brain, hear of the dead,
    the Old World brain,
Thou that lay folded like an unborn babe within its
    fold so long,
Thou carefully prepared by it so long – haply thou
    but unfoldest it, only maturest it,
It to eventuate in thee – the essence of the by-gone
    time contain'd in thee,
Its poems, churches, arts, unwitting to themselves,
    destined with reference to thee;
Thou but the apples, long, long, long a-growing,
The fruit of all the Old ripening to-day in thee.

4

Sail, sail thy best, ship of Democracy,
Of value is thy freight, 'tis not the Present only,
The Past is also stored in thee,
Thou holdest not the venture of thyself alone, not of
    the Western continent alone,
Earth's *résumé* entire floats on thy keel O ship, is
    steadied by thy spars,
With thee Time voyages in trust, the antecedent
    nations sink or swim with thee,
With all their ancient struggles, martyrs, heroes,
    epics, wars, thou bear'st the other continents,
Theirs, theirs as much as thine, the destination-port
    triumphant;
Steer then with good strong hand and wary eye O
    helmsman, thou carriest great companions,
Venerable priestly Asia sails this day with thee,
And royal feudal Europe sails with thee.

5

Beautiful world of new superber birth that rises to
 my eyes,
Like a limitless golden cloud filling the western sky,
Emblem of general maternity lifted above all,
Sacred shape of the bearer of daughters and sons,
Out of thy teeming womb thy giant babes in
 ceaseless procession issuing,
Acceding from such gestation, taking and giving
 continual strength and life,
World of the real – world of the twain in one,
World of the soul, born by the world of the real
 alone, led to identity, body, by it alone,
Yet in beginning only, incalculable masses of
 composite precious materials,
By history's cycles forwarded, by every nation,
 language, hither sent,
Ready, collected here, a freer, vast, electric world, to
 be constructed here,
(The true New World, the world of orbic science,
 morals, literatures to come,)
Thou wonder world yet undefined, unform'd,
 neither do I define thee,
How can I pierce the impenetrable blank of the future?
I feel thy ominous greatness evil as well as good,
I watch thee advancing, absorbing the present,
 transcending the past,
I see thy light lighting, and thy shadow shadowing,
 as if the entire globe,
But I do not undertake to define thee, hardly to
 comprehend thee,
I but thee name, thee prophesy, as now,
I merely thee ejaculate!

Thee in thy future,
Thee in thy only permanent life, career, thy own
unloosen'd mind, thy soaring spirit,
Thee as another equally needed sun, radiant, ablaze,
swift-moving, fructifying all,
Thee risen in potent cheerfulness and joy, in endless
great hilarity,
Scattering for good the cloud that hung so long, that
weigh'd so long upon the mind of man,
The doubt, suspicion, dread, of gradual, certain
decadence of man;
Thee in thy larger, saner brood of female, male –
thee in thy athletes, moral, spiritual, South,
North, West, East,
(To thy immortal breasts, Mother of All, thy every
daughter, son, endear'd alike, forever equal,)
Thee in thy own musicians, singers, artists, unborn
yet, but certain,
Thee in thy moral wealth and civilization, (until
which thy proudest material civilization must
remain in vain,)
Thee in thy all-supplying, all-enclosing worship –
thee in no single bible, saviour, merely,
Thy saviours countless, latent within thyself, thy
bibles incessant within thyself, equal to any,
divine as any,
(Thy soaring course thee formulating, not in thy two
great wars, nor in thy century's visible growth,
But far more in these leaves and chants, thy chants,
great Mother!)
Thee in an education grown of thee, in teachers,
studies, students, born of thee,
Thee in thy democratic fêtes en-masse, thy high
original festivals, operas, lecturers, preachers,

Thee in thy ultimata, (the preparations only now
completed, the edifice on sure foundations tied,)
Thee in thy pinnacles, intellect, thought, thy topmost
rational joys, thy love and godlike aspiration,
In thy resplendent coming literati, thy full-lung'd
orators, thy sacerdotal bards, kosmic savans,
These! these in thee, (certain to come,) to-day I
prophesy.

6

Land tolerating all, accepting all, not for the good
alone, all good for thee,
Land in the realms of God to be a realm unto
thyself,
Under the rule of God to be a rule unto thyself.

(Lo, where arise three peerless stars,
To be thy natal stars my country, Ensemble,
Evolution, Freedom,
Set in the sky of Law.)

Land of unprecedented faith, God's faith,
Thy soil, thy very subsoil, all upheav'd,
The general inner earth so long so sedulously draped
over, now hence for what it is boldly laid bare,
Open'd by thee to heaven's light for benefit or bale.

Not for success alone,
Not to fair-sail unintermitted always,
The storm shall dash thy face, the murk of war and
worse than war shall cover thee all over,
(Wert capable of war, its tug and trials? be capable
of peace, its trials,
For the tug and mortal strain of nations come at last
in prosperous peace, not war;)

In many a smiling mask death shall approach
beguiling thee, thou in disease shalt swelter,
The livid cancer spread its hideous claws, clinging
upon thy breasts, seeking to strike thee deep within,
Consumption of the worst, moral consumption,
shall rouge thy face with hectic,
But thou shalt face thy fortunes, thy diseases, and
surmount them all,
Whatever they are to-day and whatever through time
they may be,
They each and all shall lift and pass away and cease
from thee,
While thou, Time's spirals rounding, out of thyself,
thyself still extricating, fusing,
Equable, natural, mystical Union thou, (the mortal
with immortal blent,)
Shalt soar toward the fulfilment of the future, the
spirit of the body and the mind,
The soul, its destinies.

The soul, its destinies, the real real,
(Purport of all these apparitions of the real;)
In thee America, the soul, its destinies,
Thou globe of globes! thou wonder nebulous!
By many a throe of heat and cold convuls'd, (by
these thyself solidifying,)
Thou mental, moral orb – thou New, indeed new,
Spiritual World!
The Present holds thee not – for such vast growth as
thine,
For such unparallel'd flight as thine, such brood as
thine,
The Future only holds thee and can hold thee.

## *A Paumanok Picture*

Two boats with nets lying off the sea-beach, quite still,
Ten fishermen waiting – they discover a thick school of moss-bonkers – they drop the join'd seine-ends in the water,
The boats separate and row off, each on its rounding course to the beach, enclosing the mossbonkers,
The net is drawn in by a windlass by those who stop ashore,
Some of the fishermen lounge in their boats, others stand ankle-deep in the water, pois'd on strong legs,
The boats partly drawn up, the water slapping against them,
Strew'd on the sand in heaps and windrows, well out from the water, the green-back'd spotted mossbonkers.

# FROM NOON TO STARRY NIGHT

## *Thou Orb Aloft Full-Dazzling*

Thou orb aloft full-dazzling! thou hot October noon!
Flooding with sheeny light the gray beach sand,
The sibilant near sea with vistas far and foam,
And tawny streaks and shades and spreading blue;
O sun of noon refulgent! my special word to thee.

Hear me illustrious!
Thy lover me, for always I have loved thee,
Even as basking babe, then happy boy alone by some
wood edge, thy touching-distant beams enough,
Or man matured, or young or old, as now to thee I
launch my invocation.

(Thou canst not with thy dumbness me deceive,
I know before the fitting man all Nature yields,
Though answering not in words, the skies, trees,
hear his voice – and thou O sun,
As for thy throes, thy perturbations, sudden breaks
and shafts of flame gigantic,
I understand them, I know those flames, those
perturbations well.)

Thou that with fructifying heat and light,
O'er myriad farms, o'er lands and waters North and
South,
O'er Mississippi's endless course, o'er Texas' grassy
plains, Kanada's woods,
O'er all the globe that turns its face to thee shining
in space,
Thou that impartially infoldest all, not only
continents, seas,
Thou that to grapes and weeds and little wild
flowers givest so liberally,

Shed, shed thyself on mine and me, with but a
fleeting ray out of thy million millions,
Strike though these chants.

Nor only launch thy subtle dazzle and thy strength
for these,
Prepare the later afternoon of me myself – prepare
my lengthening shadows,
Prepare my starry nights.

## *Faces*

### 1

Sauntering the pavement or riding the country by-
road, lo, such faces!
Faces of friendship, precision, caution, sauvity, ideality,
The spiritual-prescient face, the always welcome
common benevolent face,
The face of the singing of music, the grand faces of
natural lawyers and judges broad at the back-top,
The faces of hunters and fishers bulged at the brows,
the shaved blanch'd faces of orthodox citizens,
The pure, extravagant, yearning, questioning artist's
face,
The ugly face of some beautiful soul, the handsome
detested or despised face,
The sacred faces of infants, the illuminated face of
the mother of many children,
The face of an amour, the face of veneration,
The face as of a dream, the face of an immobile rock,
The face withdrawn of its good and bad, a castrated
face,
A wild hawk, his wings clipp'd by the clipper,

A stallion that yielded at last to the thongs and knife
of the gelder.

Sauntering the pavement thus, or crossing the
ceaseless ferry, faces and faces and faces,
I see them and complain not, and am content with all.

2

Do you suppose I could be content with all if I
thought them their own finalè?

This now is too lamentable a face for a man,
Some abject louse asking leave to be, cringing for it,
Some milk-nosed maggot blessing what lets it wrig
to its hole.

This face is a dog's snout sniffing for garbage,
Snakes nest in that mouth, I hear the sibilant threat.

This face is a haze more chill than the arctic sea,
Its sleepy and wabbling icebergs crunch as they go.

This is a face of bitter herbs, this an emetic, they
need no label,
And more of the drug-shelf, laudanum, caoutchouc,
or hog's-lard.

This face is an epilepsy, its wordless tongue gives out
the earthly cry,
Its veins down the neck distend, its eyes roll till they
show nothing but their whites,
Its teeth grit, the palms of the hands are cut by the
turn'd-in nails,
The man falls struggling and foaming to the ground,
while he speculates well.

This face is bitten by vermin and worms,

And this is some murderer's knife with a half-pull'd
scabbard.
This face owes to the sexton his dismalest fee,
An unceasing death-bell tolls there.

3

Features of my equals would you trick me with your
creas'd and cadaverous march?
Well, you cannot trick me.

I see your rounded never-erased flow,
I see 'neath the rims of your haggard and mean
disguises.

Splay and twist as you like, poke with the tangling
fores of fishes or rats,
You'll be unmuzzled, you certainly will.
I saw the face of the most smear'd and slobbering
idiot they had at the asylum,
And I knew for my consolation what they knew not,
I knew of the agents that emptied and broke my
brother,
The same wait to clear the rubbish from the fallen
tenement,
And I shall look again in a score or two of ages,
And I shall meet the real landlord perfect and
unharm'd, every inch as good as myself.

4

The Lord advances, and yet advances,
Always the shadow in front, always the reach'd hand
bringing up the laggards.

Out of this face emerge banners and horses – O
superb! I see what is coming,

I see the high pioneer-caps, see staves of runners
  clearing the way,
I hear victorious drums.

This face is a life-boat,
This is the face commanding and bearded, it asks no
  odds of the rest,
This face is flavor'd fruit ready for eating,
This face of a healthy honest boy is the programme
  of all good.

These faces bear testimony slumbering or awake,
They show their descent from the Master himself.

Off the word I have spoken I except not one – red,
  white, black, are all deific,
In each house is the ovum, it comes forth after a
  thousand years.

Spots or cracks at the windows do not disturb me,
Tall and sufficient stand behind and make signs to me,
I read the promise and patiently wait.

This is a full-grown lily's face,
She speaks to the limber-hipp'd man near the
  garden pickets,
*Come here* she blushingly cries, *Come nigh to me
  limber-hipp'd man,*
*Stand at my side till I lean as high as I can upon you,*
*Fill me with albescent honey, bend down to me,*
*Rub to me with your chafing beard, rub to my breast and
  shoulders.*

5

The old face of the mother of many children,
Whist! I am fully content.

Lull'd and late is the smoke of the First-day morning,
It hangs low over the rows of trees by the fences,
It hangs thin by the sassafras and wild-cherry and cat-brier under them.

I saw the rich ladies in full dress at the soiree,
I heard what the singers were singing so long,
Heard who sprang in crimson youth from the white froth and the water-blue.

Behold a woman!
She looks out from her quaker cap, her face is clearer and more beautiful than the sky.

She sits in an armchair under the shaded porch of the farm-house,
The sun just shines on her old white head.

Her ample gown is of cream-hued linen,
Her grandsons raised the flax, and her grand-daughters spin it with the distaff and the wheel.

The melodious character of the earth,
The finish beyond which philosophy cannot go and does not wish to go,
The justified mother of men.

## *The Mystic Trumpeter*

### 1

Hark, some wild trumpeter, some strange musician,
Hovering unseen in air, vibrates capricious tunes to-night.
I hear thee trumpeter, listening alert I catch thy notes,
Now pouring, whirling like a tempest round me,
Now low, subdued, now in the distance lost.

2

Come nearer bodiless one, haply in thee resounds
Some dead composer, haply thy pensive life
Was fill'd with aspirations high, unform'd ideals,
Waves, oceans musical, chaotically surging,
That now ecstatic ghost, close to me bending, thy
    cornet echoing, pealing,
Gives out to no one's ears but mine, but freely gives
    to mine,
That I may thee translate.

3

Blow trumpeter free and clear, I follow thee,
While at thy liquid prelude, glad, serene,
The fretting world, the streets, the noisy hours of
    day withdraw,
A holy calm descends like dew upon me,
I walk in cool refreshing night the walks of Paradise,
I scent the grass, the moist air and the roses;
Thy song expands my numb'd imbonded spirit,
    thou freest, launchest me,
Floating and basking upon heaven's lake.

4

Blow again trumpeter! and for my sensuous eyes,
Bring the old pageants, show the feudal world.
What charm thy music works! thou makest pass
    before me,
Ladies and cavaliers long dead, barons are in their
    castle halls, the troubadours are singing,
Arm'd knights go forth to redress wrongs, some in
    quest of the holy Graal;
I see the tournament, I see the contestants incased in
    heavy armor seated on stately champing horses,

I hear the shouts, the sounds of blows and smiting steel;
I see the Crusaders' tumultuous armies – hark, how
the cymbals clang,
Lo, where the monks walk in advance, bearing the
cross on high.

5

Blow again trumpeter! and for thy theme,
Take now the enclosing theme of all, the solvent and
the setting,
Love, that is pulse of all, the sustenance and the pang,
The heart of man and woman all for love,
No other theme but love – knitting, enclosing, all-
diffusing love.
O how the immortal phantoms crowd around me!
I see the vast alembic ever working, I see and know
the flames that heat the world,
The glow, the blush, the beating hearts of lovers,
So blissful happy some, and some so silent, dark,
and nigh to death;
Love, that is all the earth to lovers – love, that mocks
time and space,
Love, that is day and night – love, that is sun and
moon and stars,
Love, that is crimson, sumptuous, sick with perfume,
No other words but words of love, no other thought
but love.

6

Blow again trumpeter – conjure war's alarums.
Swift to thy spell a shuddering hum like distant
thunder rolls,
Lo, where the arm'd men hasten – lo, mid the
clouds of dust the glint of bayonets,

I see the grime-faced cannoneers, I mark the rosy flash
amid the smoke, I hear the cracking of the guns;
Nor war alone – thy fearful music-song, wild prayer,
brings every sight of fear,
The deeds of ruthless brigands, rapine, murder – I
hear the cries for help!
I see ships foundering at sea, I behold on deck and
below deck the terrible tableaus.

7

O trumpeter, methinks I am myself the instrument
thou playest,
Thou melt'st my heart, my brain – thou movest,
drawest, changest them at will;
And now thy sullen notes send darkness through me,
Thou takest away all cheering light, all hope,
I see the enslaved, the overthrown, the hurt, the
opprest of the whole earth,
I feel the measureless shame and humiliation of my
race, it becomes all mine,
Mine too the revenges of humanity, the wrongs of
ages, baffled feuds and hatreds,
Utter defeat upon me weighs – all lost – the foe
victorious,
(Yet 'mid the ruins Pride colossal stands unshaken
to the last,
Endurance, resolution to the last.)

8

Now trumpeter for thy close,
Vouchsafe a higher strain than any yet,
Sing to my soul, renew its languishing faith and hope,
Rouse up my slow belief, give me some vision of the
future,

Give me for once its prophecy and joy.

O glad, exulting, culminating song!
A vigor more than earth's is in thy notes,
Marches of victory – man disenthral'd – the conqueror at last,
Hymns to the universal God from universal man – all joy!
A reborn race appears – a perfect world, all joy!
Women and men in wisdom innocence and health – all joy!
Riotous laughing bacchanals fill'd with joy!
War, sorrow, suffering gone – the rank earth purged – nothing but joy left!
The ocean fill'd with joy – the atmosphere all joy!
Joy! joy! in freedom, worship, love! joy in the ecstasy of life!
Enough to merely be! enough to breathe!
Joy! joy! all over joy!

## *To a Locomotive in Winter*

Thee for my recitative,
Thee in the driving storm even as now, the snow, the winter-day declining,
Thee in thy panoply, thy measur'd dual throbbing and thy beat convulsive,
Thy black cylindric body, golden brass and silvery steel,
Thy ponderous side-bars, parallel and connecting rods, gyrating, shuttling at thy sides,
Thy metrical, now swelling pant and roar, now tapering in the distance,
Thy great protruding head-light fix'd in front,

Thy long, pale, floating vapor-pennants, tinged with
 delicate purple,
The dense and murky clouds out-belching from thy
 smoke-stack,
Thy knitted frame, thy springs and valves, the
 tremulous twinkle of thy wheels,
Thy train of cars behind, obedient, merrily following,
Through gale or calm, now swift, now slack, yet
 steadily careering;
Type of the modern – emblem of motion and
 power – pulse of the continent,
For once come serve the Muse and merge in verse,
 even as here I see thee,
With storm and buffeting gusts of wind and falling
 snow,
By day thy warning ringing bell to sound its notes,
By night thy silent signal lamps to swing.

Fierce-throated beauty!
Roll through my chant with all thy lawless music,
 thy swinging lamps at night,
Thy madly-whistled laughter, echoing, rumbling like
 an earthquake, rousing all,
Law of thyself complete, thine own track firmly
 holding,
(No sweetness debonair of tearful harp or glib piano
 thine,)
Thy trills of shrieks by rocks and hills return'd,
Launch'd o'er the prairies wide, across the lakes,
To the free skies unpent and glad and strong.

## *O Magnet-South*

O magnet-South! O glistening perfumed South! my South!
O quick mettle, rich blood, impulse and love! good and evil! O all dear to me!
O dear to me my birth-things – all moving things and the trees where I was born – the grains, plants, rivers,
Dear to me my own slow sluggish rivers where they flow, distant, over flats of silvery sands or through swamps,
Dear to me the Roanoke, the Savannah, the Altamahaw, the Pedee, the Tombigbee, the Santee, the Coosa, and the Sabine,
O pensive, far away wandering, I return with my soul to haunt their banks again,
Again in Florida I float on transparent lakes, I float on the Okeechobee, I cross the hummock-land or through pleasant openings or dense forests,
I see the parrots in the woods, I see the papaw-tree and the blossoming titi;
Again, sailing in my coaster on deck, I coast off Georgia, I coast up the Carolinas,
I see where the live-oak is growing, I see where the yellow-pine, the scented bay-tree, the lemon and orange, the cypress, the graceful palmetto,
I pass rude sea-headlands and enter Pamlico sound through an inlet, and dart my vision inland;
O the cotton plant! the growing fields of rice, sugar, hemp!
The cactus guarded with thorns, the laurel-tree with large white flowers,

The range afar, the richness and barrenness, the old
 woods charged with mistletoe and trailing moss,
The piney odor and the gloom, the awful natural
 stillness, (here in these dense swamps the
 freebooter carries his gun, and the fugitive has
 his conceal'd hut;)
O the strange fascination of these half-known half-
 impassable swamps, infested by reptiles,
 resounding with the bellow of the alligator, the
 sad noises of the night-owl and the wild-cat, and
 the whirr of the rattlesnake,
The mocking-bird, the American mimic, singing all
 the forenoon, singing through the moon-lit night,
The humming-bird, the wild turkey, the raccoon,
 the opossum;
A Kentucky corn-field, the tall, graceful, long-leav'd
 corn, slender, flapping, bright green, with tassels,
 with beautiful ears each well-sheath'd in its husk;
O my heart! O tender and fierce pangs, I can stand
 them not, I will depart;
O to be a Virginian where I grew up! O to be a
 Carolinian!
O longings irrepressible! O I will go back to old
 Tennessee and never wander more.

## *Mannahatta*

I was asking for something specific and perfect for
 my city,
Whereupon lo! upsprang the aboriginal name.

Now I see what there is in a name, a word, liquid,
 sane, unruly, musical, self-sufficient,

I see that the word of my city is that word from of old,
Because I see that word nested in nests of water-bays, superb,
Rich, hemm'd thick all around with sailships and steamships, an island sixteen miles long, solid-founded,
Numberless crowded streets, high growths of iron, slender, strong, light, splendidly uprising toward clear skies,
Tides swift and ample, well-loved by me, toward sundown,
The flowing sea-currents, the little islands, larger adjoining islands, the heights, the villas,
The countless masts, the white shore-steamers, the lighters, the ferry-boats, the black sea-steamers well-model'd,
The down-town streets, the jobbers' houses of business, the houses of business of the ship-merchants and money-brokers, the river-streets,
Immigrants arriving, fifteen or twenty thousand in a week,
The carts hauling goods, the manly race of drivers of horses, the brown-faced sailors,
The summer air, the bright sun shining, and the sailing clouds aloft,
The winter snows, the sleigh-bells, the broken ice in the river, passing along up or down with the flood-tide or ebb-tide,
The mechanics of the city, the masters, well-form'd, beautiful-faced, looking you straight in the eyes,
Trottoirs throng'd, vehicles, Broadway, the women, the shops and shows,

A million people – manners free and superb – open
voices – hospitality – the most courageous and
friendly young men,
City of hurried and sparkling waters! city of spires
and masts!
City nested in bays! my city!

## *All is Truth*

O me, man of slack faith so long,
Standing aloof, denying portions so long,
Only aware to-day of compact all-diffused truth,
Discovering to-day there is no lie or form of lie, and
can be none, but grows as inevitably upon itself
as the truth does upon itself,
Or as any law of the earth or any natural production
of the earth does.
(This is curious and may not be realized
immediately, but it must be realized,
I feel in myself that I represent falsehoods equally
with the rest,
And that the universe does.)

Where has fail'd a perfect return indifferent of lies or
the truth?
Is it upon the ground, or in water or fire? or in the
spirit of man? or in the meat and blood?

Meditating among liars and retreating sternly into
myself, I see that there are really no liars or lies
after all,
And that nothing fails its perfect return, and that
what are called lies are perfect returns,

And that each thing exactly represents itself and
 what has preceded it,
And that the truth includes all, and is compact just
 as much as space is compact,
And that there is no flaw or vacuum in the amount of
 the truth – but that all is truth without exception;
And henceforth I will go celebrate any thing I see or am,
And sing and laugh and deny nothing.

## *A Riddle Song*

That which eludes this verse and any verse,
Unheard by sharpest ear, unform'd in clearest eye or
 cunningest mind,
Nor lore nor fame, nor happiness nor wealth,
And yet the pulse of every heart and life throughout
 the world incessantly,
Which you and I and all pursuing ever ever miss,
Open but still a secret, the real of the real, an illusion,
Costless, vouchsafed to each, yet never man the
 owner,
Which poets vainly seek to put in rhyme, historians
 in prose,
Which sculptor never chisel'd yet, not painter painted,
Which vocalist never sung, nor orator nor actor ever
 utter'd,
Invoking here and how I challenge for my song.

Indifferently, 'mid public, private haunts, in solitude,
Behind the mountain and the wood,
Companion of the city's busiest streets, through the
 assemblage,
It and its radiations constantly glide.
In looks of fair unconscious babes,

Or strangely in the coffin'd dead,
Or show of breaking dawn or stars by night,
As some dissolving delicate film of dreams,
Hiding yet lingering.

Two little breaths of words comprising it,
Two words, yet all from first to last comprised in it.

How ardently for it!
How many ships have sail'd and sunk for it!
How many travelers started from their homes and
ne'er return'd!
How much of genius boldly staked and lost for it!
What countless stores of beauty, love, ventur'd for it!
How all superbest deeds since Time began are
traceable to it – and shall be to the end!
How all heroic martyrdoms to it!
How, justified by it, the horrors, evils, battles of the
earth!
How the bright fascinating lambent flames of it, in
every age and land, have drawn men's eyes,
Rich as a sunset on the Norway coast, the sky, the
islands, and the cliffs,
Or midnight's silent glowing northern lights
unreachable.

Haply God's riddle it, so vague and yet so certain,
The soul for it, and all the visible universe for it,
And heaven at last for it.

## *Excelsior*

Who has gone farthest? for I would go farther,
And who has been just? for I would be the most just
person of the earth,

And who most cautious? for I would be more cautious,
And who has been happiest? O I think it is I – I think
no one was ever happier than I,
And who has lavish'd all? for I lavish constantly the
best I have,
And who proudest? for I think I have reason to be
the proudest son alive – for I am the son of the
brawny and tall-topt city,
And who has been bold and true? for I would be the
boldest and truest being of the universe,
And who benevolent? for I would show more
benevolence than all the rest,
And who has receiv'd the love of the most friends?
for I know what it is to receive the passionate
love of many friends,
And who possesses a perfect and enamour'd body?
for I do not believe any one possesses a more
perfect or enamour'd body than mine,
And who thinks the amplest thoughts? for I would
surround those thoughts,
And who has made hymns fit for the earth? for I am
mad with devouring ecstasy to make joyous
hymns for the whole earth.

## *Ah Poverties, Wincings, and Sulky Retreats*

Ah poverties, wincings, and sulky retreats,
Ah you foes that in conflict have overcome me,
(For what is my life or any man's life but a conflict
with foes, the old, the incessant war?)
You degradations, you tussle with passions and
appetites,
You smarts from dissatisfied friendships, (ah wounds
the sharpest of all!)

You toil of painful and choked articulations, you meannesses,
You shallow tongue-talks at tables, (my tongue the shallowest of any;)
You broken resolutions, you racking angers, you smother'd ennuis!
Ah think not you finally triumph, my real self has yet to come forth,
It shall yet march forth o'ermastering, till all lies beneath me,
It shall yet stand up the soldier of ultimate victory.

## *Thoughts*

Of public opinion,
Of a calm and cool fiat sooner or later, (how impassive! how certain and final!)
Of the President with pale face asking secretly to himself, *What will the people say at last?*
Of the frivolous Judge – of the corrupt Congressman, Governor, Mayor – of such as these standing helpless and exposed,
Of the mumbling and screaming priest, (soon, soon deserted,)
Of the lessening year by year of venerableness, and of the dicta of officers, statutes, pulpits, schools,
Of the rising forever taller and stronger and broader of the intuitions of men and women, and of Self-esteem and Personality;
Of the true New World – of the Democracies resplendent enmasse,
Of the conformity of politics, armies, navies, to them,

Of the shining sun by them – of the inherent light, greater than the rest,
Of the envelopment of all by them, and the effusion of all from them.

## *Mediums*

They shall arise in the States,
They shall report Nature, laws, physiology, and happiness,
They shall illustrate Democracy and the kosmos,
They shall be alimentive, amative, perceptive,
They shall be complete women and men, their pose brawny and supple, their drink water, their blood clean and clear,
They shall fully enjoy materialism and the sight of products, they shall enjoy the sight of the beef, lumber, bread-stuffs, of Chicago the great city,
They shall train themselves to go in public to become orators and oratresses,
Strong and sweet shall their tongues be, poems and materials of poems shall come from their lives, they shall be makers and finders,
Of them and of their works shall emerge divine conveyers, to convey gospels,
Characters, events, retrospections, shall be convey'd in gospels, trees, animals, waters, shall be convey'd,
Death, the future, the invisible faith, shall all be convey'd.

## *Weave in, My Hardy Life*

Weave in, weave in, my hardy life,
Weave yet a soldier strong and full for great
campaigns to come,
Weave in red blood, weave sinews in like ropes, the
senses, sight weave in,
Weave lasting sure, weave day and night the weft,
the warp, incessant weave, tire not,
(We know not what the use O life, nor know the
aim, the end, nor really aught we know,
But know the work, the need goes on and shall go
on, the death-envelop'd march of peace as well
as war goes on,)
For great campaigns of peace the same the wiry
threads to weave,
We know not why or what, yet weave, forever weave.

## *Spain, 1873–4*

Out of the murk of heaviest clouds,
Out of the feudal wrecks and heap'd-up skeletons of
kings,
Out of that old entire European debris, the shatter'd
mummeries,
Ruin'd cathedrals, crumble of palaces, tombs of priests,
Lo, Freedom's features fresh undimm'd look forth –
the same immortal face looks forth;
(A glimpse as of thy Mother's face Columbia,
A flash significant as of a sword,
Beaming towards thee.)

Nor think we forget thee maternal;
Lag'd'st thou so long? shall the clouds close again upon
thee?

Ah, but thou hast thyself now appear'd to us – we
know thee,
Thou hast given us a sure proof, the glimpse of thyself,
Thou waitest there as everywhere thy time.

## *By Broad Potomac's Shore*

By broad Potomac's shore, again old tongue,
(Still uttering, still ejaculating, canst never cease this
babble?)
Again old heart so gay, again to you, your sense, the
full flush spring returning,
Again the freshness and the odors, again Virginia's
summer sky, pellucid blue and silver,
Again the forenoon purple of the hills,
Again the deathless grass, so noiseless soft and green,
Again the blood-red roses blooming.

Perfume this book of mine O blood-red roses!
Lave subtly with your waters every line Potomac!
Give me of you O spring, before I close, to put
between its pages!
O forenoon purple of the hills, before I close, of you!
O deathless grass, of you!

## *From Far Dakota's Cañons*

### *June* 25, 1876

From far Dakota's cañons,
Lands of the wild ravine, the dusky Sioux, the
lonesome stretch, the silence,
Haply to-day a mournful wail, haply a trumpet-note
for heroes.

The battle-bulletin,
The Indian ambuscade, the craft, the fatal environment,
The cavalry companies fighting to the last in sternest heroism,
In the midst of their little circle, with their slaughter'd horses for breastworks,
The fall of Custer and all his officers and men.

Continues yet the old, old legend of our race,
The loftiest of life upheld by death,
The ancient banner perfectly maintain'd,
O lesson opportune, O how I welcome thee!

As sitting in dark days,
Lone, sulky, through the time's thick murk looking in vain for light, for hope,
From unsuspected parts a fierce and momentary proof,
(The sun there at the centre though conceal'd,
Electric life forever at the centre,)
Breaks forth a lightning flash.
Thou of the tawny flowing hair in battle,
I erewhile saw, with erect head, pressing ever in front, bearing a bright sword in thy hand,
Now ending well in death the splendid fever of thy deeds,
(I bring no dirge for it or thee, I bring a glad triumphal sonnet,)
Desperate and glorious, aye in defeat most desperate, most glorious,
After thy many battles in which never yielding up a gun or a color,
Leaving behind thee a memory sweet to soldiers,
Thou yieldest up thyself.

## *Old War-Dreams*

In midnight sleep of many a face of anguish,
Of the look at first of the mortally wounded, (of that indescribable look,)
Of the dead on their backs with arms extended wide,
I dream, I dream, I dream.

Of scenes of Nature, fields and mountains,
Of skies so beauteous after a storm, and at night the moon so unearthly bright,
Shining sweetly, shining down, where we dig the trenches and gather the heaps,
I dream, I dream, I dream.

Long have they pass'd, faces and trenches and fields,
Where through the carnage I moved with a callous composure, or away from the fallen,
Onward I sped at the time – but now of their forms at night,
I dream, I dream, I dream.

## *Thick-Sprinkled Bunting*

Thick-sprinkled bunting! flag of stars!
Long yet your road, fateful flag – long yet your road, and lined with bloody death,
For the prize I see at issue at last is the world,
All its ships and shores I see interwoven with your threads greedy banner;
Dream'd again the flags of kings, highest borne, to flaunt unrival'd?
O hasten flag of man – O with sure and steady step, passing highest flags of kings,

Walk supreme to the heavens mighty symbol – run
up above them all,
Flag of stars! thick-sprinkled bunting!

## *What Best I see in Thee*

*To U. S. G. return'd from his World's Tour*

What best I see in thee,
Is not that where thou mov'st down history's great
highways,
Ever undimm'd by time shoots warlike victory's dazzle,
Or that thou sat'st where Washington sat, ruling the
land in peace,
Or thou the man whom feudal Europe feted,
venerable Asia swarm'd upon,
Who walk'd with kings with even pace the round
world's promenade;
But that in foreign lands, in all thy walks with kings,
Those prairie sovereigns of the West, Kansas,
Missouri, Illinois,
Ohio's, Indiana's millions, comrades, farmers,
soldiers, all to the front,
Invisibly with thee walking with kings with even pace
the round world's promenade,
Were all so justified.

## *Spirit That Form'd This Scene*

*Written in Platte Cañon, Colorado*

Spirit that form'd this scene,
These tumbled rock-piles grim and red,
These reckless heaven-ambitious peaks,

These gorges, turbulent-clear streams, this naked
freshness,
These formless wild arrays, for reasons of their own,
I know thee, savage spirit – we have communed
together,
Mine too such wild arrays, for reasons of their own;
Was't charged against my chants they had forgotten art?
To fuse within themselves its rules precise and
delicatesse?
The lyrist's measur'd beat, the wrought-out temple's
grace – column and polish'd arch forgot?
But thou that revelest here – spirit that form'd this
scene,
They have remember'd thee.

## *As I Walk these Broad Majestic Days*

As I walk these broad majestic days of peace,
(For the war, the struggle of blood finish'd, wherein,
O terrific Ideal,
Against vast odds erewhile having gloriously won,
Now thou stridest on, yet perhaps in time toward
denser wars,
Perhaps to engage in time in still more dreadful
contests, dangers,
Longer campaigns and crises, labors beyond all
others,)
Around me I hear that eclat of the world, politics,
produce,
The announcements of recognized things, science,
The approved growth of cities and the spread of
inventions.

I see the ships, (they will last a few years,)
The vast factories with their foremen and workmen,
And hear the indorsement of all, and do not object to it.

But I too announce solid things,
Science, ships, politics, cities, factories, are not
 nothing,
Like a grand procession to music of distant bugles
 pouring, triumphantly moving, and grander
 heaving in sight,
They stand for realities – all is as it should be.

Then my realities;
What else is so real as mine?
Libertad and the divine average, freedom to every
 slave on the face of the earth,
The rapt promises and luminè of seers, the spiritual
 world, these centuries-lasting songs,
And our visions, the visions of poets, the most solid
 announcements of any.

## *A Clear Midnight*

This is thy hour O soul, thy free flight into the wordless,
Away from books, away from art, the day erased, the
 lesson done,
Thee fully forth emerging, silent, gazing, pondering
 the themes thou lovest best,
Night, sleep, death and the stars.

# SONGS OF PARTING

## *As the Time Draws Nigh*

As the time draws nigh glooming a cloud,
A dread beyond of I know not what darkens me.

I shall go forth,
I shall traverse the States awhile, but I cannot tell
whither or how long,
Perhaps soon some day or night while I am singing
my voice will suddenly cease.

O book, O chants! must all then amount to but this?
Must we barely arrive at this beginning of us? – and
yet it is enough, O soul;
O soul, we have positively appear'd – that is enough.

## *Years of the Modern*

Years of the modern! years of the unperform'd!
Your horizon rises, I see it parting away for more
august dramas,
I see not America only, not only Liberty's nation but
other nations preparing,
I see tremendous entrances and exits, new
combinations, the solidarity of races,
I see that force advancing with irresistible power on
the world's stage,
(Have the old forces, the old wars, played their
parts? are the acts suitable to them closed?)
I see Freedom, completely arm'd and victorious and
very haughty, with Law on one side and Peace
on the other,
A stupendous trio all issuing forth against the idea of
caste;

What historic denouements are these we so rapidly
approach?
I see men marching and countermarching by swift
millions,
I see the frontiers and boundaries of the old
aristocracies broken,
I see the landmarks of European kings removed,
I see this day the People beginning their landmarks,
(all others give way;)
Never were such sharp questions ask'd as this day,
Never was average man, his soul, more energetic,
more like a God,
Lo, how he urges and urges, leaving the masses no
rest!
His daring foot is on land and sea everywhere, he
colonizes the Pacific, the archipelagoes,
With the steamship, the electric telegraph, the
newspaper, the wholesale engines of war,
With these and the world-spreading factories he
interlinks all geography, all lands;
What whispers are these O lands, running ahead of
you, passing under the seas?
Are all nations communing? is there going to be but
one heart to the globe?
Is humanity forming en-masse? for lo, tyrants
tremble, crowns grow dim,
The earth, restive, confronts a new era, perhaps a
general divine war,
No one knows what will happen next, such portents
fill the days and nights;
Years prophetical! the space ahead as I walk, as I
vainly try to pierce it, is full of phantoms,
Unborn deeds, things soon to be, project their
shapes around me,

This incredible rush and heat, this strange ecstatic
    fever of dreams O years!
Your dreams O years, how they penetrate through
    me! (I know not whether I sleep or wake;)
The perform'd America and Europe grow dim,
    retiring in shadow behind me,
The unperform'd, more gigantic than ever, advance,
    advance upon me.

## *Ashes of Soldiers*

Ashes of soldiers South or North,
As I muse retrospective murmuring a chant in thought,
The war resumes, again to my sense your shapes,
And again the advance of the armies.

Noiseless as mists and vapors,
From their graves in the trenches ascending,
From cemeteries all through Virginia and Tennessee,
From every point of the compass out of the
    countless graves,
In wafted clouds, in myriads large, or squads of twos
    or threes or single ones they come,
And silently gather round me.

Now sound no note O trumpeters,
Not at the head of my cavalry parading on spirited
    horses,
With sabres drawn and glistening, and carbines by
    their thighs, (ah my brave horsemen!
My handsome tan-faced horsemen! what life, what
    joy and pride,
With all the perils were yours.)

Nor you drummers, neither at reveillé at dawn,
Nor the long roll alarming the camp, nor even the
muffled beat for a burial,
Nothing from you this time O drummers bearing my
warlike drums.

But aside from these and the marts of wealth and the
crowded promenade,
Admitting around me comrades close unseen by the
rest and voiceless,
The slain elate and alive again, the dust and debris alive,
I chant this chant of my silent soul in the name of all
dead soldiers.

Faces so pale with wondrous eyes, very dear, gather
closer yet,
Draw close, but speak not.

Phantoms of countless lost,
Invisible to the rest henceforth become my
companions,
Follow me ever – desert me not while I live.

Sweet are the blooming cheeks of the living – sweet
are the musical voices sounding,
But sweet, ah sweet, are the dead with their silent eyes.

Dearest comrades, all is over and long gone,
But love is not over – and what love, O comrades
Perfume from battle-fields rising, up from the foeter
arising.

Perfume therefore my chant, O love, immortal love,
Give me to bathe the memories of all dead soldiers,
Shroud them, embalm them, cover them all over
with tender pride.

Perfume all – make all wholesome,
Make these ashes to nourish and blossom,
O love, solve all, fructify all with the last chemistry.

Give me exhaustless, make me a fountain,
That I exhale love from me wherever I go like a
    moist perennial dew,
For the ashes of all dead soldiers South or North.

## *Thoughts*

### I

Of these years I sing,
How they pass and have pass'd through convuls'd
    pains, as through parturitions,
How America illustrates birth, muscular youth, the
    promise, the sure fulfilment, the absolute success,
    despite of people – illustrates evil as well as good,
The vehement struggle so fierce for unity in one's-self;
How many hold despairingly yet to the models
    departed, caste, myths, obedience, compulsion,
    and to infidelity,
How few see the arrived models, the athletes, the
    Western States, or see freedom or spirituality, or
    hold any faith in results,
(But I see the athletes, and I see the results of the
    war glorious and inevitable, and they again
    leading to other results.)

How the great cities appear – how the Democratic
    masses, turbulent, wilful, as I love them,
How the whirl, the contest, the wrestle of evil with good,
    the sounding and resounding, keep on and on,

How society waits unform'd, and is for a while
    between things ended and things begun,
How America is the continent of glories, and of the
    triumph of freedom and of the Democracies, and
    of the fruits of society, and of all that is begun,
And how the States are complete in themselves –
    and how all triumphs and glories are complete in
    themselves, to lead onward,
And how these of mine and of the States will in their
    turn be convuls'd, and serve other parturitions
    and transitions,
And how all people, sights, combinations, the
    democratic masses too, serve – and how every
    fact, and war itself, with all its horrors, serves,
And how now or at any time each serves the
    exquisite transition of death.

2

Of seeds dropping into the ground, of births,
Of the steady concentration of America, inland,
    upward, to impregnable and swarming places,
Of what Indiana, Kentucky, Arkansas, and the rest,
    are to be,
Of what a few years will show there in Nebraska,
    Colorado, Nevada, and the rest,
(Or afar, mounting the Northern Pacific to Sitka or
    Aliaska,)
Of what the feuillage of America is the preparation
    for – and of what all sights, North, South, East
    and West, are,
Of this Union welded in blood, of the solemn price
    paid, of the unnamed lost ever present in my mind;
Of the temporary use of materials for identity's sake,

Of the present, passing, departing – of the growth of
completer men than any yet,
Of all sloping down there where the fresh free giver
the mother, the Mississippi flows,
Of mighty inland cities yet unsurvey'd and
unsuspected,
Of the new and good names, of the modern
developments, of inalienable homesteads,
Of a free and original life there, of simple diet and
clean and sweet blood,
Of litheness, majestic faces, clear eyes, and perfect
physique there,
Of immense spiritual results future years far West,
each side of the Anahuacs,
Of these songs, well understood there, (being made
for that area,)
Of the native scorn of grossness and gain there,
(O it lurks in me night and day – what is gain after
all to savageness and freedom?)

## *Song at Sunset*

Splendor of ended day floating and filling me,
Hour prophetic, hour resuming the past,
Inflating my throat, you divine average,
You earth and life till the last ray gleams I sing.

Open mouth of my soul uttering gladness,
Eyes of my soul seeing perfection,
Natural life of me faithfully praising things,
Corroborating forever the triumph of things.

Illustrious every one!
Illustrious what we name space, sphere of
unnumber'd spirits,

Illustrious the mystery of motion in all beings, even
the tiniest insect,
Illustrious the attribute of speech, the senses, the body,
Illustrious the passing light – illustrious the pale
reflection on the new moon in the western sky,
Illustrious whatever I see or hear or touch, to the last.

Good in all,
In the satisfaction and aplomb of animals,
In the annual return of the seasons,
In the hilarity of youth,
In the strength and flush of manhood,
In the grandeur and exquisiteness of old age,
In the superb vistas of death.

Wonderful to depart!
Wonderful to be here!
The heart, to jet the all-alike and innocent blood!
To breathe the air, how delicious!
To speak – to walk – to seize something by the hand!
To prepare for sleep, for bed, to look on my rose-
color'd flesh!
To be conscious of my body, so satisfied, so large!
To be this incredible God I am!
To have gone forth among other Gods, these men
and women I love.

Wonderful how I celebrate you and myself!
How my thoughts play subtly at the spectacles around!
How the clouds pass silently overhead!
How the earth darts on and on! and how the sun,
moon, stars, dart on and on!
How the water sports and sings! (surely it is alive!)
How the trees rise and stand up, with strong trunks,
with branches and leaves!

(Surely there is something more in each of the trees,
some living soul.)

O amazement of things – even the least particle!
O spirituality of things!
O strain musical flowing through ages and
continents, now reaching me and America!
I take your strong chords, intersperse them, and
cheerfully pass them forward.

I too carol the sun, usher'd or at noon, or as now,
setting,
I too throb to the brain and beauty of the earth and
of all the growths of the earth,
I too have felt the resistless call of myself.
As I steam'd down the Mississippi,
As I wander'd over the prairies,
As I have lived, as I have look'd through my
windows my eyes,
As I went forth in the morning, as I beheld the light
breaking in the east,
As I bathed on the beach of the Eastern Sea, and
again on the beach of Western Sea,
As I roam'd the streets of inland Chicago, whatever
streets I have roam'd,
Or cities or silent woods, or even amid the sights of war,
Wherever I have been I have charged myself with
contentment and triumph.

I sing to the last the equalities modern or old,
I sing the endless finalés of things,
I say Nature continues, glory continues,
I praise with electric voice,
For I do not see one imperfection in the universe,
And I do not see one cause or result lamentable at last in
the universe.

O setting sun! though the time has come,
I still warble under you, if none else does,
    unmitigated adoration.

## *As at Thy Portals also Death*

As at thy portals also death,
Entering thy sovereign, dim, illimitable grounds,
To memories of my mother, to the divine blending,
    maternity,
To her, buried and gone, yet buried not, gone not
    from me,
(I see again the calm benignant face fresh and
    beautiful still,
I sit by the form in the coffin,
I kiss and kiss convulsively again the sweet old lips,
    the cheeks, the closed eyes in the coffin;)
To her, the ideal woman, practical, spiritual, of all of
    earth, life, love, to me the best,
I grave a monumental line, before I go, amid these
    songs,
And set a tombstone here.

## *My Legacy*

The business man the acquirer vast,
After assiduous years surveying results, preparing for
    departure,
Devises houses and lands to his children, bequeaths
    stocks, goods, funds for a school or hospital,
Leaves money to certain companions to buy tokens,
    souvenirs of gems and gold.

But I, my life surveying, closing,
With nothing to show to devise from its idle years,
Nor houses nor lands, nor tokens of gems or gold for my friends,
Yet certain remembrances of the war for you, and after you,
And little souvenirs of camps and soldiers, with my love,
I bind together and bequeath in this bundle of songs.

## *Pensive on Her Dead Gazing*

Pensive on her dead gazing I heard the Mother of All,
Desperate on the torn bodies, on the forms covering the battle-fields gazing,
(As the last gun ceased, but the scent of the powder-smoke linger'd,)
As she call'd to her earth with mournful voice while she stalk'd,
Absorb them well O my earth, she cried, I charge you lose not my sons, lose not an atom,
And you streams absorb them well, taking their dear blood,
And you local spots, and you airs that swim above lightly impalpable,
And all you essences of soil and growth, and you my rivers' depths,
And you mountain sides, and the woods where my dear children's blood trickling redden'd,
And you trees down in your roots to bequeath to all future trees,
My dead absorb or South or North - my young men's bodies absorb, and their precious precious blood,

Which holding in trust for me faithfully back again
give me many a year hence,
In unseen essence and odor of surface and grass,
centuries hence,
In blowing airs from the fields back again give me
my darlings, give my immortal heroes,
Exhale me them centuries hence, breathe me their
breath, let not an atom be lost,
O years and graves! O air and soil! O my dead, an
aroma sweet!
Exhale them perennial sweet death, years, centuries
hence.

## *Camps of Green*

Not alone those camps of white, old comrades of the
wars,
When as order'd forward, after a long march,
Footsore and weary, soon as the light lessens we halt
for the night,
Some of us so fatigued carrying the gun and
knapsack, dropping asleep in our tracks,
Others pitching the little tents, and the fires lit up
begin to sparkle,
Outposts of pickets posted surrounding alert
through the dark,
And a word provided for countersign, careful for
safety,
Till to the call of the drummers at daybreak loudly
beating the drums,
We rise up refresh'd, the night and sleep pass'd over,
and resume our journey,
Or proceed to battle.

Lo, the camps of the tents of green,
Which the days of peace keep filling, and the days of war keep filling,
With a mystic army, (is it too order'd forward? is it too only halting awhile,
Till night and sleep pass over?)

Now in those camps of green, in their tents dotting the world,
In the parents, children, husbands, wives, in them, in the old and young,
Sleeping under the sunlight, sleeping under the moonlight, content and silent there at last,
Behold the mighty bivouac-field and waiting-camp of all,
Of the corps and generals all, and the President over the corps and generals all,
And of each of us O soldiers, and of each and all in the ranks we fought,
(There without hatred we all, all meet.)

For presently O soldiers, we too camp in our place in the bivouac-camps of green,
But we need not provide for outposts, nor word for the counter-sign,
Nor drummer to beat the morning drum.

## *The Sobbing of the Bells*

*(Midnight, Sept.* 19–20, 1881)

The sobbing of the bells, the sudden death-news everywhere,
The slumberers rouse, the rapport of the People,
(Full well they know that message in the darkness,

Full well return, respond within their breasts, their
brains, the sad reverberations,)
The passionate toll and clang – city to city, joining,
sounding, passing,
Those heart-beats of a Nation in the night.

## *As they Draw to a Close*

As they draw to a close,
Of what underlies the precedent songs – of my aims
in them,
Of the seed I have sought to plant in them,
Of joy, sweet joy, through many a year, in them,
(For them, for them have I lived, in them my work is
done,)
Of many an aspiration fond, of many a dream and plan;
Through Space and Time fused in a chant, and the
flowing eternal identity,
To Nature encompassing these, encompassing God
– to the joyous, electric all,
To the sense of Death, and accepting exulting in
Death in its turn the same as life,
The entrance of man to sing;
To compact you, ye parted, diverse lives,
To put rapport the mountains and rocks and streams,
And the winds of the north, and the forests of oak
and pine,
With you O soul.

### *Joy, Shipmate, Joy!*

Joy, shipmate, joy!
(Pleas'd to my soul at death I cry,)
Our life is closed, our life begins,
The long, long anchorage we leave,
The ship is clear at last, she leaps!
She swiftly courses from the shore,
Joy, shipmate, joy!

### *The Untold Want*

The untold want by life and land ne'er granted,
Now voyager sail thou forth to seek and find.

### *Portals*

What are those of the known but to ascend and
enter the Unknown?
And what are those of life but for Death?

### *These Carols*

These carols sung to cheer my passage through the
world I see,
For completion I dedicate to the Invisible World.

### *Now Finalè to the Shore*

Now finalè to the shore,
Now land and life finalè and farewell,

Now Voyager depart, (much, much for thee is yet in
store,)
Often enough hast thou adventur'd o'er the seas,
Cautiously cruising, studying the charts,
Duly again to port and hawser's tie returning;
But now obey thy cherish'd secret wish,
Embrace thy friends, leave all in order,
To port and hawser's tie no more returning,
Depart upon thy endless cruise old Sailor.

## *So Long!*

To conclude, I announce what comes after me,

I remember I said before my leaves sprang at all,
I would raise my voice jocund and strong with
reference to consummations.

When America does what was promis'd,
When through these States walk a hundred millions
of superb persons,
When the rest part away for superb persons and
contribute to them,
When breeds of the most perfect mothers denote
America,
Then to me and mine our due fruition.

I have press'd through in my own right,
I have sung the body and the soul, war and peace
have I sung, and the songs of life and death,
And the songs of birth, and shown that there are
many births.
I have offer'd my style to every one, I have journey'd
with confident step;
While my pleasure is yet at the full I whisper *So long!*

And take the young woman's hand and the young
man's hand for the last time.

I announce natural persons to arise,
I announce justice triumphant,
I announce uncompromising liberty and equality,
I announce the justification of candor and the
justification of pride.

I announce that the identity of these States is a
single identity only,
I announce the Union more and more compact,
indissoluble,
I announce splendors and majesties to make all the
previous politics of the earth insignificant.

I announce adhesiveness, I say it shall be limitless,
unloosen'd,
I say you shall yet find the friend you were looking for.

I announce a man or woman coming, perhaps you
are the one, (*So long!*)
I announce the great individual, fluid as Nature,
chaste, affectionate, compassionate, fully arm'd.

I announce a life that shall be copious, vehement,
spiritual, bold,
I announce an end that shall lightly and joyfully
meet its translation.

I announce myriads of youths, beautiful, gigantic,
sweet-blooded,
I announce a race of splendid and savage old men.

O thicker and faster (*So long!*)
O crowding too close upon me,
I foresee too much, it means more than I thought,
It appears to me I am dying.

Hasten throat and sound your last,
Salute me – salute the days once more. Peal the old
cry once more.

Screaming electric, the atmosphere using,
At random glancing, each as I notice absorbing,
Swiftly on, but a little while alighting,
Curious envelop'd messages delivering,
Sparkles hot, seed ethereal down in the dirt dropping,
Myself unknowing, my commission obeying, to
question it never daring,
To ages and ages yet the growth of the seed leaving,
To troops out of the war arising, they the tasks I
have set promulging,
To women certain whispers of myself bequeathing,
their affection me more clearly explaining,
To young men my problems offering – no dallier I –
I the muscle of their brains trying,
So I pass, a little time vocal, visible, contrary,
Afterward a melodious echo, passionately bent for,
(death making me really undying,)
The best of me then when no longer visible, for
toward that I have been incessantly preparing.

What is there more, that I lag and pause and crouch
extended with unshut mouth?
Is there a single final farewell?

My songs cease, I abandon them,
From behind the screen where I hid I advance
personally solely to you.

Camerado, this is no book,
Who touches this touches a man,
(Is it night? are we here together alone?)
It is I you hold and who holds you,

I spring from the pages into your arms – decease
    calls me forth.

O how your fingers drowse me,
Your breath falls around me like dew, your pulse
    lulls the tympans of my ears,
I feel immerged from head to foot,
Delicious, enough.

Enough O deed impromptu and secret,
Enough O gliding present – enough O summ'd-up past.

Dear friend whoever you are take this kiss,
I give it especially to you, do not forget me,
I feel like one who has done work for the day to
    retire awhile,
I receive now again of my many translations, from
    my avataras ascending, while others doubtless
    await me,
An unknown sphere more real than I dream'd, more
    direct, darts awakening rays about me, *So long!*
Remember my words, I may again return,
I love you, I depart from materials,
I am as one disembodied, triumphant, dead.

# SANDS AT SEVENTY

*(First Annex)*

## *Mannahatta*

My city's fit and noble name resumed,
Choice aboriginal name, with marvellous beauty,
meaning,
*A rocky founded island – shores where ever gayly dash*
*the coming, going, hurrying sea waves.*

## *Paumanok*

Sea-beauty! stretch'd and basking!
One side thy inland ocean laving, broad, with
copious commerce, steamers, sails,
And one the Atlantic's wind caressing, fierce or gentle
– mighty hulls dark-gliding in the distance.
Isle of sweet brooks of drinking-water – healthy air
and soil!
Isle of the salty shore and breeze and brine!

## *From Montauk Point*

I stand as on some mighty eagle's beak,
Eastward the sea absorbing, viewing, (nothing but
sea and sky,)
The tossing waves, the foam, the ships in the distance,
The wild unrest, the snowy, curling caps – that
inbound urge and urge of waves,
Seeking the shores forever.

## *To Those Who've Fail'd*

To those who've fail'd, in aspiration vast,
To unnam'd soldiers fallen in front on the lead,

To calm, devoted engineers – to over-ardent
travelers – to pilots on their ships,
To many a lofty song and picture without recognition
– I'd rear a laurel-cover'd monument,
High, high above the rest – To all cut off before their
time,
Possess'd by some strange spirit of fire,
Quench'd by an early death.

## *A Carol Closing Sixty-Nine*

A carol closing sixty-nine – a *résumé* – a repetition,
My lines in joy and hope continuing on the same,
Of ye, O God, Life, Nature, Freedom, Poetry;
Of you, my Land – your rivers, prairies, States – you,
mottled Flag I love,
Your aggregate retain'd entire – Of north, south,
east and west, your items all;
Of me myself – the jocund heart yet beating in my
breast,
The body wreck'd, old, poor and paralyzed – the
strange inertia falling pall-like round me,
The burning fires down in my sluggish blood not yet
extinct,
The undiminish'd faith – the groups of loving friends.

## *The Bravest Soldiers*

Brave, brave were the soldiers (high named to-day)
who lived through the fight;
But the bravest press'd to the front and fell,
unnamed, unknown.

## *A Font of Type*

This latent mine – these unlaunch'd voices – passionate powers,
Wrath, argument, or praise, or comic leer, or prayer devout,
(Not nonpareil, brevier, bourgeois, long primer merely,)
These ocean waves arousable to fury and to death,
Or sooth'd to ease and sheeny sun and sleep,
Within the pallid slivers slumbering.

## *As I Sit Writing Here*

As I sit writing here, sick and grown old,
Not my least burden is that dulness of the years, querilities,
Ungracious glooms, aches, lethargy, constipation, whimpering *ennui*,
May filter in my daily songs.

## *My Canary Bird*

Did we count great, O soul, to penetrate the themes of mighty books,
Absorbing deep and full from thoughts, plays, speculations?
But now from thee to me, caged bird, to feel thy joyous warble,
Filling the air, the lonesome room, the long forenoon,
Is it not just as great, O soul?

## *Queries to My Seventieth Year*

Approaching, nearing, curious,
Thou dim, uncertain spectre – bringest thou life or death?
Strength, weakness, blindness, more paralysis and heavier?
Or placid skies and sun? Wilt stir the waters yet?
Or haply cut me short for good? Or leave me here as now,
Dull, parrot-like and old, with crack'd voice harping, screeching?

## *The Wallabout Martyrs*

(*In Brooklyn, in an old vault, mark'd by no special recognition, lie huddled at this moment the undoubtedly authentic remains of the stanchest and earliest Revolutionary patriots from the British prison ships and prisons of the times of* 1776–83, *in and around New York, and from all over Long Island; originally buried – many thousands of them – in trenches in the Wallabout sands.*)

Greater than memory of Achilles or Ulysses,
More, more by far to thee than tomb of Alexander,
Those cart loads of old charnel ashes, scales and splints of mouldy bones,
Once living men – once resolute courage, aspiration, strength,
The stepping stones to thee to-day and here, America.

## *The First Dandelion*

Simple and fresh and fair from winter's close emerging,
As if no artifice of fashion, business, politics, had
ever been,
Forth from its sunny nook of shelter'd grass –
innocent, golden, calm as the dawn,
The spring's first dandelion shows its trustful face.

## *America*

Centre of equal daughters, equal sons,
All, all alike endear'd, grown, ungrown, young or old,
Strong, ample, fair, enduring, capable, rich,
Perennial with the Earth, with Freedom, Law and Love,
A grand, sane, towering, seated Mother,
Chair'd in the adamant of Time.

## *Memories*

How sweet the silent backward tracings!
The wanderings as in dreams – the meditation of old
times resumed – their loves, joys, persons, voyages.

## *To-Day and Thee*

The appointed winners in a long-stretch'd game;
The course of Time and nations – Egypt, India,
Greece and Rome;
The past entire, with all its heroes, histories, arts,
experiments,
Its store of songs, inventions, voyages, teachers, books,

Garner'd for now and thee – To think of it!
The heirdom all converged in thee!

## *After the Dazzle of Day*

After the dazzle of day is gone,
Only the dark, dark night shows to my eyes the stars;
After the clangor of organ majestic, or chorus, or
perfect band,
Silent, athwart my soul, moves the symphony true.

## *Abraham Lincoln, born February 12, 1809*

(*Publish'd Feb.* 12, 1888)

To-day, from each and all, a breath of prayer – a
pulse of thought,
To memory of Him – to birth of Him.

## *Out of May's Shows Selected*

Apple orchards, the trees all cover'd with blossoms;
Wheat fields carpeted far and near in vital emerald
green;
The eternal, exhaustless freshness of each early
morning;
The yellow, golden, transparent haze of the warm
afternoon sun;
The aspiring lilac bushes with profuse purple or
white flowers.

## *Halcyon Days*

Not from successful love alone,
Nor wealth, nor honor'd middle age, nor victories of
politics or war;
But as life wanes, and all the turbulent passions calm,
As gorgeous, vapory, silent hues cover the evening sky,
As softness, fulness, rest, suffuse the frame, like
fresher, balmier air,
As the days take on a mellower light, and the apple
at last hangs really finish'd and indolent-ripe on
the tree,
Then for the teeming quietest, happiest days of all!
The brooding and blissful halcyon days!

## FANCIES AT NAVESINK

### *The Pilot in the Mist*

Steaming the northern rapids – (an old St. Lawrence
reminiscence,
A sudden memory-flash comes back, I know not why,
Here waiting for the sunrise, gazing from this hill;)
Again 'tis just at morning – a heavy haze contends
with day break,
Again the trembling, laboring vessel veers me – I press
through foam-dash'd rocks that almost touch me,
Again I mark where aft the small thin Indian helmsman
Looms in the mist, with brow elate and governing hand

## *Had I the Choice*

Had I the choice to tally greatest bards,
To limn their portraits, stately, beautiful, and
emulate at will,
Homer with all his wars and warriors – Hector,
Achilles, Ajax,
Or Shakspere's woe-entangled Hamlet, Lear,
Othello – Tennyson's fair ladies,
Metre or wit the best, or choice conceit to wield in
perfect rhyme, delight of singers;
These, these, O sea, all these I'd gladly barter,
Would you the undulation of one wave, its trick to
me transfer,
Or breathe one breath of yours upon my verse,
And leave its odor there.

## *You Tides with Ceaseless Swell*

You tides with ceaseless swell! you power that does
this work!
You unseen force, centripetal, centrifugal, through
space's spread,
Rapport of sun, moon, earth, and all the
constellations,
What are the messages by you from distant stars to
us? what Sirius'? what Capella's?
What central heart – and you the pulse – vivifies all?
what boundless aggregate of all?
What subtle indirection and significance in you?
what clue to all in you? what fluid, vast identity,
Holding the universe with all its parts as one – as
sailing in a ship?

## *Last of Ebb, and Daylight Waning*

Last of ebb, and daylight waning,
Scented sea-cool landward making, smells of sedge
    and salt incoming,
With many a half-caught voice sent up from the eddies,
Many a muffled confession – many a sob and
    whisper'd word,
As of speakers far or hid.

How they sweep down and out! how they mutter!
Poets unnamed – artists greatest of any, with
    cherish'd lost designs,
Love's unresponse – a chorus of age's complaints –
    hope's last words,
Some suicide's despairing cry, *Away to the boundless
    waste, and never again return.*

On to oblivion then!
On, on, and do your part, ye burying, ebbing tide!
On for your time, ye furious debouché!

## *And Yet Not You Alone*

And yet not you alone, twilight and burying ebb,
Nor you, ye lost designs alone – nor failures,
    aspirations
I know, divine deceitful ones, your glamour's
    seeming;
Duly by you, from you, the tide and light again –
    duly the hinges turning,
Duly the needed discord-parts offsetting, blending,
Weaving from you, from Sleep, Night, Death itself,
The rhythmus of Birth eternal.

## *Proudly the Flood Comes In*

Proudly the flood comes in, shouting, foaming, advancing,
Long it holds at the high, with bosom broad outswelling,
All throbs, dilates – the farms, woods, streets of cities – workmen at work,
Mainsails, topsails, jibs, appear in the offing – steamers' pennants of smoke – and under the forenoon sun,
Freighted with human lives, gaily the outward bound, gaily the inward bound,
Flaunting from many a spar the flag I love.

## *By That Long Scan of Waves*

By that long scan of waves, myself call'd back, resumed upon myself,
In every crest some undulating light or shade – some retrospect,
Joys, travels, studies, silent panoramas – scenes, ephemeral,
The long past war, the battles, hospital sights, the wounded and the dead,
Myself through every by-gone phase – my idle youth – old age at hand,
My three-score years of life summ'd up, and more, and past,
By any grand ideal tried, intentionless, the whole a nothing,
And haply yet some drop within God's scheme's ensemble – some wave, or part of wave,
Like one of yours, ye multitudinous ocean.

## *Then Last of All*

Then last of all, caught from these shores, this hill,
Of you O tides, the mystic human meaning:
Only by law of you, your swell and ebb, enclosing
me the same,
The brain that shapes, the voice that chants this song.

* * *

## *Election Day, November 1884*

If I should need to name, O Western World, your
powerfulest scene and show,
'Twould not be you, Niagara – nor you, ye limitless
prairies – nor your huge rifts of canyons, Colorado,
Nor you, Yosemite – nor Yellowstone, with all its
spasmic geyser loops ascending to the skies,
appearing and disappearing,
Nor Oregon's white cones – nor Huron's belt of
mighty lakes – nor Mississippi's stream:
– This seething hemisphere's humanity, as now, I'd
name – *the still small voice* vibrating – America's
choosing day,
(The heart of it not in the chosen – the act itself the
main, the quadrennial choosing,)
The stretch of North and South arous'd – sea-board
and inland – Texas to Maine – the Prairie States
– Vermont, Virginia, California,
The final ballot-shower from East to West – the
paradox and conflict,
The countless snow-flakes falling – (a swordless
conflict,
Yet more than all Rome's wars of old, or modern
Napoleon's:) the peaceful choice of all,

Or good or ill humanity – welcoming the darker odds, the dross:
– Foams and ferments the wine? it serves to purify – while the heart pants, life glows:
These stormy gusts and winds waft precious ships,
Swell'd Washington's, Jefferson's, Lincoln's sails.

## *With Husky-Haughty Lips, O Sea!*

With husky-haughty lips, O sea!
Where day and night I wend thy surf-beat shore,
Imaging to my sense thy varied strange suggestions,
(I see and plainly list thy talk and conference here,)
Thy troops of white-maned racers racing to the goal,
Thy ample, smiling face, dash'd with the sparkling dimples of the sun,
Thy brooding scowl and murk – thy unloos'd hurricanes,
Thy unsubduedness, caprices, wilfulness;
Great as thou art above the rest, thy many tears – a lack from all eternity in thy content,
(Naught but the greatest struggles, wrongs, defeats, could make thee greatest – no less could make thee,)
Thy lonely state – something thou ever seek'st and seek'st, yet never gain'st,
Surely some right withheld – some voice, in huge monotonous rage, of freedom-lover pent,
Some vast heart, like a planet's, chain'd and chafing in those breakers,
By lengthen'd swell, and spasm, and panting breath,
And rhythmic rasping of thy sands and waves,
And serpent hiss, and savage peals of laughter,
And undertones of distant lion roar,

(Sounding, appealing to the sky's deaf ear – but
now, rapport for once,
A phantom in the night thy confidant for once,
The first and last confession of the globe,
Outsurging, muttering from thy soul's abysms,
The tale of cosmic elemental passion,
Thou tellest to a kindred soul.

## *Death of General Grant*

As one by one withdraw the lofty actors,
From that great play on history's stage eterne,
That lurid, partial act of war and peace – of old and
new contending,
Fought out through wrath, fears, dark dismays, and
many a long suspense;
All past – and since, in countless graves receding,
mellowing,
Victor's and vanquish'd – Lincoln's and Lee's – now
thou with them,
Man of the mighty days – and equal to the days!
Thou from the prairies! – tangled and many-vein'd
and hard has been thy part,
To admiration has it been enacted!

## *Red Jacket (From Aloft)*

*(Impromptu on Buffalo City's monument to,
and re-burial of the old Iroquois orator,
October* 9, 1884)

Upon this scene, this show,
Yielded to-day by fashion, learning, wealth,
(Nor in caprice alone – some grains of deepest

meaning,)
Haply, aloft, (who knows?) from distant sky-clouds' blended shapes,
As some old tree, or rock or cliff, thrill'd with its soul,
Product of Nature's sun, stars, earth direct – a towering human form,
In hunting-shirt of film, arm'd with the rifle, a half-ironical smile curving its phantom lips,
Like one of Ossian's ghosts looks down.

## *Washington's Monument, February 1885*

Ah, not this marble, dead and cold:
Far from its base and shaft expanding – the round zones circling, comprehending,
Thou, Washington, art all the world's, the continent's entire – not yours alone, America,
Europe's as well, in every part, castle of lord or laborer's cot,
Or frozen North, or sultry South – the African's – the Arab's in his tent,
Old Asia's there with venerable smile, seated amid her ruins;
(Greets the antique the hero new? 'tis but the same – the heir legitimate, continued ever,
The indomitable heart and arm – proofs of the never-broken line,
Courage, alertness, patience, faith, the same – e'en in defeat defeated not, the same:)
Wherever sails a ship, or house is built on land, or day or night,
Through teeming cities' streets, indoors or out,

factories or farms,
Now, or to come, or past – where patriot wills existed or exist,
Wherever Freedom, pois'd by Toleration, sway'd by Law,
Stands or is rising thy true monument.

## *Of that Blithe Throat of Thine*

*(More than eighty-three degrees north – about a good day's steaming distance to the Pole by one of our fast oceaners in clear water – Greely the explorer heard the song of a single snow-bird merrily sounding over the desolation.)*

Of that blithe throat of thine from arctic bleak and blank,
I'll mind the lesson, solitary bird – let me too welcome chilling drifts,
E'en the profoundest chill, as now – a torpid pulse, a brain unnerv'd,
Old age land-lock'd within its winter bay – (cold, cold, O cold!)
These snowy hairs, my feeble arm, my frozen feet,
For them thy faith, thy rule I take, and grave it to the last;
Not summer's zones alone – not chants of youth, or south's warm tides alone,
But held by sluggish floes, pack'd in the northern ice, the cumulus of years,
These with gay heart I also sing.

## *Broadway*

What hurrying human tides, or day or night!
What passions, winnings, losses, ardors, swim thy
    waters!
What whirls of evil, bliss and sorrow, stem thee!
What curious questioning glances – glints of love!
Leer, envy, scorn, contempt, hope, aspiration!
Thou portal – thou arena – thou of the myriad long-
    drawn lines and groups!
(Could but thy flagstones, curbs, façades, tell their
    inimitable tales;
Thy windows rich, and huge hotels – thy side-walks
    wide;)
Thou of the endless sliding, mincing, shuffling feet!
Thou, like the parti-colored world itself – like
    infinite, teeming, mocking life!
Thou visor'd, vast, unspeakable show and lesson!

## *To Get the Final Lilt of Songs*

To get the final lilt of songs,
To penetrate the inmost lore of poets – to know the
    mighty ones,
Job, Homer, Eschylus, Dante, Shakspere,
    Tennyson, Emerson;
To diagnose the shifting-delicate tints of love and
    pride and doubt – to truly understand,
To encompass these, the last keen faculty and
    entrance-price,
Old age, and what it brings from all its past experiences.

## *Old Salt Kossabone*

Far back, related on my mother's side,
Old Salt Kossabone, I'll tell you how he died:
(Had been a sailor all his life – was nearly 90 – lived
with his married grandchild, Jenny;
House on a hill, with view of bay at hand, and
distant cape, and stretch to open sea;
The last of afternoons, the evening hours, for many
a year his regular custom,
In his great arm chair by the window seated,
(Sometimes, indeed, through half the day,)
Watching the coming, going of the vessels, he
mutters to himself – And now the close of all:
One struggling outbound brig, one day, baffled for
long – cross-tides and much wrong going,
At last at nightfall strikes the breeze aright, her
whole luck veering,
And swiftly bending round the cape, the darkness
proudly entering, cleaving, as he watches,
'She's free – she's on her destination' – these the last
words when Jenny came, he sat there dead,
Dutch Kossabone, Old Salt, related on my mother's
side, far back.

## *The Dead Tenor*

As down the stage again,
With Spanish hat and plumes, and gait inimitable,
Back from the fading lessons of the past, I'd call, I'd
tell and own,
How much from thee! the revelation of the singing
voice from thee!

(So firm – so liquid soft – again that tremulous,
manly timbre!
The perfect singing voice – deepest of all to me the
lesson – trial and test of all:)
How through those strains distill'd – how the rapt
ears, the soul of me, absorbing
*Fernando's* heart, *Manrico's* passionate call, *Ernani's*,
sweet *Gennaro's*,
I fold thenceforth, or seek to fold, within my chants
transmuting,
Freedom's and Love's and Faith's unloos'd cantabile,
As perfume's, color's, sunlight's correlation:)
From these, for these, with these, a hurried line,
dead tenor,
A wafted autumn leaf, dropt in the closing grave, the
shovel'd earth,
To memory of thee.

## *Continuities*

(*From a talk I had lately with a German spiritualist*)

Nothing is ever really lost, or can be lost,
No birth, identity, form – no object of the world,
Nor life, nor force, nor any visible thing;
Appearance must not foil, nor shifted sphere confuse
thy brain.
Ample are time and space – ample the fields of Nature.
The body, sluggish, aged, cold – the embers left
from earlier fires,
The light in the eye grown dim, shall duly flame again;
The sun now low in the west rises for mornings and
for noons continual;
To frozen clods ever the spring's invisible law returns,
With grass and flowers and summer fruits and corn.

## *Yonnondio*

*(The sense of the word is 'lament for the aborigines'.*
*It is an Iroquois term; and has been used*
*for a personal name.)*

A song, a poem of itself – the word itself a dirge,
Amid the wilds, the rocks, the storm and wintry night,
To me such misty, strange tableaux the syllables
    calling up;
Yonnondio – I see, far in the west or north, a
    limitless ravine, with plains and mountains dark,
I see swarms of stalwart chieftains, medicine-men,
    and warriors,
As flitting by like clouds of ghosts, they pass and are
    gone in the twilight,
(Race of the woods, the landscapes free, and the falls!
No picture, poem, statement, passing them to the
    future;)
Yonnondio! Yonnondio! – unlimn'd they disappear;
To-day gives place, and fades – the cities, farms,
    factories fade;
A muffled sonorous sound, a wailing word is borne
    through the air for a moment,
Then blank and gone and still, and utterly lost.

## *Life*

Ever the undiscouraged, resolute, struggling soul of
    man;
(Have former armies fail'd? then we send fresh
    armies – and fresh again;)
Ever the grappled mystery of all earth's ages old or new;

Ever the eager eyes, hurrahs, the welcome-clapping
    hands, the loud applause;
Ever the soul dissatisfied, curious, unconvinced at last;
Struggling to-day the same – battling the same.

### *'Going Somewhere'*

My science-friend, my noblest woman-friend,
(Now buried in an English grave – and this a
    memory-leaf for her dear sake,)
Ended our talk – 'The sum, concluding all we know
    of old or modern learning, intuitions deep,
'Of all Geologies – Histories – of all Astronomy – of
    Evolution, Metaphysics all,
'Is, that we all are onward, onward, speeding slowly,
    surely bettering,
'Life, life an endless march, an endless army, (no
    halt, but it is duly over,)
'The world, the race, the soul – in space and time
    the universes,
'All bound as is befitting each – all surely going
    somewhere.'

### *Small the Theme of My Chant*

(*From the* 1867 *edition* '*L. of G.*')

Small the theme of my Chant, yet the greatest –
    namely, One's-Self – a simple, separate person.
    That, for the use of the New World, I sing,
Man's physiology complete, from top to toe, I sing.
    Not physiognomy alone, nor brain alone, is
    worthy for the Muse; – I say the Form complete
    is worthier far. The Female equally with the
    Male, I sing.

Nor cease at the theme of One's-Self. I speak the
word of the modern, the word En-Masse.
My Days I sing, and the Lands – with interstice I
knew of hapless War.
(O friend, whoe'er you are, at last arriving hither to
commence, I feel through every leaf the pressure
of your hand, which I return.
And thus upon our journey, footing the road, and
more than once, and link'd together let us go.)

## *True Conquerors*

Old farmers, travelers, workmen (no matter how
crippled or bent,)
Old sailors, out of many a perilous voyage, storm
and wreck,
Old soldiers from campaigns, with all their wounds,
defeats and scars;
Enough that they've survived at all – long life's
unflinching ones!
Forth from their struggles, trials, fights, to have
emerged at all – in that alone,
True conquerors o'er all the rest.

## *The United States to Old World Critics*

Here first the duties of to-day, the lessons of the
concrete,
Wealth, order, travel, shelter, products, plenty;
As of the building of some varied, vast, perpetual
edifice,
Whence to arise inevitable in time, the towering
roofs, the lamps,
The solid-planted spires tall shooting to the stars.

## *The Calming thought of All*

That coursing on, whate'er men's speculations,
Amid the changing schools, theologies, philosophies,
Amid the bawling presentations new and old,
The round earth's silent vital laws, facts, modes
continue.

## *Thanks in Old Age*

Thanks in old age – thanks ere I go,
For health, the midday sun, the impalpable air – for
life, mere life,
For precious ever-lingering memories, (of you my
mother dear – you father – you, brothers, sisters,
friends,)
For all my days – not those of peace alone – the days
of war the same,
For gentle words, caresses, gifts from foreign lands,
For shelter, wine and meat – for sweet appreciation,
(You distant, dim unknown – or young or old –
countless, unspecified, readers belov'd,
We never met, and ne'er shall meet – and yet our
souls embrace, long, close and long;)
For beings, groups, love, deeds, words, books – for
colors, forms,
For all the brave strong men – devoted, hardy men –
who've forward sprung in freedom's help, all
years, all lands,
For braver, stronger, more devoted men – (a special
laurel ere I go, to life's war's chosen ones,
The cannoneers of song and thought – the great
artillerists – the foremost leaders, captains of the
soul:)

As soldier from an ended war return'd – As traveler
    out of myriads, to the long procession
    retrospective,
Thanks – joyful thanks! – a soldier's, traveler's thanks.

## *Life and Death*

The two old, simple problems ever intertwined,
Close home, elusive, present, baffled, grappled.
By each successive age insoluble, pass'd on,
To ours to-day – and we pass on the same.

## *The Voice of the Rain*

And who art thou? said I to the soft-falling shower,
Which, strange to tell, gave me an answer, as here
    translated:
I am the Poem of Earth, said the voice of the rain,
Eternal I rise impalpable out of the land and the
    bottomless sea,
Upward to heaven, whence, vaguely form'd,
    altogether changed, and yet the same,
I descend to lave the drouths, atomies, dust-layers of
    the globe,
And all that in them without me were seeds only,
    latent, unborn;
And forever, by day and night, I give back life to my
    own origin and make pure and beautify it,
(For song, issuing from its birth-place, after
    fulfilment, wandering,
Reck'd or unreck'd, duly with love returns.)

## *Soon Shall the Winter's Foil be Here*

Soon shall the winter's foil be here;
Soon shall these icy ligatures unbind and melt – A
little while,
And air, soil, wave, suffused shall be in softness,
bloom and growth – a thousand forms shall rise
From these dead clods and chills as from low burial
graves.
Thine eyes, ears – all thy best attributes – all that
takes cognizance of natural beauty,
Shall wake and fill. Thou shalt perceive the simple
shows, the delicate miracles of earth,
Dandelions, clover, the emerald grass, the early
scents and flowers,
The arbutus under foot, the willow's yellow-green,
the blossoming plum and cherry;
With these the robin, lark and thrush, singing their
songs – the flitting bluebird;
For such the scenes the annual play brings on.

## *While Not the Past Forgetting*

(*Publish'd May* 30, 1888)

While not the past forgetting,
To-day, at least, contention sunk entire – peace,
brotherhood uprisen;
For sign reciprocal our Northern, Southern hands,
Lay on the graves of all dead soldiers, North or South,
(Nor for the past alone – for meanings to the future,)
Wreaths of roses and branches of palm.

### *The Dying Veteran*

*(A Long Island incident – early part of the nineteenth century)*

Amid these days of order, ease, prosperity,
Amid the current songs of beauty, peace, decorum,
I cast a reminiscence – (likely 'twill offend you,
I heard it in my boyhood;) – More than a generation
  since,
A queer old savage man, a fighter under Washington
  himself,
(Large, brave, cleanly, hot-blooded, no talker, rather
  spiritualistic,
Had fought in the ranks – fought well – had been all
  through the Revolutionary war,)
Lay dying – sons, daughters, church-deacons,
  lovingly tending him,
Sharping their sense, their ears, towards his
  murmuring, half-caught words:
'Let me return again to my war-days,
To the sights and scenes – to forming the line of battle,
To the scouts ahead reconnoitering,
To the cannons, the grim artillery,
To the galloping aids, carrying orders,
To the wounded, the fallen, the heat, the suspense,
The perfume strong, the smoke, the deafening noise;
Away with your life of peace! – your joys of peace!
Give me my old wild battle-life again!'

## *Stronger Lessons*

Have you learn'd lessons only of those who admired
you, and were tender with you, and stood aside
for you?
Have you not learn'd great lessons from those who
reject you, and brace themselves against you? or
who treat you with contempt, or dispute the
passage with you?

## *A Prairie Sunset*

Shot gold, maroon and violet, dazzling silver, emerald,
fawn,
The earth's whole amplitude and Nature's
multiform power consign'd for once to colors;
The light, the general air possess'd by them – colors
till now unknown,
No limit, confine – not the Western sky alone – the
high meridian – North, South, all,
Pure luminous color fighting the silent shadows to
the last.

## *Twenty Years*

Down on the ancient wharf, the sand, I sit, with a
newcomer chatting:
He shipp'd as green-hand boy, and sail'd away,
(took some sudden, vehement notion;)
Since, twenty years and more have circled round
and round,
While he the globe was circling round and round, –
and now returns:

How changed the place – all the old land-marks
 gone – the parents dead;
(Yes, he comes back *to lay in port for good – to settle –*
 has a well-fill'd purse – no spot will do but this;)
The little boat that scull'd him from the sloop, now
 held in leash I see,
I hear the slapping waves, the restless keel, the
 rocking in the sand,
I see the sailor kit, the canvas bag, the great box
 bound with brass,
I scan the face all berry-brown and bearded – the
 stout-strong frame,
Dress'd in its russet suit of good Scotch cloth:
(Then what the told-out story of those twenty years?
 What of the future?)

## *Orange Buds by Mail from Florida*

(*Voltaire closed a famous argument by claiming that a ship of war and the grand opera were proofs enough of civilization's and France's progress, in his day.*)

A lesser proof than old Voltaire's, yet greater,
Proof of this present time, and thee, thy broad
 expanse, America,
To my plain Northern hut, in outside clouds and snow,
Brought safely for a thousand miles o'er land and tide,
Some three days since on their own soil live-sprouting,
Now here their sweetness through my room unfolding,
A bunch of orange buds by mail from Florida.

## *Twilight*

The soft voluptuous opiate shades,
The sun just gone, the eager light dispell'd – (I too will soon be gone, dispell'd,)
A haze – nirwana – rest and night – oblivion.

## *You Lingering Sparse Leaves of Me*

You lingering sparse leaves of me on winter-nearing boughs,
And I some well-shorn tree of field or orchard-row;
You tokens diminute and lorn – (not now the flush of May, or July clover-bloom – no grain of August now;)
You pallid banner-staves – you pennants valueless – you overstay'd of time,
Yet my soul-dearest leaves confirming all the rest,
The faithfulest – hardiest – last.

## *Not Meagre, Latent Boughs Alone*

Not meagre, latent boughs alone, O songs! (scaly and bare, like eagles' talons,)
But haply for some sunny day (who knows?) some future spring, some summer – bursting forth,
To verdant leaves, or sheltering shade – to nourishing fruit,
Apples and grapes – the stalwart limbs of trees emerging – the fresh, free, open air,
And love and faith, like scented roses blooming.

## *The Dead Emperor*

(*Publish'd March* 10, 1888)

To-day, with bending head and eyes, thou, too,
    Columbia,
Less for the mighty crown laid low in sorrow – less
    for the Emperor,
Thy true condolence breathest, sendest out o'er
    many a salt sea mile,
Mourning a good old man – a faithful shepherd, patriot.

## *As the Greek's Signal Flame*

(*For Whittier's eightieth birthday,*
*December* 17, 1887)

As the Greek's signal flame, by antique records told,
Rose from the hill-top, like applause and glory,
Welcoming in fame some special veteran, hero,
With rosy tinge reddening the land he'd served,
So I aloft from Mannahatta's ship-fringed shore,
Lift high a kindled brand for thee, Old Poet.

## *The Dismantled Ship*

In some unused lagoon, some nameless bay,
On sluggish, lonesome waters, anchor'd near the shore,
An old, dismasted, gray and batter'd ship, disabled,
    done,
After free voyages to all the seas of earth, haul'd up
    at last and hawser'd tight,
Lies rusting, mouldering.

## *Now Precedent Songs, Farewell*

Now precedent songs, farewell – by every name
farewell,
(Trains of a staggering line in many a strange
procession, waggons,
From ups and downs – with intervals – from elder
years, mid-age, or youth,)
*In Cabin'd Ships*, or *Thee Old Cause* or *Poets to Come*
Or *Paumanok, Song of Myself, Calamus*, or *Adam*,
Or *Beat! Beat! Drums!* or *To the Leaven'd Soil they
Trod*,
Or *Captain! My Captain! Kosmos, Quicksand Years*,
or *Thoughts*,
*Thou Mother with thy Equal Brood*, and many, many
more unspecified,
From fibre heart of mine – from throat and tongue –
(My life's hot pulsing blood,
The personal urge and form for me – not merely
paper, automatic type and ink,)
Each song of mine – each utterance in the past –
having its long, long history,
Of life or death, or soldier's wound, of country's loss
or safety,
(O heaven! what flash and started endless train of
all! compared indeed to that!
What wretched shred e'en at the best of all!)

## *An Evening Lull*

After a week of physical anguish,
Unrest and pain, and feverish heat,
Toward the ending day a calm and lull comes on,
Three hours of peace and soothing rest of brain.

## *Old Age's Lambent Peaks*

The touch of flame – the illuminating fire – the
 loftiest look at last,
O'er city, passion, sea – o'er prairie, mountain, wood
 – the earth itself;
The airy, different, changing hues of all in falling
 twilight,
Objects and groups, bearings, faces, reminiscences;
The calmer sight – the golden setting, clear and broad:
So much i' the atmosphere, the points of view, the
 situations whence we scan,
Bro't out by them alone – so much (perhaps the
 best) unreck'd before;
The lights indeed from them – old age's lambent peaks.

## *After the Supper and Talk*

After the supper and talk – after the day is done,
As a friend from friends his final withdrawal prolonging,
Good-bye and Good-bye with emotional lips repeating,
(So hard for his hand to release those hands – no
 more will they meet,
No more for communion of sorrow and joy, of old
 and young,
A far-stretching journey awaits him, to return no more,)
Shunning, postponing severance – seeking to ward
 off the last word ever so little,
E'en at the exit-door turning – charges superfluous
 calling back – e'en as he descends the steps,
Something to eke out a minute additional – shadows
 of nightfall deepening,
Farewells, messages lessening – dimmer the forthgoer's
 visage and form,

Soon to be lost for aye in the darkness – loth, O so
    loth to depart!
Garrulous to the very last.

# GOOD-BYE MY FANCY

*(SecondAnnex)*

## *Sail Out for Good, Eidólon Yacht!*

Heave the anchor short!
Raise main-sail and jib – steer forth,
O little white-hull'd sloop, now speed on really deep
waters,
(I will not call it our concluding voyage,
But outset and sure entrance to the truest, best,
maturest;)
Depart, depart from solid earth – no more returning
to these shores,
Now on for aye our infinite free venture wending,
Spurning all yet tried ports, seas, hawsers, densities,
gravitation,
Sail out for good, eidólon yacht of me!

## *Lingering Last Drops*

And whence and why come you?
We know not whence, (was the answer,)
We only know that we drift here with the rest,
That we linger'd and lagg'd – but were wafted at
last, and are now here,
To make the passing shower's concluding drops,

## *Good-Bye My Fancy*

Good-bye my fancy – (I had a word to say,
But 'tis not quite the time – The best of any man's
word or say,
Is when its proper place arrives – and for its meaning,
I keep mine till the last.)

## *On, on the Same, Ye Jocund Twain!*

On, on the same, ye jocund twain!
My life and recitative, containing birth, youth, mid-
age years,
Fitful as motley-tongues of flame, inseparably
twined and merged in one – combining all,
My single soul – aims, confirmations, failures, joys –
Nor single soul alone,
I chant my nation's crucial stage, (America's, haply
humanity's) – the trial great, the victory great,
A strange *eclaircissement* of all the masses past, the
eastern world, the ancient, medieval,
Here, here from wanderings, strayings, lessons, wars,
defeats – here at the west a voice triumphant –
justifying all,
A gladsome pealing cry – a song for once of utmost
pride and satisfaction;
I chant from it the common bulk, the general
average horde, (the best no sooner than the
worst) – And now I chant old age,
(My verses, written first for forenoon life, and for the
summer's, autumn's spread,
I pass to snow-white hairs the same, and give to
pulses winter-cool'd the same;)
As here in careless trill, I and my recitatives, with
faith and love,
Wafting to other work, to unknown songs,
conditions,
On, on, ye jocund twain! continue on the same!

## *My 71st Year*

After surmounting three-score and ten,
With all their chances, changes, losses, sorrows,
My parents' deaths, the vagaries of my life, the many
tearing passions of me, the war of '63 and '4,
As some old broken soldier, after a long, hot,
wearying march, or haply after battle,
To-day at twilight, hobbling, answering company
roll-call, *Here*, with vital voice,
Reporting yet, saluting yet the Officer over all.

## *Apparitions*

A vague mist hanging 'round half the pages:
(Sometimes how strange and clear to the soul,
That all these solid things are indeed but
apparitions, concepts, non-realities.)

## *The Pallid Wreath*

Somehow I cannot let it go yet, funeral though it is,
Let it remain back there on its nail suspended,
With pink, blue, yellow, all blanch'd, and the white
now gray and ashy,
One wither'd rose put years ago for thee, dear friend;
But I do not forget thee. Hast thou then faded?
Is the odor exhaled? Are the colors, vitalities, dead?
No, while memories subtly play – the past vivid as
ever;
For but last night I woke, and in that spectral ring
saw thee,
Thy smile, eyes, face, calm, silent, loving as ever;

So let the wreath hang still awhile within my eye-reach,
It is not yet dead to me, nor even pallid.

## *An Ended Day*

The soothing sanity and blitheness of completion,
The pomp and hurried contest-glare and rush are done;
Now triumph! transformation! jubilate!

## *Old Age's Ship & Crafty Death's*

From east and west across the horizon's edge,
Two mighty masterful vessels sailers steal upon us:
But we'll make race a-time upon the seas – a battle-contest yet! bear lively there!
(Our joys of strife and derring-do to the last!)
Put on the old ship all her power to-day!
Crowd top-sail, top-gallant and royal studding-sails,
Out challenge and defiance – flags and flaunting pennants added,
As we take to the open! take to the deepest, freest waters.

## *To the Pending Year*

Have I no weapon-word for thee – some message brief and fierce?
(Have I fought out and done indeed the battle?) Is there no shot left,
For all thy affectations, lisps, scorns, manifold silliness?
Nor for myself – my own rebellious self in thee?

Down, down, proud gorge! – though choking thee;
Thy bearded throat and high-borne forehead to the
gutter;
Crouch low thy neck to eleemosynary gifts.

## *Shakspere-Bacon's Cipher*

I doubt it not – then more, far more;
In each old song bequeath'd – in every noble page or
text,
(Different – something unreck'd before – some
unsuspected author,)
In every object, mountain, tree, and star – in every
birth and life,
As part of each – evolv'd from each – meaning,
behind the ostent,
A mystic cipher waits infolded.

## *Long, Long Hence*

After a long, long course, hundreds of years, denials,
Accumulations, rous'd love and joy and thought,
Hopes, wishes, aspirations, ponderings, victories,
myriads of readers,
Coating, compassing, covering – after ages' and
ages' encrustations,
Then only may these songs reach fruition.

## *Bravo, Paris Exposition!*

Add to your show, before you close it, France,
With all the rest, visible, concrete, temples, towers,
goods, machines and ores,
Our sentiment wafted from many million heart-
throbs, ethereal but solid,
(We grand-sons and great-grand-sons do not forget
your grand-sires,)
From fifty, Nations and nebulous Nations,
compacted, sent oversea to-day,
America's applause, love, memories and good-will.

## *Interpolation Sounds*

(*General Philip Sheridan was buried at the Cathedral, Washington, D.C., August 1888, with all the pomp, music, and ceremonies of the Roman Catholic service.*)

Over and through the burial chant,
Organ and solemn service, sermon, bending priests,
To me come interpolation sounds not in the show –
plainly to me, crowding up the aisle and from the
window,
Of sudden battle's hurry and harsh noises – war's
grim game to sight and ear in earnest;
The scout call'd up and forward – the general
mounted and his aids around him – the new-
brought word – the instantaneous order issued;
The rifle crack – the cannon thud – the rushing forth
of men from their tents;

The clank of cavalry – the strange celerity of forming
ranks – the slender bugle note;
The sound of horses' hoofs departing – saddles,
arms, accoutrements.

## *To the Sunset Breeze*

Ah, whispering, something again, unseen,
Where late this heated day thou enterest at my
window, door,
Thou, laving, tempering all, cool-freshing, gently
vitalizing
Me, old, alone, sick, weak-down, melted-worn with
sweat;
Thou, nestling, folding close and firm yet soft,
companion better than talk, book, art,
(Thou hast, O Nature! elements! utterance to my
heart beyond the rest – and this is of them,)
So sweet thy primitive taste to breathe within – thy
soothing fingers on my face and hands,
Thou, messenger-magical strange bringer to body
and spirit of me,
(Distances balk'd – occult medicines penetrating me
from head to foot,)
I feel the sky, the prairies vast – I feel the mighty
northern lakes,
I feel the ocean and the forest – somehow I feel the
globe itself swift-swimming in space;
Thou blown from lips so loved, now gone – haply
from endless store, God-sent,
(For thou art spiritual, Godly, most of all known to
my sense,)

Minister to speak to me, here and now, what word
    has never told, and cannot tell,
Art thou not universal concrete's distillation? Law's,
    all Astronomy's last refinement?
Hast thou no soul? Can I not know, identify thee?

## *Old Chants*

An ancient song, reciting, ending,
Once gazing toward thee, Mother of All,
Musing, seeking themes fitted for thee,
*Accept for me*, thou saidst, *the elder ballads*,
*And name for me before thou goest each ancient poet.*

(Of many debts incalculable,
Haply our New World's chiefest debt is to old
    poems.)
Ever so far back, preluding thee, America,
Old chants, Egyptian priests, and those of Ethiopia,
The Hindu epics, the Grecian, Chinese, Persian,
The Biblic books and prophets, and deep idyls of the
    Nazarene,
The Iliad, Odyssey, plots, doings, wanderings of
    Eneas,
Hesiod, Eschylus, Sophocles, Merlin, Arthur,
The Cid, Roland at Roncesvalles, the Nibelungen,
The troubadours, minstrels, minnesingers, skalds,
Chaucer, Dante, flocks of singing birds,
The Border Minstrelsy, the bye-gone ballads, feudal
    tales, essays, plays,
Shakspere, Schiller, Walter Scott, Tennyson,
As some vast wondrous weird dream-presences,
The great shadowy groups gathering around,
Darting their mighty masterful eyes forward at thee,

Thou! with as now thy bending neck and head, with
courteous hand and word, ascending,
Thou! pausing a moment, drooping thine eyes upon
them, blent with their music,
Well pleased, accepting all, curiously prepared for by
them,
Thou enterest at thy entrance porch.

## *A Christmas Greeting*

*(From a Northern Star-Group
to a Southern*, 1889–90)

Welcome, Brazilian brother – thy ample place is ready;
A loving hand – a smile from the north – a sunny
instant hail!
(Let the future care for itself, where it reveals its
troubles, impedimentas,
Ours, ours the present throe, the democratic aim,
the acceptance and the faith;)
To thee to-day our reaching arm, our turning neck –
to thee from us the expectant eye,
Thou cluster free! thou brilliant lustrous one! thou,
learning well,
The true lesson of a nation's light in the sky,
(More shining than the Cross, more than the Crown,)
The height to be superb humanity.

## *Sounds of the Winter*

Sounds of the winter too,
Sunshine upon the mountains – many a distant strain
From cheery railroad train – from nearer field, barn,
house,

The whispering air – even the mute crops, garner'd
apples, corn,
Children's and women's tones – rhythm of many a
farmer and of flail,
An old man's garrulous lips among the rest, *Think*
*not we give out yet,*
*Forth from these snowy hairs we keep up yet the lilt.*

## *A Twilight Song*

As I sit in twilight late alone by the flickering oak-flame,
Musing on long-pass'd war-scenes – of the countless
buried unknown soldiers,
Of the vacant names, as unindented air's and sea's –
the unreturn'd,
The brief truce after battle, with grim burial-squads,
and the deep-fill'd trenches
Of gather'd dead from all America, North, South,
East, West, whence they came up,
From wooded Maine, New-England's farms, from
fertile Pennsylvania, Illinois, Ohio,
From the measureless West, Virginia, the South, the
Carolinas, Texas,
(Even here in my room-shadows and half-lights in
the noiseless flickering flames,
Again I see the stalwart ranks on-filing, rising – I
hear the rhythmic tramp of the armies;)
You million unwrit names all, all – you dark bequest
from all the war,
A special verse for you – a flash of duty long neglected
– your mystic roll strangely gather'd here,
Each name recall'd by me from out the darkness and
death's ashes,

Henceforth to be, deep, deep within my heart
    recording, for many a future year,
Your mystic roll entire of unknown names, or North
    or South,
Embalm'd with love in this twilight song.

## *When the Full-Grown Poet Came*

When the full-grown poet came,
Out spake pleased Nature (the round impassive
    globe, with all its shows of day and night,)
    saying, *He is mine;*
But out spake too the Soul of man, proud, jealous
    and unreconciled, *Nay, he is mine alone;*
– Then the full-grown poet stood between the two,
    and took each by the hand;
And to-day and ever so stands, as blender, uniter,
    tightly holding hands,
Which he will never release until he reconciles the
    two,
And wholly and joyously blends them.

## *Osceola*

*(When I was nearly grown to manhood in Brooklyn, New York (middle of* 1838), *I met one of the return'd U.S. Marines from Fort Moultrie, S. C., and had long talks with him – learn'd the occurrence below described – death of Osceola. The latter was a young, brave, leading Seminole, in the Florida war of that time – was surrender'd to our troops, imprison'd, and literally died of 'a broken heart,' at Fort Moultrie. He sicken'd of his confinement – the doctor and officers made every allowance and kindness possible for him; then the close.)*

When his hour for death had come,
He slowly rais'd himself from the bed on the floor,
Drew on his war-dress, shirt, leggings, and girdled
 the belt around his waist,
Call'd for vermilion paint (his looking-glass was held
 before him,)
Painted half his face and neck, his wrists, and
 back-hands,
Put the scalp-knife carefully in his belt – then lying
 down, resting a moment,
Rose again, half sitting, smiled, gave in silence his
 extended hand to each and all,
Sank faintly low to the floor (tightly grasping the
 tomahawk handle,)
Fix'd his look on wife and little children – the last:
(And here a line in memory of his name and death.)

## *A Voice from Death*

(*The Johnstown, Penn., cataclysm, May* 31, 1889)

A voice from Death, solemn and strange, in all his sweep and power,
With sudden, indescribable blow – towns drown'd – humanity by thousands slain,
The vaunted work of thrift, goods, dwellings, forge, street, iron bridge,
Dash'd pell-mell by the blow – yet usher'd life continuing on,
(Amid the rest, amid the rushing, whirling, wild debris,
A suffering woman saved – a baby safely born!)
Although I come and unannounc'd, in horror and in pang,
In pouring flood and fire, and wholesale elemental crash, (this voice so solemn, strange,)
I too a minister of Deity.

Yea, Death, we bow our faces, veil our eyes to thee,
We mourn the old, the young untimely drawn to thee,
The fair, the strong, the good, the capable,
The household wreck'd, the husband and the wife, the engulf'd forger in his forge,
The corpses in the whelming waters and the mud,
The gather'd thousands to their funeral mounds, and thousands never found or gather'd.

Then after burying, mourning the dead,
(Faithful to them found or unfound, forgetting not, bearing the past, here new musing,)
A day – a passing moment or an hour – America itself bends low,
Silent, resign'd, submissive.

War, death, cataclysm like this, America,
Take deep to thy proud prosperous heart.

E'en as I chant, lo! out of death, and out of ooze and slime,
The blossoms rapidly blooming, sympathy, help, love,
From West and East, from South and North and over sea,
Its hot-spurr'd hearts and hands humanity to human aid moves on;
And from within a thought and lesson yet.

Thou ever-darting Globe! through Space and Air!
Thou waters that encompass us!
Thou that in all the life and death of us, in action or in sleep!
Thou laws invisible that permeate them and all,
Thou that in all, and over all, and through and under all, incessant!
Thou! thou! the vital, universal, giant force resistless, sleepless, calm,
Holding Humanity as in thy open hand, as some ephemeral toy,
How ill to e'er forget thee!

For I too have forgotten,
(Wrapt in these little potencies of progress, politics, culture, wealth, inventions, civilization,)
Have lost my recognition of your silent ever-swaying power, ye mighty, elemental throes,
In which and upon which we float, and every one of us is buoy'd.

## *A Persian Lesson*

For his o'erarching and last lesson the greybeard sufi,
In the fresh scent of the morning in the open air,
On the slope of a teeming Persian rose-garden,
Under the ancient chestnut-tree wide spreading its
branches,
Spoke to the young priests and students.

Finally my children, to envelop each word, each part
of the rest,
Allah is all, all, all – is immanent in every life and object,
May-be at many and many-a-more removes – yet
Allah, Allah, Allah is there.

'Has the estray wander'd far? Is the reason-why
strangely hidden?
Would you sound below the restless ocean of the
entire world?
Would you know the dissatisfaction? the urge and
spur of every life;
The something never still'd – never entirely gone?
the invisible need of every seed?

'It is the central urge in every atom,
(Often unconscious, often evil, downfallen,)
To return to its divine source and origin, however
distant,
Latent the same in subject and in object, without
one exception.'

## *The Commonplace*

The commonplace I sing;
How cheap is health! how cheap nobility!
Abstinence, no falsehood, no gluttony, lust;
The open air I sing, freedom, toleration,
(Take here the mainest lesson – less from books – less from the schools,)
The common day and night – the common earth and waters,
Your farm – your work, trade, occupation,
The democratic wisdom underneath, like solid ground for all.

## *'The Rounded Catalogue Divine Complete'*

*(Sunday — Went this forenoon to church. A college professor, Rev. Dr.—, gave us a fine sermon, during which I caught the above words; but the minister included in his 'rounded catalogue' letter and spirit, only the esthetic things, and entirely ignored what I name in the following:)*

The devilish and the dark, the dying and diseas'd,
The countless (nineteen-twentieths) low and evil, crude and savage,
The crazed, prisoners in jail, the horrible, rank, malignant,
Venom and filth, serpents, the ravenous sharks, liars, the dissolute;
(What is the part the wicked and the loathsome bear within earth's orbic scheme?)
Newts, crawling things in slime and mud, poisons,
The barren soil, the evil men, the slag and hideous rot.

## *Mirages*

*(Noted verbatim after a supper-talk out doors
in Nevada with two old miners)*

More experiences and sights, stranger, than you'd
  think for;
Times again, now mostly just after sunrise or before
  sunset,
Sometimes in spring, oftener in autumn, perfectly
  clear weather, in plain sight,
Camps far or near, the crowded streets of cities and
  the shop-fronts,
(Account for it or not – credit or not – it is all true,
And my mate there could tell you the like – we have
  often confab'd about it,)
People and scenes, animals, trees, colors and lines,
  plain as could be,
Farms and dooryards of home, paths border'd with
  box, lilacs in corners,
Weddings in churches, thanksgiving dinners, returns
  of long-absent sons,
Glum funerals, the crape-veil'd mother and the
  daughters,
Trials in courts, jury and judge, the accused in the box,
Contestants, battles, crowds, bridges, wharves,
Now and then mark'd faces of sorrow or joy,
(I could pick them out this moment if I saw them
  again,)
Show'd to me just aloft to the right in the sky-edge,
Or plainly there to the left on the hill-tops.

## *L. of G.'s Purport*

Not to exclude or demarcate, or pick out evils from
their formidable masses (even to expose them,)
But add, fuse, complete, extend – and celebrate the
immortal and the good.

Haughty this song, its words and scope,
To span vast realms of space and time,
Evolution – the cumulative – growths and generations.

Begun in ripen'd youth and steadily pursued,
Wandering, peering, dallying with all – war, peace,
day and night absorbing,
Never even for one brief hour abandoning my task,
I end it here in sickness, poverty, and old age.

I sing of life, yet mind me well of death:
To-day shadowy Death dogs my steps, my seated
shape, and has for years –
Draws sometimes close to me, as face to face.

## *The Unexpress'd*

How dare one say it?
After the cycles, poems, singers, plays,
Vaunted Ionia's, India's – Homer, Shakspere – the
long, long times, thick dotted roads, areas,
The shining clusters and the Milky Ways of stars –
Nature's pulses reap'd,
All retrospective passions, heroes, war, love,
adoration,
All ages' plummets dropt to their utmost depths,
All human lives, throats, wishes, brains – all
experiences' utterance;

After the countless songs, or long or short, all
tongues, all lands,
Still something not yet told in poesy's voice or print
– something lacking,
(Who knows? the best yet unexpress'd and lacking.)

## *Grand is the Seen*

Grand is the seen, the light, to me – grand are the
sky and stars,
Grand is the earth, and grand are lasting time and space,
And grand their laws, so multiform, puzzling,
evolutionary;
But grander far the unseen soul of me,
comprehending, endowing all those,
Lighting the light, the sky and stars, delving the
earth, sailing the sea,
(What were all those, indeed, without thee, unseen
soul? of what amount without thee?)
More evolutionary, vast, puzzling, O my soul!
More multiform far – more lasting thou than they.

## *Unseen Buds*

Unseen buds, infinite, hidden well,
Under the snow and ice, under the darkness, in
every square or cubic inch,
Germinal, exquisite, in delicate lace, microscopic,
unborn,
Like babes in wombs, latent, folded, compact,
sleeping;
Billions of billions, and trillions of trillions of them
waiting,

(On earth and in the sea – the universe – the stars
there in the heavens,)
Urging slowly, surely forward, forming endless,
And waiting ever more, forever more behind.

## *Good-Bye My Fancy!*

Good-bye my Fancy!
Farewell dear mate, dear love!
I'm going away, I know not where,
Or to what fortune, or whether I may ever see you again,
So Good-bye my Fancy.

Now for my last – let me look back a moment;
The slower fainter ticking of the clock is in me,
Exit, nightfall, and soon the heart-thud stopping.

Long have we lived, joy'd, caress'd together;
Delightful! – now separation – Good-bye my Fancy.

Yet let me not be too hasty,
Long indeed have we lived, slept, filter'd, become
really blended into one;
Then if we die we die together, (yes, we'll remain one,)
If we go anywhere we'll go together to meet what
happens,
May-be we'll be better off and blither, and learn
something,
May-be it is yourself now really ushering me to the
true songs, (who knows?)
May-be it is you the mortal knob really undoing,
turning – so now finally,
Good-bye – and hail! my Fancy.

# OLD AGE ECHOES

## (*Posthumous Additions*)

## *A Kiss to the Bride*
### *Marriage of Nelly Grant, May 21, 1874*

Sacred, blithesome, undenied,
With benisons from East and West,
And salutations North and South,
Through me indeed to-day a million hearts and hands,
Wafting a million loves, a million soulfelt prayers;
– Tender and true remain the arm that shields thee!
Fair winds always fill the ship's sails that sail thee!
Clear sun by day, and light stars at night, beam on
    thee!
Dear girl – through me the ancient privilege too,
For the New World, through me, the old, old
    wedding greeting,
O youth and health! O sweet Missouri rose! O
    bonny bride!
Yield thy red cheeks, thy lips, to-day,
Unto a Nation's loving kiss.

## *Nay, Tell Me Not To-day the Publish'd Shame*
### *Winter of 1873, Congress in Session*

Nay, tell me not to-day the publish'd shame,
Read not to day the journal's crowded page,
The merciless reports still branding forehead after
    forehead,
The guilty column following guilty column.
To-day to me the tale refusing,
Turning from it – from the white capitol turning,
Far from these swelling domes, topt with statues,
More endless, jubilant, vital visions rise
Unpublish'd, unreported.

Through all your quiet ways, or North or South, you
Equal States, you honest farms,
Your million untold manly healthy lives, or East or
West, city or country,
Your noiseless mothers, sisters, wives, unconscious
of their good,
Your mass of homes nor poor nor rich, in visions
rise – (even your excellent poverties,)
Your self-distilling, never-ceasing virtues, self-
denials, graces,
Your endless base of deep integrities within, timid
but certain,
Your blessings steadily bestow'd, sure as the light,
and still,
(Plunging to these as a determin'd diver down the
deep hidden waters,)
These, these to-day I brood upon – all else refusing,
these will I con,
To-day to these give audience.

## *To Be At All*

(*Cf. Stanza* 27, '*Song of Myself*,' *p.* 49)

To be at all – what is better than that?
I think if there were nothing more developed, the
clam in its callous shell in the sand were august
enough.
I am not in any callous shell;
I am cased with supple conductors, all over,
They take every object by the hand, and lead it
within me;
They are thousands, each one with his entry to
himself;

They are always watching with their little eyes, from
  my head to my feet;
One no more than a point lets in and out of me such
  bliss and magnitude,
I think I could lift the girder of the house away if it
  lay between me and whatever I wanted.

## *Death's Valley*

*To accompany a picture; by request. 'The Valley of the Shadow of Death,' from the painting by George Inness*

Nay, do not dream, designer dark,
Thou hast portray'd or hit thy theme entire;
I, hoverer of late by this dark valley, by its confines,
  having glimpses of it,
Here enter lists with thee, claiming my right to make
  a symbol too.
For I have seen many wounded soldiers die,
After dread suffering – have seen their lives pass off
  with smiles;
And I have watch'd the death-hours of the old; and
  seen the infant die;
The rich with all his nurses and his doctors;
And then the poor, in meagreness and poverty;
And I myself for long, O Death, have breath'd my
  every breath
Amid the nearness and the silent thought of thee.
And out of these and thee,
I make a scene, a song (not fear of thee,
Nor gloom's ravines, nor bleak, nor dark – for I do
  not fear thee,

Nor celebrate the struggle, or contortion, or hard-tied knot),
Of the broad blessed light and perfect air, with meadows, rippling tides, and trees and flowers and grass,
And the low hum of living breeze – and in the midst God's beautiful eternal right hand,
Thee, holiest minister of Heaven – thee, envoy, usherer, guide at last of all,
Rich, florid, loosener of the stricture-knot call'd life,
Sweet, peaceful, welcome Death.

## *On the Same Picture*

*Intended for first stanza of 'Death's Valley'*

Aye, well I know 'tis ghastly to descend that valley:
Preachers, musicians, poets, painters, always render it,
Philosophs exploit – the battlefield, the ship at sea, the myriad beds, all lands,
All, all the past have enter'd, the ancientest humanity we know,
Syria's, India's, Egypt's, Greece's, Rome's;
Till now for us under our very eyes spreading the same to-day,
Grim, ready, the same to-day, for entrance, yours and mine, Here, here 'tis limn'd.

## *A Thought of Columbus*

The mystery of mysteries, the crude and hurried ceaseless flame, spontaneous, bearing on itself.
The bubble and the huge, round, concrete orb!
A breath of Deity, as thence the bulging universe unfolding!

The many issuing cycles from their precedent minute!
The eras of the soul incepting in an hour,
Haply the widest, farthest evolutions of the world
    and man.

Thousands and thousands of miles hence, and now
    four centuries back,
A mortal impulse thrilling its brain cell,
Reck'd or unreck'd, the birth can no longer be
    postpon'd:
A phantom of the moment, mystic, stalking, sudden,
Only a silent thought, yet toppling down of more
    than walls of brass or stone.
(A flutter at the darkness' edge as if old Time's and
    Space's secret near revealing.)
A thought! a definite thought works out in shape.
Four hundred years roll on.
The rapid cumulus – trade, navigation, war, peace,
    democracy, roll on;
The restless armies and the fleets of time following
    their leader – the old camps of ages pitch'd in
    newer, larger areas,
The tangl'd, long-deferr'd, éclaircissement of human
    life and hopes boldly begins untying,
As here to-day up-grows the Western World.

(An added word yet to my song, far Discoverer, as
    ne'er before sent back to son of earth –
If still thou hearest, hear me,
Voicing as now – lands, races, arts, bravas to thee,
O'er the long backward path to thee – one vast
    concensus north, south, east, west,
Soul plaudits! acclamation! reverent echoes!
One manifold, huge memory to thee! oceans and lands!
The modern world to thee and thought of thee!)

# *Afterword*

I am not blind to the worth of the wonderful gift of *Leaves of Grass*. I find it the most extraordinary piece of wit and wisdom that America has yet contributed . . . I give you joy of your free and brave thought. I have great joy in it. I find incomparable things said incomparably well, as they must be. I find the courage of treatment which so delights us, and which large perceptions only can inspire.

Ralph Waldo Emerson, in a letter to
Whitman upon receiving the first edition of
*Leaves of Grass*, 21 July 1855

*Leaves of Grass* was first published on Independence Day, July 4, 1855 – an interesting date, considering the collection's obsession with the geography, population, and mentality of the United States. However, the work – which would later come to be considered the seminal piece of American poetry – got off to a very slow start. Whitman had been forced to pay for the publication of the collection himself, and only a few hundred copies of this slim green volume were issued. It was a difficult book to print, because the long lines of Whitman's verses necessitated a larger than average page – eight inches by eleven. It was a difficult book to distribute – for all Whitman's efforts, only one outlet, Fowler and Wells of New York, would stock it. And it was a difficult book to sell – after many months, only a few copies had been bought. Walt Whitman was by now middle-aged, and desperate to achieve recognition as a serious writer. He had enjoyed moderate success during the 1840s with a moral novel, *Franklin Evans*, inspired by the temperance movement, but, although it had sold over twenty thousand copies, he had come to despise the work (dismissing it as 'rot'). He felt that he had something very important and very original to communicate to the public, and was not prepared to be frustrated.

So, in the months after his book's first publication, Whitman embarked on a focused campaign of self-publicity. Using his journalistic contacts (he had worked extensively in newspapers, as a writer, editor and printer), he secured a number of reviews – all of which he wrote himself, under the cloak of anonymity. These reviews, needless to say, were, without exception, brilliant. In one he declared that *Leaves of Grass* heralded the arrival of 'An American bard at last!'; in another, he proclaimed himself 'the begetter of a new offspring out of literature.' Whether one agrees with his own judgment of himself or not (and it is hard not to, given a century and a half of critical hindsight), one has to admire his gall. However, it was the praise of his brother writers that really helped to launch *Leaves of Grass* into the public consciousness. Shortly after publication, Whitman sent his book to a wide selection of the nineteenth century's most famous writers American writers. Some of them responded with disgust (the poet John Greenleaf Whittier famously threw his copy into the fire), but many – including Henry David Thoreau, Ralph Waldo Emerson and others among the so-called 'New England Transcendentalists' – found themselves greatly impressed. Emerson wrote a congratulatory letter to Whitman (part of it is reproduced above), which he would find reprinted – against his permission – in all future editions of *Leaves of Grass*.

Having found himself an audience for his work, however, the writer then had to contend with ferocious criticism and condemnation, as well as adulation. Indeed, the ever-extending and enlarging collection of verse, which was more or less Walt Whitman's life's work, was destined always to polarize its readership. Throughout the successive, and increasingly popular, editions that came out during Whitman's lifetime, *Leaves of Grass* invariably caused a storm for all manner of reasons. Puritans and moralists took issue with its frank depictions of sex, human sexuality and sensuality: 'Children of Adam' deals with heterosexual passion in terms which were extremely graphic for the mid-Victorian era, and the following sequence, 'Calamus,' contains overtones of homosexuality which were deemed 'pornographic' and 'priapic' at the time. Others took exception to what they perceived as the irreverence of the work, highlighting sequences like those in 'Song of Myself', where Whitman places the prostitute who 'draggles her shawl' over her 'pimpled back,' alongside the President, 'holding a cabinet council . . . surrounded by great secretaries.' Similar exception was taken, in those pre-Civil War days, for the collection's sense of racial inclusivity. Perhaps most damning of all, in the eyes of the convention-bound literary establishment, Whitman's work was condemned for its total disregard of the 'normal' or established rules of verse: it did not conform to conventional meter, scansion or rhyme – his poems were simply not *poems*!

We can, I hope, assume that, since you have made it

through the not inconsiderable volume of verse that you hold in your hand, you are not overly concerned with the criticisms given above. Indeed, personally speaking – if you will pardon me such an indulgence – the more times that I return to, and re-read, *Leaves of Grass*, the more I feel that the criticisms leveled against it in the nineteenth century are, in fact, some of its greatest recommendations. Those things that the Victorians found wrong or reprehensible about the collection are, to me at least, its most important achievements.

Let us take, first of all, its sensuality, and its sexuality. Sex is not an easy subject to write convincingly about, certainly not in literary terms. Too often it is tackled in a flowery or overly poetical way, and, equally often, it is described in joyless, passionless and coldly physical terms. Although Whitman tends sometimes toward the former, he manages, on the whole, to convey sex and sexual desire in erotic and sensual language that, as he himself noted, keeps it out of the realm of both the Puritan and the pornographer. Creating a realistic and well-worded description of sex was important to Whitman, as he strongly felt that human beings were half body and half soul, the one depending on, and influencing, the other. His poems needed to be as physical as they were spiritual, otherwise he would not be capturing the whole of the human experience.

This leads us on to the next point of criticism that the nineteenth century held for Whitman: the fact that he tended to describe and depict humanity as a complete entity, with no qualitative judgments made about race, sex, age or color. For me, the most compelling and immediately noticeable aspect of

*Leaves of Grass* is its inclusivity: the way Whitman ranges across the whole of America, including all of its people and its frontiers, and manages to define each as part of a common, joyful experience. This shines through nearly every passage of 'Song of Myself,' and manifests itself in dozens of places elsewhere: in 'I Hear America Singing,' in the Civil War poems, in 'Our Old Feuillage.' One is left with a strong impression of a writer who sees mankind, in all its infinite color, as made up of the same stuff, as joined by a common fraternal bond. Everyone, high or low, President or prostitute, is an equal part of the tribe, with an equal right to be heard and appreciated.

Part of this egalitarian attitude toward the Family of Man may have been actuated by Whitman's own unusual family background. His father, a frequently unemployed alcoholic, and his mother, neurotic but essentially kind-hearted, produced a brood of nine children (Walt junior – his father also being called Walt – was the second). This family (by no means large by nineteenth-century standards) went onto enjoy drastically varying degrees of success and failure. One brother went insane and lived out his life in a lunatic asylum; another took after his father and died prematurely of drink; another was a great military hero, having been decorated in the American Civil War; another found fortune as a builder and engineer; another was mentally and physically handicapped from birth. Walt himself, of course, became a celebrated poet of international renown. It seems no coincidence in this context that he often describes God as an 'elder brother': Whitman's own family must have demonstrated to him, from an early age, the infinite potential variety of man's experience, as well as the necessity of appreciating and understanding this variety, whether it be happy or sad.

Whatever biographical reasons one can put forward, however, the expansiveness of the volume has its most visible roots in the geography and sensibility of the United States. First and foremost, Whitman considered himself an American poet – indeed, he believed that he was *the* American poet. America was still a young country when Whitman first sat down to write *Leaves of Grass*. The American Revolution was within living memory, and the upheavals of the Civil War were yet to come. America was – as it still is – a country of boundless possibilities, of amazing variety, both physical and political, and Whitman's extensive travels throughout it must have deeply engrained this within his mind. This collection is a celebration of his country. The way it juxtaposes an intensely subjective, personal outlook with the outlook of a whole continent is an early manifestation of that most American of traits: fierce individuality coupled with a strongly felt sense of national identity and national pride. The death of Abraham Lincoln, to whom Whitman felt a strong personal bond, having often encountered the President on the streets of Washington (when the poet was working as a clerk), provides the inspiration for two of the most touching and memorable pieces in the collection: 'O Captain, My Captain,' and 'When lilacs last in the dooryard bloom'd' (which are arguably two of the most perfect elegies ever written in English). The Civil War provides the rhythms and melancholy memories of *Drum-Taps* and its various sequels. But above and beyond these obvious touchstones, the emerging American identity informs nearly every sentence and every word.

Lastly, let us consider the remaining contemporary criticism of Whitman: his unusual poetical style, his innovation. The line-length and blank verse of his poetry was certainly out of place in the rigidly formal literary scene of the nineteenth century, and has few obvious precursors; however, one can perhaps trace some of their roots from the circumstances of the writer's career. Clearly, the expansiveness and spontaneity of Whitman's poetry demands a fluid and flexible length of meter and verse. However, after acknowledging this, it is interesting to note that many of his lines are of approximately the same length, and actually form a similar picture upon the page. Whitman was trained as a 'jour' (journeyman) printer and compositor (one who arranges the letters in the frames), and was therefore fascinated with *shape* that poetry makes on the page. He had been drawn to the look of lengthened lines when he read the *libretti* of his favorite operas, which tended to be published in attenuated, uneven lines. He wanted his poetry to appeal, like the words of these operas, to the eye as well as to the heart and the voice; so, perhaps he structured it that way – uneven and interesting to look at.

Similarly, one wonders whether the fact of his being a printer for much of his working life had some bearing on Whitman's free-flowing style. Printers and compositors, though fantastically fast with their hands, cannot hope to match the speed with which the word is written on the page. To a man like Whitman, it must have seemed an intensely laborious process carefully to select each letter, space and punctuation mark in any given text before racking them up in a frame to be printed. Perhaps this accounts in some small way to the feeling of complete release, of freedom and spontaneity, that Whitman displays. His pen seems almost to be running away with itself; the words seem to be tumbling uncontrollably out of him. He seems to be trying to write as fast and as fluidly as he can to escape the snail-like pace of the printing shop.

These conjectures aside, Whitman's verse – thanks to its unusual, arrhythmic composition – has a truly visionary quality, which puts one in mind of the Ancient Greek poets, as well as certain books of the Bible, and some of the work of later writers such as John Milton or Percy Bysshe Shelley. Whitman also bears certain similarities to the eighteenth-century English poet, William Blake. Blake, author of *Songs of Innocence and of Experience* and *The Marriage of Heaven and Hell*, writes in an equally spontaneous and loose-structured style. He is similarly free-flowing and wide-ranging, and also encountered equivalent difficulty and rejection because of the unusual and radical morality he advocated in his work. However, these similarities are all essentially fleeting. Whitman was a true original. Nothing like *Leaves of Grass* had ever been done before. And, although Whitman's influence would be strongly felt for the next century and up until the present day, shaping various literary movements from Modernism to the Beat Poets, nothing like it has ever been done since. It is truly a masterpiece.

## Further Reading

Allen, Gay Wilson, *The Solitary Singer: A Critical Biography of Walt Whitman* (New York University Press, 1955)

Kaplan, Jerome, *Walt Whitman: A Life* (Simon and Shuster, 1980)

Killingsworth, M. Jimmie, *Whitman's Poetry of the Body: Sexuality, Politics and the Text* (University of North Carolina Press, 1989)

## Biography

Walt Whitman was born on Long Island in 1819 – the second of nine children. His formal education was brief, and at the age of eleven he began work as an office boy, quickly becoming apprenticed to various printing firms. He would remain employed in different aspects of printing and publication throughout most of his adult life, working as a journalist and editor on such publications as the *Long-Islander*, *The Evening Tattler* and *The New York Democrat*. He began to write poetry and fiction in the early 1840s, and achieved his first success with the novel *Franklin Evans*. *Leaves of Grass* was first published in 1855, and from thereon, Whitman's literary output was devoted to compiling new editions of the collection, which grew prodigiously in size over the six versions which were printed during his lifetime. Ill-health dogged him through his later years, and he died at the age of 72.

## *Index of the Poem Titles*

## *Index of the Poems' Opening Words*